THE
GLOBAL
COUP D'ÉTAT

THE
GLOBAL
COUP D'ÉTAT

THE FOURTH INDUSTRIAL
REVOLUTION AND
THE GREAT RESET

JACOB
NORDANGÅRD

Skyhorse Publishing

Skyhorse Publishing books may be purchased in bulk at special discounts for sales promotion, corporate gifts, fund-raising, or educational purposes. Special editions can also be created to specifications. For details, contact the Special Sales Department, Skyhorse Publishing, 307 West 36th Street, 11th Floor, New York, NY 10018 or info@ skyhorsepublishing.com.

Skyhorse® and Skyhorse Publishing® are registered trademarks of Skyhorse Publishing, Inc.®, a Delaware corporation.

Visit our website at www.skyhorsepublishing.com.

Please follow our publisher Tony Lyons on Instagram @tonylyonsisuncertain

10 9 8 7 6 5 4 3 2 1

Library of Congress Cataloging-in-Publication Data is available on file.

Cover design by David Ter-Avanesyan
Cover image from Getty Images

Print ISBN: 978-1-5107-8203-7
Ebook ISBN: 978-1-5107-8205-1

Printed in the United States of America

Contents

Preface

In the spring of 2019, when I had just finished writing my previous book, *Rockefeller: Controlling the Game*, I could not imagine how events would unfold the following year. However, the warning signs had been there. The Greta Thunberg fever was at its peak and there were indications that 2020 would be a dramatic year.

This was the year when the implementation of the 2015 Paris Agreement on Climate and the 17 Global Goals of Agenda 2030 were set to begin. 2020 marked the start of what the United Nations had dubbed the "Decade of Action."

In early 2020, the COVID-19 pandemic hit the world. As the seriousness of the situation intensified, resulting in democratic rights and freedoms almost overnight being replaced by authoritarian mandates, curfews, and riots, I felt an urgent need to write this book.

Everything I had warned about for years in my books, articles, lectures, and songs suddenly became a reality. The inhumane control society of the Fourth Industrial Revolution was rapidly unfolding. It became clear that the COVID-19 crisis was part of a global coup, in which the old system was about to be replaced by a new one where humankind was fully integrated into a technological system.

This book, first published in Swedish December 14, 2020, includes some amended and expanded articles written during 2020 and 2021 as a reaction to the events following the COVID-19 crisis, as well as updates on how it unfolded and what comes next. This is an ongoing story.

The purpose of this book is to give a brief background to what is happening in the world, and also to continue the story presented in *Rockefeller*. Even though public focus shifted away from the climate issue during the

COVID-19 crisis, the climate agenda was still permeating everything and is briefly summarised here.

The pandemic became the perfect "trigger event" needed to implement some of the draconian climate strategies called for by proponents such as James Lovelock, Torbjörn Tännsjö, and the Club of Rome, in order to "save the planet" and kick-start the Great Transformation.

My aim is to clarify how decisions are made at a global level, what the Fourth Industrial Revolution is, what consequences this agenda is likely to have for humankind, and to identify the individuals and organizations involved, including the World Economic Forum (and its Young Global Leaders program), the United Nations, G20, and the European Union.

My concern is that the consolidation of global power may have dire consequences for humanity, even if the intention is well-meaning. The global public-private partnership between the United Nations and World Economic Forum to fulfill the global goals of Agenda 2030 appears to combine the worst sides of capitalism with the worst sides of socialism, with a techno-totalitarian technocracy as the end result.

My style of writing is to present facts, quotes, and sources that my readers can check for themselves. I also try to have a helicopter perspective and analyze all sides of the "grand chessboard." This means that you as a reader may find some chapters challenging, especially if you have chosen a specific team or put your faith in a specific savior figure.

My belief is that we as a species have to be our own saviors by learning to discriminate facts from propaganda and misinformation from all sides. Hopefully, this book will be of some help in that process.

I would like to convey my gratitude to other freedom fighters across the world who have helped spread my work, such as researcher and author Patrick Wood (editor in chief of Technocracy.news), Catherine Austin Fitts (Solari Report), Karen Siegemund (American Freedom Alliance), Ivor Cummins (Ireland), Rypke Zeilmaker (Netherlands), Urszula Klimko (who has published my books in Poland), Skyhorse Publishing, and many others.

Musical greetings to my band Wardenclyffe, Kristian Karlsson, Koen van Baal, and Stella Tormanoff.

And an extra thank-you to Hans Holmén for proofreading and book description, Johan Laurell for good advice and statistical data, Johan Eddebo for help with translation, and Staffan Wennberg for invaluable help with the publishing as well as the original idea for this book. Last but not least to my beloved wife Inger for her editing and partial translation of this book, and compiling appendixes A and B.

This book is dedicated to my daughters Celia and Alva, who I hope will not have to live through the dystopian future that the powerful "planetary custodians" have planned for humanity. In any case, I will do what I can to prevent this plan from being realized by studying, compiling, and making essential information available. This book is offered as a contribution to that struggle.

The success of the plan hinges on everyone believing in the propaganda and playing along. But truth always finds a way. With more and more people waking up and seeing through the illusions, I believe this ongoing technocratic coup is doomed to fail.

Jacob Nordangård
Norrköping, Sweden
June 7, 2024

Foreword

Catherine Austin Fitts

"His work is fantastic. You have to meet him. You have to read his books. You must interview him on the Solari Report." These were the words of a great Swedish ally. A solid businessman, my friend is not usually so enthusiastic. He was talking about his discovery of Swedish researcher and author Dr. Jacob Nordangård.

And so it was that on a trip to Stockholm early this year, I had dinner with Jacob and his wife Inger and learned more about their work. Intrigued, I read Jacob's book on the Rockefeller family and its investments over many decades designed to institutionalize numerous technocratic controls: *Rockefeller—Controlling the Game*. Published in 2019, this book provides solid evidence of the deliberate engineering of central control, including the weaponization of environmental concerns. As the existing fiat currency systems debase, the Rockefeller interests and syndicate are promoting the control of energy and carbon to undergird their central banking cartel.

After meeting again and presenting with Dr. Nordangård at the Northern Lights Convention in Malmö, Sweden, this spring, I invited him to join me on the Solari Report. In anticipation of our discussion, he shared an advance copy of his new book, *The Global Coup d'État*.

The Global Coup d'État extends the analysis in *Rockefeller* and does so with the benefit of the global unmasking of tyranny that has occurred since 2019—spurred by the COVID-19 pandemic and its acceleration of what I call "the great poisoning," as well as by the central bankers' Going Direct Reset, which has engineered global financial consolidation on a previously unimaginable scale.

Engineering central control takes a lot of work—and it leaves a document trail. Dr. Nordangård has taken great care to map out the people, groups, events, and regulatory frameworks that have been and are being used to consolidate and justify global power. His attention to detail alongside a remarkable ability for synthesis create a work that is unusually well done and easy to follow.

He is also skilled in translating the official narratives used to market the changes underway into the actual technocratic details—the nuts and bolts of tyranny.

The Global Coup d'État makes it much easier to see the control grid slowly closing in around us. It also makes it much easier for you to back out of that control grid—in your work, in your choice of media and banks, in your investments, and in your choice of companions and communities.

We don't have to slide into tyranny, especially if we can see it coming. So, take a deep breath and dive in—you are about to get a heavy dose of actionable intelligence, one that can help you avoid an enormous number of deep-state traps.

Catherine Austin Fitts
Stavoren, Netherlands
September 2, 2022

Prologue

WHO has been assessing this outbreak around the clock and we are deeply concerned both by the alarming levels of spread and severity, and by the alarming levels of inaction. We have therefore made the assessment that COVID-19 can be characterized as a pandemic.[1]

The year 2020 will go down in history as the Year of Crisis and the year when the global coup d'état was initiated. On March 11, 2020, the World Health Organization (WHO) declared that the outbreak of the novel coronavirus SARS-CoV-2 had developed into a pandemic. This kick-started a dramatic chain of events that would have a momentous impact on the world.

Nation after nation began shutting down large sections of society, restricting travel, closing borders, declaring curfews, mandating social distancing and mask-wearing, and whole populations of healthy people were forced into isolation at home for months at a time as a proactive measure.

In many countries, penalties ware harsh for those who did not adhere to the new rules. In authoritarian countries like the Philippines, there was even a risk of being shot on the spot. The pandemic became the perfect excuse for implementing surveillance technologies on a larger scale, without meeting much public resistance.

Almost overnight, the world had become harsh, cruel, and authoritarian. Economic activity slowed down markedly, resulting in many bankruptcies, especially among smaller businesses in the service, entertainment, travel, and tourist sectors, with mass unemployment and great suffering for many people as a result.

In the midst of this growing chaos, Black Lives Matter began mass protests around the world after the murder of George Floyd by a police officer. These were followed by mass protests against the lockdowns. The world was on fire and people were scared.

However, when viewed from a higher perspective, and in a historical context, these events appear rather as part of a well-directed chess game, a sort of global coup d'état, with complete control of the whole planet as the final goal.

During the crescendo of this drama, the powers behind the coup emerged quite openly, offering a techno–totalitarian and very far-reaching solution to the world. This solution, which they call *The Great Reset*, means that humankind must be fully integrated and merged with a world-wide technological system, through the application of the technologies of the Fourth Industrial Revolution—all for our own safety, security, and well-being.

World Control

1

The Vision

We are now at the year nineteen hundred and eight, which was the year that the Carnegie Foundation began operations. And, in that year, the trustees meeting, for the first time, raised a specific question, which they discussed throughout the balance of the year, in a very learned fashion. And the question is this: Is there any means known more effective than war, assuming you wish to alter the life of an entire people? And they conclude that, no more effective means to that end is known to humanity, than war. So then, in 1909, they raise the second question, and discuss it, namely, how do we involve the United States in a war?[1]

For some, the pursuit of power is one of the major driving forces in life. The dream of completely dominating one's subjects has been present throughout history and has been demonstrated in the most appalling ways, and the common people have often been heavily burdened by the dictates of powerful rulers.

The Rule of Power

Historically, this type of domination has mostly been exercised in limited geographical areas; in clans, city states, feudal principalities, and nation states, but also in grand empires that have expanded to encompass a large portion of a continent, with the Roman Empire as perhaps the foremost and most well-organized historical example.

For a power-hungry ruler, it is of essence to appear like a benevolent leader with noble goals, in order to make subjects dependent and willing to submit. In Rome, bread, circuses, and protection from enemies were the main baits to keep citizens loyal and less prone to revolt. An additional mechanism was severe punishment for those who disobeyed the dictates of power.

Today, people in power have at their disposal completely different means of control and, unlike the previous geographically limited empires, now have within their reach the possibility of gaining control of the whole planet, with its natural and human resources.

The British Empire was the first to truly span the globe through trade, conquest, and cunning strategy. The British colonial empire, lasting from the seventeenth century until just after World War I, encompassed a third of the world. Eventually, however, the colonial system began to disintegrate, and colonies demanded greater sovereignty. New paths to dominance were sought. The more loosely knit cooperation of the Commonwealth of Nations became a reality during the 1920s.

The League of Nations

After World War I, the victors (mainly British and American interests) created the League of Nations. The initiative was presented at the Paris Peace Conference in 1919 by US President Woodrow Wilson but had been prepared behind the scenes for a long time by, among others, South African prime minister and philosopher general Jan Smuts.

Smuts was a great admirer of the British imperialist Cecil Rhodes and his ideas of gathering the English-speaking countries (including the United States) into a single union. Rhodes, in turn, had been influenced by Oxford professor John Ruskin's call for the English to colonize and control all fertile land and to spread the ideals of the British upper class to all parts of the world.

The world would be socially reformed and provided with the "higher morals" of the British elite. Ruskin had Plato's *Republic* as his guiding light. It was a vision of the perfect society, the kingdom of God on earth. This kingdom was to be ruled by the British elite, whose members saw themselves as genetically superior.

This message was heeded by future leaders such as Cecil Rhodes, Lord Milner, and Arnold Toynbee.[2] What they had in mind was a global utopia.

This vision eventually led to the formation of the Round Table movement, founded in 1909, based on the ideas of Rhodes and Ruskins, with Jan Smuts as one of the most active proponents. Rhodes, whose wealth came from the diamond trade in South Africa, also instituted the Rhodes scholarships for recruiting leaders to advance this vision for the world.

During the negotiations for the Paris Peace Treaty, members of the Round Table movement also founded the front organizations and think tanks the Royal Institute of International Affairs (RIIA) in England in 1919 and the Council on Foreign Relations (CFR) in the United States in 1921, in order to advance their far-reaching agenda for the world.[3] Through these institutes, the American East Coast elite, dominated by the financial interests of banker J. P. Morgan and the Rockefeller oil and finance empire, became close allies for the cause.

The founding of RIIA and CFR was followed by other foreign policy institutes around the world, such as the Pacific Institute of International Affairs.

Another strong proponent of the League of Nations was Scottish-born steel magnate Andrew Carnegie, who in 1911 had founded the foreign policy think tank the Carnegie Endowment for International Peace and financed the Peace Palace in the Hague (inaugurated in 1913 and housing the UN International Court of Justice).[4]

Carnegie died only a year before his dream was fulfilled, but his foundations would come to have a close relationship with the League of Nations, United Nations, and Council on Foreign Relations.[5]

Through the US House of Representatives Special Committee on Tax Exempt Foundations (1952–1954) and its main investigator Norman Dodd, it was revealed how the Carnegie Endowment provisional board, during its first meetings in 1908 and 1909, had discussed the most effective means to change the lives of an entire population. They found that "no more effective means to that end is known to humanity, than war." Whereupon efforts were focused on trying to involve the United States in a war by taking control over the Foreign Office and its diplomatic relations (see appendix A).[6]

The end goal was the creation of a world federal government and the implementation of collectivism "administered with characteristic American efficiency" (scientific management). A new way of running first the United States and then the whole world. This vision was also shared by John D. Rockefeller and pervaded his foundations the General Education Board (founded in 1902) and the Rockefeller Foundation (founded in 1913), which came to have a close collaboration with the Carnegie foundations in order to realize this goal.

As chairman of the Carnegie Endowment and the Carnegie Corporation of New York, Andrew Carnegie chose his friend and adviser Elihu Root, former US secretary of war and secretary of state. In 1918, Root founded the precursor to the Council on Foreign Relations and in 1921 became its honorary chairman.[7] In April 1917, after intense anti-German propaganda, the United States finally joined the Allies in World War I. Root had been a strong driving force behind the efforts to persuade the United States to abandon its neutrality and fight on the side of the British and the French.[8] Ironically, only a year before the war broke out, he had been awarded the Nobel Peace Prize.[9]

In November 1918, after a series of successful Allied offensives in connection with the deployment of American troops into the war, Germany and Austria-Hungary capitulated. In order to create a peace organization, war was obviously deemed a necessity. Nine million soldiers lost their lives for Andrew Carnegie's "pacifist" ideals.

The League of Nations was a loosely knit collaboration between the nations of the world, forming the embryo of a world government.[10] However, the League of Nations failed to unite all countries (the United States never ratified it) and it suffered several setbacks in the 1930s when countries such as Germany and Italy withdrew. The agreement was full of loopholes, and the organization was toothless, lacking the mandate to intervene in conflicts. Few countries were prepared to relinquish their sovereignty at this time. The war, which the League of Nations was instituted to prevent, soon became a horrid reality. In the background, however, new plans were drawn up by powerful forces behind the scenes.[11] These plans included the founding of the Council on Foreign Relations and its *War & Peace Studies* (1939–1945) which spawned the idea of the new international organizations such as the United Nations, the World Bank, and the International Monetary Fund (IMF). The study was funded by the Rockefeller Foundation and the Carnegie Corporation.[12]

Jan Smuts was also one of the coauthors of the UN Charter and the Declaration on Human Rights. His metaphysical ideas, from the book *Holism and Evolution*, about the world as an organism evolving toward unity, would soon find fertile soil within the UN system.[13]

The United Nations

On October 24, 1945, United Nations was founded by the Allied victors of World War II. There were great ambitions and the organization grew rapidly. Its aim was to promote cooperation between the nations of the world, prevent new conflicts, and improve living conditions in the poorer nations.

The United States now took the lead, succeeding the near-bankrupt British Empire. The UN headquarters were located in New York (on land donated by John D. Rockefeller Jr.) while the old League of Nations headquarters in Geneva became the center of UN organizations such as the World Health Organization (WHO), the World Trade Organization (WTO), and the World Meteorological Organization (WMO).[14]

According to the UN Charter, the organization's primary objectives are:

1. To maintain international peace and security, and to that end: to take effective collective measures for the prevention and removal of threats to the peace, and for the suppression of acts of aggression or other breaches of the peace, and to bring about by peaceful means, and in conformity with the principles of justice and international law, adjustment or settlement of international disputes or situations which might lead to a breach of the peace;

2. To develop friendly relations among nations based on respect for the principle of equal rights and self-determination of peoples, and to take other appropriate measures to strengthen universal peace;

3. To achieve international co-operation in solving international
   problems of an economic, social, cultural, or humanitarian character, and in promoting and encouraging respect for human rights
   and for fundamental freedoms for all without distinction as to
   race, sex, language, or religion; and
4. To be a centre for harmonizing the actions of nations in the
   attainment of these common ends.[15]

The numerous subdivisions of the United Nations system have over time
grown to cover virtually every area of human activity—an endeavor that
had already been initiated by its predecessor, the League of Nations.

The Six Main Bodies of the UN Organization

1. **The General Assembly,** where each nation has one delegation
   and one vote (197 nations), is the very heart of the organization.
   During September to December every year, their meetings take
   place. The purpose is to discuss issues relating to the UN's main
   objectives (this is where sustainable development has grown
   into an overriding issue), review reports from main UN bodies,
   elect new members, approve the Security Council's proposal for
   Secretary-General, and decide on the UN budget. The General
   Assembly adopts resolutions on the issues discussed. These are
   not legally binding and only provide recommendations to the
   member states (who may, however, choose to make them legally
   binding in their respective countries).
2. **The Security Council** consists of fifteen members, of which five
   are permanent (France, China, Russia, United Kingdom, and
   United States). The other members are elected by the General
   Assembly for two-year terms. The Council, which does not hold
   regular meetings but is convened when necessary, discusses peace
   and security issues and the decisions taken are binding for all
   member states. However, the permanent members (the victors of

World War II) have veto powers and can thereby prevent adoption of a proposal.

3. **The Economic and Social Council** (ECOSOC) handles economic issues related to population, children, housing, women's rights, discrimination, drug abuse, crime, social welfare, youth, environment, and food. Its stated purpose includes promoting higher living standards, full employment, and economic and social progress; solutions to international economic, social, and health-related problems, as well as international cultural and educational cooperation. ECOSOC has fifty-four members elected by the General Assembly over a three-year term. Due to its large and broad remit, the Council consists of a number of commissions, including the High Level Panel on Sustainable Development. Their decisions involve recommendations to the member states, based on documentation from the UN's many sub- and professional bodies.

4. **The International Court of Justice** in the Hague, Netherlands, is the main UN body for legal issues. It settles disputes between states and advises on international legal issues. The Court of Justice has fifteen judges, elected by the General Assembly and the Security Council.

5. **The Trusteeship Council** was created to oversee and manage territories lacking a functioning state of affairs and therefore temporarily placed under UN administration. This applied to former colonies and territories that came under UN management after World War I. Following Palau's self-sovereignty in 1994, the Council lacks responsibilities and convenes only if the need arises. A chairman and vice-chairman are still appointed.

6. **The Secretariat** administers the activities of the UN agencies, arranges meetings, prepares decision documents, and implements UN decisions. Since 2017, António Guterres (former president of the Socialist International) has been Secretary General. He manages over 44,000 employees, of whom 6,500 work in New York.[16]

In the years following World War II, a number of organizations (all members of the World Federalist Movement) were actively working toward establishing the UN as a world government.

INTERNATIONAL COURT OF JUSTICE

Settles international legal disputes

The Hague

THE TRUSTEESHIP COUNCIL

Oversees trust territories (currently not in use)

New York

THE SECURITY COUNCIL

Keeps international peace and security

New York

THE UN SECRETARIAT

Executive body

Led by the Secretary-General

New York

THE UN GENERAL ASSEMBLY

193 MEMBER STATES

Adopts resolutions

New York

THE ECONOMIC & SOCIAL COUNCIL

Makes reports, coordinates sub- and professional bodies

New York

DEPARTMENTS:

DCO
DESA
DGACN
DGC
DMSPC
DOS
DPO
DPPA
DSS
OCHA
OCT
ODA
OHCHR
OIOS
OLA
OSAA
SRSG
UNDRR
UNODC
UNOG
UN-OHRLLS
UNON
UNOP
UNOV

PROFESSIONAL BODIES:

FAO
ICAO
ICSID
IFAD
ILO
IMF
IMGA
IMO
ITU
UHIDO
UPU
UNESCO
WHO
WIPO
WMO

WORLD BANK GROUP:

IBRD
IDA
IFC

SUB-BODIES:

UNCHS
UNCTAD
UNDP
UNEP
UNFCCC
UNFPA
UNHCR
UNICEF
UNODC
UNOPS
UNRWA
UNWOMAN
UNU
UNV
WFP

The UN System

The European Union

Meanwhile in Europe, the ground was being prepared for the European integration project. Jacques Delors in a speech before the Royal Institute of International Affairs later described the European Union (EU) as a "laboratory" where the world government concept could be tested on a smaller scale.[17]

> Thirty-five years after the European Community was set up, I believe it is not too presumptuous to claim that it still has something revolutionary about it, that it is something of a "laboratory" for the management of interdependence. (Jacques Delors, chairman of the EU Commission 1985–1995)

As many nations were still reluctant, the ultimate goal of a full-fledged world government had to be shelved for the time being. In the background, however, strategies were developed and measures taken to gradually bolster the power of the UN through the use of manipulation and persuasion. The UN would be marketed as the key organization for maintaining peace and order in a politically fractured world.

In the early twentieth century, the Carnegie Endowment and the Rockefeller Foundation, in collaboration with other foundations such as the Ford Foundation and the Guggenheim Foundation, started gaining influence over the education system (see appendix A for details)[18] while buying up leading newspapers and periodicals.

Through effective indoctrination through schools and the media, the worldview of the aristocracy would eventually become accepted by the majority: only the UN would be able to save the world from the specter of nuclear war after World War II. This threat would soon be accompanied by other issues of a global nature, all of which prompted a closer international cooperation and control.

The Rockefeller circle and the Council of Foreign Relations (CFR) came to work intensely at creating legitimacy for internationalism. It was also the purpose of the Trilateral Commission, a think tank founded in 1973 by banker David Rockefeller, "to respond in common to the opportunities and challenges that we confront and to assume the responsibilities that we face.[19]

Richard N. Gardner (member of the CFR and the Trilateral Commission) clarified both the goal and the recommended means in an article published in the CFR journal *Foreign Affairs*:

> In short, the "house of world order" will have to be built from the bottom up rather than from the top down. It will look like a great "booming, buzzing confusion," to use William James' famous description of reality, but an end run around national sovereignty, eroding it piece by piece, will accomplish more than the old-fashioned frontal assault.[20]

The project had ambitions that few comprehended. The idea was to technologically fuse together all nations and peoples to create a world organism. Nations as well as individuals would in the end lose their sovereignty and instead be governed by central dictates. Everything was founded upon scientific rationalism and management techniques inspired by Frederick Taylor and Henry Ford. Efficiency was the motto.

The World Brain

In his essay collection *The World Brain*, author and Fabian Society member H. G. Wells elaborated the idea of a global brain, where all human knowledge would be stored. In *The Open Conspiracy*, he describes a world governed by a scientific elite.[21] In 1940, Wells finally summarized his views on this global utopia in *The New World Order*, outlining this new system—which he did not expect to be welcomed by everyone.

> Countless people, from maharajas to millionaires and from pukkha sahibs to pretty ladies, will hate the new world order, be rendered unhappy by frustration of their passions and ambitions through its advent and will die protesting against it.[22]

In the science fiction novel *The Shape of Things to Come* (1933), adapted for the movie screen as *Things to Come* by Alexander Corda in 1936, Wells sketches a hypothetical future up until the year 2106, in which a financial crisis causes war in Europe, followed by a plague which causes insanity. Out of the ruins then emerges a coalition of benevolent engineers with a superior air force. They create a perfect permanent utopia with peace and order through abolishing nations, establishing a world language (English), prohibiting religion, and supporting the sciences. This utopia is populated by a new race of enlightened supermen. They live in a harmonious collective and begin to explore space. Such utopian visions of technocratic progressivism were typical of its time.

Wells's thoughts were inspired by his former teacher, the English biologist Thomas Huxley (also known as "Darwin's bulldog" due to his apologias for Darwin's theory of evolution). This implies that Wells was strongly influenced by eugenics (the genetic perfection of humankind) and social Darwinism.

During the same period, the Jesuit priest and paleontologist Pierre Teilhard de Chardin introduced his theories on developing a collective psychic sphere through the use of communications technology (the noosphere), and how this rapport would inherently progress toward unity, perfection, and the emergence of the cosmic Christ (the omega point). His teachings consisted of a peculiar mixture of evolutionary theory and Christian faith. Julian Huxley embraced his ideas (apart from the Christian aspects) and wrote in the foreword of the English version of Teilhard's *Le phénomène humain*:

> The incipient development of mankind into a single psychosocial unit, with a single noosystem or common pool of thought, is providing the evolutionary process with the rudiments of a head. It remains for our descendants to organise this noosystem more adequately.[23] (*The Phenomenon of Man*, 1959)

Wells's and Teilhard de Chardin's ideas in turn influenced the philosopher Oliver L. Reiser who, in his *World Sensorium: The Social Embryology of World Federation* (1946), introduced the idea of developing a "planetary socialism" based in scientific humanism (also known as scientism or secular humanism)—a view proposing that all societal developments should be based in the scientific method.[24] Reiser was also one of the signatories of the Humanist Manifesto (1933) which advocated the establishment of a new humanist religion.[25] The world brain was to constitute the body for world planning, able to execute operations universally. This would be headed by a group of world coordinators and a world parliament.

> If society is not to collapse from unresolved conflicts and resulting failures at integration, the nations of the world must surrender some measure of their sovereignty and begin to function within the texture of the world-whole. This social nervous system, center of intellectual–social unification, is called the world brain.[26]

Reiser called for a global consciousness and an international morality. For these reasons, he suggested that the newly founded UN should establish an International Institute of Educational and Cultural Cooperation. It was supposed to function as a global university with the purpose of disseminating scientific humanism across the globe. His plea was heeded, and in November of 1945, the specialized UN agency of UNESCO was formed with this very purpose.[27] The eugenicist and internationalist Julian Huxley (the brother of author Aldous Huxley and the grandson of H. G. Wells's teacher, Thomas Huxley) was appointed its first secretary-general.

Reiser's utopia surely had benevolent purposes. It was nonetheless contradictory, and his ideas would come to attract power-hungry factions with no qualms about promising paradise while hell was to be found in the fine print of the contract.

Reiser's ideas bore a close resemblance to those presented in Francis Bacon's utopian tract *The New Atlantis*, which envisioned a world governed by the scientific elite. These visions were also deeply rooted within the contemporary technocratic movement of the 1930s and influenced politics both in the United States and in Nazi Germany.[28] Reiser saw three potential future trajectories for the postwar era:

1. World destruction
2. World fascism
3. World federation (planetary socialism)

His own dream was the development of a peaceable world federation, while being aware that a darker future could become reality. He described how world fascism could lead to international cartels and large mono-polistic corporations taking total control over "development, distribution and marketing of resources like oil, rubber, metals and the like—goods we eat, wear, or use in one form or another." This would mean an anti-humanitarian unification of the world. Yet, this very type of monopolist, who had collaborated with Hitler, would after the war help fund the new UN headquarters in New York and join forces with the idealists, hiding behind the noble endeavors of an equal and just world while furtively preparing their techno–totalitarian solutions.

Cosmic Humanism

In his book *Cosmic Humanism and World Unity*, Reiser later described his plan for the world in greater detail. Through the book, published by the UN-associated organization World Institute in 1975, it was emphasized that technology would play a significant role in constructing the world utopia and for the evolution of the human race. By the application of technological solutions, Reiser considered that a peaceful and harmonious world would emerge.

> As an alternative to Marxism—already long obsolete—we propose a more futuristic orientation—the theory of planetary humanism. Our view is that the coming universal civilization will fuse many of the features of a variety of political, economic, and religious systems.[29]

Reiser also described how the new religion would be created, and that the end goal was to rebuild the Temple of Solomon—not *physically* in Jerusalem, but as a technological "temple" consisting of satellites and communications technology, in which the individual would be reduced to a mere cell in the great global organism. The individual would serve the greater good, yet also be transformed with the help of technology. This was supposed to be achieved through developing the method of "radio-eugenics," which meant that evolution could be remotely guided to upgrade the functions, behavior, and health of each individual with the help of technological tools. This would engender a new "super-human."

> Mankind must now take the next step: the conscious control or guid-
> ance of human evolution. (Oliver Reiser)

Reiser called this new high-tech religion cosmic humanism, whereas Julian Huxley coined its modern name, transhumanism. These thoughts were clearly inspired by the evolutionary principles of theosophy and freemasonry, according to which humankind will be alchemically transformed and ascend to perfection or a godlike status.

Reiser frequently published articles in Lucis Trust's theosophical periodical *The Beacon*. In Reiser's vision, this would not be attained through the individual voluntary self-improvement, but through the use of technological and scientific tools to manipulate people—with or without their knowledge or consent. The vision demanded careful strategic planning in order to be implemented. Reiser's and Teilhard de Chardin's ideas were anchored in UNESCO and were mainly promulgated by systems theorist Ervin László through the Club of Rome, World Future Society, and the United Nations' project the New International Economic Order (NIEO).

The Club of Rome

In the 1970s, The Club of Rome began sounding the alarm about the downsides of industrialism and about coming resource shortages if the population and the economy continued to grow. Through NIEO, the

United Nations, in partnership with a number of other influential institutions, would make this grandiose utopia come true.

The doomsday messages from the Club of Rome were closely connected to the type of solutions suggested in Reiser's utopian global civilization. A revolution in information technology that would bring about a peaceful world in balance. A resilient system run by cybernetic central planning. The alternative was Armageddon.

In 1977, Ervin László wrote the report *Goals for Mankind* for the Club of Rome, relaying this message (see chapter 10). According to their computer models, a sustainable utopia should ideally have a global population of 500 million, with the world divided into interdependent regions.[30]

Georgia Guidestones

The eugenic dreams of controlling population and reproduction were also reflected in some (1, 2, and 10) of the new "commandments" of the Georgia Guidestones monument of Elberton, Georgia.

The ten guidelines were carved in stone in eight modern languages, with shorter texts in four ancient languages, like a Rosetta Stone for the future. The inscription read:

1. Maintain humanity under 500,000,000 in perpetual balance with nature.
2. Guide reproduction wisely—improving fitness and diversity.
3. Unite humanity with a living new language.
4. Rule passion—faith—tradition—and all things with tempered reason.
5. Protect people and nations with fair laws and just courts.
6. Let all nations rule internally resolving external disputes in a world court.
7. Avoid petty laws and useless officials.
8. Balance personal rights with social duties.
9. Prize truth—beauty—love—seeking harmony with the infinite.
10. Be not a cancer on the Earth—Leave room for nature—Leave room for nature.

Georgia Guidestones

The monument was inaugurated March 22, 1980, and its origin has been shrouded in mystery from the beginning. In the book *Common Sense Renewed* (1986), written by one of the founders under the pen name "Robert Christian," a detailed explanation was given:

> The most pressing world environmental problem is the need to control human numbers. In recent centuries technology and abundant fuels has multiplied humanity far beyond what is prudent or long sustainable. We can foresee the impending exhaustion of certain energy sources and the depletion of many vital raw materials. To control reproduction is crucial. This will require major changes in our attitudes and customs.[31]

In the investigative documentary *Dark Clouds over Elberton* (2015), it was revealed that the man behind the monument was Dr. Herbert Kersten, a physician from Fort Dodge, Iowa.[32] According to a local historian interviewed in the documentary, this doctor had shocked his local country club by openly voicing racist and white supremacist views.

He also wrote an opinion piece for a Florida newspaper in which he supported David Duke, Grand Wizard of the Knights of the Ku Klux Klan, and was proud of his acquaintance with controversial Nobel laureate William Shockley (inventor of the transistor) who had also expressed racist and eugenicist opinions. He claimed that blacks were intellectually inferior to whites and proposed that people with an IQ below 100 should be paid to undergo voluntary sterilization.

On the morning of July 6, 2022, an explosion went off by the monument. One of the stones was totally shattered and others damaged. Later that same day, after the forensic investigation was concluded, the remains of the monument were removed for safety reasons. On August 8, the Elbert County Board of Commissioners decided that the remains would be returned to the builders, the Elberton Granite Association, and the land returned to its previous owner.[33] No perpetrators have yet been found.

The Initiative for Eco-92 Earth Charter

During a meeting in Des Moines of the United Nations Association of Iowa on September 22, 1991, in preparation of the UN's environmental conference in Rio de Janeiro the following year, a disturbing document was issued. It was called "The Initiative for Eco-92 Earth Charter" by the Secretariat for World Order.

The tone of the document had similarities to Robert Christian's ideas and contained the following draconian recommendations:

> The Security Council of the UN, led by the Anglo-Saxon Major Nation Powers, will decree that henceforth, the Security Council will inform all nations that its sufferance on population has ended, that all nations have quotas for REDUCTION on a yearly basis, which will be enforced by the Security Council by selective or total embargo of credit, items of trade including food and medicine, or by military force, when required.
>
> The Security Council of the UN will inform all nations that outmoded notions of national sovereignty will be discarded and that the

Security Council has complete legal, military and economic jurisdiction in any region of the world . . .

The Security Council of the UN will take possession of all natural resources, including the watersheds and great forests, to be used and preserved for the good of the Major Nations of the Security Council.

The Security Council of the UN will explain that not all races and peoples are equal, nor should they be. Those races proven superior by superior achievements ought to rule the lesser races, caring for them on sufferance that they cooperate with the Security Council. Decision making, including banking, trade, currency rates, and economic development plans, will be made in stewardship by the Major Nations.

All of the above constitute the New World Order, in which Order, all nations, regions and races will cooperate with the decisions of the Major Nations of the Security Council.

These chilling views can be traced back to Rhodes's and Milner's vision for the world. The authors were a group devoted to British supremacy and global control, with the United Nations' Security Council as executive organ. This is openly stated in the document:

We are the living sponsors of the great Cecil Rhodes will of 1877, in which Rhodes devoted his fortune to: "The extension of British rule throughout the world . . . the colonization by British subjects of the entire continent of Africa, the Holy Land, the Valley of the Euphrates, the islands of Cyprus and Canada, the whole of South America, the islands of the pacific not heretofore possessed by Great Britain, the whole of the Malay Archipelago, the seaboard of China and Japan, the ultimate recovery of the United States of America as an integral part of the British Empire. . . .

We stand with Lord Milner's Credo. We too, are "British Race patriots" and our patriotism is "the speech, the tradition, the principles, the aspirations of the British Race." Do you fear to take this stand, at the very last moment when this purpose can be realized?

> Do you not see that failure now, is to be pulled down by the billions of Lilliputians of lesser race who care little or nothing for the Anglo-Saxon system?[34]

These racist views were not necessarily shared by the UN in general, or by the many genuine idealists within the organization seeing the UN as a protector of world peace and justice, but it illustrates how the fears of over-population and proposed solutions based on neo-Malthusianism and eugenics have a created fertile ground for ideas with a very dangerous potential.

Unfortunately, similar scenarios seem to be under implementation in the wake of the COVID-19 crisis. But instead of the open racism of earlier times, we today have an inverted form. Tension between ethnic groups seem stronger than for many decades and have been aggravated by activist organizations and campaigns, backed by critical race theory and intersectionality. In order to succeed, those identified as belonging to underprivileged groups are considered in need of "positive discrimination" in higher education, on corporate boards, and in politics—where they can be influenced to become loyal agents of change, and perhaps even set up as convenient future scapegoats for an agenda originally drawn up by privileged white male racists. So, after decades of relative color blindness, gender equality, and a wider acceptance of differences, once again people are to be evaluated collectively as members of a specific group—this time in an inverse order—based on attributes such as gender, sexual orientation, and pigmentation, instead of as individuals and fellow human beings.

Atomic bomb

2

The Threats

If the world government cause is to triumph it will need more than sympathetic endorsement by the majority. People must be made to feel that their own security, freedom, and prosperity, yes their very own survival, depend on the creation in our time of a world rule of law. They must be made to believe that the establishment of a world government is more urgent than the maintenance of a high domestic standard of life and as, if not more, practical than the pursuit of a deceptive security by military preparedness.[1] (Eugene Rabinowitch, 1947)

In addition to propaganda about the excellence of the United Nations, there was a need to build a solid foundation for the development of a pure World Government and an implementation of the Great Transformation. This is where the global threats come in. Convincing threats and global crises are needed to gain popular support for changing society at a profound level. Invisible threats, such as nuclear radiation, climate change, ozone holes, viruses, and lurking terrorists can be extra frightening.

Background

During the postwar decades, a number of new global issues requiring more intense international cooperation were raised. The United Nations was again presented as the key organization to address these threats. The United States and the organizations and institutes of the Rockefeller sphere took the lead. In the Rockefeller Brothers Fund's *Special Studies*

Project from the late 1950s, three areas of special importance were listed: the climate (carbon dioxide), global health (pandemics), and nuclear war.[2]

The Nuclear Threat

The greatest fear during the Cold War (1945–1991) was the nuclear threat and later the threat of an "atomic winter" (the global cooling due to blocked solar radiation that was likely to follow a major nuclear conflict).

The Doomsday Clock at Rockefeller's University of Chicago became a representation of this looming nuclear threat. The symbolic clock was created by the same nuclear physicists who were involved in the Manhattan Project (the research project that led to the development of the atomic bomb) to illustrate how close the world was to an apocalypse. In December 1945, they started the periodical *Bulletin of the Atomic Scientists* to warn about the dangers of the nuclear weapons they themselves had just developed.

As indicated by the opening quote, their solution to world threats was from the very beginning the establishment of a world government. According to the *Bulletin*'s editor in chief Eugene Rabinowitch, the task of the scientists was to guide the populace to the conclusion that a world government was absolutely indispensable to solving the world's pressing issues:

> Scientists must remember the path which brought them to the unanimous realization of the necessity of world government. Their special task, which none else can perform with equal authority and chance for success, is to lead others along the same path, so that more and more people may arrive at the same conclusion—that political likes or dislikes must be subordinated to the urgent common cause of establishing, within this generation, a community of mankind under enforceable law.[3]

The University of Chicago was one of the main strongholds for these visions. Between 1945 and 1948, its president Robert Hutchins and professor Giuseppe Borgese helped draft the World Constitution.[4] They also founded the Aspen Institute for Humanistic Studies which is closely associated with the UN.*

In 1947, the Doomsday Clock was launched. It has since warned of the danger of a nuclear war. Until the fall of the Berlin Wall in 1989, the warnings were mainly focused on a possible conflict between the United States (NATO) and the USSR (The Warsaw Pact). Later, other existential threats were added. According to the atomic scientists, the world had been close to Armageddon on two particular occasions. In 1953, the hands of the clock were set to two minutes to midnight, due to the fact that both the United States and the USSR had recently developed and tested hydrogen bombs. The second occasion was the Cuban Missile Crisis of 1961.

The man behind the hydrogen bomb was Edward Teller, nuclear physicist at the Institute for Atomic Studies at the University of Chicago. It is worth noting that he was part of the editorial team of the *Bulletin of the Atomic Scientists*, and had five years earlier posed the question of whether nuclear war was at all possible to avoid, also arguing for a world government as a solution.

Edward Teller 1958

* See my book *Rockefeller: Controlling the Game* for more details.

Teller was a close friend of Nelson Rockefeller (US Vice President 1974–1977) and was part of the Rockefeller Brothers Fund's Special Studies Project during the late 1950s. This ambitious project advised the United States to expand its nuclear arsenal to counter the threat from the Soviet Union.

When the Cold War ended in 1991, the hands were moved back to seventeen minutes to midnight. After the fall of the Berlin Wall, the peace movement that had been very active during the 1980s became integrated into the green movement.

Overpopulation

In 1948, the books *Our Plundered Planet* by Fairfield Osborn and the *Road to Survival* by William Vogt were published. Both authors were part of the conservationist organization Conservation Foundation founded in the same year with support from Laurance Rockefeller. The Conservation Foundation was characterized by Malthusian ideas on the planet's carrying capacity in relation to population and available resources. To address these problems, global, centrally planned solutions, and preferably a world government, were suggested. Vogt coldly remarked that "Large scale bacterial warfare would be an effective, if drastic, means of bringing back the earth's forests and grasslands."[5]

Four years later, John D. Rockefeller III and Frederick Osborn (Fairfield Osborn's cousin) founded the Population Council for the purpose of curbing population growth. Its head office was located at the Rockefeller University campus in New York. Its ideals, as well as its representatives, were deeply entrenched in eugenics, and would inspire both the founding of the Club of Rome and its views on humans. In 1956, Osborne wrote in the *Eugenics Review* that "We need the greatest possible number of births from genetically superior individuals."

In the 1960s, Paul Ehrlich's book *The Population Bomb* helped spread a wider awareness of the population issue, both within the nascent environmental movement and in politics. John D. Rockefeller III was appointed by President Nixon to head the Rockefeller Commission on Population Growth and the American Future (1969–1972).[6]

In 1974, the United Nations held the World Population Conference, with John D. Rockefeller III as chief representative of the United States. These efforts were thereafter continued through the Rockefeller Brothers Fund's report *The Unfinished Agenda* (1977) and the US Congress report *Global 2000* (1980). The reports, both compiled under the auspices of Gerald O. Barney, presented a specific action plan for curbing global population growth (very similar to the national plan presented to President Nixon by the Rockefeller Commission in 1972). The reports had a strong impact on the environmental debate of the 1980s and also on the shaping of China's one-child policy. The population issue was closely connected to issues of environment and resources.[7] Even today, overpopulation is often emphasized as a major problem, despite falling birth rates even in developing countries and a historically low population growth rate.[8]

Pollution

In 1948, the International Union of Conservation of Nature and natural Resources (IUCN) was founded by Julian Huxley and the UNESCO. IUCN focuses upon conservation, biodiversity, and sustainable development.

In 1961, Julian Huxley, president of the British Eugenic Society, also took part in launching the World Wildlife Fund (WWF) with Prince Bernhard of the Netherlands (founder of the Bilderberg group) and Prince Philip of the United Kingdom. Bernhard became its president, and Godfrey Rockefeller, cousin of the Rockefeller brothers, was appointed as the first executive director. Its foundational capital came from Royal Dutch Shell, the president of which, John Loudon, in 1976 would succeed Prince Bernhard as president of the WWF. In 1962, DDT was picked up on by Rachel Carson in her book *Silent Spring* as an environmental toxin affecting birdlife. The modern-day environmental movement was born.

A decade later, the threats facing our common environment became the theme of the first UN environmental conference in Stockholm, led by the Rockefeller family's trusted henchman Maurice Strong, with Russell Train as head of the US delegation. The call for the conference came from

Sweden (Sverker Åström and Hans Palmstierna), and the agenda was planned in concert with the Aspen Institute in the United States.

The Club of Rome, founded in 1968, was influential in the debate ahead of the conference. In 1972, the book *Limits of Growth* were published, warning of a complete system collapse unless economic growth was reduced. All important minerals and resources were predicted by computer models to run out if population continued to grow. The Malthusian views of the elite were then popularized by environmental organizations like Greenpeace and Friends of the Earth, giving the impression of a genuine grassroots awakening.

Environmental debate in the 1970s and 1980s focused primarily on overfishing, whaling, environmental toxins, desertification, the ozone hole, and potential nuclear reactor accidents. This led to the launching of the Brundtland Commission in 1983 at the behest of the UN, with Maurice Strong as participant. Both Gro Harlem Brundtland and Strong were also members of the elite think tank the Trilateral Commission.

These efforts resulted in the 1992 Rio conference on the environment. Again Maurice Strong was chosen as secretary-general of the conference. The concluding document, Agenda 21 (Agenda for the 21st Century), resulted in a long-term plan encompassing every aspect of human and social evolution. Everything was to be controlled through the UN. The first step was adopting the Millennium Goals (for the time period 2000–2015).

After the Rio meeting, work also began on the Earth Charter. Queen Beatrix of the Netherlands (daughter of Prince Bernhard), appointed Club of Rome members Mikhail Gorbachev and Maurice Strong as heads of the authoring commission. The main coordinator was Nelson Rockefeller's son, Steven, a professor of religious studies. The work was directed from the Rockefeller property Pocantico outside New York and funded by the Dutch government. In March of 2000, the Earth Charter final text was approved at a meeting at UNESCO headquarters in Paris and three months later given official status at a ceremony in the Hague Peace Palace, funded by Andrew Carnegie, in the presence of Queen Beatrix.

The following year, the Earth Charter was written down on papyrus and placed in a new Ark of the Covenant—the Ark of Hope (designed by artist Sally Linder). After the inauguration ceremony on September 9, 2001, it was carried in procession from Shelburne Farms, Vermont, to the UN headquarters and put on public display in anticipation of the environmental conference in Johannesburg 2002. For security reasons (due to the 9/11 attacks), the procession had a stopover at the Rockefeller Interfaith Center (nicknamed "The God Box").

The second Rio Environmental Summit (Rio+20) was held in 2012 with the motto "The Future We Want." Here, it was decided that the Millennium Goals were to be succeeded by new Sustainable Development Goals (Agenda 2030, for the period 2015–2030). These new goals were accepted by the world's heads of state in September 2015.[9] The goals were very similar to the Earth Charter (more on the global goals in chapter 3).

Global Warming

Climate change is also viewed as an environmental threat and has become closely linked with the population issue. Toward the end of the 1980s, it succeeded thermonuclear war as the main threat and functions as the engine of the contemporary agenda of global change.

The carbon dioxide theory was formulated by Swedish physicist Svante Arrhenius as early as 1896, but was initially not taken very seriously. As a board member of the Swedish State Institute for Racial Biology in Uppsala, Arrhenius was deeply involved with eugenics, which also held true for the researchers who came to study the issue more closely a few decades later.

German climatologist and meteorologist Hermann Flohn was one of the first to explore the theory more seriously. His article "Die Tätigkeit des Menschen als Klimafaktor" ("Man's activity as a climate factor") was published in 1941 during his service with the Luftwaffe (the Nazi Germany air force). Flohn, who took part in planning the attack on the Soviet Union, continued work on establishing the carbon dioxide theory in concert with mainly American and Swedish researchers after the war.

Roger Revelle, who took part in the Population Council's first conference of 1952, became a leading researcher in terms of promoting the idea of anthropogenic climate influence during the 1950s, together with Arrhenius's disciple Carl-Gustaf Rossby and his PhD student Bert Bolin. This work was supported by the Rockefeller Foundation in relation to a project exploring the effects of nuclear weapons upon atmosphere, land, and ocean.

Revelle's paper received much attention and gave the issue scientific credibility during the International Geophysical Year (1957–1958). In relation to this program, one started to measure the carbon dioxide content of the atmosphere, This brought about the first international conference on human carbon dioxide emissions and their influence on the climate, arranged by Laurance Rockefeller's Conservation Foundation in 1963. Thereupon, Revelle lobbied to put these issues on Lyndon Johnson's environmental agenda, which resulted in the 1965 report *Restoring the Quality of the Environment*. Revelle was awarded a population institute at Harvard University by the Rockefeller Foundation. From then on, the issue was present in the international arena.

In 1971, Nelson Rockefeller's close friend, the MIT professor and Club of Rome member Carrol L. Wilson, set up the conference Study of Man's Impact on the Climate. Carbon dioxide was here implicated as a possible cause of climate change, while one participant also warned of possible cooling due to aerosols. The report was circulated during the 1972 Stockholm conference on the environment where it was decided that the WMO and the ICSU would tackle the issue in tandem with the newly formed UNEP under the supervision of Maurice Strong.

These organizations arranged the first World Climate Conference in 1979 (with an agenda founded upon the SMIC report), as well as the succeeding Villach and Bellagio conferences funded by the Rockefeller Brothers Fund (RBF) and the Rockefeller Foundation. With the 1985 Villach meeting as a starting point, the UNEP president Mostafa Tolba advised the Reagan administration and the trilateral member George Schultz to erect an interstate organization to assemble research on anthropogenic climate effects. This resulted in the founding of the IPCC in

1988, at the same time as the UN declared climate change a critical issue for all of humanity. The climate emergency was considered a global problem, only possible to address within a global framework.

In 1992, the environmental treaty UNFCCC was adopted. Its purpose was to "stabilize the amount of atmospheric greenhouse gases at a level preventing the detrimental effects of human action upon the climate system." The negotiations within UNFCCC led to the 1997 Kyoto Protocol on emissions reduction, a treaty which was never ratified by the United States.

The great breakthrough of the climate emergency took place after the 2005 Hurricane Katrina and was also catalyzed by Al Gore's film *An Inconvenient Truth* from 2006. In relation to this, climate propaganda and activism were intensified. Major climate protests were held during the UN week in New York in 2014 and globally in 2015, arranged by 350.org with funding from the RBF. Everything led up to the Paris Climate Accords of December 2015, with the purpose of "maintaining global warming below two degrees, but preferably below 1.5 degrees." This treaty was initially signed on Earth Day, April 22, 2016.[10]

Terrorism

During the 1970s, apart from the politically motivated IRA attacks in London and the PLO operations in Israel, a number of terrorist attacks were perpetrated by left-wing extremists such as the Red Army Faction (aka the Baader-Meinhof group) in Germany, the Red Brigades in Italy, and the Symbionese Liberation Army (SLA) in the United States—famously kidnapping and converting Patty Hearst to join their cause. Between 1978 and 1995, the "Unabomber" Ted Kaczynski terrorized the United States with his homemade mail bombs. There were also a number of spectacular airplane hijackings in the 1970s, resulting in a permanent intensification of airport security and control of passengers and luggage.

However, the notion of terrorism as a *global* threat did not emerge until the attacks on the World Trade Center and the Pentagon on September 11, 2001. This tragic event was very convenient for US war hawks. The think tank Project for the New American Century (PNAC) had already advocated for a more aggressive US foreign policy the year before, in opposition to the more pacifist position of the Democrats. PNAC had also explicitly stated the need for a trigger event enabling the execution of their agenda:

> Further, the process of transformation, even if it brings revolutionary change, is likely to be a long one, absent some catastrophic and cata-lyzing event—like a new Pearl Harbor.[11]

This think tank included a several members of the upcoming Bush administration, including the neoconservative hawks John Bolton, Paul Wolfowitz, Donald Rumsfeld, and the later World Bank president Robert Zoellick. The neocon ideology originated with Leo Strauss, professor at the University of Chicago.

The World Trade Center was a Rockefeller initiative made possible by the influence of the brothers David and Nelson. The complex was finished in 1972, and the twin towers were nicknamed "David" and "Nelson." After the towers were turned to rubble in the 9/11 event, the "War on Terror" was launched, intrusive surveillance measures were established without public opposition, and the wars against Afghanistan and Iraq were initiated.

The attacks, attributed to Al Qaeda and its founder Osama bin Laden, were followed by the terrorist attacks in Madrid in March 2004 and in London in July 2005, and a wave of Islamic terrorism during the follow-ing decade, including the attacks on the *Charlie Hebdo* office in Paris in January 2015.

The Saudi bin Laden family were old business partners of the Bush family, and the Al Qaeda network had emerged out of the mujahideen of Afghanistan, backed by the United States during the Soviet occupation of 1979–1989. The Trilateral Commission cofounder Zbigniew Brzezinski and the CIA funded and armed these groups.

During the 2010s, terror attacks have increasingly been characterized by right-wing extremism, such as the attack on the Oslo government quar-ters and the Utøya massacre in 2011 (as a response to Islam and mass immigration from the Middle East, according to the perpetrator Anders Breivik). Later examples include the attack on the Al Noor mosque of Christchurch, New Zealand, in 2019, and many more.

In the wake of the 2015 refugee crisis during the Syrian civil war, provoked and inflamed by foreign interests that turned four million people into refugees, these tensions have kept increasing.

Economic Crises

A number of economic crises have contributed to changing the global landscape. The Great Depression during the 1930s cut international trade in half, with ensuing mass unemployment. It enabled a more intrusive governmental interference in Western economies (Keynesianism). In the United States, the New Deal was introduced. In Europe, the Nazi regime in Germany started building its Thousand-Year Empire with borrowed funds out of the debris of the global economic recession.

The 1973 oil crisis increased oil prices by 400 percent, which sent shock waves through the economy. The postwar growth was brought to a halt. The crisis raised awareness of oil dependence and resource consumption, and an outsourcing of energy-intensive industry to low-wage countries in Asia was initiated. The crisis was triggered by the Yom Kippur War when Israel was attacked and successfully fended off its neighbors. Ahead of this crisis, the effects of a 400 percent increase in oil price had specifically been discussed at a Bilderberg Meeting in Saltsjöbaden, Stockholm. Additionally, the Aspen Institute had arranged a workshop on global energy issues the previous year (funded by the Rockefeller Brothers Fund).

The dot-com bubble in the late 1990s, caused by the overvaluation of budding IT companies, burst in 2000 causing the early 2000s recession.

The Global Financial Crisis of 2007–2008 was attributed to the overleveraged housing market in the United States. Several nations were facing bankruptcy. The crisis resulted in actions such as the G20 being established as a forum for addressing global challenges such as financial crises and climate change.

Refugee Crises

Both before and after World War II, there were major waves of migration when borders were redrawn and people were driven from their homelands. In Europe, millions of Germans and Poles were forced to leave cities and regions they had inhabited for generations.

The persecution of Jews in Nazi Germany led to a mass migration into Palestine. When Israel was proclaimed a sovereign nation in 1948, Arab Palestinians were in turn driven out to live in refugee camps in Lebanon and Jordan.

At the partition of India in 1947, 15 million Muslims and Hindus became refugees—one of the largest population displacements in history thus far, creating great challenges, much suffering, and the deaths of several hundred thousand, perhaps up to two million, people.

During the Yugoslavian Wars of 1991–2001, Europe once again saw major waves of refugees. This in turn gave rise to right-wing nationalist parties painting the large influx of asylum seekers as a threat. The conflict was also used to persuade more countries to join the European Union "for peace and the environment."

Then, in the second half of 2015, there was another refugee crisis with mass immigration to Europe, mainly from Syria, Afghanistan, Iraq, and Africa. This crisis was highlighted in the media with dramatic images of refugees precariously crossing the Mediterranean in small rafts, and put much pressure on social institutions in receiving countries. Many did their best to welcome these refugees, but the situation soon generated conflict between immigration-positive groups and more xenophobic groups. These tensions intensified during the following years, fomented by reports of increased crime, including rapes, robberies, shootings, and gang crime.

The crisis also resulted in a reintroduction of border controls between EU member states and demands for more stringent control of the external EU borders. As early as 2013, the European Commission had introduced proposals for Smart Borders and an automated entry/exit system using biometric data (fingerprint and iris scans).

Conveniently, a pilot study for such a system could be conducted during the cusp of the crisis between March and September 2015.[12] This all took place during the general consultation for the European Commission's proposal, which in 2018 resulted in the European Travel Information and Authorization System (ETIAS). The system, designed to identify potential security risks and illegal immigration, is expected to become operational in Spring 2025.

> ETIAS will be a largely automated IT system created to identify security, irregular migration or high epidemic risks posed by visa-exempt visitors traveling to the Schengen States, whilst at the same time facilitate crossing borders for the vast majority of travelers who do not pose such risks.[13]

Pandemics

Throughout history, there have been a number of serious pandemics eliminating large parts of the global population, with the Black Death during the middle ages considered the most fatal.

The most serious pandemics in modern times were the Spanish flu, a bacterial infection killing around 50 million people between 1918 and 1920, and AIDS, with a death toll of 32 million since the 1980s.

Pandemics transcend borders. This threat is thus one of the most effective means by which to bring about fundamental changes of society. As early as 1913, the Rockefeller Foundation was searching for diseases that could be controlled or extinguished within a few decades, and founded the International Health Division that same year. IHD was the model for—and shared its expertise and resources with—the League of Nations Health Organization (with the Rockefeller Foundation as a significant financier).

After the disbandment of the League of Nations, its work was continued by the World Health Organization (WHO), founded in 1948, which had emerged as a central agency with the purpose of addressing global health issues. Up until the turn of the millennium, the Rockefeller Foundation was one of the most important sources of funding, succeeded by the increasingly influential Bill & Melinda Gates Foundation during the 2000s (more on this in chapter 4).

The Paris terror attacks in the Bataclan club November 13, 2015—
which coincided with the 2015 G20 Antalya summit in Turkey two days
later, only two weeks before the crucial UN Climate Change Conference
in Paris—is another example of how the various threats have tended
to converge.

These crises always result in the same solution being offered—global
governance. As the master manipulator Henry Kissinger wrote in the *New
York Times* in 2009:

> The ultimate challenge is to shape the common concern of most
> countries and all major ones regarding the economic crisis, together
> with a common fear of jihadist terrorism, into a common strategy
> reinforced by the realization that the new issues like proliferation,
> energy and climate change permit no national or regional solution.[14]

Handshake

The Partnership

This Agenda is a plan of action for people, planet and prosperity. It also seeks to strengthen universal peace in larger freedom. We recognise that eradicating poverty in all its forms and dimensions, including extreme poverty, is the greatest global challenge and an indispensable requirement for sustainable development. All countries and all stakeholders, acting in collaborative partnership, will implement this plan. We are resolved to free the human race from the tyranny of poverty and want and to heal and secure our planet.[1]

A clear and well-defined solution to the threats is needed. This solution should be presented in a way that it sounds irresistible and is difficult to reject. In this case, the various threats and crises are used to justify the implementation of the Great Transformation—Agenda 2030 and the global goals. According to proponents, this will guarantee a sustainable world in balance.

The Global Goals

On September 25, 2015, the global framework Agenda 2030, with its seventeen sustainable development goals (SDGs), was signed by the member states of the United Nations.[*] According to UNEP, Agenda 2030 "is the

---

[*] Agenda 2030 (for the period 2015–2030) replaced the Millennium Goals (for the period 2000–2015). Both are sub-goals of the overarching *Agenda 21* ("Action Plan for Sustainable Development for the 21st Century") that was signed in 1992.

most ambitious agenda for sustainable development the world's nations have ever undertaken." The historical significance of this cannot be overstated. If the goals are implemented as intended, it will lead to a *total transformation* of *all* aspects of life for *all* beings on this planet.

The colorful goals are clearly written to gain broad support from member states. Who does not want to save the planet and see justice, equality, and security for all?

The Seventeen SDGs of Agenda 2030

In practice, however, the vague wording of the goals would soon turn out to be interpreted by the UN, G20, EU, and WEF in favor of the interests of the largest global institutions, multinational corporations, banks, and the world's richest billionaires, and made legally binding for all inhabitants on Earth, without their informed consent or a chance to vote on this radical global transformation.

Agenda 2030 is founded in the same notions of overpopulation, eugenics, and population control that were held by the founders of the League of Nations and the UN. These goals will now be implemented using the scientific management techniques of Frederick Taylor and Henry Ford. The global utopia comes at a price.

World Economic Forum

The World Economic Forum (WEF) was originally founded as the European Management Forum in 1971 and renamed in 1987. As of 2015, it calls itself "the world's leading organization for public–private partnerships" dedicated to "improving the world."

Members and partners are leading transnational corporations, foundations, and financial institutions. Its head office is located in Geneva, Switzerland, a few kilometers from the Palace of the Nations and the WHO.

When WEF founder and president Klaus Schwab studied at Harvard Kennedy School in the 1960s, Henry Kissinger was his mentor, and Harvard has remained closely associated with WEF. Schwab has also been a member of the Bilderberg group's steering committee.

Since 2017, Börge Brende, former foreign minister of Norway, has been the president of WEF. Brende is also a member of the steering committee of the Bilderberg group and has been a board member of Statoil. WEF board members also include David Rubenstein (member of the Trilateral Commission and president of the Council on Foreign Relations), Al Gore (climate guru, ex–Trilateral Commission), Marc Benioff (Salesforce, member of the CFR, president of the WEF Center for the Fourth Industrial Revolution), as well as representatives of the World Bank, the IMF, BIS, and also national banks such as Russian Sberbank, Bank of China, and Bank of England.

The WEF gathers the world's major players in business, finance, and politics to shape the global agenda, as well as select celebrities and influencers. Besides the annual Davos meeting, there is the Meeting of the Champions in China each summer or fall, emphasizing technology, science, and innovation.

The price for membership or partnership is tiered between $60,000 and $600,000, depending upon degree of involvement.[2] For access to the January Davos meeting, participants must add another $28,000, including the costs of the stay itself.[3] "Associated Members" take part in select activities of interest, while "Strategic Partners" fund and run many of the forum's activities. For these fees, WEF members and partners can more or less purchase both problems and solutions in order to increase demand for their corporation or organization's particular goods or services.

WORLD
ECONOMIC
FORUM

MANAGING BOARD	WEF BOARD OF TRUSTEES	EXECUTIVE COMMMITTEE
President Börge Brende	Chairman Klaus Scwhab	Chairman Klaus Scwhab
Geneva	Geneva	60 nationalities

Strategic Partner	Strategic Partner Associate	Partner	Associate Partner

REGIONS

Africa, ASEAN, Europe/Eurasia, Latin America, Middle East, China, South Asia

SYSTEMS INITIATIVES

Shaping the Future of:

1. Consumption
2. Manufacturing & Production
3. Cities & Infrastructure
4. Cybersecurity
5. Digital Economy
6. Energy & Materials
7. Financial & Monetary Systems
8. Global Public Goods
9. Health & Healthcare
10. Investing
11. Media Entertainment & sports
12. Mobility
13. AI & Machine Learning
14. Blockchain and Digital Assets
15. Technology Governance
16. Global Economic Governance
17. Internet of Things
18. New Economic Society
19. Covid Action Platform

COMMUNITIES

1. Geostrategic Collaboration
2. Book Club
3. CEO Action for the EU Green Deal
4. Civil Society
5. Cultural Leaders
6. Global Future Council
7. Fellows
8. Global Leadership Fellows
9. Global Shapers
10. Global University Leaders
11. Partnering Against Corruption
12. Values for a Decentralised Future
13. Social Innovators
14. Family Business
15. Strategic Intelligence Co-curators
16. Technology Pioneers
17. Young Global Leaders
18. Young Scientists

CENTER FOR THE FOURTH INDUSTRIAL REVOLUTION

San Fransisco, China, India, Japan

SUBDIVISIONS

Brazil, Colombia, Israel, Norway, Rwanda,
Saudi Arabia, South Africa, Turkey, United Arab Emirates

WORLD ECONOMIC FORUM – board members 2021

KLAUS SCHWAB (Switzerland) WEF Chairman		**Laurance Fink** (USA) Blackrock; MoMA
Mukesh D. Ambani (India) Reliance Industries	COUNCIL on FOREIGN RELATIONS	**Mark Benioff** (USA) Salesforce
Christine Lagarde (France) European Central Bank		**David Rubenstein** (USA) Carlyle Group; CFR Chair
Jim Hagemann Snabe (Denmark) Siemens	TRILATERAL COMMISSION	**Orit Gadiesh** (Israel, USA) Bain & Co.
Kristalina Georgieva (Republic of Bulgaria) IMF		**Mark Carney** (Canada, UK) UN Climate Action; G30 Bank of England; BIS; FSB
Thomas Buberl (Germany) AXA	BILDERBERG MEETINGS	**Al Gore** (USA) Apple; Google Climate Reality Project
André Hoffman (Switzerland) Roche		**Angel Gúrria** (Mexico) OECD
Mark Schneider (Switzerland) Nestlé		**Julie Sweet** (USA) Accenture; ID2020
Peter Brabeck-Letmathe (Switzerland) Nestlé	**Queen Rania** (Jordania) UN SDG; UN Foundation	**L. Rafael Reif** (USA) MIT
Peter Mauer (Switzerland) Red Cross	**Zhu Minh** (People's Republic of China) IMF	**Yo-Yo Ma** (USA) Aspen Institute
Feike Sybesma (Netherlands) Philips	**Heizo Takenaka** (Japan) Keio University	**Chrystia Freeland** (Canada) Minister of Finance
Fabiola Gianotti (Italy) CERN	**Tharman Shanmugaratnam** (Singapore) Senior Minister of Singapore	**Luis Moreno** (Colombia) Intl. Olympic Committée
Herman Gref (Russian Federation) Sberbank	**Paula Ingabire** (Rwanda) Minister of Communications	**Patrice Motsepe** (Republic of South Africa) African Rainbow Minerals

The WEF manages eighteen different major initiatives where international political agendas are shaped, with the participation of the forum's partners. Central to discussions are how global issues can be addressed through public–private partnerships. One significant example, relevant to global events during 2020, is the project Shaping the Future of Health and Health Care.[4] Partners include Bill & Melinda Gates Foundation, GAVI—The Vaccine Alliance, GlaxoSmithKline, Henry Schein, Johnson & Johnson, Moderna, the European Commission, Rockefeller Foundation, US National Institute of Health, Wellcome Trust, WHO, and the World Bank Group.

Another initiative of major importance for the technological development is Shaping the Future of Digital Economy and New Value Creation.[5] This systems initiative "helps companies leverage technology to be agile in the face of disruption and to create the new digitally enabled business models for a new normal—post-COVID, purpose driven, sustainable and inclusive." Partners include Accenture, AliBaba Group, the European Commission, Generation Investment Management (Al Gore), Google, GSMA, Huawei, Mastercard, Microsoft, Salesforce, SAP, and the International Telecommunications Union.

WEF members are also involved in various communities and networks, such as:

- **Family Business Community**: Owners and heirs of the world's leading family businesses.
- **Global Shapers**: A rapidly growing "grassroots" network of over 10,000 youth under the age of 30 from more than 150 countries with over 500 local city-based "hubs."
- **Social Entrepreneurs**: 330 established entrepreneurs from 70 states collaborating on global issues.
- **Technology Pioneers**: Tech developers within health, environment, and IT.
- **Young Global Leaders**: A yearly batch of between 100 and 200 promising individuals below the age of 40, selected to assume leading roles in future society.[6]

Young Global Leaders

In 1992, Klaus Schwab launched a one-year WEF program, initially called Global Leaders of Tomorrow. Schwab's vision was to create a proactive group of promising young leaders with a mission to influence decision-making and mobilize a transformation toward "a better world." In 2004, the program was restructured into a five-year program led by his daughter Nicole Schwab and renamed Forum of Young Global Leaders.

The initial nomination committee, led by Queen Rania of Jordan, comprised leaders from "eminent" international media houses such as Reuters, Forbes, the *New York Times*, the *Washington Post*, China Central Television (CCTV), and the Swedish Bonnier Group.[7]

The criteria for inclusion are rigorous so that only the very best will be selected, and no self-nominations are accepted. The nominee is expected to:

- be forty years of age or younger at the time of nomination;
- have a recognized record of extraordinary achievement and a proven track record of substantial leadership experience;
- have demonstrated a commitment to serve society at large through exceptional contributions, and have a global perspective;
- have an impeccable record in the public eye and good standing in his/her community, as well as show great self-awareness and a desire for learning;
- have leading positions within the company if coming from the business sector.[8]

The candidates are expected to be ready to "commit time and energy in the purposes and activities of the organization." They will then be educated into the visions and ideas of the WEF.

The Young Global Leaders are chosen from fields such as public service, business innovation, tech development, arts and culture, education, research and development, philanthropy, journalism, and activism, plus young members of royal families from across the world.

The program is free of charge, all expenses covered. This is how the technocrats of the future global society have been and are being recruited. The stated objectives of the Forum of Young Global Leaders are to:

- Convene a diverse global community of peers by bringing together Young Global Leaders at summits, regional events, leadership development programs, and community-organized gatherings around the world. YGLs are encouraged to learn from each other, and with each other, in a search for forward-looking and innovative solutions to present-day problems. YGL events are dynamic, interactive gatherings that focus on collaboration across traditional "divides" and where every participant is an active one.
- Catalyze the next generation of leaders through personal experiences that enable YGLs to build knowledge and engender a better understanding of global challenges and trends, as well as to further enhance their unique role as leaders within their organizations and the broader community. Insights come from dedicated educational modules (such as the "Leadership and Public Policy for the 21st Century" module at the Harvard Kennedy School of Government); informal, interactive, off-the-record sessions with high-profile world leaders; and peer-to-peer coaching opportunities.
- Positively impact the global agenda by engaging the YGL community in initiatives and task forces related to specific global challenges which they identify collectively. YGLs bring their diverse skill set to tackle a range of issues using their expertise, knowledge, and networks to make a sound contribution to the world. In that sense, the YGL Community is a distinctive balance of rights and responsibilities.[†]

The very first year, 237 young global leaders from all over the world were invited to join and every year, between 100 and 200 new recruits are chosen. To date, over 4,000 Global Leaders of Tomorrow and Young Global

---

†   The strategy of selecting gifted youth and reeducating them into activists has been employed by agenda-setting foundations for at least a century (see appendix A).

Leaders have been selected to join the program. Notable participants include:

Politicians

1993: **Tony Blair**, Prime Minister of the UK (1997–2007)

1993: **Angela Merkel**, Chancellor of Germany (2005–2021)

1993: **Vladimir Putin**, President of Russia (2012–)

1993: **Viktor Orbán**, Prime Minister of Hungary (2010–)

1993: **Nicolas Sarkozy**, President of France (2007–2012)

1993: **José Manuel Barroso**, President of the EU Commission (2004–2014)

2000: **Chrystia Freeland**, Minister of Finance, Canada (2019–)‡

2002: **Ilir Meta**, President of Albania (2017–2022)

2003: **Greg Hunt**, Minister of Health and Aged Care, Australia (2017–2022)§

2005: **Gavin Newsom**, Governor of California (2019–)

2005: **Justin Trudeau**, Prime Minister of Canada (2015–)⁵

2006: **Thani bin Ahmed Al Zeyoudi**, Minister of State for Foreign Trade, United Arab Emirates (2020–)

2006: **Sanna Marin,** Prime Minister of Finland (2019–2023)

2008: **Karien van Gennip**, Minister of Social Affairs, Netherlands (2022–)

2009: **Anies Baswedan**, Governor of Jakarta, Indonesia (2017–2022)

2009: **Sebastian Kurz**, Chancellor of Austria (2017–2021)

2010: **Alexander De Croo**, Prime Minister of Belgium (2017–)

2010: **Vincent van Quickenborne**, Minister of Justice, Belgium (2020–2023)

2013: **Ida Auken**, Minister of Environment, Denmark (2011–2014)**

2014: **Jacinda Ardern**, Prime Minister of New Zealand (2017–2023)

2016: **Emmanuel Macron**, President of France (2017–)

2016: **Jens Spahn**, Minister of Health, Germany (2021–2021)††

2018: **Jagmeet Singh**, New Democratic Party of Canada (2017–)‡‡

2019: **Carlos Alvarado Quesada**, President of Costa Rica (2018–2022)

---

‡   Freeland froze bank accounts connected to the Freedom Convoy protests in February 2020.

§   Overseer of the Australian response to the COVID-19 pandemic.

⁵   Trudeau used the Emergencies Act against peaceful protesters Freedom Convoy 2022.

** Author of "Welcome To 2030: I Own Nothing, Have No Privacy and Life Has Never Been Better," published by WEF and *Forbes* in November 2016.

†† Spahn said that by the end of winter "pretty much everyone in Germany will be vaccinated, recovered or dead," November 22, 2021.

‡‡ Acted as Canadian "opposition" but still supported Trudeau's use of the Emergencies Act against the protesting truckers.

2019: **Mamuka Bakhtadze**, Prime Minister of Georgia (2018–2019)

2019: **Kamissa Camara**, Minister of Digital Economy, Mali (2019–2020)

2019: **Annika Saarikko**, Deputy Prime Minister of Finland (2020–2023)

2019: **Juan Guaidó**, President of Venezuela (2019–2023)

2020: **Faisal F. Alibrahim**, Minister of Economy & Planning, Saudi Arabia (2021–)

2020: **Shauna Aminath**, Minister of Environment, Climate Change and Technology, Maldives (2021–2023)

2020: **Hammad Azhar**, Minister of Energy, Pakistan (2021–2022)

2020: **Annalena Baerbock**, Minister of Foreign Affairs, Germany (2021–)

2020: **Karina Gould**, Minister of Families, Children & Social Development, Canada (2021–)

2020: **Paula Ingabire**, Minister of Information Communication Technology & Innovation, Rwanda (2008–), WEF trustee

2021: **Vera Daves de Sousa**, Minister of Finance, Angola (2019–)

2021: **Martín Guzmán**, Minister of Economy, Argentina (2019–2022)

2021: **Ronald Lamola**, Minister of Justice & Correctional Services, South Africa (2019–)

Business and Tech Entrepreneurs

1993: **Richard Branson**, founder of Virgin

1995: **Paul Allen**, cofounder of Microsoft

1995: **Michael O'Brien**, VP, Goldman Sachs International

1997: **David Filo,** cofounder of Yahoo

1998: **Jeff Bezos**, founder of Amazon

1999: **Pierre Omidyar**, founder of eBay

2001: **Jack Ma**, founder of Alibaba and Alipay

2002: **Larry Page**, founder of Google

2005: **Niklas Zennström**, founder of Skype

2005: **Ali Y. Koç**, president, Koç Holdings, Turkey

2005: **Marc Benioff**, CEO of Salesforce

2007: **Jimmy Wale**, founder of Wikipedia

2009: **Chad Hurley**, cofounder of Youtube

2010: **Evan Williams**, cofounder of Twitter

2010: **Ricken Patel**, founder of Avaaz

2010: **Mark Zuckerberg**, founder of Facebook/Meta

2014: **Leah Busque**, founder of TaskRabbit

2014: **David Karp**, founder of Tumblr

2016: **Joe Gebbia**, founder of Airbnb

2019: **Anjali Sud**, CEO of Vimeo

2021: **Zhengyu He**, head of systems engineering, Ant Financial[§§]

Media and Celebrities

1993: **Bono**, singer and cofounder of the ONE campaign

1993: **David Roy Thomson,** chairman of Thomson Reuters

2002: **Carlos Lozada**, managing editor, *Foreign Policy* (CFR)

2003: **Carina L. Dennis**, senior editor, *Nature Magazine*

2006: **Debo Adesina**, editor, *The Guardian*

2008: **Anderson Cooper**, anchor, CNN

2008: **Leonardo DiCaprio**, actor, UN Messenger of Peace on Climate Change

2008: **Kristine Stewart**, CBC and Twitter Canada

2008: **Shakira**, singer

2013: **Chelsea Clinton**

2015: **Ivanka Trump**

2019: **Gary Liu**, CEO, *South China Morning Post*

Note how many of these examples are in *recent* or *current* top political positions. And these are just a few examples of hundreds.[¶¶] In an interview by David Gergen at the John F. Kennedy School of Government, Harvard University, 2017, Schwab proudly bragged about how his YGLs are now to be found in governments around the world.

> Gergen: . . . that when you brought the Young Global Leaders here [to Harvard] for executive education and then the Schwab Fellows, but there are two countries in the world now in which the Young Global Leaders have emerged. Tell us just a bit about that, in terms of governance.
>
> Schwab: I have to say when I mention our names like Mrs. Merkel, even Vladimir Putin and so on—they all have been Young Global Leaders of the World Economic Forum. But what we are very proud of now—the young generation like Prime Minister Trudeau, President of Argentina [Mauricio Macri] and so on—that we penetrate the cabinets.

[§§] Ant financial (now Ant Group) is a spinoff of Alipay, creating the social credit system in China.

[¶¶] A complete vetted and updated GLT/YGL list can be downloaded from: blog.jacobnordangard.se/wef-ygl-list.

> So yesterday I was at a reception with Prime Minister Trudeau and I would know that *half* of this cabinet, or even more than half of this cabinet, are our . . . actually Young Global Leaders.
>
> Gergen: It's true in Argentina, as well?
>
> Schwab: It's true in Argentina and it's true in France now, with the President [Macron].[9]

In 2005, the Young Global Leaders project "Initiative 2020" was launched, aiming to realize the vision of a better world by the year 2020. The recruited young future leaders were to:

- use scenario and visioning exercises to understand current and future trends, risks, and opportunities both at global and regional levels. This will require challenging existing assumptions, addressing knowledge gaps, and mapping interrelationships
- formulate a shared vision of the world in 2020
- create task forces on priority issues and develop global and regional strategies, concrete actions, and measurable benchmarks to advance toward their vision.[10]

Among the "challenges and opportunities" discussed in the working groups were health (pandemics); environmental issues (climate change); global control and security; and poverty and global development. Every working group was then to elaborate a plan of action and a schedule for its implementation. In 2007, "Initiative 2020" was changed into "The 2030 Initiative."

Board members for the Forum of Young Global Leaders during the first years included Klaus Schwab himself, his daughter Nicole Schwab (founding director of the YGL Forum), Queen Rania of Jordan, and Joseph Nye (a Rhodes Scholar and member of the Trilateral Commission, CFR, and Aspen Strategy Group). In 2020, the board included the Deputy Secretary-General of the UN, Amina Mohammed. The organization is supported by CFR president David Rubenstein. Strategic partners in later years have included the Bill & Melinda Gates Foundation, Google, and JPMorgan Chase.

Today, the Forum of Young Global Leaders includes several hundred active members and alumni.[11] These are the agents of change, contributing to shaping the trends of global development into what they have been led to believe will be a sustainable utopia—a global tech revolution "with mankind at the centre."

> As stewards of the Forum of Young Global Leaders, the YGL Alumni Community embodies and sustains the YGL ethos. The Community fosters members' continued growth as responsible leaders, strengthens lifelong connections, and drives solutions to complex social, environmental, and economic global issues.[12]

In October 2018, six hundred Young Global Leaders gathered in San Francisco under the slogan "Co-Creating a Sustainable Future" under the auspices of Mark Benioff, CEO of Salesforce. The world was to be transformed through the technologies of the Fourth Industrial Revolution, and the young leaders were summoned to assist in fulfilling this mission.[13]

Besides the Young Global Leaders, there is the even younger and more numerous WEF army of Global Shapers, ready and eager to change their communities.[14] They have a growing number of "hubs" all over the world.

The Fourth Industrial Revolution

On December 12, 2015, the last day of the UN Climate Summit in Paris and four months after the signing of Agenda 2030, Klaus Schwab, in an article in the Council on Foreign Relations' journal *Foreign Affairs*, announced the beginning of the Fourth Industrial Revolution (4IR):

> We stand on the brink of a technological revolution that will fundamentally alter the way we live, work, and relate to one another. In its scale, scope, and complexity, the transformation will be unlike anything humankind has experienced before.[15]

This revolution will, according to its proponents, literally fuse humankind with technology in order to create a highly efficient surveillance society where human beings are seen as manageable units.

Only a month later, in January 2016, the Fourth Industrial Revolution was the main theme of the annual WEF meeting in Davos, Switzerland. Just in time for this meeting, the book *Fourth Industrial Revolution* was published, in which Schwab presents a futuristic agenda in which all problems of humankind will be solved with the technologies developed and marketed by the leading business partners of the WEF. In this book, twenty-three "deep shifts" are introduced,[16] intended to fundamentally reshape the world and humankind during coming decades:

1. Implantable Technologies
2. Our Digital Presence
3. Vision as the New Interface
4. Wearable Internet
5. Ubiquitous Computing
6. A Supercomputer in Your Pocket
7. Storage for All
8. The Internet of and for Things
9. The Connected Home
10. Smart Cities
11. Big Data for Decisions
12. Driverless Cars
13. Artificial Intelligence and Decision Making
14. AI and White-Collar Jobs
15. Robotics and Service
16. Bitcoin and Blockchain
17. The Sharing Economy
18. Governments and the Blockchain
19. 3D Printing and Manufacturing
20. 3D Printing and Human Health
21. 3D Printing and Consumer Products

22. Designer Beings
23. Neuro-technologies

These new technologies were the results of decades of work in think tanks and organizations like the RAND Corporation, the Institute for the Future, and the World Future Society.

In October 2016, the World Economic Forum launched its Centre for the Fourth Industrial Revolution in San Francisco, with the purpose of advancing inter-sector collaborations and guidance of the Fourth Industrial Revolution.

In November that same year, the Network of the Global Future Councils was also initiated in tandem with leading experts. The idea was to explore possible "systemic shifts" in important areas such as energy, mobility, and infrastructure, while at the same time reflecting upon the effects of technological breakthroughs in the fields of artificial intelligence, biotech, and other areas relating to the Fourth Industrial Revolution. The task was to shape a more resilient, inclusive, and sustainable future. This network now convenes annually in Dubai.[17]

In 1918, the succeeding work *Shaping the Fourth Industrial Revolution* was published, with Klaus Schwab as author and a foreword by Satya Nadella, CEO of Microsoft.[18] It chiefly consists of contributions from the numerous WEF working groups, describing the new revolution in greater detail. Its sections cover WEF's four main goals:

I. **Extending Digital Technologies** (Internet of Things)
II. **Reforming the Physical World** (artificial intelligence and robotics)
III. **Altering the Human Being** (neuro- and biotechnologies)
IV. **Integrating the Environment** (space technology and geoengineering)

This includes the integration of superfast computers into both the urban environment and into our bodies, connecting us to a global network called the Internet of Things—80 billion machines and human beings in constant communication with each other.

The collected data is to be analyzed using AI, and everything linked together with a blockchain-based digital currency. These new technologies are considered crucial for the realization of the UN Sustainable Development Goals and for regulating CO_2 emissions.

By always being online, human behavior and functions are to be "influenced and improved in open as well as subtle ways." This interconnection is predicted to influence decisions, nudging us to become more health-conscious and prolong our lives. Medical professionals will be able to monitor our health status in real time. Another goal is to increase the efficiency of manufacturing processes through more thorough supervision of the interconnected production chains and identification of any weak links.

In the book, humankind as well as nature are viewed as objects to be perfected through the application of technology. This vision seems to have direct ideological links to twentieth-century eugenics and dreams of a superhuman: the foundations for the Nazi worldview. This vision of perfection is also to be implemented through less-than-democratic means.

In the end, the Fourth Industrial Revolution will, according to Schwab, "challenge our ideas of what it means to be human." When technology moves into our bodies and brains, this raises the question of where to draw the line between human and machine. This dilemma, however, is presented more as an opportunity than a risk. As Rodney Brooks, AI researcher at MIT and agenda contributor of Word Economic Forum, predicted in 2000: "We don't have to fear robots taking over from us because there will be no 'us' to take over from . . . we will have become one with our machines."[19]

Schwab also matter-of-factly states that these technologies can be used "to manipulate our worldview and influence our behavior," indicating that this opens up for total control of humankind—and that this is not a problem. Society is thus to be reshaped and made "resilient" with the aid of technology, and shall on all levels become balanced according to the principle of equality. No person left behind. That this at the same time implies a total surveillance of every human process through the Internet of Things, smart borders, sensors, and drones—and that a

Western version of China's social credit system is incipient—is not mentioned. Instead, everything is painted in rainbow colors and the global tech giants are happy to disregard these ethical dilemmas in view of the profit opportunities.

Among the many corporations and organizations connected to the Center for the Fourth Industrial Revolution are Microsoft, Accenture, IDEO, Salesforce, Palantir, Chinese Huawei, drone manufacturer DJI, and Bill Gates's GAVI—The Vaccine Alliance.[20]

The UN–WEF Partnership

On June 13, 2019, a strategic partnership was signed between the United Nations and the World Economic Forum.[21] This historic event received very little media attention, despite its enormous implications for humanity. By and large, the partnership meant that the power over our lives with the stroke of a pen was transferred to leading global corporations, their respective owners, and their visions for the future.

It was more than obvious for whom the UN had been created. Even before the partnership was signed, many UN organizations were already members of World Economic Forum's working groups. Amina Mohammed is listed as a WEF Agenda Contributor and a member of the Young Global Leaders board of directors.

Börge Brende & Claus Schwab (WEF) with António Guterres & Amina Mohammed (UN) after signing the WEF–UN Partnership 2019

The UN–WEF partnership covers six focus areas:

1. **Financing the 2030 Agenda:** Mobilize systems and accelerate finance flows toward the 2030 Agenda and the UN Sustainable Development Goals, taking forward solutions to increase long-term SDG investments.
2. **Climate change:** Achieve clear, measurable and public commitments from the private sector to reach carbon neutrality by 2050, help create public-private platforms in critical high-emitting sectors, and scale up the services required to adapt to the impacts of climate change.
3. **Health**: Support countries in achieving good health and well-being for all, within the context of the 2030 Agenda, focusing on key emerging global health threats that require stronger multi-stakeholder partnership and action.
4. **Digital cooperation**: Meet the needs of the Fourth Industrial Revolution while seeking to advance global analysis, dialogue, and standards for digital governance and digital inclusiveness.
5. **Gender equality and the empowerment of women**: Foster multi-stakeholder partnerships and coalitions for full participation and equal opportunities for women at all levels of decision-making and for productive participation of women in the labour force, and promote equal pay for work of equal value across sectors and occupations as well as within them.
6. **Education and skills**: Promote public-private partnerships to address global re-skilling and lifelong learning for the future requirements for work, and empower youth with competencies for life and decent work.

The purpose of the partnership is accelerating implementation of the seventeen global goals of Agenda 2030.

Meeting the Sustainable Development Goals is essential for the future of humanity. The World Economic Forum is committed to

supporting this effort, and working with the United Nations to build
a more prosperous and equitable future. (Klaus Schwab)

The partnership specifies the World Economic Forum's Fourth Industrial
Revolution as a crucial component for implementing the agenda and digitalization as the key to success. This becomes even more obvious when
looking closer at the leading partners for the Global Goals.[22]

1. The first leading partner is the **Bill & Melinda Gates
   Foundation**, founded with the fortune from Microsoft and run
   by the company's former CEO, Bill Gates. The Foundation is
   one of the key operatives in implementing the Agenda 2030 plan,
   together with foundations like the Rockefeller Foundation, the
   Rockefeller Brothers Fund, the Ford Foundation, Bloomberg
   Philanthropies, the UN Foundation, and the Open Society
   Foundation. They all have their roots in population control and
   eugenics and represent the global elite that ultimately shapes the
   agenda on a global scale.
2. The second partner is **Avanti Communications**, a world-leading
   British provider of satellite technology to military and government
   projects. Their satellites are said to "provide secure, rapid and reliable connectivity for government digital inclusion programmes."
   They deliver a world-spanning connectivity which may be used
   to finally realize the old dream of a World Brain where all human
   activity can be tracked and analyzed in real time.
3. The third partner is **2030Vision**, a technology partnership "that
   connects businesses, NGOs and governments with the technology and expertise they need to realize the Goals." 2030Vision was
   founded and chaired by British semiconductor company ARM. It
   consists of corporations like Microsoft and the German software
   company SAP, together with a number of tech advocacy groups.
   2030Vision, which recently merged with WEF's Frontier 2030,
   is a partnership that connects cross-sector organizations with the

advanced tech solutions needed to support the implementation of the Global Goals. Its secretariat is run by the WEF.[23]

4. The fourth partner is the global tech giant **Google**, provider of cloud computing, leading search engine and web browser, Android cell phone operating system, YouTube, and AI solutions. An everyday companion for billions of people, it already intimately tracks users and their behaviors. Google is also a strategic partner with WEF.

5. The fifth partner is the American multinational financial services corporation **Mastercard**. A key player in developing the Digital ID which will be needed to access basic services and payment in the New International Economic Order that will rise out of the ashes of the old world system. Mastercard is of course also a strategic partner with WEF. Its CEO Ajaypal Singh Banga is a member of the Council on Foreign Relations as well as WEF's International Business Council.

6. The sixth partner is American corporation **Salesforce**, a cloud-based software company headed by Marc Benioff, Young Global Leader 2005 and board member of World Economic Forum. Salesforce is a global leader in customer relationship management through the use of cloud computing, social media, Internet of Things, and AI.

7. The seventh partner is **UNICEF** (United Nations Children's Fund), an agency now focused on ensuring that no child will be left behind from being integrated in the global digital panopticon. Through the UN–WEF partnership, UNICEF is also included in and has a close collaboration with both corporations and foundations (such as the Rockefeller Foundation).

Global Goals Week

Coinciding with the United Nations Week in late September every year, the Global Goals Week is "a shared commitment between 100+ partners across civil society, business, academia, and the UN system to accelerate action on the Sustainable Development Goals." The Global

Goals Week initiative was launched in 2016 by Project Everyone, initiated by British film director Richard Curtis in 2015 "to raise awareness of the UN Global Goals,"[24] UNDP (United Nations Development Programme), and its main financier, the UN Foundation.[25]

Despite its official-sounding name, the UN Foundation is a private tax-exempt foundation, founded in 1998 by media mogul Ted Turner "to support the UN and serve as a strategic partner and resource for the UN in solving global problems."[26]

Turner, founder of **CNN**, **TNT** (Turner Network Television), and **TCM** (Turner Classic Movies), holds the opinion that world population must be reduced to between 2 and 2.5 billion people to be sustainable.[27]

> In order to arrest climate change or reverse it, first of all you got to stabilize the population. And hopefully reduce the population by having a voluntary *one child family* for a hundred years. (Ted Turner, father of five)

In 1990, he founded the **Turner Foundation**, focused on philanthropic grants related to conservation and overpopulation. Board members include **Gro Harlem Brundtland (Brundtland Commission)**, **Queen Rania of Jordan (WEF)**, and US Senator **Tim Wirth (member of the Trilateral Commission)**.

Global Goalkeepers

In 2017, Bill & Melinda Gates Foundation launched the Global Goalkeepers with the purpose of gathering leaders, accelerating the implementation of the Global Goals, and awarding its pioneers.

> Goalkeepers are leaders who take a stand on the issues they care about and innovate in their communities to achieve the Global Goals.[28]

On many levels, Bill Gates has gained a growing influence on the UN agenda. During Global Goals Week, Bill and Melinda Gates issued Global Goals Awards to "remarkable individuals taking action to help achieve the

Global Goals by 2030." Among the 2019 award winners were Narendra Modi, Prime Minister of India (one of the major G20 nations) and in 2020 Dr. John Nkengasong, Cameroon, director of Africa Centres for Disease Control and Prevention (Africa CDC).[29]

The Decade of Action

During the United Nations Summit in September 2019, Secretary-General António Guterres declared that the sustainability agenda needed accelerating on three levels in order to fulfill the Sustainable Development Goals by 2030:

1. Global action to secure greater leadership, more resources, and smarter solutions for the Sustainable Development Goals
2. Local action embedding the needed transitions in the policies, budgets, institutions and regulatory frameworks of governments, cities, and local authorities
3. People action, including by youth, civil society, the media, the private sector, unions, academia, and other stakeholders, to generate an unstoppable movement pushing for the required transformations.[30]

The time had come for immediate action in order to create the promised paradise without poverty, hunger, or inequality. In his speech to the United Nations General Assembly on September 24, 2019, Guterres praised the Swedish climate activist Greta Thunberg's Atlantic crossing by racing sailboat to highlight the climate crisis. He called upon member states to add to the global funds for both health and the climate, and on "the world of science, research and technology to ensure that new technologies narrow the digital and broader technological divide and are geared toward the common good." 2020 was to initiate the Decade of Action on a global scale.[31]

The recommendations on how the digital agenda should be implemented came from the United Nations High Level Panel on Digital Cooperation. This group, formed on July 12, 2018, was headed by

Melinda Gates and Jack Ma (founder of Alibaba and board member of World Economic Forum).[32] Their final report, *The Age of Digital Interdependence* (June 10, 2019), was financed by foundations such as the Ford Foundation, the UN Foundation, the Global Challenges Foundation, and eight governments (including China, Norway, Finland, Denmark, and Israel). Partners included the WEF and its Center for the Fourth Industrial Revolution.[33]

The World Economic Forum's technology partnership 2030Vision was a direct response to the panel's recommendations.

> Building on the call from the UN High Level Plan on Digital Cooperation for a multi-stakeholder approach that brings together technology companies, government, civil society and international organizations leaders to collaborate on the responsible deployment of new technologies to deliver positive impact.[34]

This "inclusive" strategy was firmly anchored among policymakers around the world and a part of the G20 agenda.

G20—The Executive Council

The G20 (Group of 20) is an important and often overlooked forum that, since 2008, has emerged as one of the most important associations for global cooperation. It comprises the nineteen largest economies, plus the European Union. The chairmanship is rotated among member states. G20 was formed in 1999 and grew out of G7/G8 as an international forum for governments and central bank executives, with invited international organizations, nations, and interest groups. The UN Secretary-General is a permanent guest, along with the World Bank and the IMF, the WTO, APEC, ASEAN, and the African Union (which became a permanent G20 member as of January 2024). Every year, temporary guests are also invited.

The initiative can be traced back to the United States and Great Britain and to the goals set out by Zbigniew Brzezinski and David Rockefeller before their founding of the Trilateral Commission in 1973. G20 got its central role in connection with the financial crisis in 2008 and since then, focus areas such as climate/energy, trade, employment, development, the empowerment of women, health, and innovations have been added to its agenda. Meetings are held in the hosting nation throughout the year. Today, it functions in many ways as an informal world government, aiding the great transformation into the high-tech surveillance society that is now being implemented at a rapid pace. The last leader of the Soviet Union, Mikhail Gorbachev, called the G20 "a global politburo."

G20 is led by a troika consisting of this year's presidency, the previous year's presidency, and the next year's presidency (during 2020, the troika thus consisted of Japan–Saudi Arabia–Italy). This structure ensures that the agenda is kept continuous and intact. Several proposals for creating a permanent secretariat have been made in recent years, but they have so far been blocked. The OECD in Paris, however, has a close link to the G20 and can be said to function as a quasi-secretariat. In addition to ministerial meetings, a number of other complementary meetings are held by various "engagement groups."

- **Business 20** gathers business lobby organizations (2019 meetings focused specifically on the lucrative expansion of surveillance for the Global Goals under the motto "Society 5.0 for SDGs").
- **Civil 20** gathers leading NGOs ("civil society") for input on how the Great Transformation can be implemented with maximum efficiency.
- **Foundations 20** gathers philanthropic foundations, including RBF, WWF, and the World Future Council in its steering committee (unofficial).
- **Interfaith 20** gathers religious organizations (unofficial).
- **J20** gathers supreme courts and constitutional courts.
- **Labor 20** gathers trade unions from around the globe.
- **Science 20** gathers science academies.
- **SAI 20** gathers supreme audit institutions.
- **Startup 20** gathers new start-ups (new group 2022).

- **Think 20** gathers leading think tanks to provide G20 with research and policy recommendations (2019 discussions included how the world should be governed and how to manage "the political spring").
- **Urban 20** gathers mayors from the world's largest cities to discuss how the urban environment can contribute to a "sustainable and inclusive" future (which means building more "smart cities").
- **Women 20** gathers women's organizations to demand equal participation in all professions.
- **Youth 20** gathers youth organizations and speaks for the world's youth (people under 30).

Official engagement groups may vary from year to year. The stated objective of these interest groups—restructuring the global financial system into a new international economic order—was declared on the W20 website during Japan's chairmanship in 2019: "Engagement groups influence G20 leaders to create new international economic order by making policy recommendations"[35]

G20 and the Global Goals

Already under China's chairmanship in 2016, G20 committed to the implementation of Agenda 2030 and the 17 Global Goals. During the same meeting, a new Industrial Revolution Action Plan was presented, where the goals of the Fourth Industrial Revolution were integrated into the G20 agenda.[36] This fusion was further solidified by Angela Merkel during the German chairmanship in 2017, who stated that "Digital transformation is a driving force of global, innovative, inclusive and sustainable growth and can contribute to reducing inequality and achieving the goals of the 2030 Agenda for Sustainable Development."[37]

In June 2019, at the G20 Summit in Osaka, the Global Goals were firmly fused with the Fourth Industrial Revolution, "Society 5.0 for SDGs."

19 MEMBER STATES + the European Union & the African Union

GROUP 1	GROUP 2	GROUP 3	GROUP 4	GROUP 5
Australia	India	Argentina	France	China
Canada	Russia	Brazil	Germany	Indonesia
Saudi Arabia	S. Africa	Mexico	Italy	Japan
USA	Turkey		UK	S. Korea

G20 TROIKA

PREVIOUS YEAR'S HOST NATION	CURRENT HOST NATION	COMING YEAR'S HOST NATION

OECD as quasi-secretariat

PERMANENT G20 GUESTS

ASEAN (Association of Southeast Asian Nations)

NEPAD (New Partnership for Africa's Development)

OECD (Organisation for Economic Co-operation and Development)

FSB (Financial Stability Board)

ILO (International Labor Organization)

IMF (International Monetary Fund)

UN (United Nations)

WBG (World Bank Group)

WTO (World Trade Organization)

Spain

G20 ENGAGEMENT GROUPS

Business 20 (2013): Business Associations

Civil 20 (2013): NGOs ("civil society")

Foundations 20 (2016): Philanthropies (unofficial)

Interfaith 20 (2014): Religions (unofficial)

J 20 (2018): Supreme courts and constitutional courts

Labour 20 (2008): Labor unions

Oceans 20 (2024)

Parliament 20 (2015): Parliamentarians

Science 20 (2016): Science academies

SAI 20 (2022): Supreme audit institutions

Startup 20 (2022): Startups

Think 20 (2012): Think tanks

Urban 20 (2014): Leading mayors

Women 20 (2016): Women organisations

Youth 20 (2016): Youth organisations

The G20 structure

Society 5.0 is a vision of human-centered future society promoted by the Japanese government to achieve an advanced society, which realizes economic growth and solves social challenges, by advancing toward Sustainable Development Goals (SDGs) through the increasing convergence of the physical world and the virtual world.[38]

This summit took place only a few weeks after the partnership between the UN and the World Economic Forum, with invited guests such as the UN General-Secretary, the executive of the World Bank Group, and the chairman of the IMF.

The G20 works toward fulfilling the Global Goals by implementing the "disruptive" technologies of the 4IR. In their vision, the digital transformation will ensure a sustainable and resilient planet. The G20 summit in Japan discussed how it would be financed and how cooperation with NGOs could be strengthened. One of the methods proposed was to use the immense assets of pension funds to finance the expansion of the "green infrastructure" needed to reshape the world into a single manageable unit.

These far-reaching interventions in our future development have hardly been debated during any national elections. Yet, every member state is now obliged to adapt its national policies to the interpretations of the Global Goals dictated by the United Nations, the G20, and the World Economic Forum. This means the power to regulate our lives down to the smallest detail, with scant possibility of objecting. The only "choice" we are left with is the freedom to elect which national and local officials get to enforce the supranational decrees and make sure we obey them.

Extinction Rebellion, theatrical and provocative climate activists

The Emergency

You have stolen my dreams and my childhood with your empty words. And yet I'm one of the lucky ones. People are suffering. People are dying. Entire ecosystems are collapsing. We are in the beginning of a mass extinction, and all you can talk about is money and fairy tales of eternal economic growth. How dare you! (Greta Thunberg)[1]

In order to increase public receptivity to the Grand Plan, and even have us beg for its introduction, tears and appeal to emotion are used. Most effective is the use of innocent children and youth demanding the solution already waiting to be offered. This makes it difficult to criticize the agenda, as such critique will appear heartless and selfish.

The 2019 UN General Assembly

Just before the UN High-Level Political Forum (HLPF) 24–25 September 2019, the United Nations had pointed out the need for a faster transition into sustainability than the current pace. Member states had not taken their commitments seriously enough. Time was running out, and immediate action was required.

The day before the HLPF, another climate summit, Climate Action Summit 2019—A Race We Can Win, was held, led by Secretary-General António Guterres with around a hundred world leaders attending. Here, the young Swedish climate activist Greta Thunberg (pronounced *Toonberg*) delivered a passionate speech.

Global Climate Strike

During the week of the UN General Assembly, well-coordinated and professionally organized Global Climate Strike events were held across the world, demanding that leaders take responsibility and implement a new international economic order. The Global Climate Strike, starting on Friday, September 20, coincided with the Climate Action Summit and Climate Week New York (arranged by the Rockefeller-initiated Climate Group) and gathered hundreds of international organizations.

School strike for the climate 2020

However, this was not a grassroots or youth initiative. The idea for a global climate strike, with Greta Thunberg as a poster child, was hatched in May 2015, during the Global Youth Summit at the Evangelical Academy in Tutzing, Germany. The organizer was the German Plant for Planet Foundation (closely related to the Club of Rome) with UNEP (United Nations Environment Programme) and its youth program TUNZA.[2] This youth summit gathered high-profile names such as Bill McKibben (350.org), Franz-Josef Radermacher (Club of Rome), Christiana Figueres (UNFCCC), Ottmar Edenhofer (Potsdam Institute for Climate Impact Research), and Vandana Shiva (World Future Council).

The goal of the summit was to develop strategies for how children and youth could best help spread awareness of the "climate crisis." This was seen as essential before the upcoming Paris Climate Summit (COP 21) a few months later. Another objective was to "prepare a proposal for solutions to ensure our survival and send a message to world leaders" who were to meet at the G7 summit at Schloss Elmau, Bavaria, and the Bilderberg Meeting in Telfs-Buchen, Austria (a one-hour drive from the Youth Summit).

Franz-Josef Radermacher, (1959–), Club of Rome

With assistance from Radermacher—who had not been a teenager since the Beatles era—a Youth Manifesto was crafted, in which world leaders were asked to strengthen global governance to achieve economic, ecological, social, and cultural sustainability and to integrate the WTO, financial markets, and United Nations into one global governance system with taxation of the "Global Commons," such as the atmosphere and the Arctic, under UN control.[3] The manifesto was then sent to German Chancellor Angela Merkel (WEF Global Leader of Tomorrow 1993 and chairman of the G7 summit), with the following plea: "We, the 3 billion children and youths of the world, are terrified about our future and ask you, Chancellor Merkel, for your support."[4] The letter, signed by the six young board members of Plant for the Planet, astoundingly gave themselves the mandate to speak for the three billion children and youths of the world on the climate issue.

Plant for the Planet was founded in 2007 by the then nine-year-old Felix Finkbeiner (1997–) to "fight the climate crisis by planting trees." The son of the vice president of the German chapter of the Club of Rome, Frithjof Finkbeiner, he soon received media attention and powerful backers. Prince Albert II of Monaco and Klaus Töpfer from UNEP became patrons, while Harrison Ford and German billionaire and Club of Rome member Michael Otto praised the initiative.[5]

In 2008 Felix became a member of the UNEP youth organization and was invited to speak in the European Parliament, at the conference A Global Contract Based on Climate Justice—The Need for a New Approach Concerning International Relations, organized by the Club of Rome, the Potsdam Institute, the Tällberg Foundation, the Eco-Social Forum, and the Global Marshall Plan. The panel included Hans Joachim Schellnhuber, Johan Rockström, Anders Wijkman (chairman of the Club of Rome), Ottmar Edenhofer, and Franz-Josef Radermacher.[6]

The influences from these gentlemen's perceptions and philosophies on both Plant for the Planet and the Youth Conference manifesto, concerning how the world should best be governed and humanity controlled, clearly shine through. Both wording and content have striking similarities with the stated goals of these organizations and individuals.

However, in order to reach out to the world and make the climate a top priority for the world's children and youth, something more was needed. Under the heading, "How to ensure our survival? Activities and campaigns," the question of how to move forward was discussed. This resulted in the idea of climate-striking schoolchildren—a concept to be implemented only a few months later.

On the opening day of the Paris Climate Summit, COP21, on November 30, 2015, the first climate strike was arranged, encouraging schoolchildren to help highlight the climate crisis and create "The Future We Want." For this purpose the organization Climate Strike was founded, with financial support from Bill McKibben's 350.org and Global Greengrants Fund (a member of Rockefeller's Environmental Grantmakers Association).[7]

In the following years, 2016 and 2017, Climate Strike initiated repeated climate strikes. What was still missing, however, was a teenager who could be the literal poster child for the movement. This person was eventually found in Sweden by Bo Thorén from Fossil Free Sweden, a divestment movement founded in 2013 under 350.org.

In early 2018, Thorén invited a select group of well-known environmental activists to discuss "how youth can become involved and help increase the speed of the transformation to a sustainable society." Participants included Anders Wijkman and Johan Kuylenstierna.[8] A few months later, Greta Thunberg was approached by Bo Thorén with the notion of a school strike for the climate.

In April 2018, Greta and her mother, opera singer Malena Ernman, had received some media attention in connection with Malena's new book about her family's lifestyle changes prompted by Greta's climate-related depression.[9] Malena, who had been named "Sweden's Environmental Hero of the Year 2017" by the World Wildlife Fund (WWF), later took part in the "Climate Parliament" event at Stockholm University in early May 2018 with Anders Wijkman and Ahmed Al-Qassam (president of climate activist organization Push Sverige). The main sponsors of the event were the organizations Klimataktion and We Don't Have Time).[10]

On May 30, Greta Thunberg was appointed one of the three winners of a climate competition for youth, arranged by Swedish daily paper *Svenska Dagbladet*, with Al-Qassam included in the jury.[11]

Greta went along with Thorén's idea. On August 20, 2018, right at the start of the fall semester, she made a name for herself by initiating a one-person climate school strike outside the Swedish Parliament. The purpose was to bring attention to the climate crisis, and major publicity quickly followed.

The very first day, *Aftonbladet*, one of the leading Swedish evening tabloids, reported on the young climate striker.[12] A Swedish documentary film team also "coincidentally" happened to pass by and immediately started following Greta on her journeys across the world.[13]

Three days later, her mother Malena's book *Scenes from the Heart* was released and the media attention on Greta likely helped bolster sales. Greta's success may also partly be due by the fame of her parents (her father, Swedish actor Svante Thunberg, was distantly related to the above-mentioned Svante Arrhenius). Greta was quickly embraced by the global elite. In only a few months she had become an international superstar. In December 2018, she was invited to address the COP24 UNFCCC Climate Conference in Katowice, Poland.

In January 2019 Greta was welcomed to the World Economic Forum in Davos, where she delivered her famous speech.[14]

> I don't want you to be hopeful. I want you to panic. I want you to
> feel the fear I feel every day. And then I want you to act. I want you
> to act as you would in a crisis. I want you to act as if the house was
> on fire—because it is!

These successful addresses were followed by appearances in the European Parliament and the UK Houses of Parliament, followed by Arnold Schwarzenegger's international climate meeting in Austria.

As Greta's activism inspired more youth and started spreading across the world, the movement Fridays for Future was formed, organizing a number of well-publicized manifestations throughout 2019. Fridays for Future was closely connected to Plant for the Planet, which in 2018 registered the trademark Fridays for Future, and oversaw the group's donations account.[15]

When Greta was invited to participate in the 2019 UN Climate Action Summit in New York and refused to fly, she was offered a seat on a racing sailboat across the Atlantic (on August 14–28), belonging to Prince Albert of Monaco (benefactor of Plant for the Planet), with Albert's nephew Pierre Casiraghi at the helm. The ship had the curious name *Malizia II*.[16]

Greta's backers and advisers had close ties to the Club of Rome, 350.org, the Plant for the Planet foundation, and their associated organizations—especially We Don't Have Time, with its president Ingmar Rentzhog, where Greta functioned as an adviser until January 2019.

The climate strike was held on September 27 and ended with a global general strike, Earth Strike, to save the planet and avoid overheating of the Earth ("Hothouse Earth"). The climate strike took place exactly sixty years after the climate had been chosen as the problem most suitable for uniting the nations of the world.

Extinction Rebellion

The climate frenzy also ignited the more extreme activist organization Extinction Rebellion (XR). It was founded in 2018 by British activists Gail Bradbrook, Simon Bramwell, and Roger Hallam.

Beginning in the autumn of 2018 and throughout 2019, XR performed a number of spectacular and well-publicized manifestations in the UK, USA, Australia and elsewhere, including provocative theatrical public performances; occupying public spaces; blocking streets, bridges, and train tracks; splashing fake blood on sculptures; smashing windows; placing a sailboat by Times Square in New York; provoking mass arrests as a tactic; and supergluing their hands to surroundings to prevent removal by the police.

Hothouse Earth

The "Hothouse Earth" concept was coined in 2018 by Johan Rockström and Hans Joachim Schellnhuber (his predecessor as head of the Potsdam Institute). In an article published by the US Academy of Sciences, they argued that "time was now running out" and we would have to reorient society completely to avoid "self-reinforcing feedback loops" in the climate system. To avoid this scenario they called for "a redirection of human actions from exploitation to stewardship of the Earth system."[17]

Their doomsday scenario was presented by Rockström during the World Economic Forum's annual Davos meeting on January 21–23, 2019.[18] It spread like wildfire. According to Rockström, an important aspect of climate change mitigation was the implementation of the technologies of the Fourth Industrial Revolution. This was also expressed in an article published by World Economic Forum, coauthored by Rockström and the CEO of Ericsson, Börje Ekholm (also a board member of Alibaba Group), where they wrote that "we have growing evidence that exponential innovations in both infotech and biotech, as we enter deeper into the Fourth Industrial Revolution, have the potential to realise a sustainable and wealthier future for all."[19]

On September 25, 2019, Greta Thunberg was awarded the Right Livelihood Award, which she received at a ceremony a few months later from the hands of Johan Rockström.[20] The international award, also known as the "alternative Nobel Prize," was established in 1980 by Swedish-German politician Jakob von Uexkull and his Right Livelihood Foundation (for which Anders Wijkman was adviser). Both are members of the World Future Council, based in Hamburg, Germany, which includes fifty global agents of change. In December 2019, Greta was also named Person of the Year by *Time Magazine*.[21]

The Green New Deal

The very same day Greta received the Right Livelihood Award, the UNCTAD (The United Nations Conference on Trade and Development) presented a report on the Global Green New Deal, the plan for financing the digital "green" agenda—Agenda 2030. In relation to this presentation, the General Secretary of UNCTAD wrote that "meeting the financing demands of the Agenda 2030 requires rebuilding multilateralism around the idea of a Global Green New Deal, and by implication a financial future very different from the recent past."[22]

As expected, the EU took the UN recommendations very seriously. EU preparations in support of the above had also gone on for some time before the UNCTAD report was introduced.

The notion of a Green New Deal, which is a central aspect of the European Commission's strategy for implementing Agenda 2030 and the Global Goals, arose simultaneously in the United States and Great Britain in 2007–2008. It was thereafter picked up by Green parties around Europe, the Obama Presidential Campaign, and UNEP. The term was first used in an editorial by CFR member Thomas L. Friedman, published in the *New York Times* in 2007.[23]

However, it took ten years for the idea to bear political fruit. In December 2018, the Sunrise Movement launched a campaign for a Green New Deal in the United States. That same month, young socialist activist Alexandra Ocasio-Cortez (AOC) was elected to congress. She was supported by activist organizations such as Black Lives Matter, MoveOn, and Democracy for America. In February 2019, AOC together with senator Ed Markey presented her first proposal to Congress, "Recognizing the duty of the Federal Government to create a Green New Deal." The proposal included a complete phasing out of fossil fuels, the upgrading or replacement of every building in the country (!), and the fundamental reorganization of the transport sector so that air travel would be rendered unnecessary. The goals of the Green New Deal were:

- to achieve net-zero greenhouse gas emissions
- to create millions of good, high-wage jobs
- to invest in the infrastructure and industry of the United States
- to secure clean air and water, climate, and community resiliency
- to promote justice and equity for underprivileged minorities.[24]

Ed Markey, president of the Senate's Climate Change Taskforce, had previously worked closely with former senator Jay Rockefeller on the Senate Committee on Commerce, Science and Transportation (led by Rockefeller between 2009 and 2015). Their collaboration was mainly about the expansion of IT infrastructure in the school system.[25]

Digitization was to be a main part of the Green New Deal. The suggestion was supported by Greenpeace and the Sunrise Movement, but was voted down in the Senate. AOC nonetheless became quite famous through this initiative. The process had been set in motion.

The Sunrise Movement was founded as a youth movement in 2017 with funding from the Rockefeller Family Fund, the Rockefeller Brothers Fund, the Tides Foundation, and the Wallace Global Fund and shares offices with the US Climate Action Network.[26] The movement's purpose is to stop climate change, and it would now work intently on marketing the Green New Deal in the United States:

> In 2019, we'll build support for the Green New Deal in every corner of the country and cement it as a litmus test for every politician seeking the Presidency. Then, in 2020, we will unite by the millions to defeat corrupt politicians and the fossil fuel billionaires who aid them, and we'll elect a President and Congress who will make the Green New Deal law in 2021.[27]

Soon thereafter, the UN system also sprang into action. On April 10, 2019, Richard Kozul-Wright, head of the globalization and development strategy at UNCTAD, with Kevin Gallagher of Boston University, wrote that "the Green New Deal" (GND) proposed by progressives in the United States cannot be achieved in isolation. To tackle climate change and inequality together, all countries will need to agree to new rules for international cooperation.

For the Green New Deal to work, the idea would need to be applied globally, and the old institutions replaced with new "smart" ones. Through this, the authors argued, the weak nations would be protected from the strong. However, a crisis would be necessary to generate the proper conditions. The international community had failed to heed Winston Churchill's advice "to never let a good crisis go to waste."[28]

Two days later, Kozul-Wright and Gallagher published the report *A New Multilateralism for Shared Prosperity: Geneva Principles for a Global Green New Deal* through their respective institutions, UNCTAD and Boston University, which delineated the five steps needed to "mend the social contract" and structure a new, just world order. The financier of the project was, unsurprisingly, the Rockefeller Brothers Fund (whose board president at the time was Jay Rockefeller's daughter Valerie). To implement their five-step plan, investments at the level of trillions of dollars were needed from both private and public investors.[29]

Covering Climate Change

On April 30, 2019, the *Columbia Journalism Review*, *The Guardian*, and *The Nation* held the conference Covering Climate Change. The panels included a number of well-known climate activists and journalists such as Bill McKibben, Naomi Klein, Kyle Pope, Chris Hayes, and the young American climate protester Alexandria Villaseñor.

Once again, the Rockefeller family footed the bill through the Rockefeller Family & Associates, which sponsored the event held at Columbia University. Both Klein and McKibben, as well as the university itself, had previously been funded by the Rockefeller family. During the very first session, "How we got here and where we need to go," the campaign "Exxon Knew" was discussed—a rather surreal feature at an event sponsored by *the founders of Exxon*).

The second session, "A TV Case Study: Covering the Green New Deal," discussed how to favorably portray the Green New Deal in the media. A PR video, *A Message From the Future*, produced by *The Intercept* and Naomi Klein, was viewed and debated.[30] It contained a "message" from a utopian future, narrated by Alexandria Ocasio-Cortez and illustrated by young artist Molly Crabapple in order to appeal to a younger audience. According to Naomi Klein and Kyle Pope, it was now also time for journalism to abandon its foundation of objectivity (!) and replace it with climate activism.[31] This proposal was met with astonishing enthusiasm from both the panel and the audience.

> There's an absolute fetish for centrism, for seriousness as defined by splitting the difference, and not getting too excited about anything, and just looking for that middle path and being profoundly distrustful of people saying "actually, the house is on fire." But guess what? The house is on fire! (Naomi Klein)

The event resulted in initially 170, later 220, newspapers, TV channels, educational institutions, and journalists pledging to report intently on the climate during the week leading up to the UN Climate Summit in New York on September 23, 2019.

Green New Deal for Europe

Meanwhile in Europe, also in September 2019, the campaign "The Green New Deal for Europe" was launched by the organization Democracy in Europe Movement 2025 (DiEM25) and its representative Pawel Wargan (previously adviser to the UK Ministry of Finance) and David Adler.

DiEM25 is styled as a "revolutionary" organization. Its vision makes fanciful promises of a strengthened European democracy reining in the greed of major corporations, the solution to the climate crisis, and securing a just, sustainable future for all. As they state on their website:

> Europe is ruled by oligarchs. They own the apartments we live in, the
> banks that keep our money, the vaccines that save our lives, the apps
> we need to work, the data these apps collect about us, the oil and gas
> that heat up our planet—and, more importantly, they own the poli-
> ticians that were supposed to defend us against them.[32]

Inspiration for the movement was taken from the Sunrise Movement as well as the climate activism of Fridays for Future. Just like the Sunrise Movement, the message was tailored to attract a young progressive audience. DiEM25 has political parties called MERA25 in Italy, Germany, Greece, and Sweden.[33]

In the DiEM25 report *The Green New Deal for Europe: Blueprint for Europe's Just Transition*, with foreword by Bill McKibben and Ann Pettifor, Johan Rockström's Planetary Boundaries Framework and Hothouse Earth were used as theoretical foundations. Climate activism organizations, such as Extinction Rebellion and Earth Strike, participated in writing the report.[34] One of the report's recommendations was the proclamation of a "climate emergency" in the European Union which would "commit to continuously updating climate targets to align with scientific consensus."[35]

This would soon become a priority for the new European Commission, headed by Ursula von der Leyen. Yet, the Commission's interpretation of the Green Deal would also be merged with the goals of the WEF and the Club of Rome, and fused together with the tech solutions of the Fourth Industrial Revolution.

A Global Marshall Plan

This green plan, now intended to be implemented all over the world, had clear affinities with Al Gore's plan to save the global environment in the 1992 book *Earth in Balance*, Mikhail Gorbachev's *My Manifesto for the Earth,* and not least the Dutch throne's Earth Charter Initiative which between 1992 and 2000 had been coordinated by Steven Rockefeller from the Rockefeller Brothers Fund.

From these ideas, the Global Marshall Plan initiative was formed by a number of Club of Rome members (including Franz-Josef Radermacher and Frithjof Finkbeiner) in 2003. Supporters were individuals and organizations such as Jakob von Uexkull, Ernst Ulrich von Weizsäcker (previous Club of Rome president 1999–2007), Prince of Jordan El Hassan bin Talal, Ervin László (Club of Budapest), and venture capitalist George Soros.

The purpose was to create a global eco-social market economy that implemented the millennium goals, stabilization of global population, fostering a global partnership, an effective stewardship of resources, and a digital transformation. The same goals would later be inserted into the Plant for the Planet's youth manifesto. The EU was considered a key ally to realize the vision.[36]

Yet, to carry out this plan, some sort of catalyzing event was necessary. In 2005, the British psychoanalyst and governmental adviser David Wasdell[*] had encouraged Prince El Hassan bin Talal and the Club of Rome

---

* In February 2019, Wasdell was adviser to Extinction Rebellion.

to proclaim a global emergency with the purpose of initiating the program and begin the long-term reduction of global population.[37] The prince was a member of two of the Club of Rome's influential partners working on the project, the Council of Foreign Relations and the Trilateral Commission.[38]

The launching of the plan, however, had to be postponed until the Global Goals of Agenda 2030 and the Paris Agreement were signed.

A Climate Emergency

In November 2018, Anders Wijkman and Ingemar Rentzhog (from We Don't Have Time) introduced the Club of Rome Climate Emergency Plan (authored by Club of Rome president Sandrine Dixson-Declève, Ian Dunlop, and Anders Wijkman). The plan, which was announced in the European Parliament the following week, included ten recommendations pertaining to the strategy of transition. The report cites Hans Joachim Schellnhuber's doomsday warning stating that: "Climate change is now reaching an end-game scenario, where very soon humanity must choose between taking unprecedented action, or accepting that it has been left too late and bear the consequences."[39]

The report's ten recommendations were to:

1. Halt fossil fuel expansion.
2. Triple annual investments in renewable energy.
3. Put a price on carbon to reflect the true cost of fossil fuel use and embedded carbon by 2020.
4. Replace GDP growth as the main objective for societal progress
5. Improve refrigerant management by 2020.
6. Create an International Task Force to explore alignment of exponential technologies and business models with the Paris Agreement.
7. Ensure greater materials efficiency and circularity by 2025.
8. Triple annual investments in large-scale REDD+ reforestation and estuarine marshland initiatives in developing countries.

9. Ensure that population growth is kept under control by giving priority to education and health services for girls and women and promoting reproductive health and rights, including family planning programmes.
10. Call upon the top 10% earners of the world to cut their GHG emissions by half till 2030.

The Club of Rome report also proposed supporting the development of technology by appointing a work group to examine

> state-of-the-art technology and optimisation of potential technology for reduction of greenhouse gas emissions by adapting digitalisation, exponential technology (such as AI) and business models to the Agenda 2030 and the Paris Agreement, in concert with every state's own particular contributions (the NDC) to the UNFCCC-process.

With the aid of technology, the world was to be put back in balance. It was also necessary for the EU to declare a climate emergency.

> Our historical recognition of the existential nature of this threat, the need for an emergency response, and the opportunity such planning can present, is the unique contribution which the Club of Rome wishes to bring to this debate. We are calling on governments, business leaders, the science community, NGOs and citizens to rise to the challenge of climate action, so that our species can survive and create thriving civilizations in balance with planetary boundaries.[40]

This was enthusiastically accepted. The MEPs Jo Leinen and Heidi Hautala (members of the GLOBE EU network, closely affiliated with the Club of Rome) gave their full support, stating that they were "proud to host the launch of the Club of Rome's Climate Emergency Plan and fully support the Club of Rome's call for urgency."

The plan was right on track. It was now time to declare the planetary emergency. On September 24, 2019, at the UN Climate Action Conference in New York, the Club of Rome presented the report *The Planetary Emergency Plan,* authored in collaboration with the Potsdam Institute (of which Rockström had become supervisor after Schellnhuber).

> Declaring a Planetary Emergency provides a new compass for nations and injects the essential urgency into decision-making. It will ensure that all action from 2020 will be taken in light of its impact on the stability of Earth's life-support systems, and be underpinned by the social and economic transformations needed to secure the long-term health and well-being of people and planet.[41]

The Club of Rome was thereafter invited by the cabinet of the vice president of the European Commission in Brussels to discuss how the report could help anchor the European Green Deal. The Club of Rome also held a number of advisory meetings with the European Commission president-elect Ursula von der Leyen.[42]

Their efforts were successful. On November 29, 2019, the European Parliament declared a climate and environment emergency, with the admonition that the EU must be carbon dioxide neutral by 2050 and that payments to the Global Green Fund would be doubled. Support for the European Green Deal was also expressed.[43] The European Parliament called on the Commission, the Member States, and all global actors "to urgently take the concrete action needed in order to fight and contain this threat before it is too late."[44]

Behind this resolution was the newly elected Member of Parliament and former French minister for development Pascal Canfin. He was previously adviser to the World Resources Institute during the Paris Climate Accords and supervisor of WWF France and was a close associate of 350. org and the Rockefeller Brothers Fund.[45] A few German MEPs, however, protested about the choice of words since Hitler had proclaimed an emergency, Notstand, with the purpose of seizing power right after the Reichstag fire of February 27, 1933.[46]

The 1933 Reichstag Fire

The Reichstag Fire Decree (which had been written beforehand) gave the government full license to implement measures "in protection of the general public" without approval from the Parliament. Thereby, all freedoms of press, speech, and assembly were tacitly abolished and the state was given the authority to censor correspondence and to search and seize property as it saw fit. The horrors of World War II and the Nazi dictatorship still seem to influence the discourse.

The 1933 Reichstag Fire (followed by the textbox Timeline of Adolf Hitler's legal coup d'état)

Timeline of Adolf Hitler's Legal Coup d'Etat

Jan 30, 1933 Hitler is voted Reich Chancellor

Feb 1, 1933 The German Parliament is dissolved

Feb 2, 1933 Hitler initiates rearmament of Germany's defense

Feb 20, 1933 Hitler in secret meeting with industrialists for funding

Feb 27, 1933 **The Reichstag fire**

Feb 28, 1933 A four-year **emergency** is declared

Mar 23, 1933 The Enabling Act (power to pass laws by chancellor decree)

Apr 7, 1933 Prohibitions against jews and communists in public office

Apr 26, 1933 Hermann Göring founds Gestapo (the secret police)

May 10, 1933 Public book burnings

July 14, 1933 All parties but NSDAP are banned

Jun 30, 1934 "The night of the long knives" (purges within the SA)

Aug 2, 1934 Reich President Hindenburg dies

Aug 19, 1934 Hitler becomes Führer

Sep 15, 1935 The Nuremberg Laws

The European Union

Two years after the Schuman Declaration, authorized in 1950 by French foreign minister Robert Schuman and which stated that "world peace cannot be maintained without constructive countermeasures against threatening hazards," the interstate collaboration the European Coal and Steel Community (ECSC) was instituted between Germany, France, Italy, and the Benelux nations. The seed had been sown. From this grew the European Economic Community (EEC) in 1958 to finally emerge in the form of the world's most extensive supranational community, the European Union comprising twenty-seven states. The goal of unifying Europe was an old one, present in one form or another since the collapse of the Roman Empire. In 1941, Adolf Hitler proclaimed his intention of creating a Neuordnung (New Order) unifying Europe under Germany.[47] This was the given path toward total global domination.[48] As Hitler's propaganda minister Joseph Goebbels put it, "Whoever dominates Europe will thereby assume the leadership of the world."

Almost eighty years later, after Britain's exit from the European Union, Germany once again emerges as a leader and the economic engine of Europe. Soon the EU Commission would have a new German president—leading a European Union that has gradually been turning into a Federation, at least in practice.

The EU governance system comprises seven main institutions:[49]

1. **The European Council** (EUCO) defines the political priorities of the EU but lacks legislative power. Besides its president (Charles Michel since 2019), it includes heads of state or government of member states, as well as the president of the EU Commission and the high representative of the Union for Foreign Affairs and Security Policy.

2. **The European Commission** is the government or executive institution of the EU, comprising one commissioner from each member state. It is divided into thirty-six departments, "directorates-general." It proposes new legislation, implements it, and safeguards the common interests of the Union. Members are proposed by the European Council and approved by the European Parliament, which can also dismiss the Commission. The Commission president since 2019 is Ursula von der Leyen, succeeding Jean-Claude Juncker (2014–2019).

3. **The European Parliament** and the Council of the European Union decide on the Commission's legislative proposals. Members of the European Parliament are elected by the people and consist of 736 MEPs and 20 permanent committees.

The Parliament president is David Sassoli (since 2009). The Parliament addresses the commission's legislative proposals and forms a consensus position. The various committees are assigned proposals relating to their expertise and function, and their work is led by a rapporteur. The consensus position is then forwarded to the Council of the European Union.

4. **The Council of the European Union** (also known as the Council of Ministers or just the Council) comprises ministers from member states. It has a legislative function and is responsible for entering into treaties and agreements. On many issues, its authority is shared by the European Parliament. The presidency is shared by member states on a rotational basis. It addresses the consensus developed by the parliament. If not approved, another position is advised, and the issue is returned to the parliament, which may reject or approve the council's position.

5. **The Court of Justice** of the European Union is the judicial branch of the EU. It interprets legislation and regulations and determines whether member states fulfill their obligations. Its president since 2015 is Koen Lenaerts, and its seat is in Luxembourg.

6. **The European Court of Auditors** audits the EU. It reports "fraud, corruption or other illegal activities," and is also seated in Luxembourg.

7. **The European Central Bank** is the central bank of those nineteen EU states that have adopted the Euro as their currency. Its purpose is to maintain price stability. Its main office is located in Frankfurt, and its president since 2019 is Christine Lagarde (also a board member of the World Economic Forum).

Ursula von der Leyen

Ursula von der Leyen (1958–), president of the European Commission

On December 1, 2019, Ursula Von der Leyen took office as the thirteenth president of the European Commission. She had previously held the position as minister of defense of Germany (2013–2019), and had also been a board member of the World Economic Forum (2016–2019)—a circumstance that would later turn out to be of crucial importance. When von der Leyen ran for office, she clearly stated her intentions in an address to the European Parliament on July 19, 2019, "I will put forward a Green Deal for Europe in my first 100 days in office. I will put forward the first ever European Climate Law which will set the 2050 target into law."[50]

This promise she has kept to the letter. On December 11, while the UN Climate Change Conference (COP25) was held in Madrid and Greta Thunberg was appointed person of the year of *Time Magazine*, the newly instated Commission presented the European Green Deal.

That very same day, Sandrine Dixson Declève, president of the Club of Rome, wrote to von der Leyen:

> We firmly believe that the European Green Deal could be a game-changer for Europe and European citizens if executed with the right time and scale. The enabling legislation and market frameworks are now urgently required to set in motion the necessary transformations over the next two decades.[51]

However, the Club of Rome wanted the commission to rename the proposal, instead preferring the name "New Deal for Europeans," since the "European Green Deal" could be interpreted as an initiative by the Greens, which could be exploited by climate skeptics and others in opposition. This suggestion was not heeded, but the ideas of the Club of Rome were still firmly planted and had, in concert with the Rockefeller network, successfully influenced the agenda of the EU. Despite these efforts, recalcitrant nations like Poland, the Czech Republic, and Hungary blocked the proposals in the Council of the European Union.[52] Something more was required to gain political support for the process.

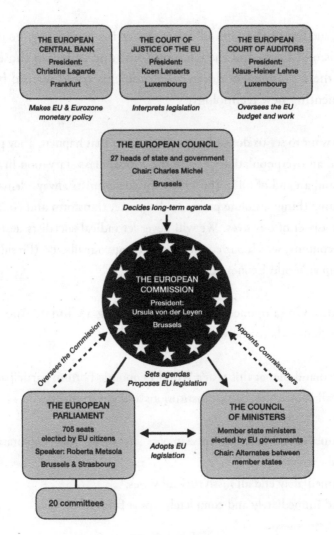

The EU structure

The 2020 World Economic Forum Summit

On January 21, at the annual summit of the World Economic Forum in Davos, Switzerland, US president Donald Trump and Greta Thunberg each held an address at two separate sessions. Trump's message was of course very different from Greta's, and not without merit. After bragging about the success of the United States under his presidency, he criticized the alarmism of Greta and the Club of Rome and called on those present to ignore these prophets of doom. The problems could instead be solved by implementing new technology.[53]

> They want to see us do badly, but we don't let that happen. They predicted an overpopulation crisis in the 1960s, mass starvation in the 70s, and an end of oil in the 1990s. These alarmists always demand the same thing: absolute power to dominate, transform and control every aspect of our lives. We will never let radical socialists destroy our economy, wreck our country or eradicate our liberty. (President Trump at World Economic Forum 2020)

After Trump, Greta opened the session "Averting a Climate Apocalypse," stating her demands to the world leaders:

> We demand that at this year's World Economic Forum, participants from all companies, banks, institutions and governments:
>
> • Immediately halt all investments in fossil fuel exploration and extraction;
> • Immediately end all fossil fuel subsidies:
> • And immediately and completely divest from fossil fuels.
>
> We don't want these things done by 2050, 2030, or even 2021, we want this done *now*. Our house is still on fire![54]

Coincidentally, her request for an end to fossil fuel subsidies were the very same as the World Bank had recommended in 2015,[55] while the demand for divesting from fossil fuels was initiated by the Rockefeller Family Fund in 2016.[†] The leaders were not hard to convince. This was precisely this

---

†   See Nordangård, *Rockefeller*.

type of youth response anticipated by António Guterres a few months earlier. Soon, the games could begin.

After Greta's address, a panel of experts took the stand, which included Rajiv Shah, executive director of the Rockefeller Foundation, succeeding Judith Rodin in 2017 (he had been recruited by the Bill & Melinda Gates foundation in 2001 and became one of WEFs Young Global Leaders in 2007).

In a speech the next day, Greta's demand for immediate action was supported by Prince Charles (now Charles III of the UK): "We simply cannot waste anymore time . . . the time to act is *now.*"[56]

At this fiftieth Davos Summit, with the theme "Stakeholders for a Cohesive and Sustainable World," the connections between the Fourth Industrial Revolution and the climate emergency became even more apparent:

> In responding to the need for further public–private action in this area, the World Economic Forum at its Annual Meeting in Davos in January 2020 brought together leaders from industry and business with Executive Vice-President Frans Timmermans to explore how to catalyze the European Green Deal.[57]

Just before the summit, the report *Unlocking Technology for the Global Goals* was released by the WEF working group Global Future Council on 4IR for Global Public Goods in collaboration with audit consulting firm PwC.[58]

This project was part of the new WEF initiative Frontier 2030: Fourth Industrial Revolution for Global Goals Platform (now 2030Vision), supervised by Danish Anne Marie Engtoft Larsen (who also collaborated with Klaus Schwab on his *Shaping the Fourth Industrial Revolution*).

It may be worth noting that six of the seven main authors of the *Unlocking Technology* report were women. Among these were Dr. Celine Herweijer (key adviser to the UN, member of G20's Digital Economy Taskforce and WEF Young Global Leader 2013) and Antonia Gawel (head of the WEFs Circular Economy Initiative and member of the executive committee of the WEF).[59]

The report presented detailed suggestions on how the advanced IT technologies of the Fourth Industrial Revolution could be used to reach each of the 17 Global Sustainability Goals by 2030. It was made crystal clear that the lofty and idealistic sounding goals are more about profit and control than about saving the planet.

According to WEF's technocratic vision, everyone and everything will be monitored and controlled through the use of AI, satellites, robotics, drones, self-driving vehicles, blockchain, genetic engineering, nanotech, and the Internet of Things, with synthetic food on the menu. In effect, a global panopticon where all human activity is to be gauged, analyzed, and corrected in real time using a form of social credit—not just in China but *everywhere*.

The stage was set. All that was needed now was a trigger event to kick-start the process.

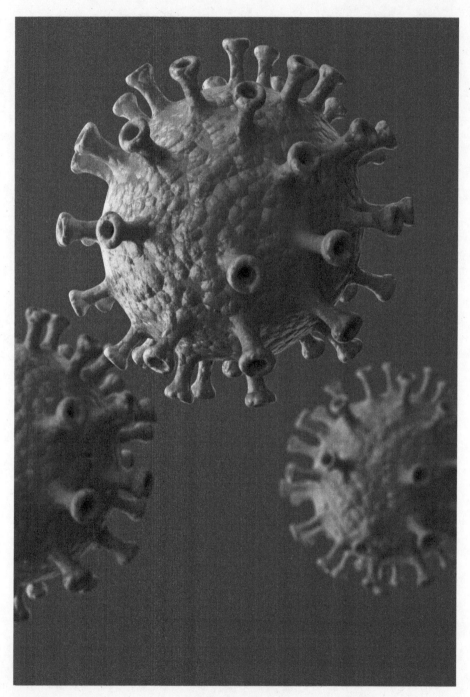

Coronavirus

5

The Trigger

At first, the notion of a more controlled world gained wide acceptance and approval. Citizens willingly gave up some of their sovereignty—and their privacy—to more paternalistic states in exchange for greater safety and stability. Citizens were more tolerant, and even eager, for top-down direction and oversight, and national leaders had more latitude to impose order in the ways they saw fit. (Rockefeller Foundation, 2010)

A trigger event, so shocking and frightening that no one can escape its effects, is crucial for the plan to work. The threat needs to be at least partly realized. This will send waves of shock and terror through society, and thereby make it easier for those affected to accept the solutions offered.

COVID-19

On January 30, 2020, one week after the annual World Economic Forum meeting in Davos, Switzerland, the World Health Organization (WHO) declared a global health emergency. This was around one month after reports of a serious virus outbreak in Wuhan, China, had begun leaking out to the rest of the world. In order to contain the outbreak, Wuhan had been closed off as of January 23, and its inhabitants quarantined. The reports were dramatic and showed Chinese authorities using harsh authoritarian methods to contain the outbreak.

CEPI

The same day as the Chinese lockdown, a press conference was held by the Coalition for Epidemic Preparedness Innovations (CEPI) at World Economic Forum about the development in China. Participants included Stéphane Bancel (CEO of biotech company Moderna and Young Global Leader 2009), Jeremy Farrar (of the Wellcome Trust, WHO, and the Global Preparedness Monitoring Board), and Richard Hatchett (representing CEPI). At the press conference, CEPI declared that they had just formed a partnership with Moderna and the US National Institute of Allergy and Infectious Diseases (NIAID) to develop a vaccine against COVID-19—an experimental vaccine that would use messenger RNA to "inject instruction into humans, for humans to make their own medicine."[1]

The virus had now spread to several continents and countries, including Australia, New Zealand, Germany, and Italy. Air traffic was being shut down or restricted. It all happened very quickly.

The Pandemic

On March 11, 2020, WHO General Secretary Tedros Adhanom Ghebreyesus declared COVID-19 a pandemic. This statement kick-started the immediate implementation of more or less draconian measures to contain the contagion across the world:

- Social distancing
- Quarantines and lockdowns, even for asymptomatic people
- Curfews
- Bans or limitations on public meetings
- Travel bans or travel restrictions
- Closed borders
- Shutting down factories and other workplaces
- Closing of schools and universities
- Canceled culture and sports events
- Forced closing of pubs, clubs, and nonessential shopping
- Isolation of the elderly and visiting restrictions
- Mandatory mask wearing, even for schoolchildren

These mandates were unparalleled. Never before in history have such extreme measures been taken to contain a novel influenza virus.

The chain of events were largely based on statistical modelling of the *expected* spread of the virus, developed by epidemiologist Neil Ferguson and his COVID-19 Response Team at the MRC Centre for Global Infectious Disease Analysis, Imperial College, London.[2] Financiers included the Bill & Melinda Gates Foundation, the World Bank Group, the WHO, and the Wellcome Trust.

Ferguson predicted *huge* death tolls unless strict measures were swiftly put in place. Through Ferguson's role as adviser to the British government and the WHO* his predictions were widely disseminated and had an immediate impact on the containment policies implemented across the globe.

> We show that in the UK and US context, suppression will minimally require a combination of social distancing of the entire population, home isolation of cases and household quarantine of their family members. This may need to be supplemented by school and university closures, though it should be recognized that such closures may have negative impacts on health systems due to increased absenteeism.

According to Ferguson, the measures would have to remain in place until a vaccine had been developed (up to eighteen months later).[3] Ferguson was later disgraced and forced to resign when he was found breaking the very restrictions he himself had recommended, in order to see his mistress. Moreover, his history of prognosing mad cow disease (BSE), the bird flu, the swine flu, and the Ebola epidemic had been grievously misleading, with significantly overstated predictions of mortality. He was known among colleagues as the Master of Disaster.[4] His prognosis of COVID-19 mortality also turned out to be overestimated by orders of magnitude. His abysmal track record did, however, not perturb the trust placed in his models by the WHO or the nations taking extreme measures to contain the current pandemic.

---

*   His mission from WHO was to "upon request of WHO provide rapid analysis of urgent infectious disease problems, notably outbreaks and events of international concern."

Global Lockdown

In the beginning of April 2020, more than half of the global population was under so-called "lockdown" (a very peculiar term, normally only used to contain prison riots).

In large parts of the world, people were only allowed to leave their homes for shopping or recreation for a few hours per day, if at all. In many cases, violating the new rules or voicing criticism of the official policy could result in shockingly high fines or even imprisonment. Authoritarian powers saw an opportunity to tighten control over their citizenry. Police and armed forces began patrolling the streets, and the general public was encouraged to inform on their neighbors' infractions. Government elections were postponed in several countries, including Bolivia and Ethiopia. Surveillance with tracking apps, CCTV, or the location data of cell phones was used to trace the infected, and temporary tracking bracelets for the recovered were used in Hong Kong.[5] In some instances, "robot dogs" or drones were used to disperse crowds or to inform, surveil, register, and photograph those who violated the new restrictions.[6]

In India, a national lockdown was put in place on March 24 after "500 cases of infection." The following day, almost all factories and all services, including airline and railway transport for anything except goods, was shut down. Migrant workers who suddenly became unemployed had to make their way back to their home villages as best they could. Many more died from exhaustion, starvation, traffic accidents, suicide, and police brutality than from the virus.[7]

Such draconian measures, implemented through hasty emergency legislation, were used not only by traditionally authoritarian regimes but also in liberal democracies such as Denmark, Germany, Canada, and Great Britain.

In Germany, a female lawyer questioning government measures was brutally taken to a psychiatric clinic by the police.[8]

Australia (under Minister of Health Greg Hunt, WEF Global Leader of Tomorrow 2003) and New Zealand (led by Jacinda Ardern, Young Global Leader 2014) implemented exceptionally severe measures, intended to *completely eradicate* the virus:

- Mandatory face masks
- Outdoor activities for one hour per day only
- Activities limited to basic shopping, dog walking, and exercise
- Traveling restricted to a radius of five kilometers
- Military checkpoints[9]
- Borders between states closed down
- 5,000 AU$ in fines for non-permitted outdoor activities[10]
- Suspending package services from outside Australia
- Later, even "COVID camps" for detaining infected people.

In South Africa, Trade and Industry minister Ebrahim Patel (WEF Global Leader of Tomorrow 1994) was one of the main administrators of the waves of lockdowns that shut down most activities from March 23, 2020, and was criticized for irrational measures such as banning cooked hot meals being served.

In Denmark, a rushed emergency law, which included the option of mandatory vaccination and the isolation of afflicted areas, was approved on March 23, 2020. The proposal also suggested that public health authorities without a court order should be allowed to enter private property in the case of suspected infection, but that part was dismissed.[11]

In New Zealand, a new COVID–19 law was approved in May 2020. It gave law enforcement far-reaching powers to enforce new infection control regulations:

20 Powers of Entry

1. An enforcement officer may enter, without a warrant, any land, building, craft, vehicle, place, or thing if they have reasonable grounds to believe that a person is failing to comply with any aspect of a COVID-19 order.
2. However, subsection (1) does not apply to a private dwellinghouse.
3. A constable may enter a private dwellinghouse without warrant only if they have reasonable grounds to believe that people have

gathered there in contravention of a COVID-19 order and entry is necessary for the purpose of giving a direction under Section 21.[12]

A similar legislation was implemented in Great Britain.

> The rapidly implemented corona legislation, invoked on ministerial authority in every part of Great Britain, with no debate or vote held, affords the government extensive authority unlike any other legislation. It has no sunset clause, meaning that the legislation expires after a number of years, but contains the option of extension for six month intervals for purposes of flexibility. For instance, the laws authorise law enforcement to detain a citizen for testing if he or she is suspected to be infected, to shut down non-essential businesses, as well as to prevent freedom of movement and assembly.[13]

Nations across the world increasingly became governed by decrees from their respective health authorities, in turn following the guidelines from World Health Organization. Many online communities were alarmed by a statement at a WHO press conference on March 20:

> In some senses transmission has been taken off the streets and pushed back into family units. Now we need to go and look in families to find those people who may be sick and remove them and isolate them in a safe and dignified manner.[14] (Dr. Michael Ryan, senior adviser, WHO)

Yes, he really *did* say this (even if not specifying that it would be *children* taken into custody, as some internet rumors claimed).

Meanwhile, the United States and China took turns accusing each other of releasing the virus.[15]

Most concerning were not the immediate panicked measures taken in the beginning of the situation, when fears that the virus might be extremely lethal were rampant, but rather the extensive restrictions of civil liberties implemented by many states which can forthwith be activated or reintroduced whenever a new variant or virus appears.

In Sweden, often considered among one of the most liberal nations in addressing the crisis, restrictions were mainly limited to recommendations. This was likely due to the legal protections in the Swedish constitution, as well as the comparatively high degree of public trust in the competence and benevolence of public institutions, resulting in a high level of compliance without harsh enforcement.

Still, the recommendations eventually turned into a "soft lockdown" where everyone able to work or study from home was recommended and expected to do so. Service homes for the elderly stopped permitting visits, restaurants closed early, and public assembly was restricted to groups of fifty, later only eight.

More shockingly is that from early on in the pandemic, Swedish doctors, often via telephone, in many cases prescribed palliative care (respiratory-inhibiting morphine and benzodiazepines and no food or water) for elderly persons with symptoms in care homes instead of oxygen, hydration, nutrition, and access to emergency care.

This new practice was based on the Stockholm Regional Council's triage guidelines for different groups of patients, written with the purpose of alleviating *expected* or *possible* (not *actual*) pressure on emergency care resources.[16] In combination with poor information, guidance, and equipment to nursing home staff, this resulted in many avoidable deaths among the elderly, and can be considered as a form of euthanasia—especially as it turned out that many countries had issued very similar guidelines, including Australia, Denmark, England, France, Germany, Ireland, and Switzerland.[17]

This practice also got death statistics up among the most vulnerable enough to scare the majority into not only accepting, but actually *begging* for stricter measures.

How many more countries seized the opportunity to discreetly euthanize some of their elderly and infirm while relatives were prohibited from visiting and noticing what went on? The two initiatives American Frontline Nurses The Remembrance Project[18] and the

COVID-19 Humanity Betrayal Memory Project[19] have collected a growing number of chilling personal stories of how loved ones were mistreated, maimed, or killed in hospitals during the pandemic in the United States alone.

Economic Disaster

The social and economic consequences worldwide were devastating. The economic downturn was marked and the stock markets initially plummeted. Cultural life was ground to a halt and small shops and restaurants had to struggle to survive. Many perished, despite government financial support. Even as the infection and death rates sharply decreased when the flu season was over, the measures in large parts of the world remained. Some countries gradually eased their restrictions during the summer and autumn of 2020—only to reintroduce them when the next flu season began, often with even sharper restrictions.

The Digital Transformation

The COVID-19 crisis catalyzed the great digital transformation by the "smart" solutions and strict surveillance measures that various governments of the world quickly implemented.

Big Tech and Big Pharma stood ready to aid a world stricken by shock and fear. Here was a golden opportunity to begin harvesting previously restricted health data from the population and using AI and cell phone data to more intrusively analyze peoples' movement patterns, contacts, and compliance with the new restrictions.

Leading performers and talk show hosts all over the world immediately manifested their loyalty by airing their shows digitally from home, like good role models.

Together at Home

As early as April 18, 2020, a music gala broadcast online, *One World: Together at Home*, was arranged by Global Citizen and WHO to raise funds for the WHO's COVID-19 Solidarity Response Fund and to create an artificial sense of unity during the forced isolation. The event was sponsored by supporters and associates of the WHO (including Cisco, Citi, Coca-Cola, GSK, IBM, Johnson & Johnson, P&G, Pepsi, State Farm, Tenco, Verizon, and Vodaphone).

Global Citizen was founded in 2008 in Melbourne, Australia, by Hugh Evans (Young Global Leader 2015), Simon Moss, and Wei Soo, originally as the Global Poverty Project, working for a world without extreme poverty by 2030 (SDG #1).

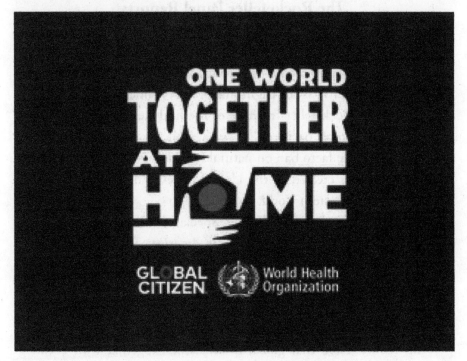

One World: Together at Home poster

Global Governance

In the wake of the crisis, there were also renewed demands for global governance, a transformation of the economic system, and the inclusion of the European New Deal in the stimulus package that was now necessary to restart the global economy.

The fear of climate change that had more or less dominated the news cycles of 2019 and prioritized by the World Economic Forum in January 2020 was immediately replaced by another invisible threat. Yet, the measures to win the war against this new enemy being debated were eerily similar to those suggested in the fight against the old one. This can be explained in relation to the fact that both shared common origins as useful threats promulgated with the purpose of changing the world at the global scale. The entire process appears to be carefully planned and calculated.

The Rockefeller Panel Reports

Through their early interest in medical research, the Rockefeller foundations and institutions have had a huge impact on the development of modern healthcare and medicine throughout the world.

This began as early as the beginning of the twentieth century with the founding of the Rockefeller Institute of Medical Research in New York. Through philanthropic partner Carnegie's publication and support for the *Flexner Report*, a de facto ban on natural remedies in favor of petrochemical medicines was created in the United States and Canada. This then spread across the Western world.

The Rockefeller Brothers Fund's Special Studies Project from the late 1950s, resulting in the *Prospect for America: The Rockefeller Panel Reports*, can be seen as a starting point for the mission of the Rockefeller family and the Council on Foreign Relations, "to shape a new international order in all its dimensions—spiritual, economic, political, and social."[20]

This report stated that global health issues, together with oceanography and meteorology, were important areas to support due to their international scope, as they would require global solutions and multilateral cooperation. One of the main architects of the project was Henry Kissinger, appointed by Nelson Rockefeller.

The Rockefellers, who were also involved in the creation of World Health Organization (WHO) in 1948, have since been deeply involved in sounding alarms about global health and climate issues, as well as building support for global solutions.[21]

Global Risks Report 2006

Another important player in the development of a global health regime is the World Economic Forum (WEF). Its Global Risk Program, initiated in 2004, was led by economist Thierry Malleret (previously senior partner of IJ Partners, an investment firm for ultra-high-net-worth individuals).

In June 2006, WEF released the report *Global Risks 2006*, in cooperation with management consulting firm Mercer Oliver Wyman, insurance company Swiss Re, and Merrill Lynch (the investment branch of Bank of America). The report warned about global problems and offered Big Business solutions. The purpose was to "advance the thinking around more effective mitigation of global risks." The first report identified four main threats:

1. Terrorism
2. Climate Change
3. Oil price shock
4. Pandemics

According to the report, the consequences of a lethal flu could be severe and in the end, reshape the world.

> A lethal flu, its spread facilitated by global travel patterns and uncontained by insufficient warning mechanisms, would present an acute threat. Short-term economic impacts would include severe impairment of travel, tourism and other service industries, as well as manufacturing and retail supply chains. Global trade, investor risk appetites and consumption demand could suffer for more extended periods. Deep shifts in social, economic and political relations are possible.[22] (WEF, *Global Risks 2006*)

WEF concluded that "the impact on society might be as profound as that which followed the Black Death in Europe in 1348." The advice was to develop a strategy to mitigate these risks:

- Top-down surveillance of threats at the global level (such as satellite monitoring of the environment);
- Effective dissemination of information from the bottom up (such that transparency allows for the quick responses needed to contain, for example, SARS or avian flu);
- Appropriate mechanisms to inform the public about risk (such as the Centers for Disease Control and Prevention) to prevent "infodemics" and create appropriate expectations of risk;
- Exchanges on global best practice (including through trade associations), and advice that can be shared between governments and businesses on their risk assessments and mitigation strategies.

Another piece of advice was to harness expertise from the private sector, said to be "ahead of the public sector in its mitigation of risks."

The Bellagio Meeting 2006

Around the same time, the Johns Hopkins Bloomberg School of Public Health gathered international experts from WHO, World Bank, CARE International, and other top institutions in economy, epidemiology, ethics, human rights, health, and animal health at the Rockefeller Foundation conference center in Bellagio, Italy, to formulate principle on pandemic prevention and response planning (in the event of a new serious pandemic).

The meeting resulted in the Bellagio Statement of Principles with a stated purpose to "specifically make available accurate, up-to-date and easy-to-understand information about avian and human pandemic influenza for disadvantaged groups."

With the Bellagio Statement of Principles, we have a better sense of how we might move forward to prevent or at least mitigate unjust outcomes for the world's most vulnerable populations. It's not only better public policy, but the right thing to do.[23] (Judith Rodin, the Bellagio Statement of Principles)

The Swine Flu

Not long after the release of the Global Risk Report, news reports about the bird flu (H5N1) started to make headlines and scare the public. It did, however, soon blow over without making the profound impact on society that had first been anticipated. What it did accomplish was to make governments, in cooperation with the business community, take precautionary measures. This became obvious during the 2009 swine flu outbreak.

One month before a global pandemic was declared by the US CDC and the World Health Organization in June 2009, the WHO changed its definition of what constitutes a pandemic. The requirement "enormous numbers of deaths and illness" was simply removed from the definition on the WHO website:

> An influenza pandemic occurs when a new influenza virus appears against which the human population has no immunity, resulting in several simultaneous epidemics worldwide.[24]

Removing those seven words suited the profit-hungry pharmaceutical industry perfectly.

In Sweden, for example, authorities had, after pressure from the WHO, signed a binding agreement with GSK (GlaxoSmithKline) for the purchase of 18 million doses (for a population of only 9.3 million) of the Pandemrix vaccine for 1.3 billion SEK, automatically going into effect when/if a pandemic was declared. Aside from waste of public funds through an unfavorable agreement, hundreds of young people had their lives ruined by chronic narcolepsy after taking the vaccine, with the global number reaching at least 1,300. The experiment was criticized in the Swedish press for how it was handled.[25]

This was an early example of the Public-Private Partnership that the World Economic Forum believes to be the solution to all the world's problems. Just as during the COVID-19 outbreak, the swine flu pandemic was top focus of the media and there was a strong social pressure to accept the vaccine.

The Rockefeller Foundation's Prophetic Scenarios

In 2010, the Rockefeller Foundation and the consulting firm Global Business Network released the eerily prophetic report *Scenarios for the Future of Technology and International Development*, presenting four future scenarios for the world (Lock Step, Clever Together, Hack Attack, and Smart Scramble) and investigating how each of these might promote or hinder technological development.[26] Judith Rodin, president of the Rockefeller Foundation, stated in the report that, "The results of our first scenario planning exercise demonstrate a provocative and engaging exploration of the role of technology and the future of globalization."

The report was based on a workshop held in Bellagio on March 16–20, 2009, on how technology could help the world's poor, and the technical innovations analyzed by RAND Corporation in their report *The Global Technology Revolution 2020: In-Depth Analyses*, 2006.[27]

One of the scenarios in *Scenarios for the Future*, "Lock Step" ("A world of tighter top-down government control and more authoritarian leadership, with limited innovation and growing citizen pushback"), dealt with a severe pandemic and had quite chilling similarities to the development and response to the COVID-19 crisis.

> The pandemic also had a deadly effect on economies: international mobility of both people and goods screeched to a halt, debilitating industries like tourism and breaking global supply chains. Even locally, normally bustling shops and office buildings sat empty for months, devoid of both employees and customers. (p. 18)

It made predictions of tight control over citizens to contain the outbreak.

> During the pandemic, national leaders around the world flexed their authority and imposed airtight rules and restrictions, from the mandatory wearing of face masks to body-temperature checks at the entries to communal spaces like train stations and supermarkets. Even after the pandemic faded, this more authoritarian

control and oversight of citizens and their activities stuck and even intensified. (p. 19)

Initially, this did not elicit much protest but rather the opposite.

At first, the notion of a more controlled world gained wide acceptance and approval. Citizens willingly gave up some of their sovereignty—and their privacy—to more paternalistic states in exchange for greater safety and stability. Citizens were more tolerant, and even eager, for top-down direction and oversight, and national leaders had more latitude to impose order in the ways they saw fit. In developed countries, this heightened oversight took many forms: biometric IDs for all citizens, for example, and tighter regulation of key industries whose stability was deemed vital to national interests.

China was seen as a role model and other nations soon followed their example, implementing totalitarian strategies which persisted even after the pandemic.

The Chinese government's quick imposition and enforcement of mandatory quarantine for all citizens, as well as its instant and near-hermetic sealing off of all borders, saved millions of lives, stopping the spread of the virus far earlier than in other countries and enabling a swifter postpandemic recovery. (p. 18)

Even the technological solutions somewhat coincided with the 2020 situation.

- Scanners using advanced functional magnetic resonance imaging (fMRI) technology become the norm at airports and other public areas to detect abnormal behavior that may indicate "antisocial intent."

- New diagnostics are developed to detect communicable diseases. The application of health screening also changes; screening becomes a prerequisite for release from a hospital or prison, successfully slowing the spread of many diseases.
- Tele-presence technologies respond to the demand for less expensive, lower bandwidth, sophisticated communications systems for populations whose travel is restricted.
- Driven by protectionism and national security concerns, nations create their own independent, regionally defined IT networks, mimicking China's firewalls. Governments have varying degrees of success in policing internet traffic, but these efforts nevertheless fracture the "world wide web."

The report predicted that the strict control measures would not be accepted by the public in the long run, but the already implemented technology would still remain. This included biometric identification for all citizens (see chapter 11).

Contagion

The following year, 2011, the film *Contagion* premiered. The plot was inspired by the SARS and swine flu outbreaks and the screenwriter had consulted the WHO and medical experts. With extremely high mortality rates and A-list actors dying shortly after exposure just minutes into the film, the film likely helped lay a solid foundation of fear just at hearing the word "pandemic." The solution to the global health and social crisis in the film was a rapidly developed experimental vaccine. The hero was the scientist who tried it on himself and the villain, an outspoken conspiracy theorist (likely modeled after Alex Jones) who initially seemed to have reasonable criticism against Big Pharma but later turned out to only be in it for personal profit.[28]

Contagion was produced by Participant Media, created by eBay founder and tech billionaire Jeff Skoll. Participant's stated purpose is to "inspire positive social change."[29] Participant also produced Al Gore's documentary *An Inconvenient Truth* (2006), and *Food, Inc.* (2008).

Skoll, together with the Rockefeller Foundation and Bill & Melinda Gates Foundation, is also a core partner in the philanthropic collaboration Co-Impact, founded to enable "meaningful systems change for millions of people" (primarily in developing nations).[30]

Ebola

In 2014, the Ebola virus made headlines but was limited to West Africa. The Ebola outbreak had, however, become a real concern for the World Economic Forum, resulting in a report called *Managing the Risk and Impact of Future Epidemics: Options for Public–Private Cooperation* (written with Boston Consulting Group in 2015). Advisers included Jeremy Farrar from Wellcome Trust and Christopher Elias from the Bill & Melinda Gates Foundation (previously with Population Council).[31] The report recommended building up global preparedness to manage future outbreaks, using public-private partnerships. WEF continued the work at hand with advice from, among others, the WHO, UNICEF, the Bill & Melinda Gates Foundation, Henry Schein, Inc., GSK, and Johnson & Johnson, "aiming to start a dialogue between the private sector, the international community and the leaders who will form collaborations moving forward."

Bill Gates Warns of a New Pandemic

In March 2015, World Economic Forum partner Bill Gates, in an article in the *New York Times*, warned of a new pandemic and of limitations in public authorities' capacity to map and manage it correctly. Using the recent Ebola crisis as an example, he wrote that "Even once the Ebola crisis was recognized last year, there were no resources to effectively map where cases occurred, or to use people's travel patterns to predict where the disease might go next."[32]

However, an upside, according to the article, was that we now had technology that could make a difference. Smartphones and satellites could inform and track people's movement and new, more precise, vaccines could be used.

As Rajiv Shah, president of the Rockefeller Foundation and former associate of Bill Gates, would later put it: "Once we started to get transparent, location-specific, real-time data on where someone had perished from Ebola, and who their relatives and other contacts were, we could target prevention and response efforts much more precisely."

What was lacking, according to Gates's article, was a global health system and better global coordination. This was something he intended to remedy. The Bill & Melinda Gates Foundation would soon become one of the major contributors to the WHO (in 2020, after President Trump withheld US funding for WHO, the foundation became the top funder).

In April 2015, UN Secretary-General Ban Ki-moon initiated a High-Level Panel on Global Response to Health Crises for the purpose of strengthening the international and domestic systems to prevent and address coming health risks.[33] The Ebola situation was a trigger in this case. The panel included Rajiv Shah. One of the recommendations was to "carry out simulation exercises for all relevant responders, including security forces."

In order to implement the recommendations of the global panel, the UN launched the Global Health Crises Task Force in 2016, headed by the vice Secretary-General Amina J. Mohammed, World Bank president Jim Yong Kim, and the director-general of the WHO, Margaret Chan. Among members were Christopher Elias from the Bill & Melinda Gates Foundation and Anthony P. Fauci of the National Institute of Allergy and Infectious Diseases, a top adviser of the White House. In his report, Secretary-General Ban Ki-moon stated that increased travel and climate change had heightened the risk of a serious outbreak of disease.

I believe that the threat to millions of lives of a pandemic has so far been underestimated, as has the importance of global preparedness and capacity. I recognize that, in the current global political and economic environment, many priorities place pressure on limited resources. However, unless we act now to strengthen the public health capacities of countries, to empower WHO, the United Nations and other responders and to invest to prevent disease outbreaks, the next health crisis may cause even greater devastation than the Ebola outbreak.[34] (Ban Ki Moon, *Strengthening the Global Health Architecture,* 2016)

This same year, the Trilateral Commission, of which Rajiv Shah is a member, addressed this topic in its report *Global Health Challenges*.[35] The report discussed global health issues like pandemics and how to manage them. The title of chapter 4, "Global One Health: A New Integrated Approach," indicated the kind of solutions they had in mind, coincidentally one of the long-term goals of the Rockefeller Family, and exactly what Bill Gates had called for.

One of the authors, Harvard professor Julio Frenk, had previously held top positions at the Bill & Melinda Gates Foundation and the WHO, and had also been a board member of Ted Turner's United Nations Foundation with Gro Harlem Brundtland. As usual, there were close ties between the top players.

The Founding of CEPI

At the World Economic Forum annual meeting in January 2017 the public-private partnership Coalition for Epidemic Preparedness Innovations (CEPI) was presented. Its purpose was to develop vaccines to stop future pandemics. Behind the initiative were the WEF, the Wellcome Trust, and the Bill & Melinda Gates Foundation. Richard Hatchett was appointed CEO of CEPI, with Jeremy Farrar as one of the board members. Bill Gates stated that governments and foundations needed to join forces to create the proper conditions for handling future pandemics, and that a new experimental vaccine implementing RNA and DNA technology could be a solution. This would be the task of CEPI.

The following month, at a security conference in Munich in February 2017, Gates warned of a severe pandemic and requested investments in vaccine development: "Whether it occurs by a quirk of nature or at the hand of a terrorist, epidemiologists say a fast-moving airborne pathogen could kill more than 30 million people in less than a year."[36]

Things were heating up.

At the next World Economic Forum annual meeting in January 2018, Gates addressed the session "A New Era for Global Health" on how new forms of leadership, policies, and business models were changing the global health scene. He was himself very much involved in this transformation.

Later in 2018, Gates raised alarms about the population growth in southern Africa. He found it imperative to limit this growth and encourage women to raise fewer children through education.[37] This was exactly what the Club of Rome had advocated in its *Climate Emergency Report*.

Johns Hopkins Scenarios

The School of Hygiene and Public Health at Johns Hopkins University in Baltimore was founded in 1916 by the Rockefeller Foundation. In 1998, the school established a think tank advising the US government, the WHO, and the UN Biological Weapons Convention. In October 2017, this think tank, Johns Hopkins Center for Health Security, hosted the exercise "The SPARS pandemic 2025–2028: A Futuristic Scenario to Facilitate Medical Countermeasure Communication," an exercise focused on communications dilemmas around medical interventions that could arise during a pandemic and how to centralize control of recommendations for the general public so that everyone would get the same message.[38]

In order to overcome the public's disinterest, the CDC and FDA, in concert with other government agencies and their social media experts, began developing a new public health messaging campaign about SPARS, Kalocivir, and the forthcoming vaccine, Corovax. The purpose of this campaign was to create a core set of messages that could be shared by all public health and government agencies over the next several months during which time the SPARS vaccine would be introduced.[39]

On May 15, 2018, another exercise was arranged, Clade X, with funding from the Open Philanthropy Project. The purpose was to "illustrate high-level strategic decisions and policies that the United States and the world will need to pursue in order to prevent a pandemic or diminish its consequences should prevention fail."

World Economic Forum 2019

Before its 2019 annual meeting, the WEF published the white paper *Outbreak Readiness and Business Impact: Protecting Lives and Livelihoods across the Global Economy*. The report, written in collaboration with the Harvard Global Health Institute, and aimed at the business community, concluded that,

> with increasing trade, travel, population density, human displacement, migration and deforestation, as well as climate change, a new era of the risk of epidemics has begun.[40]

The paper included a number of recommendations and pointed out that "effective readiness for outbreaks requires reliable public-private. cooperation."

The Fourth Industrial Revolution Health Regime

September 20, 2019, a few months before WHO declared the pandemic, the WEF released its report *Health and Healthcare in the Fourth Industrial Revolution*. Among the authors was Victor Dzau, president of the US National Academy of Medicine. The report discussed how new technologies could be employed to build the healthcare system of the future:

> It is now possible to join the dots between personal digital devices, connected medical devices, implants and other sensors so that sensors collect data, micro-controllers process and analyse and wirelessly communicate data, and microprocessors enable rich graphical user interface.[41]

This was a system for merging man with technology, and a response to the appeals from Bill Gates and the Rockefeller Foundation. Just a few days after the release of this report, during the UN General Assembly, September 25, 2019, Rajiv Shah from the Rockefeller Foundation presented a partnership with UNICEF, GAVI, WHO, and the World Bank Group, where one of the goals was "identifying and testing new ways to use digital maps, road networks, climate patterns, and social media data from the private sector to better predict public health challenges such as infectious disease outbreaks before they occur." The Rockefeller Foundation invested $100 million in the project, which would use "precise tools for decision-making, based on large amounts of integrated data, predictive analysis, artificial intelligence and machine learning." Everything was to be done in real time and would, according to their predictions, save six million lives before 2030.[42]

The time was now ripe for the business community to step up and protect the planet from contagious diseases.

Event 201

On October 18, 2019 (coinciding with the opening day of the 2019 Military World Games in Wuhan, China), Johns Hopkins Center for Health Security joined forces with the World Economic Forum and Bill & Melinda Gates Foundation for a live simulation of a global "corona virus pandemic."[43]

All in accordance with the recommendations from the UN High-Level Panel on Global Response to Health Crises, participants included the US and Chinese Centers for Disease Control, the United Nations, the Rockefeller Foundation, Ted Turner's UN Foundation, GAVI, the WHO, CEPI, Lufthansa, Henry Schein, and Johnson & Johnson.

The result of the simulation was dramatic, with a total lockdown of most of society, followed by an economic recession. This very much resembled the Rockefeller Foundation's Lock Step scenario from 2010.

The sequence of events in the Event 201 simulation soon became a shocking reality. The first cases of COVID-19 were reported around the same time—even if the Chinese government didn't publicly admit to the crisis until December.

A Green Deal for Europe

This all took place around the time the Green Deal package was presented by the European Commission, led by former WEF board member Ursula von der Leyen. The European Green Deal was an ambitious plan to implement a circular economy and transform society with digital technology in order to fulfill the Sustainable Development Goals of the UN Agenda 2030, including reaching carbon neutrality by 2050. The digital transformation was seen as a "key enabler for reaching the Green Deal objectives."

In late November 2019, the previously mentioned "climate emergency" was declared by the European Parliament. Our house was again said to "be on fire" and the European Union would now lead the fight against this "existential threat." There had, however, been some opposition, and not all EU countries approved the policies.

On March 4, 2020, the Green Deal proposal was followed by a proposal for a new Climate Framework and a European Climate Pact in order to engage EU citizens in "the battle against climate change."[44]

A week later, March 10, A New Industrial Strategy for Europe was adopted.[45] The day after, the European Commission presented the EU Green Deal, which included an EU action plan for a circular economy.[46]

This took place just as the World Health Organization declared a global pandemic on March 11. According to von de Leyen, the digital transformation was now more urgent than ever, both for the environment and for public health "as Europe embarks on its ambitious green and digital transitions in a more unsettled and unpredictable world."[47]

Crisis and Opportunity

The COVID-19 crisis almost overnight introduced measures closely related to the criticized climate policy. All over the world, large sections of society were quarantined (despite lack of symptoms) and prevented from attending school, work, and social gatherings. Consumption and real-life culture and entertainment were put on hold and travel and air traffic minimized, with resulting impact on the economy.

At the same time, the pandemic created an unprecedented opportunity to quickly roll out and test the technologies of the Fourth Industrial Revolution. A large portion of office work, education, health care, business meetings, entertainment, and shopping was transferred to the digital realm—though not without problems. In many countries, control and tracking of both COVID-19 patients and whole populations became accepted strategies.

Initially, there was little opposition, as the pandemic measures perfectly combined nationalist aims of stricter border control and surveillance of refugees, with the left's ambitions to control and tax the very air we breathe.

The Club of Rome Reacts

As both Johan Rockström and the Club of Rome were quick to point out shortly after the pandemic had been declared, both the pandemic and climate change were perfect threats for implementing the same agenda: "Here lies an opportunity to weld together the EU Green Deal with the work to save EU from the Corona Crisis. It is the same agenda." (Johan Rockström, March 29, 2020)[48]

The agenda was the EU Green Deal and the introduction of new economic models. If this was not done, we could expect new crises, according to the Club of Rome.

> COVID-19 reflects a broader trend: more planetary crises are coming. If we muddle through each new crisis while maintaining the same economic model that got us here, future shocks will eventually exceed the capacity of governments, financial institutions, and corporate crisis managers to respond. Indeed, the "corona-crisis" has already done so.

The COVID-19 crisis had demonstrated that society was capable of transfer practically overnight. Now there was a golden opportunity for creating the world they desired.

> Rather than simply reacting to disasters, we can use the science to design economies that will mitigate the threats of climate change, biodiversity loss, and pandemics. We must start investing in what matters, by laying the foundation for a green, circular economy that is anchored in nature-based solutions and geared toward the public good.[49]

The Club of Rome would now continue leading the way. In 2019, a partnership had been formed by the Club of Rome and WWF, including 250 organizations devoted to implementing a Planetary Emergency Plan. Now, pandemics were also included in this concept.[50]

G20 Reacts

This new crisis soon became a priority for the G20. The uncoordinated responses indicated that a firm global leadership and coordination of the corona crisis was needed. At an extraordinary general meeting held online on March 26, the following statement was made:

> The unprecedented COVID-19 pandemic is a powerful reminder of our interconnectedness and vulnerabilities. The virus respects no borders. Combatting this pandemic calls for a transparent, robust, coordinated, large-scale and science-based global response in the spirit of solidarity. We are strongly committed to presenting a united front against this common threat.[51]

G20 decided on an urgent action plan:

1. Strengthen WHO's mandate to coordinate the international fight against COVID.

2. On a voluntary basis commit resources to WHO: COVID-19 Solidarity Response Fund, Coalition for Epidemic Preparedness and Innovation, and GAVI, The Vaccine Alliance.
3. Increase research on vaccines and medicines, leverage digital technologies, and strengthen scientific international cooperation.
4. Ask the Central Bank Governors to develop a G20 action plan in response to COVID-19. Work closely with international organizations to deliver international financial assistance.
5. Ask ILO [the International Labor Organization] and OECD to monitor the pandemic's impact on the employment.
6. Enhance global cooperation through frontline organizations like WHO, IMF, World Bank Group, and multilateral and regional banks.
7. Ask top relevant officials to coordinate the pandemic's impact, including through border management measures and providing assistance to repatriate citizens (if necessary).

The development of a vaccine became a priority for G20, which supported the goal of the Global Preparedness Monitoring Board to raise $8 billion for vaccine research.

> Global challenges demand global solutions and this is our time to stand and support the race for a vaccine and other therapeutic measures to combat COVID-19. We commend the existing funding efforts from around the world and underscore the urgency to bridging the financing gap.

A month later, G20 ministers in charge of the digital economy held a summit.[52] They stressed the importance of using digital solutions and AI to fight COVID-19.

> This present crisis carries with it an opportunity for governments to encourage the use of our most advanced technologies in order to

prevent, mitigate, treat, and defeat future pandemics, and to facilitate the development of digital innovations that will enable a full
economic recovery. The Digital Economy Task Force will encourage
the dissemination of current and emerging digital tools for fighting
this pandemic.

This opened up a path for large investments in digital technology and
vaccine research. The G20 also assumed that the pandemic mitigation
strategies would continue through 2021 when Italy became host nation
for G20 summits. The devastating impact of the pandemic measures on
ordinary people's economy and social life at the same time also created
winners. The monopoly capitalists from Big Tech and Big Pharma now
had a chance to make huge profits from the crisis.

Bill Gates Reacts

In interviews, Bill Gates could hardly contain his excitement over the
fact that the pandemic that he'd been warning about for years had now
finally arrived.

> There will be the ability, particularly in rich countries, to open up if
> things are done well over the next few months. But for the world at
> large, normalcy only returns when we have vaccinated largely all of
> the world's population.[53]

His unsavory glee may also have been related to the huge profit potential
for vaccine developers.

The Rockefeller COVID-19 Testing Plan

The Rockefeller Foundation was, as always, well prepared. On April
21, 2020, they issued the report *National Covid-19 Testing Action Plan:
Pragmatic Steps to Reopen our Workplaces and Our Communities,* with a
foreword by Rajiv Shah.[54] The report focused on measures in the United
States and proposed three goals:

1. Launch a 1-3-30 plan to dramatically expand COVID-19 testing
2. Launch a COVID community healthcare corps for testing and contact tracing
3. Create a COVID-19 data commons and digital platform

This plan included using digital surveillance technology for contact tracing and monitoring people's health data in real time. Rockefeller Foundation invested $15 million to make "the plan of plans" operational.

> When integrated into national and state surveillance systems, such innovations may enable the same level of outbreak detection with fewer tests. Promising techniques include anonymous digital tracking of workforces or population-based resting heart-rate and smart thermometer trends; continually updated epidemiological data modelling; and artificial intelligence projections based on clinical and imaging data.

A few weeks later, on May 1, 2020, US Congress introduced H.R.6666, COVID-19 Testing, Reaching, and Contacting Everyone (TRACE) Act.[55] The man behind the act was Rep. Bobby L. Rush.

Nine months earlier, in August 2019, Rush had participated in a conference in Rwanda on the US role in African development (part of an Aspen Institute Congressional Program). The travel expenses for Rush and his wife ($19,000) were paid by the Bill & Melinda Gates Foundation, the Henry Luce Foundation, the Rockefeller Brothers Fund, the Democracy Fund, and the Eleanor Crook Foundation.[56]

At this conference, Rush had discussed a contact tracing program with representatives of the Bill & Melinda Gates Foundation.[57] The conference report also pointed out how thermal scans had been used at Rwanda-Congo border checkpoints to identify and turn away travelers with a fever.[58] Tech companies were quick to offer solutions. On the same day that the Rockefeller Foundation report was issued, VSBLTY and Photon-X announced that they were developing a heat sensor camera with facial recognition for building entrances to identify individuals with a fever. It could also be used to measure heart rate and oxygen level.[59]

Black Lives Matter

The drama of 2020 escalated further when the African American George Floyd died during a police intervention on May 25. He suffocated due to an officer pressing down his head with a knee, and the event was recorded by bystanders with smartphones and transmitted virally across the globe. The next day, protests began in Minneapolis against police brutality and violence against Black people. This was rapidly picked up by the Black Lives Matter (BLM) movement and within a week, the protests had spread all over the world.[60] Thousands gathered to show their sympathy in cities like London, Paris, and Stockholm, despite the new pandemic measures restricting public assembly. BLM and its slogans proliferated. In several US cities there were riots and violent clashes between protesters and the police.

Black Lives Matter was founded in 2013 by the activists Patrisse Cullors, Alicia Garza, and Opal Tometi to challenge police brutality and racism.[61] Their ideas are based in critical theory, Marxism, and the defense of minorities, including racial minorities and sexual minorities such as LGBTQ people. Both Cullors and Garza identify as queer.

Their cause has received much support from the higher echelons. Garza, a professional activist, became a WEF Young Global Leader in 2020 and was also the supervisor of the Black Futures Lab (funded by the Tides Foundation and the Rockefeller Brothers Fund). This organization has since 2018 worked toward strengthening black influence in politics (which is of course commendable). The question remains, however, *whose* politics are they meant to work for? Garza, who supports the Green New Deal, works closely with her financier the Rockefeller Brothers Fund (RBF). She has been handpicked by the wealthy elite behind the Fourth Industrial Revolution.

In October 2019, the RBF board visited the US South, with Garza and representatives of two other organizations (Team Blackbird and Color of Change) as part of their Democracy Practices program.[62] Team Blackbird focuses on building a civil rights movement where climate politics is a central component.

> We helped build the cultural and political engine known as the Movement for Black Lives. We're working hard to help build the next stage of a climate movement that highlights those most likely to suffer the impacts of climate change.[63]

This is one of the core issues of the RBF. Garza is also a board member of the women's rights organization Supermajority (founded in 2019), intending to "reshape our nation and build an intergenerational, multicultural movement for women's equality."[64] Cofounders were Cecile Richards (board member of the Ford Foundation and former director of Planned Parenthood) and Ai-jen Poo (a Ford Foundation board member and Young Global Leader 2013).[65]

In 2014, the umbrella organization Movement for Black Lives (M4BL) and the fundraising foundation Borealis Philanthropy were founded. The latter entered into a partnership with the Ford Foundation and the W. K. Kellogg Foundation to collect funds. Contributions came from a large number of US corporations. The Rockefeller Brothers Fund also helped fund the M4BL and their "Electoral Justice Project."[66]

Walker (CFR member and board member of Rockefeller Philanthropy Advisors) was previously employed by the Rockefeller Foundation. The Ford Foundation and the Rockefeller Foundation are old partners and share the same agenda (see chapter 1 and appendix A).

> We have an obligation to interrogate how our own practices and institutions may reinforce structural racism and inequality in our society.[67] (Darren Walker, Ford Foundation)

In 2016, M4BL launched their platform, A Vision for Black Lives, with a corresponding pamphlet listing demands:

1. **End the war on black people**.
2. **Reparations**: "for past and continuing harms."
3. **Invest-Divest**: "investments in Black communities, determined by Black communities, and divestment from exploitative forces including prisons, fossil fuels, police, surveillance and exploitative corporations."
4. **Economic Justice**: "economic justice for all and a reconstruction of the economy to ensure Black communities have collective ownership, not merely access."
5. **Community Control**: "a world where those most impacted in our communities control the laws, institutions, and policies that are meant to serve us—from our schools to our local budgets, economies, police departments, and our land—while recognizing that the rights and histories of our Indigenous family must also be respected."
6. **Political power**: "independent Black political power and Black self-determination in all areas of society."[68]

While some of these demands may be reasonable, M4BL is an openly anti-capitalist movement, advocating for the view that the current system needs a complete overhaul, and calls for a total restructuring of global power. Coincidentally, this also happens to be the plan of their funders. Just not in the way M4BL envisions.

Earth in the hands of the global public private partnership

6

The Coup

We have a choice to remain passive, which would lead to the amplification of many of the trends we see today. Polarisation, nationalism, racism, and ultimately increasing social unrest and conflicts. But we have another choice, we can build a new social contract, particularly integrating the next generation, we can change our behavior to be in harmony with nature again, and we can make sure the technologies of the Fourth Industrial Revolution are best utilized to provide us with better lives. (Klaus Schwab)

In the middle of the crisis, brought about by the trigger event, the usurper may step forward and offer safety, protection, and security, and thereby seem like a benevolent savior. The necessary support can thus be garnered for carrying out the actual agenda.

The Great Reset

After several months of extreme measures where whole continents were shut down and authoritarian control measures were implemented all over the world, Klaus Schwab appeared as a global authority in a video released on the World Economic Forum platform on June 3, 2020, offering a solution to all of our problems: The Great Reset. This was less than a year after the UN and World Economic Forum had signed their partnership on June 13, 2019.

The COVID-19 crisis has shown us that our old systems are not fit anymore for the 21st century. It has laid bare the fundamental lack of social cohesion, fairness, inclusion and equality. Now is the historical moment in time, not only to fight the real virus but to shape the system for the needs of the Post-Corona era.[1] (Klaus Schwab)

Schwab also stated that The Great Reset would be the theme of the following year's Davos meeting. Now the possibility had come of founding a new economic and social order for a "more just, sustainable and resilient future."

Klaus Schwab declares The Great Reset

Schwab's opening speech was followed by an address by Prince Charles (now King Charles III): "We have a golden opportunity to seize something good from this crisis. Its unprecedented shockwaves may well make people more receptive to big visions of change."

The UN Secretary-General António Guterres in his address said that this "human tragedy" (not mentioning that it was initiated by the WHO declaring COVID-19 a "global pandemic") was a "wake-up call" for humanity, and that the Great Reset was the solution: "We must build more equal, inclusive and sustainable economies and societies that are more resilient in the face of pandemics, climate change and the many other global changes we face."[2]

These dignitaries were followed by statements from Kristalina Georgieva (managing director of IMF and a WEF board member) and "voices from all interest groups in global society" such as Bradford L. Smith (CEO of Microsoft) and Ajay P. Banga (executive chairman of MasterCard).

The Digital Agenda

Only a week after Schwab's appearance on the WEF platform, a UN report with an action plan was presented, based on the recommendations from the United Nations High Level Panel on Digital Connectivity (headed by Melinda Gates and Jack Ma, president of Alibaba and at the time a WEF board member). The purpose was to implement the digital agenda, "CONNECT, RESPECT, and PROTECT all people in the digital age."

The report stated that the pandemic had demonstrated the benefits of digitalization—such as research collaborations on vaccine development, working from home, online education, and e-commerce, while the pandemic had also emphasized the divide between those who had internet access and those who did not. This now had to be remedied. The goal was, once again, to include every human in the digitalization agenda (i.e., to carry out Oliver Reiser's and H. G. Wells's old utopian dreams of a world brain). According to Guterres, this would entail:

1. Achieving universal connectivity by 2030—everyone should have safe and affordable access to the internet.
2. Supporting the availability of digital services and products to create a more equal world—such as the open source code of the internet. Citizen-based initiatives should be supported.
3. Promoting digital public goods to unlock a more equitable world—the internet's open source, public origins should be embraced and supported.

4. Strengthening digital capacity building—skills development and training are needed around the world.
5. Ensuring the protection of human rights in the digital era— human rights apply both online and offline.
6. Supporting global cooperation on artificial intelligence that is trustworthy, human rights–based, safe, and sustainable and promotes peace.
7. Promoting digital trust and security—calling for a global dialogue to advance the Sustainable Development Goals.
8. Building a more effective architecture for digital cooperation— make digital governance a priority and focus the United Nation's approach.[3]

Digitalization was the backbone of Agenda 2030 and the artificial world envisioned.

Through the leading role of the World Economic Forum in the agenda, they were also well prepared. In July, WEF published the report *Accelerating Digital Inclusion in the New Normal* (with Boston Consulting Group). According to the report, the crisis had highlighted the importance of ubiquitous high-speed internet connections and the implementation of the UN Secretary-General's plan for digital cooperation:

> The economic and behavioural trends brought about by the COVID-19 pandemic will challenge public and private sectors to rethink and prioritize digital in the future.

The WEF working group behind this report had been formed in 2016, the same year that Klaus Schwab declared the advent of the Fourth Industrial Revolution, with experts from corporations such as Microsoft, Google, Facebook, AT&T, Ericsson, Dell, Nokia, Telenor, and Huawei.[4] They could now all reap the benefits of this "new normal" and "successfully navigate" the Great Reset and the Fourth Industrial Revolution.

The Decade of Action

In the report *The Sustainable Development Goals Report 2020* published by the UN on July 7, 2020, António Guterres, under the heading "Launching the Decade of Action at a Time of Crisis," remarked that "[t]he 17 Sustainable Development Goals (SDGs) demand nothing short of a transformation of the financial, economic and political systems that govern our societies today to guarantee the human rights of all."[5]

COVID-19, which in the report was described as a "crisis of health, economy and society without measure," had stymied these goals. Health care systems were severely strained, unemployment increasing, 1.6 billion lacked basic education while tens of millions had fallen into extreme poverty. Yet these problems only emphasized the importance of increasing the efforts. They advised that: "A transformative recovery from COVID-19 should be pursued, one that addresses the crisis, reduces risks from future potential crises and relaunched the implementation efforts to deliver the 2030 Agenda and SDGs during the Decade of Action."[6]

In other words, these crises demonstrated why Agenda 2030 and the Paris Agreement on climate were absolutely necessary to implement.

COVID-19: The Great Reset

Two days later, July 9, 2020, the WEF published the book *COVID-19: The Great Reset*, where these ideas were developed by Klaus Schwab and coauthor Thierry Malleret (head of the WEF Global Risk Network). The book's stated purpose is to prepare us for the future changes we need to make. It is divided into three main sections:

1. **Macro Reset**: Reviews the effects on economy, society, geopolitics, environment, and technology.
2. **Micro Reset**: Analyses effects on industry and private enterprises.
3. **Individual Reset**: Discusses consequences at the individual level.

According to the authors, we are at a crossroads. One path will lead us to a better world: more inclusive, more equal, and better respecting Mother Earth. The other path will lead to a world reminiscent of the one we have just left behind, only worse and with recurring unpleasant surprises. Below follows a summary of the most relevant sections of *COVID-19: The Great Reset*, with chapter headings and quotes from the book.[7]

"Geopolitical Reset"

According to the authors, COVID-19 has reminded the world that the major issues we face (climate, pandemics, terrorism, international trade) are *global*, but that the international organizations have not been adequately equipped and have lacked effective leadership. The present system has therefore not been capable of dealing with the COVID-19 crisis, but has rather been characterized by disorganized national counter-measures. This, supposedly, is evidence of a need for more effective and better coordinated leadership, and of nationalism being a dead end. The concern was that "without appropriate Global Governance, we will become paralysed in our attempts to address and respond to global challenges. (p. 115)

This was especially the case in Africa, Latin America, and Asia, where nations come close to collapse under the pressure of the crisis. They stated that: "[a]ny lockdown or health crisis caused by the coronavirus could rapidly create widespread desperation and disorder, potentially triggering massive unrest with global knock-out effects." (p. 129)

Violence, hunger, unemployment, and chaos would follow. Starvation of biblical proportions could emerge. This threatened to generate a new wave of refugees and mass migration, akin to the one in 2015–2016. The world could be a poorer and more dangerous place without the leadership from global institutions, argued Schwab and Malleret. Without their guidance and leadership, there would be no reset of the global economy.

"Environmental Reset"

Pandemics, climate change, and the collapse of ecosystems are, according to the authors, evidence of the complex interaction between humankind and nature. They argue that COVID-19 had given the world a preview of what a more full-blown climate crisis and ecosystem collapse would mean for the economy, for geopolitics, and for technological progress. The crises also share common traits, such as being global in scope, and only possible to address through international coordination.

One difference is that pandemics necessitate immediate action with quick results, whereas climate change is less conspicuous and thus generally considered less urgent to address. During a pandemic, the majority will accede to forceful measures, while they will resist constraints on their life choices if the purpose is to address climate change, with leeway to question the scientific evidence.

The book mentions studies where pandemics like COVID-19 are considered related to human effects on the environment. As usual, it is we humans who are to blame, and since carbon dioxide emissions have only been reduced by 8 percent during the lockdowns, the conclusion is that we need a radical transformation of the energy systems, as well as structural changes to our consumption habits. (It is, however, not mentioned if the proposed restrictions will also apply to Schwab himself and his billionaire friends and associates.)

> If, in the post-pandemic era, we decide to resume our lives just as
> before (by driving the same cars, by heating our homes the same way
> and so on), the COVID-19 crisis will have gone to waste as far as
> climate policies are concerned. (p.142)

The authors predict that the pandemic will dominate politics for several years, and thus risk overshadowing climate politics. COP26 was, for instance, postponed. This, Schwab and his allies want to avoid, and instead suggests that the COVID-19 crisis may bring new opportunities to implement the Sustainable Development Goals.

In this scenario, governments and corporations will be influenced into making the "correct" decisions through the majority of the population developing a "social conscience," emphasizing that other ways of life are possible. This will be brought about by strategic activism. Since governments may be tempted to return to the old order, four focus areas will be used to nudge them in the desired direction:

1. **Enlightened leadership**: leaders taking charge in the fight against climate change (indicating Prince Charles and others).
2. **Risk awareness**: the pandemic has made us aware of our relations of dependence and the effects of not submitting to scientific expertise.
3. **Change in behavior**: the pandemic has forced us to adapt our travel and consumption patterns to a "greener way of life."
4. **Activism**: the virus has inspired changes and created new strategies. Climate activists who have reduced pollution during the lockdowns will double their efforts to influence investors and private corporations.

The massive Europe Green Deal, where the European Commission plans to invest one trillion euro to reduce emissions and pave the way for a circular economy, is highlighted as "the most significant example" of how authorities are not letting the COVID-19 crisis go to waste.

"Technological Reset"

The pandemic will accelerate innovation even more, catalysing technological changes already under way and "turbocharging" any digital business or the digital dimension of any business. (pp. 152–53)

According to the authors, the COVID-19 crisis has enabled digital development to make two years' progress in just a month. Almost everything has moved online. Tech companies are the winners, and their profits during the crisis have been astounding, while all business models focusing on personal interaction (such as the culture and hospitality sectors) are the major losers. This is a situation which the authors think will persist. The COVID-19 crisis has effected thoroughgoing changes to our work, education, trade, medicine, and culture. Also, it has enabled a significant violation of our privacy.

> We will see how contact tracing has an unequalled capacity and a quasi-essential place in the armoury needed to combat COVID-19, while at the same time being positioned to become an enabler of mass surveillance. (p. 153)

This development has also forced governments across the world to abandon the practice of investigating the effects of new and emerging technology and regulating it before introduction. Instead, all bets are off. Temporary regulations emerging during the crisis may, according to the authors, remain after the crisis, and this may also include social distancing. Societies will emphasize the restructuring of work spaces to minimize human contact. For employees within the service and education sectors, the future looks bleak. The authors predict rapid automatization in the name of hygiene and cleanliness, which in turn will accelerate the digital transformation. Domestic productivity is predicted to increase due to the further implementation of robotics.

> From the onset of the lockdowns, it became apparent that robots and AI were a natural alternative when human labour was not available. (p. 157)

But all of this comes at a price. It renders humans obsolete, with especially menial workers being at risk. The entire narrative is presented in a cold and misanthropic tone. But it gets worse. According to the authors, the lockdowns have had a huge cost, which aggravates the need for new methods to address the virus situation. This opens the way for permanent technological solutions such as contact tracing, tracking, and analyzing all of our movement patterns in order to be able to quarantine the infected.

> A tracking app gains insight in real time by, for example determining
> a person's current location through geodata via GPS coordinates or
> radio signals. (p. 160)

The point is to keep us separated at all costs, but also to study our behavior over time. Several nations, like South Korea, China, and Hong Kong, used intrusive and mandatory tracking methods in real time during the pandemic.

In Hong Kong, electronic bracelets were used, while other states used cell phone apps to make sure the infected did not break quarantine. Singapore's Trace Together app, which alerts the user if they approach within two meters of a registered infected person and automatically sends a notification to the Health Ministry, is seen as a reasonable compromise by the authors. However, they also address the problems entailed in basing these surveillance systems on voluntary compliance.

> No voluntary contract-tracing app will work if people are unwill-
> ing to provide their own personal data to the governmental agency
> that monitors the system, if any individual refuses to download the
> app (and therefore to withhold information about a possible infec-
> tion, movements and contacts), everyone will adversely be affected.
> (p. 164)

In light of these different systems, common standards for contact tracing may be adopted (especially with regard to the EU). Schwab and Malleret write that contact tracing enables early interventions against "super spreading environments" such as family gatherings. It is not difficult to see that the system can easily be used against any form of political dissidence against this diabolic structure.

The book also reports how private corporations all over the world, even after states have reopened, have implemented digital surveillance of their employees "in order to minimize the risk of recurring infection." This is of course a gross violation of all conceivable human rights charters and rules of ethics. The authors indicate that once these systems are in place, it is not likely that they will be removed even if the risk of infection would be temporarily reduced.

"The Risk of Dystopia"

Schwab and Malleret add that a number of analysts, decision makers, and security advisers predict that a dystopian future will emerge in the wake of these measures. The book gives a clear warning that a global techno-totalitarian surveillance state is being instated, with the coronavirus as rationale! Yet, there is little doubt that the authors feel that the benefits outweigh the risks—a sentiment that is also obvious from Schwab's previous two books on the 4IR.

> It is true that in the post-pandemic era, personal health will become a much greater priority for society, which is why the genie of tech-surveillance will not be put back in the bottle. (p. 171)

The authors end this chapter by indicating that it is up to us and our governments to "control and harness the benefits of technology without sacrificing our individual and collective values and freedoms." Despite the World Economic Forum's central role in creating this tyrannical surveillance system, what Schwab is telling us is that it is now *our* responsibility to use it wisely!

"Micro Reset"

For private entrepreneurs, there is no going back to the previous system. COVID-19 has changed everything. Business-as-usual is declared dead.

> When confronted with it, some industry leaders and senior executives may be tempted to equate reset with restart, hope to go back to the old normal and restore what worked in the past: traditions, tested procedures and familiar ways of doing things – in short, a return to business as usual. This won't happen because it can't happen. For the most part business as usual died from (or at least was infected by) COVID-19 (p. 173)

According to the authors, the "new normal "is:

- Working from home
- Virtual meetings
- More efficient decision processes
- Acceleration of digitalisation and technological solutions

Businesses refusing or unable to follow the recommendations on this total digital transformation will find it difficult to survive. The winners will be major e-trade companies and streaming services such as Alibaba, Amazon, Netflix, and Zoom. Jeff Bezos, the CEO of Amazon, has for instance increased his already astronomical fortune by 60 percent during the crisis. Trade has in a very short time span come to be totally dominated by a small number of monopolistic opportunists. The same holds true for the videoconference business Zoom. Its rise in valuation during the spring of 2020 was exceptional.

In the book, almost everything is predicted to move into cyberspace. In 2019, only 1 percent of consultations with doctors in the UK were online. During the corona crisis, they have been at almost 100 percent. E-trade is also predicted to grow when customers are forced online, with Big Tech and Big Pharma as the major winners.

In the "post-corona era," as Schwab calls it, governments are also expected to attain greater control over private business. The stimulus packages have come with detailed conditions regarding how their businesses are to be conducted.

According to the authors, we are to expect a form of stakeholder capitalism with environmental, social, and corporate governance (ESG).* This means that the private corporations must resume their responsibility and invest "sustainably."

---

*   Stakeholder Capitalism was also the name of Schwab's next book, *Stakeholder Capitalism: A Global Economy that Works for Progress, People and Planet.* (Geneva: World Economic Forum Publishing, January 29, 2021).

Through activism from NGOs like Greenpeace, the private sector will be pressured to make the "correct choices." This brings to mind Pieter Winsemius's sustainability formula for major corporations, outlined in his book *A Thousand Shades of Green: Sustainable Strategies for Competitive Advantage* (2002), and of the Trilateral Commission report *Beyond Interdependence* (1991).

"Individual Reset"

In the final chapter, authors examine the individual effects of the pandemic. They point out that unlike other catastrophes such as earthquakes and floods, which generate sympathy and bring people closer together, this situation has had the opposite effect. It has been devastating. The pandemic is a slow-moving process, combining a strong fear of death with uncertainty as to when the danger is over. It can always strike again. It has also generated authoritarian and unpredictable measures from governments. All of this results in fear and anxiety.

We may also refrain from helping others out of the fear of disease and death, which generates guilt and shame. It is impossible to do what is right, something which is also seen at the macro level, with states closing borders and strongly limiting travel. These measures have also been the cause of racism and a growth in nationalism. The authors consider this a "toxic mixture."

The authors display a chilling awareness of the psychological effects of social distancing:

> Humans are inherently social beings. Companionship and social interactions are a vital component of our humanness. If deprived of them, we find our lives upside down. Social relations are to a significant extent, obliterated by confinement measures and physical and social distancing, and in the case of the COVID-19 lockdowns, this occurred at a time of heightened anxiety when we needed them most. (p. 226)

During the pandemic, many have been restricted from seeking support from family and friends. Especially our elderly have been isolated from the contact that may have meant everything to them. We have been robbed of the intimacy we need to stay well.

The situation is akin to a prolonged torture session slowly breaking us down (there is a reason why solitary confinement is considered one of the most severe forms of punishment).

The increased cases of mental illness during lockdowns are coldly anticipated in the book:

- People with previous mental issues will face even more severe anxiety attacks.
- Social distancing will increase mental problems, even after the restrictions are lifted.
- The loss of income and employment will increase deaths through suicide or from drug and alcohol abuse (deaths of despair).
- Domestic violence will increase during the pandemic.
- "Vulnerable" people, especially children, patients, social outcasts, and the disabled, will face a decline in mental health.

They point out that all of this will create an increased need for psychiatric and mental health care in the coming years. This area will therefore need to be prioritized by decision-makers after the crisis. This exemplifies their cold and ruthless attitude.

They are keenly aware of the untold suffering they have caused. These are the very effects they have been seeking to create in order to "nudge" us all to make the "correct choices" and embrace their technological dictatorship.

In the chapter on private enterprise, we are given a preview of how the future of health care will manifest:

> Like for any other industry, digital will play a significant role in shaping the future of wellness. The combination of AI, the IoT and sensors and wearable technology will produce new insights into personal well-being. They will monitor how we are and feel, and will

progressively blur the boundaries between public health care systems and personalized health creation systems—a distinction that will eventually break down. (p. 206)

The new technology will also measure our carbon footprints, our effects on biodiversity, and the "toxicity" of everything we consume! The technocrats' need for control seems insatiable.

According to the book, the pandemic has also given us "time to reflect upon what we truly value in life." The time in isolation has "given us insights as to our previous unsustainable ways of life, neglecting the climate and the environment." These errors can now be corrected:

> The pandemic gives us this chance: "it represents a rare but narrow window of opportunity to reflect, reimagine and reset our world."
> (p. 244)

Somewhat surprisingly, in the book's conclusions, the authors present the *very low mortality numbers* of the pandemic. It is pointed out that COVID-19 by the end of June 2020 had only caused the death of 0.006% of the global population! This can be contrasted to the Black Death (killing 30–40 percent of the global population); the Spanish Flu (2.7 percent); and ischemic heart disease (16 percent of global mortality as of 2020).[8]

The death toll of COVID-19 was thus obviously not warranting a total shutdown of the entire world, even if every death is a personal tragedy and some of the recovered have suffered persistent neurological issues.

* * *

The Enlightened Prince

On September 20, 2020, just before World Economic Forum's Sustainable Development Impact Summit in New York, Prince Charles delivered the message that the global pandemic was "a wakeup call" that must not be ignored. And that a global "military-style Marshall plan" was needed in order to save humankind and the planet: "We must now put ourselves on a warlike footing, approaching our action from the perspective of a military-style campaign."[9]

The plan included:

1. Implementing effective and equitable carbon pricing;
2. Scaling up development and implementation of carbon capture and storage;
3. Establishing a credible and trusted global carbon offset market;
4. Tackling subsidies for fossil fuels;
5. Creating a recognized global ecosystems services market;
6. Advancing sustainable urbanism.

Already back in 2007, Prince Charles had launched the Prince's May Day Network to gather together private corporations with the purpose of addressing climate change. "May Day," the international call of distress, was chosen to emphasize the urgency. In this venture, the Prince was supported by Bank of America CEO Bill Mohnihan, who argued that the major private corporations now had to collaborate to create workable solutions. Klaus Schwab concurred and declared that, "Now it's really the moment and window of opportunity to reset the world to make it more sustainable, more resilient and more inclusive."[10]

The hypocrisy was glaring. The prince's own royal lifestyle with fox hunting, global travel, opulent banquets, and luxurious residences was far removed from the austere reset he was promulgating for the rest of the world. The changes and restrictions he envisioned as necessary for the general public were obviously not meant to include himself and his peers.

* * *

In 2021, during Italy's G20 chairmanship, digitalization was again lifted as a priority for the G20 members and a catch-all solution to every problem.

> The pandemic has highlighted the benefits of digitalisation for the economy and the society: to support employment, health and education (People), to contribute to sustainability (Planet) and to enable the economic resilience of businesses (Prosperity).[11]

The challenge now was to get businesses and employees to adapt to this new emerging artificial world with the implementation of a purported human-centered "Trustworthy Artificial Intelligence" and a digital government.

Bill Gates with an earlier vaccine deal

7

The Club

> *The year 2020 will forever be associated with crises. First came the Covid-19 pandemic, a joint public health and economic emergency that spread around the world with unprecedented speed and scope. Next came a crisis of international cooperation, as countries struggled to coordinate their efforts in tackling a common viral foe. Then came a compounding social crisis— anchored in the United States but reverberating around the world—focused on issues of systemic racism and police brutality.[1] (Rockefeller Foundation)*

Besides control, it is crucial for a usurper to also make financial gains from his measures. Careful planning for coming events gives foreknowledge that makes investments potentially very profitable. At the same time, unprepared competitors face ruin, and the general public poverty.

Bill and Melinda Gates

For Bill and Melinda Gates, and their mentors in the Rockefeller family, the COVID-19 crisis has been an enormous boon. Their investments in pharmaceutical companies and manufacturers of surveillance technology have been extremely successful.

After the turn of the millennium, the Bill & Melinda Gates Foundation has emerged as the leading philanthropy in the field of healthcare, assuming the position previously held by the Rockefeller Foundation. The structure of the COVID-19 narrative is further evidence of this, as will be shown in this chapter. There are many connections between the two organizations, including a shared history, leaders, focus areas, goals, and modus operandi. In many ways, Bill Gates can be seen as the major "heir" of the Rockefeller family in fields such as global health, agriculture, and population control.

After a successful career making Microsoft the global leader in IT, Bill and Melinda Gates, with the help of Bill's father William H. Gates, in 1994 created the foundations William H. Gates Foundation and the Gates Library Foundation. Inspiration and advice came from David Rockefeller.

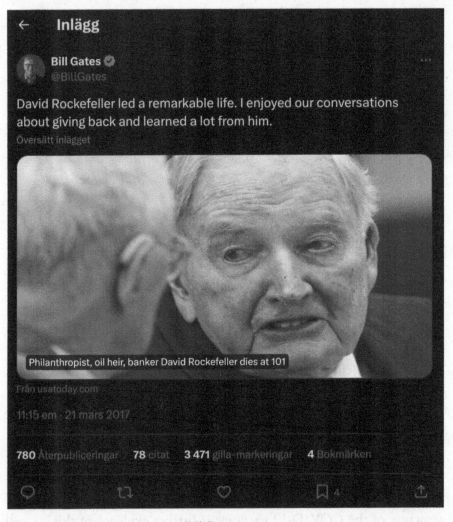

← **Inlägg**

Bill Gates ✓
@BillGates

David Rockefeller led a remarkable life. I enjoyed our conversations about giving back and learned a lot from him.

Översätt inlägget

Philanthropist, oil heir, banker David Rockefeller dies at 101

Från usatoday.com

11:15 em · 21 mars 2017

780 Återpubliceringar   **78** citat   **3 471** gilla-markeringar   **4** Bokmärken

Bill Gates tweet

Bill Gates and his father had thoroughly studied the pioneering work of the Rockefeller Foundation during the early twentieth century. Bill wanted his own foundations to be structured after the Rockefeller model. As such, they would address global issues "ignored by governments" while supporting their own business interests through Public-Private Partnerships.[2] As Bill's father put it in his book *Showing up for Life*: "A lesson we learned from studying and working with the Rockefellers is that to succeed in pursuing audacious goals you need like-minded partners with whom to collaborate."[3]

This method was called "venture philanthropy," a term coined by John D. Rockefeller III in 1969.[4] Just like the latter's grandfather and namesake John D. Rockefeller Sr., Gates had created a hugely lucrative monopoly for himself through ruthless business practices. In 1998 he faced charges for "illegally thwarting competition in order to protect and extend [Microsoft's] software monopoly." The path was set for Gates to follow, learning from the family that had turned monopoly capitalism, merged with philanthropy, into an art form. They shared the same business philosophy and the same worldview.

During the first years, just before of the turn of the millennium, the foundations' main focus was on "bridging the digital divide" between those who did and did not have access to IT technology. Part of the agenda was to expand the use of computers in education, as well as digitizing libraries—which also helped the Microsoft founder spread the use of his company's products and services. To the digital agenda were then added more of the old pet projects of the Rockefeller Foundation: agriculture (GMO), global health (medical technology and vaccines), and population control (family planning).[5]

> This Foundation helped invent the discipline that exists today. We created tests and vaccines, and built a network of thousands of scientists, doctors, and community health workers around the world. Today, thousands of scientists (some of whom received their training via Rockefeller Foundation grants and refer to themselves as "Rocky Docs"), first responders, and frontline health workers are working

against the clock to protect all of us, often at great personal risk.[6] (Rajiv Shah, Rockefeller Foundation)

Right from the start, IT and health were closely linked. To assist them, the Gates couple hired Gordon W. Perkin (previously with Planned Parenthood and the Ford Foundation), Suzanne Cluett (from Planned Parenthood), and Patricia Q. Stonesifer (from Microsoft; close friend of the Rockefeller Foundation's former president Judith Rodin, and today a board member).

The close connections to Planned Parenthood may also be related to the fact that Bill's father was involved in the organization for a long time, and for a period served as its president.[7]

The Bill & Melinda Gates Foundation would not be what it is today without my dad. More than anyone else, he shaped the values of the foundation.[8] (Bill Gates)

Planned Parenthood

The Planned Parenthood Federation of America was founded in 1916 by Margaret Sanger, and has since the early 1920s been closely affiliated to, as well as funded by, the Rockefeller family. Both John D. Rockefeller Jr. and his wife Abby were close friends of Sanger's, and the support continued through their son John D. III.[9]

Sanger was a passionate advocate for eugenics and family planning, and surrounded herself with eugenicists, Fabian socialists, sexologists, and futurists such as the eugenicist and social reformer Havelock Ellis (Sanger's mentor and lover), the author George Bernard Shaw (cofounder of the Fabian Society), H. G. Wells (yet another of Sanger's lovers), and Henry Fairchild (president of the American Eugenics Society) who was recruited by Sanger to the institute's advisory board.[10]

Together with the Rockefeller Foundation, the Ford Foundation, and the Population Council, Planned Parenthood became a leading organization in population control and eugenics during the entire twentieth century, not only in the United States, but all over the world.

The International Planned Parenthood Federation was founded in India in 1952 by Margaret Sanger and Lady Rama Raui, following the first International Population Conference in Stockholm, 1946 (arranged by the Swedish RFSU, an association for sex education founded in 1933 by Elise Ottesen-Jensen).[11]

Since the turn of the millennium, the task of curtailing population growth now also includes Bill Gates, who soon became an influential contributor to both Planned Parenthood (of which his father had been a board member) and to John D. Rockefeller III's Population Council.

The Bill & Melinda Gates Foundation and GAVI

In 1999, Bill Gates's two foundations were merged into the Bill & Melinda Gates Foundation.

One of the first projects this new organization entered into was GAVI (Global Alliance for Vaccines and Immunization, later GAVI, the Vaccine Alliance). This public-private partnership was the immediate successor to the Rockefeller-founded Children's Vaccine Initiative, founded in 1990. The mission was to vaccinate children in the world's poorest countries.

GAVI was launched at the annual Davos Summit 2000 by the Bill & Melinda Gates Foundation and the Rockefeller Foundation, with partners UNICEF, WHO, and the World Bank, after a preparatory World Bank meeting at the Rockefeller Bellagio Centre in Italy.[12] Other donating partners were the vaccine industry and national governments. Bill Gates rapidly became the most significant contributor, and former Rockefeller employee Dr. Seth Berkley was appointed CEO. GAVI would later come to play a key role during the COVID-19 crisis.

At a 2011 pledging conference hosted by the governments of the United Kingdom and Liberia and the Bill & Melinda Gates Foundation, GAVI raised $4.3 billion to immunize more than 250 million children in developing countries by 2015.[13]

Ellen Johnson Sirleaf (president of Liberia), Seth Berkley (GAVI CEO), Bill Gates (GAVI cochair), David Cameron (UK prime minister), Andrew Mitchell (UK secretary of state for international development), Dagfinn Høybråten (GAVI board member) at GAVI pledging conference 2011

The Carnegie Medal of Philanthropy

In 2001, both Bill and Melinda Gates and the Rockefeller family received the first Carnegie Medal of Philanthropy for their philanthropic efforts and their initiatives to create the future Andrew Carnegie had envisioned: "a smarter, cleaner, healthier, safer and better place for all of us."

> We Honor the Gates family for their faith in Andrew Carnegie's "Gospel of Wealth," and for celebrating it as a true clarion call to those who have great resources, urging them to use their wealth in the service of humanity. Indeed despite the pressures of shepherding one of the world's leading companies, Bill and Melinda have had the wisdom and foresight to understand that their true legacy will arise from the great good they have done—and will do—as philanthropists, working to help develop and deploy life-saving vaccines, ease human suffering by improving global health equity, and to promote education and learning on a worldwide basis.[14]

Among recipients were also Brooke Astor, George Soros, and Ted Turner. Presenters included Dr. Anthony Fauci and Richard Parsons from Time Warner.[15] Others to receive the award in later years have been Michael Bloomberg, investor Jeremy Grantham, the CFR president David Rubenstein, eBay founder Jeffrey Skoll, as well as the Bilderberg group president Marie-Josée Kravis and her husband Henry Kravis.

In 2005 Bill Gates was dubbed "Knight Commander of the Order of the British Empire" by Queen Elizabeth II. This is awarded to persons who have performed important services to British interests. Gates received it for his philanthropy and the founding of Microsoft.[16] Perhaps also for expected future efforts, since his work had only just begun?

The Grand Master of the Order, Prince Philip (consort of Elizabeth II and father of Prince Charles) was deeply troubled by the effects of over-population. During his tenure as the president of the World Wildlife Fund in 1981, he had stated:

> Human population growth is probably the single most serious long-term threat to survival. We're in for a major disaster if it isn't curbed—not just for the natural world, but for the human world. The more people there are, the more resources they'll consume, the more pollution they'll create, the more fighting they'll do. We have no option. If it isn't controlled voluntarily, it will be controlled involuntarily by an increase in disease, starvation and war.[17]

The Malthusian agenda of the old British elite was alive and well, and has since expanded significantly.

In 2006, investor Warren Buffet announced that he would surrender a large part of his fortune ($31 billion) to the Gates Foundation, and also become a member of the board. Around the same time, Dr. Tadataka (Tachi) Yamada, who then was a board member of the Rockefeller Brothers Fund, was recruited as head of the Bill & Melinda Gates Foundation's Global Health Program.

That same year, the Bill & Melinda Gates foundation launched its Global Development Program. This was a major expansion of another of the key program areas of the Rockefeller Foundation.[18]

AGRA

In 2006, the Rockefeller Foundation and the Bill & Melinda Gates Foundation entered into a partnership through the launch of Alliance for a Green Revolution in Africa (AGRA), headed by former UN Secretary-General Kofi Annan (1913–2018), a close friend and partner of the Rockefeller family.

The purpose of AGRA was increasing yields for small farmers in Africa by modernizing agriculture, including the use of GMOs.[19] Critics have pointed out that their activities mostly seem to revolve around making farmers dependent upon patented seeds from corporations such as Syngenta and Monsanto.

The head of AGRA at the Gates Foundation was Rajiv Shah (previously involved in fundraising for GAVI). After serving as the head of AGRA's partner USAID (the US foreign aid agency) from 2010 to 2015, he accepted the position as CEO for the Rockefeller Foundation in 2017 while remaining a board member at AGRA.[20] As of 2015, he is also a member of the Trilateral Commission.[21]

In 2007, Melinda and Bill Gates with Bill's father William Sr. were awarded the "David Rockefeller Bridging Leadership Award" by David Rockefeller's daughter Peggy Dulany's organization Synergos. An award presented the first time in 2003, then to Bill Gates's own favorite adviser—Peggy's father David. Thereafter, the award has been given to other philanthrocapitalists in David's fold, such as Ted Turner, Michael Bloomberg, Bill Clinton, and Richard Branson.[22] As Bill Gates was now quite accomplished, the time was ripe for a greater mission.

The Good Club

In 2009, the billionaires of the self-styled "Good Club" gathered in the president's apartments of the Rockefeller University (situated close to the UN headquarters) summoned by David Rockefeller, Bill Gates, and Warren Buffet. Some of the other participants were George Soros, Michael Bloomberg, Ted Turner, Oprah Winfrey, and the venture capitalist Peter G. Peterson from the Blackstone Group.

Several of the participants were members of the Council on Foreign Relations and represented some of the wealthiest foundations in the world, such as the Rockefeller Brothers Fund, Bill & Melinda Gates Foundation, Open Society, Bloomberg Philanthropies, and the UN Foundation. One reason for their meeting was that Gates had decided to invest a major part of his fortune for "improving" and "saving" the world. Philanthrocapitalism was now ready to take over.

During the meeting, classical global threats such as overpopulation and pandemics were discussed. Gates was apparently very enthusiastic about the conference.[23] The meeting resulted in the Gates and Buffet initiative "The Giving Pledge," aiming to convince other billionaires to pledge 50 percent of their fortunes to "charity."

First in line to offer contributions were, among others, IT billionaires such as Elon Musk, Jeffrey Skoll, and Mark Zuckerberg, but also the "Grand Master" himself, David Rockefeller.[24]

The following year, Bill Gates declared that the "Decade of Vaccines" had begun. Both the Bill & Melinda Gates Foundation and GAVI took part, in collaboration with the WHO and UNICEF.[25]

The billionaires had a shared vision for the world—a cybernetic biological tech revolution for the whole of humanity, with the Gates and Rockefeller families playing some of the leading roles.

Jeffrey Epstein

Both the Rockefeller family and Bill Gates were closely affiliated with the infamous financier Jeffrey Epstein (1955–2019). As early as the mid-1990s, Epstein was elected a member of both the Council on Foreign Relations and the Trilateral Commission, and was a significant contributor during his membership.[26] In 1995, he also became a board member of Rockefeller University, together with Henry Kissinger's wife Nancy.[27]

In 2008, Epstein's reputation became tarnished when he was sentenced for procuring a 14-year-old girl for prostitution and "soliciting a prostitute." Epstein, however, got a very lenient sentence, probably due to his close connections with the upper echelons of the elite (who might have had their own motives for keeping the scandal to a minimum).

It was the US attorney for the Southern District of Florida, Alexander Acosta, who gave Epstein the "sweetheart deal": a 13-month part-time prison sentence in a private wing of the local prison—which he was allowed to leave to go to his office six days a week! Acosta later became Trump's secretary of labor.

Only a few years later, Bill Gates enters the picture. He met with Epstein on at least six occasions between 2011 and 2014 in Epstein's townhouse in New York. They clearly had a much closer relationship than Gates later would admit. Present at one of these meetings were, among others, Lawrence H. Summers (Trilateral Commission member and former secretary of the treasury) and representatives from the Rockefeller bank JPMorgan Chase.

The Gates Foundation and JPMorgan Chase had already begun constructing the Global Health Investment Fund which was launched in 2012. Its purpose was to invest in global health technologies, with the stated potential of "saving millions of lives in developing countries" (the partnership also included GSK, Merck, and Pfizer).

Epstein suggested that they create a separate foundation to finance health-related projects across the globe, with money from the Gates Foundation. Epstein also offered to collect donations from his wealthy contacts for a fee of 0.3 percent of the total amount.[28] Epstein's offer was, however, rejected. Bill and Jeffrey then met up frequently until 2014, when the relationship seems to have faded, as did the relationship between Bill and Melinda, due to Bill's association with Epstein. In May 2021, the couple announced their divorce, and Melinda publicly explained why.

> So, in October 2019, when the relationship between Mr. Gates and Mr. Epstein burst into public view, Ms. French Gates was unhappy. She hired divorce lawyers, setting in motion a process that culminated this month with the announcement that their marriage was ending.[29]

Epstein was also closely affiliated with the scientific community and was connected to many prominent scientists. He supported prestigious universities like Harvard.

Epstein had an elitist worldview and entertained eugenic and transhumanist ideas, which included the founding of a breeding farm in New Mexico where select women were to be inseminated with the sperm of Nobel laureates to improve the human gene pool.

He also planned to have his head and penis put in cryostasis at the time of death, to be resurrected when the appropriate technologies had been developed.[30] Such eugenicist and transhumanist views are, unfortunately, not uncommon in the circles around the Trilateral Commission, Council on Foreign Relations, and the World Economic Forum.

On July 6, 2019, Epstein was again arrested on charges of sex trafficking involving minors and the shocking extent of his exploitation and abuse of underage girls was unraveled.

Only one month later, Epstein was found dead in his cell. According to official accounts, he had committed suicide by hanging. Many doubted this narrative. A trial would likely have been too revealing for Epstein's influential associates and could have implicated many of the powerful men who had been invited aboard his "Lolita Express" and flown to his private island in the Caribbean to be entertained by girls in their lower teens. Here were former presidents, actors, Nobel Prize laureates, and investors. His friends included prominent people such as the Harvard professor of law Alan Dershowitz, Les Wexner of Victoria's Secret, Prince Andrew, Bill Clinton, and Donald Trump.

Bill Gates, the New Climate Expert

In February 2020, the Bill & Melinda Gates Foundation announced an investment of $100 million to address COVID-19 and develop a vaccine. The couple (who were still very involved in the foundation despite their divorce as a couple) also stated that they would be directing resources to two new areas. Bill had developed an interest in climate issues, and Melinda in equality.[31] These, too, had been among the Rockefeller family's main focus areas.

Climate change is one of the most difficult challenges the world has ever taken on.[32] (Bill Gates)

As patron of the Global Goals, Bill now become a climate expert. In August 2020, he wrote about the connections between COVID-19 and climate change and argued that the modest reductions in emissions seen during the crisis meant that the solution was not just about stopping air travel and driving less. More drastic measures would be needed to fight climate change.

> To understand the kind of damage that climate change will inflict, look at COVID-19 and spread the pain out over a much longer period. The loss of life and economic misery caused by this pandemic are on par with what will happen regularly if we do not eliminate the world's carbon emissions.[33] (Bill Gates)

According to Gates, a long-term plan was needed to address climate change. He did not, however, mention what he himself would be willing to sacrifice. As of 2020, he owned four private jets, a helicopter, an amphibious aircraft, a luxury yacht, and two Porsches.[34] He also owns a number of properties. His main residence, Xanadu 2.0 outside Seattle, contains seven bedrooms, six kitchens, twenty-four bathrooms, a reception hall for two hundred people, an eighteen-meter swimming pool, a spa, a movie theater, a library (where Leonardo da Vinci's notebook *Codex Leicester* is kept), a boathouse, a conference hall, offices, several garages, a gym of 232 square meters, and a dining hall of ninety-three square meters.[35] Bill Gates has been the world's wealthiest person for eighteen of the last twenty-four years.*

John D. Rockefeller III's focus on population control had now been inherited by Bill Gates III, and included the ability to profit from one's

---

* In 2018, Bill Gates's fortune was surpassed by that of Amazon founder Jeff Bezos who owns numerous mansions, the world's largest private yacht, a Gulfstream G-650ER jet, and a space rocket.

ostensibly philanthropic investments. Gates left the board of Microsoft on March 13, 2020, but remains as one of the most significant private share-holders, with 1.3 percent of total shares.

Melinda Gates stepped down from her role as co-chair of the founda-tion on June 7, 2024. Bill remains as sole chairman while the name has been changed to the Gates Foundation.[36]

The Rockefeller Reset

Together with Bill Gates, the Rockefeller Foundation and the Rockefeller Brothers Fund has taken the initiative with regard to shaping "our com-mon future." After the Great Reset was declared, several new initiatives were launched. On June 11, 2020, RBF announced its intention to address the "systemic errors" they claimed to have found behind the COVID-19 pandemic, as well as the "crisis of racial justice" emerging in the wake of the murder of George Floyd. According to CEO Stephen Heintz, one must now use this opportunity to act:

> As protests around the country have demonstrated, this is a hinge moment in history that we must seize to ensure our democracy swings forward, and not back. It is time for reforms in the institu-tions and processes of our democracy, as well as major investments in civil society and civic culture. We must reinvent our democracy to serve our common purpose in the 21st century.[37]

Heintz was also part of the team behind the report *Our Common Purpose* by the American Academy of Arts and Sciences, released in June 2020 but finished before the COVID-19 pandemic was declared and the BLM protests erupted. The report, centered on a revitalized US democracy, included suggestions such as mandatory voting (with fines upon refusal), creating a digital informational architecture sup-porting the pursuit of common goals (giving third parties access to digital user data), and instituting one year's compulsory social service for youth (within the military, local authorities, civil society, or at news stations).[38]

The report was funded by the Rockefeller Brothers Fund and the Stephen Bechtel Fund which was now to support the implementation of the report's recommendations. Forty-eight million dollars over the next five years were to be invested in new initiatives on racial justice, climate change, and economic equality. The coinciding crises made it imperative to implement systemic changes at every level, according to the RBF.

One week later, on June 19, 2020, the Rockefeller Foundation announced its intentions to use the crisis as an opportunity: "The world needs to make the most of the moment at hand. To chart a path through the complex uncertainty, we suggest three distinct forms of action— Response, Recovery and Reset."[39]

Response was about the near-term protection of lives and livelihoods. Recovery related to restarting and rebuilding the economy and social life in a way that "protects public health, promotes societal healing, and preserves the environment." Reset meant establishing "a new equilibrium among political, economic, social, and environmental systems toward common goals."

"Fortunately," according to the foundation, a solution already existed—the 17 Global Sustainability Goals of UN Agenda 2030. Together with the Brookings Institution, the foundation would now present these goals as the theme of the "17 Rooms Flagship Meetings," held during the United Nations week in September since 2018. This time, however, the meetings would be held virtually via Zoom. The goal was to prepare the ground for decisive action in 2021. Digitization and the technologies of the Fourth Industrial Revolution were key.

On September 9, the Rockefeller Foundation released the report *Digital Health.*[40] Through the COVID-19 crisis, an opportunity had come to roll out and test digital technology, and the results could now be evaluated. The study was based on China which had been a spearhead of digital transformation, implementing camera surveillance and smart systems within health care. Health care was now to be reshaped using AI and massive data collection.

Digital Investments

The new surveillance technologies and control over our data is like the new petroleum. This is where money and power lie, something which has long since been realized and anticipated by the old oil barons. The Rockefeller family's financial bastion Rockefeller Capital Management (RCM) has, since the end of 2019, increased its presence in Silicon Valley and begun a major expansion of its operations all over America. In September 2019 they acquired Financial Clarity Inc., an institution known to serve those who first built Silicon Valley (among others, the heads of Apple and Google).[41] In the words of Tim O'Hara, CEO of the Rockefeller Global Family Office: "The opportunity to grow in Silicon Valley is accelerated just given the wealth creation in this area, which is pretty extraordinary."[42]

During 2020, this corporation has purchased more than 23 asset management businesses all across the United States.[43] When RCM was founded in 2018 (and replaced the Rockefeller Financial Services), the goal was to multiply its capital by a factor of ten within five years.[44]

Bill Gates has become a close ally in realizing this goal. But while the Bill & Melinda Gates Foundation has pledged to spend the foundation's capital at most twenty years after the couple's deaths, the Rockefellers have made no such promises. Gates is a player in a game he ultimately does not control, nor has he himself designed it. He cannot trump the Rockefeller family's astonishing influence over the global development of the twentieth century, and is really only contributing to an older agenda.

So, how then has the Rockefeller Family handled these current and future challenges? Which were the opportunities revealed by this crisis?

Unsurprisingly, Rockefeller Capital Management (RCM) had placed its largest investments within the fields of information technology and health. Besides Microsoft, Apple, Facebook, and Amazon, which all did spectacularly well during the lockdowns, RCM had also invested in

GlaxoSmithKline (GSK), one of the pharmaceutical companies at the forefront of developing COVID-19 vaccines.[45]

GSK is a legacy partner of the Bill & Melinda Gates Foundation, and is part of a consortium initiated by the foundation to develop vaccines, diagnostic tools, and treatment for COVID-19.[46] From January 2020 until March 31, RCM had increased its GSK holdings from 25,059 shares to 3,819,379 (at a value of $140 million)—an increase by 15,241 percent![47]

Rockefeller Capital Management's top holdings, March 31, 2020:

Microsoft (information technology)
Apple (information technology)
Facebook (communication)
Amazon (online shopping)
Verizon (telecom)
Progressive (finance)
Comcast (telecom)
SPDR (finance)
Alphabet/Google (communication)
GlaxoSmithKline (health)

Operation Warp Speed

On May 15, 2020, President Trump announced "Operation Warp Speed" with the aim of having 300 million doses of vaccine ready by the end of 2020. As chief scientist for Warp Speed, Trump appointed Dr. Moncef Slaoui, former head of the vaccines department at GSK.[48]

> To date, Operation Warp Speed has brought together all of the experts across the federal government from places like the NIH, CDC, FDA, and many other agencies. This historic partnership will now bring together the full resources of the Department of Health and Human Services with the Department of Defense. And we know what that means. That means the full power and strength of military—the

military. And that—really, talking about the logistics—if we get it, when we get it. That means the logistics, getting it out, so that everybody can take it. (President Trump)

GSK was one of the eight companies, with AstraZeneca, Merck, Moderna, Pfizer, Vaxart, Novavax, and Johnson & Johnson, invited to take part in the project.[49]

When Joe Biden became president, Operation Warp Speed was transferred to the White House COVID-19 Response Team, with David A. Kessler, the previous head of Warp Speed, and Anthony Fauci as board members.

It was obvious who was pulling the strings and profited from this public-private partnership, regardless of who was in the White House. Bill Gates had now proven that he had fully mastered the Rockefeller business model.

As John D. Rockefeller said: "I have always tried to turn every disaster into an opportunity."

To sum it up: astronomical profits can be made from promising to alleviate the misery caused by the virus and the pandemic measures. The bringers of solutions will appear as heroes, even when they put the world in chains. This is a well-known formula from the world of monopoly capitalism—as well as from the world of organized crime.

The Trump Card

8

The Trump Card

The future does not belong to globalists. The future belongs to patriots. The future belongs to sovereign and independent nations who protect their citizens, respect their neighbors, and honor the differences that make each country special and unique.[1]
(Donald Trump)

Reaction and resistance to a swiftly changing world is bound to arise. This makes it necessary to control the opposition. With a rhetoric that promises everything your opponents want to hear, they can be misled and even made to work indirectly for the agenda.

The Maverick President

When Donald Trump was elected president of the United States in November 2016, he assumed the role as opposer of "the globalist agenda" who would fight the powers that be and "drain the swamp." Many of his supporters seemed to view him as a messiah who was going to fix everything that was broken in America and the world. How well did he live up to this image? Was Trump what he claimed to be?

One thing that can be said about him, whether you admire or despise him, is that he is a natural media whiz who knows how to attract attention, spark controversy, and stir public debate. His uniquely simplified rhetoric style leaves no one unmoved. As president, he immediately started doing things his own way—to the shock and horror of some and to the amusement or hope of others.

However, for those who put their hopes in him as a savior against globalism, technocracy, and the financial-political elites of the world, he has certainly had some eyebrow-raising friends, supporters, and funders. On his path to fame, fortune, and power, he has been surrounded by proponents of the Fourth Industrial Revolution, Big Data, and a totalitarian surveillance regime.

Trump's Financiers and Advisers

One of Trump's most important financiers has been Robert Mercer, a hedge-fund billionaire who formerly was an AI scientist at IBM. In 1993, he was recruited to the position as CEO at Renaissance Technologies and later became known as a supporter of Brexit. Mercer is the main investor in Cambridge Analytica—a company surrounded by scandals, such as trying to influence elections in several countries by collecting information about millions of Facebook users and targeting them with customized political propaganda.[2] The 2016 US presidential election, which Trump won against all odds, is probably the most publicized example.

Another central Trump financier was Peter Thiel, cofounder of Palantir Technologies and PayPal. He was Trump's technical adviser, belonging to his inner circle and part of the president's transition team, with Mercer's daughter Rebekah. Eight of Thiel's fifteen closest men were given top positions in the Trump administration.[3] Thiel worked closely with Trump's son-in-law Jared Kushner and played a central part in building the close ties to the tech giants of Silicon Valley.[4] Thiel also had significant stakes in Facebook 2004 (10 percent of its funding capital) and has since had a place in the board of directors with Zuckerberg.

Just like Mercer, Thiel has been working with data analysis. His own private data-mining company Palantir (named after Sauron's all-seeing stones in *The Lord of the Rings*) was partly funded by the CIA and frequently contracted by the intelligence services of Israel and the United States. Palantir is also a founding partner of WEF's Centre for the Fourth Industrial Revolution.[5] Both Thiel and Zuckerberg are alumni from the World Economic Forum's Global Young Leaders program. Thiel is another eager proponent of the transhumanist concepts of singularity, artificial intelligence, and life-extending technologies (he, too, planned to be frozen with cryogenics when he dies so he can be revived when or if future technologies allow it). He has been one of the major financiers of the transhumanist movement.[6]

Trump's high-tech solutions to problems like mass shootings (pre-crime software), migration (biometric identification and tracking), and "the war on terror" have had great commercial value for Thiel and Palantir. Through Trump, Thiel (often portrayed by his opponents as a techno-cratic fascist) has secured lucrative contracts with the American military for technology to track illegal immigrants.[7]

Technologies of this kind were also promoted to handle pandemics in the wake of the COVID-19 crisis. Thiel (with other venture capitalists such as the late Jeffrey Epstein) had already invested in the Israeli company Carbyne, which offers remote-control tracking and monitoring of infected individuals.

As part of the Trump Administration's pandemic measures during the spring of 2020, Palantir was awarded several pandemic response contracts by the U.S. Department of Health and Human Services, including one for building a new platform, HHS Protect, to aid the White House Coronavirus Task Force in tracking the spread of the virus.[8]

Despite his support for Trump and the lucrative contracts with the federal government, in July 2020, Thiel announced that he would withdraw from Trump's reelection campaign because the economic crisis reduced Trump's chances of being reelected and because he was dissatisfied with Trump's handling of the COVID-19 crisis.[9] His strong influence over the White House tech agenda has, however, remained.

Thiel is also a recurring attendee at Bilderberg Meetings, was present in 2019, and is a member of the Steering Committee together with Swedish banker and leading industrialist Marcus Wallenberg, Eric Schmidt from Google, and Thiel's colleague from Palantir, Alex Karp.

The chairman of the Bilderberg Steering Committee, Marie-Josée Kravis, is a part of the Rockefeller circle and is the chair of Rockefeller's MoMA (Museum of Modern Art, New York), board member of Sloan

Kettering Institute, and a member of the Council on Foreign Relations (CFR).[10]

Her husband, businessman Henry Kravis (board member of CFR 2006–2012), the mastermind behind Kohlberg Kravis Roberts (KKR), donated a million dollars to the inauguration of Trump as US president. Kravis is notorious as one of the most ruthless capitalists in the United States and one of the role models for Gordon Gekko in the 1987 film *Wall Street*.[11] Still, Trump has continued to express his admiration for Kravis and invited him and other powerful entrepreneurs to his first state dinner.[12] Kravis in turn praised Trump for his business-friendly politics and tax cuts. Kravis was Trump's first choice for secretary of the treasury but declined the offer.

Another Gordon Gekko role model, Carl Icahn, for a time served as Trump's adviser on financial regulation, but later resigned due to conflicts of interest.

Instead of Kravis and Icahn, Trump appointed CFR member Steven Mnuchin as a minister of finance.[13] Once again, Goldman Sachs was back in the White House! After seventeen years at Goldman Sachs, Mnuchin was recruited as head of SFM Capital Management by Trump's "archenemy," billionaire George Soros.[14] During the last financial crisis, Mnuchin as CEO of the IndyMac bank became known as the "King of Foreclosures" when thousands of homeowners were forced from their homes and property through dirty methods.

Billionaire Stephen Schwarzman became Trump's trusted outside adviser and also the biggest contributor to his reelection campaign.[15] Together with his mentor Peter G. Peterson (ex-president of CFR and successor to Lehman Brothers and David Rockefeller), Schwarzman cofounded investment firm Blackstone Group, which has been sharply criticized for its aggressive property acquisitions all over the world, causing a global housing crisis by pushing people from their homes.[16]

In December 2016, another billionaire businessman, Larry Fink, CEO of investment firm BlackRock and member of CFR, Trilateral Commission, and the board of WEF, was invited by Trump to join a business forum to provide strategic and policy advice on economic issues. Fink also advised Trump on how to handle the COVID-19 crisis, while BlackRock helped the Federal Reserve stabilize the financial market.[17] BlackRock could thereby directly profit from Fink's advice to the president.

> Under one of the programs that BlackRock will help lead, the Fed can buy exchange-traded funds that hold stakes in investment-grade bonds, a type of investment that BlackRock sells.[18]

This was the same procedure as after the financial crisis of 2008. That time, too, BlackRock worked closely with the Federal Reserve. Politics and finance tend to work smoothly together, regardless of which party is in power. Fink's investment firm BlackRock is one of the most powerful players on the financial market. Together with Vanguard Group and State Street, they control a majority of American companies and numerous companies in Europe. Fink was also Trump's personal fund manager: "Larry did a great job for me. He managed a lot of my money. I have to tell you, he got me great returns."

Fink, a lifelong Democrat sympathizer and supporter of Hillary Clinton, in 2016 received the David Rockefeller Award at the Museum of Modern Art, New York. This was the last prize ceremony David himself attended.[19] Fink is also a MoMA board member.

Trump's Secretary of Commerce, Wilbur L. Ross Jr., had previously worked at N.M. Rothschild & Sons and was known for acquiring and reconstructing failing companies and selling them at a profit. While working at Rothschild & Co. in the 1980s, he saved Trump's casinos in Atlanta from bankruptcy and gave him a second chance.[20] Trump was very grateful, and the "King of Foreclosures" became a close friend after this. Despite Ross being accused by close colleagues of stealing close to $120 million and described as a "notorious liar" by a close associate, Trump saw him as a "legendary Wall Street genius."[21]

On top of this, sixty-four members of Trump's cabinet have had close connections to the globalist power center such as Council of Foreign

Relations and/or the Bilderberg group—central nodes in the "deep state" which Trump supporters expected him to oppose.

In the final analysis, Trump appears more like pawn in a Hegelian game than as genuine opposition—almost as if he had been given a prominent role in an epic stage play with religious overtones, aiming to gather support both from the left and the right, and to help kick-start the great global digital transformation. In light of his financiers, ministers, and advisers, his promises of "draining the swamp" seemed more like a bad joke. If anything, he invited the swamp to move into the White House.

Trump's Friend Kissinger

At the Bilderberg Meeting 2019, under the motto "A Stable Strategic Order" and with an agenda obviously connected to AI and monitoring technologies, there were several prominent participants closely connected to Donald Trump; his son-in-law and senior adviser Jared Kushner (business partner with another participant of that particular meeting, Peter Thiel), secretary of state Mike Pompeo (former head of the CIA), and Trump's close friend Henry Kissinger, one of the world's most influential globalists (who worked tirelessly to further the agenda until he passed away on November 29, 2023).

Their friendship was all the more remarkable considering Trump's passionate patriotic and protectionist speeches about "making America great again"—the exact opposite of everything Kissinger worked for during his long career as a political strategist.[22] After Trump became president, he met with Kissinger on three occasions to get advice from one of the most experienced geopolitical strategists, for whom he has expressed a great admiration. Trump and Kissinger became friends back in the 1980s. "Henry Kissinger has been a friend of mine. I've liked him, I've respected him. But we've been friends for a long time, long before my emergence in the world of politics, which has not been too long."[23]

Kissinger seemed equally pleased: "It's always a great honor to be in this office, and I'm here at a moment when the opportunity to build a constructive, peaceful world order is very great."

Donald Trump and Henry Kissinger

In an interview in December 2016, Kissinger commented on Trump's coming presidency:

> I believe he has the possibility of going down in history as a very considerable president, because every country now has two things to consider, one, their perception that the previous president or the outgoing president basically withdrew America from international politics, so that they had to make their own assessment of their necessities, and, secondly, that here is a new president who is asking a lot of unfamiliar questions. And because of the combination of the partial vacuum and the new questions, one could imagine that something remarkable and new emerges out of it. I'm not saying it will. I'm saying it's an extraordinary opportunity.[24]

According to Kissinger, here was a new opportunity to create the "new world order" he had openly called for. Trump's patriotic and populist rhetoric seemed to be part of this game. The opposition is always attracted by the hope of change, and its force can be used to create the desired synthesis between the liberal call for a global climate dictatorship to save the planet, and the conservative call for a national police state with increased surveillance to keep the nation safe from illegal immigrants, drugs, and crime.

Like a shadow Secretary of State, Kissinger had also had meetings with Vladimir Putin and Xi Jinping. It was Kissinger, a frequent guest in the Kremlin, who helped arrange the meeting between Trump and Putin in Helsinki in 2018.

Increased Surveillance

Despite the image built around Trump, he was never a real threat to the global financial elite, which he himself was born into. He appeared rather as their trump card in the process of implementing the technocratic dystopia. The newly proclaimed global emergency, first due to the "climate crisis" and then the "COVID-19 pandemic," rather helped pave the way for its rapid implementation, with Trump playing a vital part.

Early on in his presidency, Trump announced that the United States would take a leading role in the development and implementation of new technologies such as AI, 5G, and the use of biometric monitoring systems.[25] Even during his first election campaign in 2016, Trump had declared his intention to implement a biometric entry/exit visa tracking system to keep track of illegal immigrants: "It will be on land, it will be on sea, it will be in air. We will have a proper tracking system."[26] In 2017, this was included in one of Trump's executive orders.

> The Secretary of Homeland Security shall expedite the completion
> and implementation of a biometric entry exit tracking system for in-
> scope travelers to the United States, as recommended by the National
> Commission on Terrorist Attacks Upon the United States.[27]

During the Trump administration, business executive Michael Kratsios (previously principal at Thiel Capital Management) was the president's top technology adviser. In 2019, he was appointed chief technology officer of the United States and, in 2020, under-secretary of defense for research and engineering. Mark Esper, US Secretary of Defense commented: "In seeking to fill this position we wanted someone with experience in identifying and developing new technologies and working closely with a wide range of industry partners."[28]

Under the leadership of Kratsios, the United States launched strategic plans for AI, 5G, autonomous vehicles, quantum computing, and the COVID-19 High Performance Computing Consortium (with members such as Amazon, Google, Microsoft, IBM, and Intel). He was the US representative at OECD and at the G20 summits on digital economy. According to Kratsios, the Trump administration largely continued the policies of the Obama administration on AI.[29]

Kratsios (formerly the principal of Thiel Capital Investment) became a member of Trump's transition team through Bilderberg attendee Peter Thiel.[30] Kratsios was also a Young Global Leader 2020 (with Black Lives Matters cofounder Alicia Garza). Just as Klaus Schwab had intended, Kratsios's counsel to the White house was perfectly in line with the principles and technocratic agenda of the World Economic Forum.

President Trump and Bill Gates

In March 2018 (!) Bill Gates had a meeting with President Trump in the White House. Gates voiced his concerns over a possible pandemic with high mortality rates and how new technologies could be used to meet such a threat.

> The president was kind enough to spend time with me, and one of the issues I brought up is this opportunity to build new tools that would help us deal with a pandemic.[31] (Bill Gates)

When Gates mentioned a universal flu vaccine, the president "got all fired up." During the meeting, he even offered Gates the position as scientific adviser (which had been vacant after John Holdren in the Obama administration). Gates, however, declined and said "that's not a good use of my time."[32] He was clearly busy preparing for the great pandemic he had predicted in Munich the year before.

The Bill & Melinda Gates Foundation intended to fund an experimental vaccine that would be ready for human trials by 2021.[33] This ambition would two years later become part of the Trump administration's Project Warp Speed.

Preparations in the White House started early on. On September 19, 2019, Donald Trump issued Executive Order 13887—Modernizing Influenza Vaccines in the United States To Promote National Security and Public Health.[34] This order stated that:

> While it is not possible to predict when or how frequently a pandemic
> may occur, there have been 4 pandemics in the last 100 years. The
> most devastating pandemic occurred in 1918–1919 and is estimated to
> have killed more than 50 million people worldwide, including 675,000
> Americans. Vaccination is the most effective defense against influenza.[35]

As the speed of manufacturing and delivery of vaccines was deemed "insufficient to meet the response needs in the event of a pandemic, which can emerge rapidly and with little warning," a National Influenza Vaccine Task Force was established with the secretary of defense and secretary of health and human services as cochairs. The Department of Defense would have a key role, which among others meant to "assess the feasibility of using DOD's advanced manufacturing facility for manufacturing cell-based or recombinant influenza vaccines during a pandemic."[36]

Other departments and agencies included Department of Justice, Centers for Disease Control and Prevention (CDC), Biomedical Advanced Research and Development Authority (BARDA), and National Institutes of Health. CDC would one month later participate in Event 201.

The Task Force was obliged to present a report to the President with a "5-year national plan (Plan) to promote the use of more agile and scalable vaccine manufacturing technologies." A strategy was published, to the benefit of Bill Gates, in June 2020 with the guiding principle of expanding public-private partnerships.[37]

The Peace Treaty

After Trump's success in securing peace with North Korea, he had the White House draft the "deal of the century"—a peace treaty and two-state solution for Israel and Palestine. It was drafted under the leadership of Trump's son-in-law and senior adviser Jared Kushner, with external consultation from Henry Kissinger and Tony Blair.[38]

The plan, *Peace and Prosperity: A Vision to Improve the Lives of the Palestinian and Israeli People,* was introduced in the shadow of the COVID-19 pandemic at the end of January 2020 (the first part was presented June 22, 2019). The treaty gave obvious benefits exclusively to Israel, including the right to annexation of the Jordan Valley. At the press conference in the White House, Benjamin Netanyahu announced his firm intention to implement this paragraph.[39] Unsurprisingly, the Peace Plan was unilaterally discarded by both the League of Arab States and Palestinian leaders and was more likely to incite new conflict than any lasting peace. Trump's frequent taunting of Iran was also not helping his new image as the Prince of Peace.

Solomon's Temple

Among orthodox Jews and Christian evangelists, there was also the hope that Donald Trump, if reelected, would attempt to rebuild Solomon's temple.

> With Trump recognizing Jerusalem as the capital, evangelicals are eagerly anticipating what might come next—perhaps the rebuilding of the temple, the rapture of all true Christians from earth, then, for the rest of us left behind, tribulation, war and the battle of Armageddon.[40]

In 2018, Israel's seventieth anniversary as a nation, and after Trump had ordered moving the American Embassy from Tel Aviv to Jerusalem, the Mikdash Educational Center in Israel minted a commemorative "Temple Coin" depicting President Trump side by side with the Persian king Cyrus II (who saved the Jews from the Babylonian captivity with a promise that the temple would be rebuilt)![41] With a plan seemingly hatched with a literal interpretation of Bible prophecies in mind, this epic power play got truly surreal—especially when followed by a global pandemic and ensuing financial crisis that resulted in extreme measures.

The 2020 Presidential Election

The chaos of 2020 continued through the presidential election in November. After an unusually drawn-out ballot count, due to the large number of mail votes, Trump declared that the election must have been rigged. Even during the 2016 election, he had made accusations of voting fraud due to many states not demanding identification from voters. In April 2020, Trump again voiced concerns that the expected increase in postal votes due to COVID-19 could lead to voting fraud.

This risk required a system that could both handle and prevent manipulation of the election results—as well as keep track of undocumented refugees.

> Now, mail ballots—they cheat. Okay? People cheat. Mail ballots are a very dangerous thing for this country, because they're cheaters. They go and collect them. They're fraudulent in many cases. You got to vote. And they should have voter ID, by the way. If you want to really do it right, you have voter ID.[42] (President Trump)

As Trump saw it, this had now been confirmed. At a press conference on November 5, he claimed that the postal voting had unilaterally benefited Biden, that the Democrats had tried to steal the election through electoral fraud, and that he would take the matter to the Supreme Court. The Trump administration then went on to sue several states, urging them to stop counting votes.[43] By his side Trump had his lawyer and faithful friend, Rudy Giuliani, former mayor of New York, who in January 2017 had been appointed Trump's cybersecurity adviser and in 2018 his personal attorney.[44]

Operation Warp Speed Delivers

On November 13, 2020, President Trump in a White House press conference announced that a vaccine developed by Pfizer was now available and that three other vaccines were expected within weeks—all thanks to his own Operation Warp Speed: "The average time of development for the vaccine, including clinical tests and manufacturing, can take 8 to 12 years. Through Operation Warp Speed we do it in less than a year."[45] The President also announced that the vaccine would be available for every American citizen by April 2021.

Bill Gates was very pleased: "With the very good news from Pfizer and Moderna, we think it's now likely that AstraZeneca, Novavax, and Johnson & Johnson will also likely show very strong efficacy."[46]

At the virtual G20 Leaders Summit in Saudi Arabia, November 12–22, 2020, COVID-19 continued to be a priority as well as accelerating "the development and delivery of vaccines, diagnostics and treatments."[47] During this summit, which was Donald Trump's last major international representation as US president, he declared that he wanted the US population to be vaccinated first.[48]

After the mass vaccination, there would still remain the problem of ascertaining who had received a COVID-19 test or vaccine. The solution to this dilemma already existed. In early 2019, the Rockefeller Foundation had initiated the project ID2020 (see chapter 11).

The Storming of the Capitol

The turmoil continued through the last weeks of Trump's presidency. Even though he had lost his Supreme Court appeal, he was not yet ready to hand over the reins. On January 6, as the Congress gathered in the Capitol building in Washington to formalize Biden's victory, a large rally was held outside with tens of thousands of participants where Trump (with Rudy Giuliani and Donald Trump Jr. by his side), in a final attempt to influence the

Congress, got his supporters fired up and urged them not to give up on the "stolen election."

> We have come to demand that Congress do the right thing and only
> count the electors who have been lawfully slated. Lawfully slated.
> I know that everyone here will soon be marching over to the Capitol
> building to peacefully and patriotically make your voices heard.[49]
> (President Trump)

After Trump's speech, protesters made their way up to Capitol Hill and a smaller group stormed the Congress building, occupying it for several hours. Both sides accused each other of trying to stage a coup.

World leaders were quick to express outrage at this "attack on democracy." In many cases, these were the same leaders who had just put a shocking number of civil liberties on hold and used draconian measures in order to "contain the pandemic."

After that last desperate attempt at retaining power, and after having had his Twitter account suspended, the next day Trump held an official speech where he condemned the attack, acknowledged the results from the Congress, and called for a peaceful transition of power.

> Now, Congress has certified the results. A new administration will
> be inaugurated on January 20. My focus now turns to ensuring a
> smooth, orderly and seamless transition of power. This moment calls
> for healing and reconciliation.[50]

That same day, president-elect Joe Biden declared that the rioters were not peaceful demonstrators but "domestic terrorists."[51] Even before the election, Biden had vowed to clamp down harder on domestic terrorism. This was something he had earlier experience with. After the 9/11 attacks in 2001, the civil rights–eroding USA Patriot Act was introduced just a week later, and passed the next month.

This exceptional swiftness was made possible by the fact that it was largely based on the Omnibus Counterterrorism Act of 1995, introduced by senator *Joe Biden.*

> Months before the Oklahoma City bombing took place, [then-Senator Joe] Biden introduced another bill called the Omnibus Counterterrorism Act of 1995. It previewed the 2001 Patriot Act by allowing secret evidence to be used in prosecutions, expanding the Foreign Intelligence Surveillance Act and wiretap laws, creating a new federal crime of "terrorism" that could be invoked based on political beliefs, permitting the U.S. military to be used in civilian law enforcement, and allowing permanent detention of non-U.S. citizens without judicial review. The Center for National Security Studies said the bill would erode "constitutional and statutory due process protections" and would "authorize the Justice Department to pick and choose crimes to investigate and prosecute based on political beliefs and associations."[52] (Caitlin Johnstone 2021, quoting CNET 2008)

Too extreme to be passed at its first introduction, it could be reintroduced under a new name when national sentiments were in an uproar after the 9/11 attack.

* * *

On January 20, Joe Biden was inaugurated as president without further incidents—and without Trump, who had retired to Florida, planning his next move.

During Biden's presidency, pandemic measures continued and the new experimental mRNA "vaccines" were administred to the public and made manatory for federal employees.

Freedom rally in Stockholm on June 6, 2021

9

The Resistance

The best way to control the opposition is to lead it ourselves.

(Vladimir Lenin)

To neutralize the resistance, it needs to be influenced. The powers that be can either create oppositional organizations from scratch or infiltrate existing movements and insert problematic individuals or exaggerated narratives that make the whole movement look unhinged or even dangerous, while drowning out more balanced and well-founded criticism. Thereby, many would-be supporters in the establishment or mainstream are discouraged from joining the cause. Those involved in genuine action groups also risk being led astray—sometimes right into the arms of the very forces against which the movement was created.

Anti-Lockdown Protests

During the spring of 2020, popular resistance started to grow in response to the often excessively harsh, illogical, and constantly shifting pandemic measures, including lockdowns, curfews, mask mandates, fines, and other restrictions. Meanwhile, authorities did everything to control the narrative with massive propaganda, varying degrees of censorship, and what appear to be cleverly designed disinformation campaigns.

As many people lost their only means of earning a living, hunger protests erupted across the world. In Europe, there were anti-lockdown protests in Spain, France, Bulgaria, Italy, Ireland, England, Germany, and many other countries. One of the largest was the massive anti-lockdown protest in Berlin on August 29, 2020.[1]

These protests were as a rule reported negatively in the media. While the BLM demonstrations, following the murder of George Floyd on May 25, tended to be met with sympathy from authorities, media, and the general public—even as some of the peaceful protests erupted in vandalism, plunder, and attacks on federal buildings—the anti-lockdown protesters were as a rule described as conspiracy theorists, extremists, and a danger to public safety.

World Wide Demonstration

One initiative was the World Wide Demonstration, a project initiated in Kessel, Germany, during the spring of 2020. Mini posters and hashtags were spread via social media and resulted in synchronized demonstrations in over 120 cities around the world, the first in March 2021 and another one in May 2022. The anonymous organizers called themselves Freie Bürger Kessel (Free Citizens of Kessel).

Physicians and Lawyers Speak Out

On October 4, *The Great Barrington Declaration* was published, initiated by experts from Oxford, Harvard, and Stanford, with demands of focusing on the elderly instead of total lockdown, as there was now more information about the virus. Two months later it had been signed by over 36,000 physicians, over 12,000 scientists in the healthcare sector, and over 660,000 concerned citizens.[2] As of May 2023, it has over 937,000 signatures.

Since 2020, there have been similar initiatives in different countries. In Sweden, a group of medical doctors started the Doctors Appeal, which received over 26,000 signatures.[3]

In early October 2020, German-born lawyer Dr. Reiner Füllmich (Anglicized as Fuellmich) publicly declared that a group of lawyers had initiated preparations for a class action lawsuit for what they called "probably the greatest crime against humanity ever" against those responsible for the pandemic measures and the PCR tests.[4] Their case has yet to be accepted by any court of law.

World Freedom Alliance

> We are leading the world into a global reset. . . . We need to be the
> people that shape the next stage. We have to present a better world to
> people because no one else is going to do that. (Nigel Utton, World
> Freedom Alliance)

On August 29, 2020, there was a huge "Unite for Freedom Rally" in
London. Among the speakers were meteorologist Piers Corbyn (brother
of former Labour leader Jeremy Corbyn), nurse Kate Shemirani, Professor
Dolores Cahill, Dr. Kevin Corbett, Dr. Mohammed Adil, controversial
Swedish physician Dr. Mikael Nordfors, and controversial author David
Icke.[5] Corbyn was later fined £10,000 for his part in organizing the rally.[6]
A co-organizer was Stand Up X, created in May 2020 to challenge the
pandemic restrictions.[7]

On September 19, there was another rally at Trafalgar Square in
London with many of the same speakers.[8] These two events laid the foun-
dation for the founding of the World Doctors Alliance (WDA) and World
Freedom Alliance (WFA).

On October 10, doctors Adil, Cahill, Cox, Kaufman, and Nordfors
met in Berlin to found World Doctors Alliance, joined by German physician Heiko Schöning. Professor Cahill was elected chairman (she was
also party leader of the EU-skeptic Irish Freedom Party, a position she
left in March 2021). Participating in this meeting were also Danish former banker Mads Palsvig (party leader of JFK21), Irish activist Fiona
Hine (founder of CoviLeaks), and Nordfors's daughter Maneka Helleberg
(introducing herself as chairman of the People's Court and core member
of the New Earth Project).[9]

This was also the day of the Great March through Berlin. Among
the speakers were lawyer and activist Robert Kennedy Jr., founder of
Children's Health Defense, who finished his speech by reiterating the
famous words of his uncle, JFK, "*Ich bin ein Berliner!*" to thundering
applause. Everything was filmed by Oracle Films.

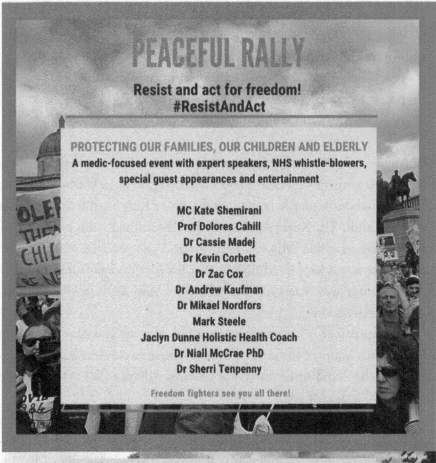

Poster for the London rally, September 19, 2020

On Halloween, October 31, 2020, another rally was held in Stockholm, Sweden, with both Swedish and international speakers (including, via virtual link, Robert Kennedy Jr. and New Age influencer Sacha Stone). The following day, the organization World Freedom Alliance was officially founded. The board included Dolores Cahill (president), Dr. Heiko Schöning (vice president), Manneka Helleberg (chair), Mads Palsvig (treasurer), Fiona Hine (secretary-general), and barrister/musician Martin Byrne.

World Freedom Alliance has members in most European countries, USA, Canada, Australia, South Africa, Russia, Costa Rica, Chile, Saudi Arabia, India, and Thailand. The leadership of both WFA and WDA is, however, dominated by Scandinavians and Northern Europeans. The stated purpose of WFA was to link professionals in health care, law, and education all over the world.[10] But it was also about something bigger than to protest against pandemic mandates. Dr. Cahill had great ambitions about building a new and better world.

> You are with us as freedom fighters building the new world, a new health system, a new banking system, a better world.[11]

Such utopian visions and New Age ideals seem to dominate much of the resistance, at least in the most vocal organizations and individuals highlighted by media. Most people involved in the resistance movement seem to be well-meaning, freedom-loving people. However, once a movement has formed, it can be led in a direction that renders it harmless to the powers that be. Infiltration can happen on several levels, including on an ideological level, and by injecting terminology and symbolism which may be off-putting to the majority.

The Swedish Freedom Movement

In Sweden, the WFA subdivision Frihet Sverige was formed in early 2021 by former *Swedish Idol* contestant Filip Sjöström, with himself as vice chairman and Dr. Nordfors as chairman.

Together with his friend, health coach Max Winter (CEO of Optiself), Filip Sjöström initiated the sister organization Frihetsrörelsen (the Freedom Movement). Max was also elected chairman of the World Freedom Alliance's youth movement Youth For Freedom and also created Freedom Defence Sweden, a small group of young men trained to defend protesters if the need should arise.[12]

In the spring of 2021, this Freedom Movement arranged several marches through Stockholm, protesting the new temporary pandemic law in Sweden that allowed gatherings of only eight people, and the EU plans for a COVID passport. Already a semi-celebrity, Filip became the movement's spokesperson and was interviewed on Swedish morning news and talk shows. While the first protests during 2020 had been completely ignored by establishment media, the spring 2021 protests were now extensively covered—although not in a positive light. Instead, there were the same accusations of conspirituality (a neologism to describe the intermingling of conspiracy theory with spiritual movements) and right-wing extremism as in many other countries.

It didn't exactly help that many of the leaders and invited speakers talked about their spiritual visions for the world, or that *some* of the alternative health enthusiasts and freedom advocates were lured into association with a small network of fringe alt-right organizations, political parties, or generously welcoming alternative media channels—some of which appear to have been created for this very purpose.

The Swedish Inquisition

In the spring of 2021, Andreas Önnerfors, a Swedish historian, became known as the appointed expert on the resistance. He had just published a report on conspiracy theories for the Swedish Civil Contingencies Agency (MSB). According to his report, conspiracy theories are "based on an assumed coalition or group that together make plans and have the knowledge, will and means to carry them out." This constitutes a "threat to society": "Conspiracy theories break down trust and contribute to a process of radicalization. They can lead to a questioning of scientific expertise, mistrust of political leadership, government, and how a country is run."[13]

The report was part of a campaign initiated by the Swedish government (following a political decision on December 22, 2020 "to increase awareness of how conspiracy theories contribute to the spread of disinformation and misleading information"). The report points out that a typical characteristic of a conspiracy theory is "to place blame and assign scapegoats." Ironically, this is exactly what Önnerfors does when labeling individuals and groups critical of COVID restrictions and mass vaccination programs as "conspiracy theorists": "The views on diseases and treatments within the alternative health community is a breeding ground for adopting conspiratorial thinking patterns regarding both the pharmaceutical industry and governmental health agencies." (MSB, p. 13)

So, those who harbor the least bit of doubt regarding the altruistic motives of pharmaceutical companies or criticize the policies of government agencies are considered delusional and dangerous. Önnerfors specifically named World Freedom Alliance as a "corona-critical international network" with connections both to "right-wing extremism" and the "wellness industry" and to spreading the view that a global elite is seeking to dominate the world. The report goes on: "Grossly simplified views of a group and their properties (stereotyping) is another contributing factor which can either be built on (cultural) perceptions and communicated during a long time period or on real personal experiences which are generalized in an unscientific manner." (MSB, p. 39) Önnerfors does not reflect on the paradox that he himself in this report has created a simplistic stereotype—which can then be freely attacked by the media and the general public alike.

After the report was published, Önnerfors was invited to many talk shows and panels as an expert. Curiously, Önnerfors is himself actually a high-ranking Freemason and an expert on the history of freemasonry. As such, he is also a dedicated supporter of the establishment of supranational political structures with a World Parliament and World Citizenship (with "individual responsibility for the whole").[14] The masonic ideal of a universal brotherhood is a core component of his beliefs. As he describes it in an interview in the masonic journal *The Gavel*:

> In masonic ritual—at least in a self-contained system like the Swedish Rite, which has ten subsequent degrees that interrelate— there is a level of path-dependency with little leeway for free choices, like a script, a musical score, or even an algorithm. We imagine that by going through the ritual and experiencing it again and again, we internalize the values of Freemasonry so that, when leaving the virtuality of time and space in the lodge, we can apply them out in the world. Would it be different to program an A.I. robot to act as a Freemason? To insert a printed circuit board which instructs it to make the "right" decisions? Is it possible to initiate a cyborg? What makes initiation different from programming a machine?[15]

The plan is not only to perfect oneself but also the world, with the use of the technologies of the Fourth Industrial Revolution, as explained in the masonic book *The Art and Science of Initiation* by Jedediah French and Angel Millar, cited by French in the same issue of *The Gavel* (of which he is also the editor):

> Masons should not become better men, but the best. The duty of every true Mason must be to view the world— regardless of race, skin tone, sex, class, or creed—as one human family, as one interconnected lodge. When economists today speak of the Fourth Industrial Revolution (4IR), this is where Masons should be especially active as the work force and foundational infrastructure of our societies yield to advanced technologies and robotics. Masons must make sure this new industry does not lose sight of the spiritual implications of this massive change and help guide these technologies toward the spiritual wellbeing and betterment of everyone on the planet. (French, *The Gavel*, p. 19)

In the MSB report, Önnerfors gives a clear indication that those he labeled "conspiracy theorists," "antivaxxers," and "climate deniers" will not be welcome in the "universal brotherhood" of this masonic utopia. Or perhaps they need some reeducation procedure in order to become "perfected"?

Sacha Stone

A central profile, who at an early stage stepped forward as a guru for the international resistance against lockdowns and repressive laws, was former rock musician and New Age influencer Sacha Stone, a well-known profile in alternative circles. He was born in Rhodesia in 1966, lives in a mini palace at his retreat in Ubud, Bali, and has a luxurious apartment in London.

In May 2021, an investigative article in a leading Swedish newspaper highlighted the connections between World Freedom Alliance and the outspoken Stone, with compromising revelations about his activities that cast WFA in a bad light. Önnerfors was also interviewed for the article and given an opportunity to formulate his own conspiracy theory: "I can well imagine that there will be some kind of attack against an institution in Sweden due to all these conspiracy theories."[16]

This speculation is all the more ironic considering that several of the leaders of the resistance, including Sacha Stone, share the very same visions of a future peaceful utopia with a global democratic governance as in freemasonry: "Speculative Masonry aims at bringing, not only a building, but a new society—dare we say a world—into existence, a world that is founded on universal brotherhood (or humanity), certain rational principles, and aesthetic ideals." (French, *The Gavel*, p. 17)

New Earth Project

New Earth Project (NEP) was founded in 2012 by Sacha Stone as an "open platform to unite humanity in ushering in a new era of planetary wellbeing, peace and prosperity."[17] NEP comprised several subprojects:

- **New Earth Nations**: An early vision of "a federation of self-governing sovereign nations, creating villages and communities in which we can live peacefully, abundantly, and in harmony with nature."[18]

- **New Earth University**: "Online new-paradigm learning community of the NewEarth Project," started in 2014 and led by Rev. Nancy Ash.
- **New Earth Haven**: Sacha's beautiful retreat and conference center, built in organic architecture, finished in 2016.
- **New Earth Festival**: Annual festivals at the Bali center, starting 2017.
- **International Tribunal of Natural Justice**: "A world court – for the people and by the people" (a mock tribunal), founded in 2015 and led by John Walsh, usually held during the annual festival.
- **World Health Sovereignty Summit**: a conference for alternative medicine held during the annual festival, starting 2019.

New Earth Nations was separated from the New Earth Project in 2020 and now appears to be defunct. Over the years, Sacha has initiated a host of other visionary projects which are no longer active or never took off, such as Natural World Organization,[19] New Earth Exchange (finance and commerce using blockchain), New Earth Youth Council (a New Age version of WEF's Forum of Young Global Leaders), New Earth Institutes, Earth Sanctuary, and Exemplar-Zero. NEP was recently relaunched as New Earth Horizon and given a new website.[20]

Humanitad

The economic entity behind New Earth is the Humanitad Foundation, founded by Sacha Stone in 1999. Humanitad is "committed to ushering in a new era of truth, transparency and right-mindedness whilst inspiring growth in the spiritual framework within which we function as a species."[21]

According to Sacha's former manager and close friend, Ciro Orsini, Humanitad has "exceptional government support"[22] and several prominent members from UNESCO and World Federalists among its coworkers and supporters—visionaries, dreaming of a new world to emerge out of the crises of the old order. The list also includes Club of Rome and Club of Budapest member Dr. Bernhard Lietaer (1942–2019) who was involved in the creation of the EURO system and had proposed a global currency called TERRA.[23]

Another member was neo-theosophist Dr. Robert Müller (1923–2010), one of the signatories to systems theorist Ervin László's *Manifesto on the Spirit of Planetary Consciousness* (1996). He worked within the United Nations for forty years, for a time as deputy secretary-general, and was deeply influenced by theosophy and new age philosophy.[24] On Humanitad's website, his plan for how a world government could be realized is commented on by Sacha's former technical adviser Elliott Maynard:

> Perhaps the most efficient way to achieve Global Transformation is to launch the most colossal media campaign in history. Funding for this campaign could be provided by Key Individuals like Ted Turner, Bono, Paul McCartney, Leonardo DiCaprio, Prince Charles and similar philanthropists. Such individuals (and countless others) have great concerns for Social Justice, and Environmental Reform. The Major Global Media Organizations are already beginning to air stories about Global Warming, Conservation, and the Environment on a daily basis.[25]

Maynard, who "worked with Dr. Robert Müller on developing and implementing his visionary concepts for a new model of planetary government,[26] called this a "Gaia Media Blitzkrieg."

Hippie Technocracy

The New Earth Project is a utopian plan for the evolution of humanity and the future management of the planet. It is presented as a pioneering venture for "social experiments serving as nationwide examples for the ideal sustainable, conscious community." A New Age paradise where all problems will go away if we only join together as one happy family in the new enlightened era.

NEP appears as an offshoot of the same futurism as that of World Future Society (in which Maynard is involved) and may be described as a form of hippie technocracy. Just like in Young Global Leader Ida Auken's WEF article "Welcome To 2030: I Own Nothing, Have No Privacy And Life Has Never Been Better," New Earth individuals will own nothing. Sacha himself says that "ownership is a toxic notion." Instead everything is to be owned collectively, through the New Earth Trust. The original land owners, who are invited to offer their land for New Earth centers, will be reduced to trustees and "guardians of the land."

> We are launching the universal trust that belongs to the earth and designates the earth as the beneficiary and the people of the earth as beneficiary and we are inviting people in dwellings, in farms, in communities who own land. All of those land holdings are invited to simply leave the earth and dock into the supranational trust structure.[27]

Donations to the project are administered and controlled by the New Earth Trust and its board. Who controls the trust is shrouded in mystery. It costs upward of $50,000 to get a home built in New Earth.

The first to be built was Sacha's own beautiful lush new age conference center on Bali for hosting conferences and festivals. It was built as a prototype for New Earth Nations centers and as an example of bio-architecture and sacred geometry. As of 2024, it still seems to be the only center that has actually been built. The other planned community in Mexico, which is linked to on the new website, only shows renderings of the planned center, said to be under construction.[28]

New Earth seems like an agrarian version of Jacques Fresco's explicitly technocratic Venus Project.[29] Through Exemplar Zero, which used vision images from the Venus Project in its presentation material, Sacha even gave an award to his friend Fresco for his lifelong achievements.

World Health Sovereignty Summit

As of 2019, the New Earth Festival also includes a World Health Sovereignty Summit, under the (almost Masonic) slogan "One Earth—One Humanity" with subjects related to vaccines, Big Pharma, Big Agro, weather modification, and 5G. It has attracted many well-known representatives from the alternative health movement. The first summit had well-known and respected establishment critics such as Del Bigtree, G. Edward Griffin, and Dr. Joseph Mercola as speakers.[30] In 2020, the pandemic lockdowns were added to the list of causes.

The New Earth Project has in many ways been an important hub in the growing global resistance against lockdowns and overly repressive pandemic mandates. For a couple of decades, Sacha's wide social network and new age image have effectively captured many of the well-meaning visionaries and advocates of alternative health who dream of a better world in unity, freedom, and harmony.

Earth Sanctuary and the UN Millennium Goals

In the late 1990s, Sacha Stone was involved with the United Nations and, during a few years, executive producer for the Millennium Development Goals Award.[31] He was also involved in the United Nations Global Impact Forum, with support from Club of Budapest members such as Ervin László, Bernhard Lietaer, Deepak Chopra, and Jane Houston, as well as Sacha's long-term associate, Bishop Riah Abu El Assal of Jerusalem. The forum was to launch the largest online platform for democracy in history around the "Millennium Development Goals" project. Two of Sacha's previous projects, Earth Sanctuary and Exemplar Zero, were created to support United Nations Millennium Development Goals (precursors to Agenda 2030).

> Earth Sanctuaries will evolve as semi-autonomous nation-by-nation community "'protectorates" which will find one another across national and cultural borders and begin to emerge as a pan-global human family. This "supra-national" and "supra-cultural" global movement will flourish as a self-determining conscious and

sustainable framework for all humanity—serving our higher purpose and fulfilling our higher aspirations. The Earth Sanctuary project is a planetary social experiment with extraordinary possibilities.[32]

These aspirations were then channeled into the New Earth Project. Earth
Sanctuary also had an overt climate and environmental profile.

Long haul passenger jets, global pandemics and "climate-change"
make it clear to everyone that we live in a finite world. It should
therefore also be clear that a harmonised world economic system that
depends on constant growth must have an end date. Growth requires
more consumption by more people—but we have a finite world—it
is as simple as that.[33]

In other words, ideas coming directly from the Club of Rome, the UN,
and the Rockefeller Brothers Fund. This was also true of the project
Exemplar Zero (developing tech solutions for Earth Sanctuary) of which
Sacha was general manager, together with futurists Dr. David Martin and
the previously mentioned Elliot Maynard. EZ advocated zero tolerance for
continued debate and "Zero-growth in CO_2-emissions":

This pioneering global initiative heralds the dawn of a new cooper-
ative approach toward manifesting a just and sustainable world. It
invites and challenges all nations to demonstrate their stated obligations toward mitigating climate-change and carbon-emissions whilst
ensuring a sustainable future.[34]

Lately, Sacha Stone has done a complete 180 and started to viciously attack
both the climate agenda and the UN Agenda 2030, describing them as an
"evil globalist plan" where people will be forced from rural areas into cities
to be "poisoned by glyphosate, fluoride, and chemtrails." At the Stockholm
manifestation on October 31, 2020, when the World Freedom Alliance
was founded, he made the following statement (in a video link from Bali):

It is a sub-human agenda. I am a former director-general in the IGO-sector at the United Nations. I know first hand. Climate Change, your paper says, is one of the greatest longtime challenges for humanity. It has direct and rapid growing security consequences. The 2015 Paris agreement blah, blah, blah, blah... It is all trying to sell you on scarcity. That we are running out of water, we are running out of land, we are running out of wilderness, we are running out of rainforests, we are running out of everything. This scarcity economics modelling is written in to the agenda. It is a Fabianist agenda, it is a Tavistock agenda, it is a Jesuit agenda.[35]

Despite this dramatic turn, the New Earth Project seems like a new age version of Agenda 2030, now repackaged in conspirituality terminology to appeal to audiences skeptical of the technocratic and corporate model advocated by the World Economic Forum.

International Tribunal for Natural Justice

In June 2015, Stone founded the International Tribunal for Natural Justice (ITNJ) as a part of New Earth Project and Humanitad. The stated purpose was to "apprehend the abuses and tyranny of systems and institutions; restore truth and reason to the delivery of justice in the world; and uphold natural justice as the foundational tenet of human expression beyond the artifice of borders and boundaries."[36]

This may sound like a worthwhile objective. Initially, ITNJ focused on trafficking, pedophilia, and the handling of child protection services. In 2019, the focus shifted to the "weaponization of our biosphere" (5G, geoengineering, bioweapons, and GMOs) and in 2020 toward lockdowns and other pandemic measures.

In May and June 2020, ITNJ and Sacha Stone held a "tribunal," inviting vocal vaccine critics such as Dolores Cahill and Mikael Nordfors from WFA, Ole Dammegård (*Light on Conspiracies*), and controversial physicians Andrew Wakefield, Rashid Buttar, and Judy Mikovits.[37] ITNJ is also a partner of World Freedom Alliance.

The organization is led by the well-paid judge "Sir John Walsh of Brannagh" (with one of the most pretentious CVs ever seen). Of all people, Walsh recruited former (?) CIA agent Robert David Steele (1952–2021) as chief adviser.[38] The ITNJ website describes itself as:

> the world's first people-powered tribunal that operates independently of governments and corporations, and is therefore willing to issue rulings against those organizations based on Natural Law and Natural Justice, where agents of governments and/or corporations have caused harm or loss to living men and women.[39]

Their impact has, however, been disputed. In December 2015, the Australian organization National Child Protection Alliance (NCPA) sought legal assistance from ITNJ in a case against the Commonwealth of Australia. One year later, NCPA made three serious charges against ITNJ, including:

> False presentation of a Legal Service by John Walsh and his staff Julie-Anne Pho and Shae Woodward. i.e. that an organization titled the International Tribunal for Natural Justice has recognition, reputation, and status in Australia and other countries, when in fact it has no such lawfully recognised authority in Australia, nor recognition by any government, government body, nor among the general populace of any country.[40]

ITNJ has become more and more questioned as it lacks any legal power to enforce its rulings. It seems to be just one more of several "people's tribunals" masquerading as legitimate courts when they are not. Former volunteers have officially warned against getting involved, including one US representative of ITNJ:

> LET IT BE KNOWN that those of us who understand the goal of the ITNJ has nothing to do with justice, and everything to do with the status quo with a new face, that we will inform the public of the

dangers of getting involved, thinking any justice for the people will be served. It is a sideshow that distracts and detracts from the real culprits and provides no enforcement whatsoever.[41]

Conspirituality

From initially attracting primarily a new age audience, and as late as 2016 calling Donald Trump "a clown," Sacha Stone has more and more joined the Q narrative where "good people" like Trump, the "white hats," and Vladimir Putin will deal with the "evil Luciferian elite." As Sacha said in 2020: "The President [Trump] in my view is possessed with the Christ of Light, the grace of God incarnate."[42]

In the spring of 2020, Stone helped spread a viral claim from his friend Michael Tellinger (South African author, explorer, and founder of the Ubuntu Party) that Trump had taken the Federal Reserve back from the "cabalistic demons"—when Trump in fact had just appointed Larry Fink from BlackRock and WEF to run it![43]

As a new age influencer, Sacha promises that a New Earth paradise will appear once the old order has fallen. But looking more closely, he seems to rather represent the very forces he claims to expose. Through his presence in so many alternative channels and events, his influence has been substantial. Unfortunately, his dramatically exaggerated conspirituality rhetoric both bedazzles and contaminates the opposition by squeezing in as many controversial statements, blatant lies, and far-out theories as possible into every single interview and public appearance. Both his followers, associates, and the many high-profile system critics all over the world who have been invited to his initiatives and interviews risk getting their reputations severely compromised by the association.

Q

As is probably well known by now, the Q phenomenon started in October 2017 as cryptic messages, Q-drops, from a mysterious "Q" profile on the anonymous internet forum 4Chan, later 8Chan.[44] During the spring of

2020, the Q narrative spread as swiftly as the fear of the virus and grew into a significant movement.

The main theme was that both the United States and the world are governed by an evil cabal of top politicians, corrupt secret services, cultural leaders, and the global financial elite. So far so good; there is clearly a higher degree of ruthlessness, narcissism, and psychopathy among many of the top players in national and global politics, business, media, education, and entertainment, and there does seem to be an agenda with ulterior motives, as well as a real global child-trafficking problem.

However, what might have been a well-founded critique against the system seemed in this case to be something else. On one hand, it could have been a clever part of the presidential campaign (by spreading anonymous internet rumors of political opponents as blood-drinking satanists). The narrative also included so many outlandish insinuations, easily debunked claims, and unfulfilled promises that followers would appear unhinged for believing *any* of it, despite *some* legitimate questions being raised.

In the very first post in 2017, Q claimed that Hillary Clinton was just about to be arrested. In August 2018, and again in January 2020, Q wrote that "45 000+ sealed indictments" against the global elite were about to be made public, followed by mass arrests and purges within the FBI, CIA, and the US government. The fact that Trump was *sitting President* from 2017 to 2021 and that few or none of Q's many promises and predictions came true during or after Trump's presidency does not seem to deter believers.

To be fair, Trump *did* order an initiative to combat trafficking,[45] and he *did* pull US funding from the WHO—but instead gave even more taxpayer funds to Bill Gates's GAVI via USAID.[46]

Fall of the Cabal

Very helpful in disseminating the Q narrative to a wider audience via social media just as the pandemic was declared was the almost parodically exaggerated *Fall of the Cabal*, a low-budget ten-part video series by

Dutch crop circle researcher Jane Ossebaard (1966–2023).[47] After nine episodes of ever more extreme allegations against the Clintons, George Soros, and Hollywood celebrities, with grains of verifiable truth thrown in here and there, the final episode culminates in an almost religious tribute to "Trump the Savior" who, together with JFK Jr. (claimed to still be alive), was going to "save the children," "execute the cabal," give us "free Tesla energy," abolish the income tax and the Federal Reserve, and many other fantastic things. *Soon.*

This, however, is an *old* tale, dating back to when Trump was known only for his taste in supermodels and glitzy skyscrapers and starring in *The Apprentice*. Back then, it was the Pentagon's "White Hats" who were just about to "arrest the cabal" and give us a new economic system and free energy. Some of the most active in spreading this type of "hope porn" have been Ben Fulford (Canadian-born former Asian bureau chief of *Forbes* in Japan, from 2006 turned full-time conspiracy theorist), the self-styled "dreaming prophet" David Wilcock, and "insiders" like Drake Bailey.

> I heard from another insider this morning who has a variety of contacts with intelligence agency personnel, central bankers, military officials, et cetera. He specializes in trying to get free energy out to the public. The news from this insider, directly connected to the so-called "Pentagon White Hats," is extremely positive – if indeed true. // There have been critical nuclear attacks against underground cities and sub-shuttle systems. The mass arrests have already begun, aggressively – but they are still "below the radar." As a result of these events, we are told the cabal has now formally agreed to surrender. (David Wilcock, 2011)[48]

Following these early disinformation agents, many other self-styled "insiders" have peddled the same narrative. The previously mentioned Robert David Steele (who passed away with COVID-19 in 2021, allegedly after intubation at the hospital) was very active online. He, too, spread rumors of impending mass arrests and executions of the "deep state henchmen" and praised Donald Trump as the savior who would deal with "globalists such as Hillary Clinton."[49] Steele also became a guru among Q followers. His website hosted the *Fall of the Cabal* series, and he made statements such as: "We actually believe that there is a colony on Mars that is populated by children who were kidnapped and sent into space on a 20-year ride, so that once they get to Mars, they have no alternative but to be slaves on the Mars colony."[50]

Steele was also a vaccine critic and thereby perfectly connected well-founded hesitancy toward new untested medical treatments with Q, Trump worship, unabashed anti-Semitism, and the crudest form of conspiracism.

Another website hosting Ossebaard's films is *Stop World Control*, by Belgian-born David Sörensen, evangelist and former White House aide in the Trump administration (until reports of alleged violence against his former wives and current girlfriend). Sörensen's exceptionally well-styled website mixes serious critique of the economic system and the World Economic Forum's transhumanist agenda with populist memes and conspiracy theories about everything from the pandemic to Ukraine—where Putin and Trump are again heralded as "chosen by God."

It all appears like a massive psyop, where any legitimate criticism of governmental overreach or concern for real trafficking victims is drowned out by, associated with, or mixed with so many absurd and unsubstantiated claims that their chances of being heard or taken seriously are severely diminished. The flood of obvious disinformation campaigns, as well as a sudden surge of satire sites and "flat earth" believers over the last decade, have also helped legitimize the growing trend of online censorship indiscriminately hitting anyone questioning the official narrative.

Waiting for NESARA

In April 2020, Robert David Steele, in a video pod with Sacha Stone, stated that Donald Trump was just about to announce NESARA.[51] This, however, is a *decades-old* internet scam.

The story began in 1991 with a bill written by Harvey Barnard (1942–2005), an engineer and teacher from Louisiana. He called it the National Economic Stabilization and Recovery Act. It proposed replacing the privately owned Federal Reserve with a US Treasure Reserve, reforming the tax system, and reducing private debt. Barnard claims to have sent it to one thousand members of the US Congress. However, no congressman was interested in sponsoring the bill. He still kept working for his vision by writing the book *Draining the Swamp: Monetary and Fiscal Policy Reform* (1996), founding the NESARA Institute (2001), and posting the proposal online on his nesara.com website, hoping to gain public support.

In the early 2000s, when the 1990s Omega Trust swindler Clyde Hood was sentenced to fourteen years in prison, one of his followers, Shaini Goodwin (calling herself the "Dove of Oneness") saw an opportunity to get some of her money back. She simply took over Hood's still-waiting audience of hoodwinked investors and kept their futile hope alive. Goodwin had found Barnard's NESARA website online and saw its potential. She created a faux website with a similar name, redefined the acronym, made her own NESARA logo (featuring a dove), and embellished the original bill with total debt forgiveness, abolishment of all taxes, world peace, free energy, and generous "prosperity programs" in a new precious metal–backed "rainbow currency"—to be distributed as soon as "the secret NESARA Law" was officially announced. She kept her followers hoping (and paying) for nearly a decade until her alleged death in 2010.[52]

The scam was then taken over by other grifters, such as new age channeler Beth Trutwin, new age author Sheldan Nidle, and the ever-present David Wilcock and Ben Fulford.

Since 2020, as the pandemic measures wreaked havoc on the economy, Q, Sacha Stone, Robert David Steele, Ole Dammegard, and countless other YouTubers have reignited desperate people's hope in this old pipe dream. Variations on the theme include GESARA ("Global NESARA"), GCR ("Global Currency Reset"), RV ("Revaluation of Currencies"), and QFS ("Quantum Financial System").

The source of the QFS fantasy is British Charlie Ward, who claims to have been moving money around for the elite for thirty years. Describing QFS in the new online version of the late JFK Jr.'s magazine *George* (restarted in 2022 by Trump and Q fan Gene Ho), it sounds exactly like CBDC (central bank digital currency) but Ward assures us that QFS is a "good" version of CBDC.[53] How do we know this to be true? Well, because he *says* so.

Looking into Wards's background, however, reveals a character that seems more than shady. Besides promoting NESARA/GESARA and QFS and lying about being a doctor, he has previously promoted the fake "King John III" story with his friend, the real estate con man David O. Mahoney. In a candid interview, Ward also happily admits to having procured underage girls (about five to ten per week) for Top of the Pops host Jimmy Savile (!)—fully aware of what would likely happen to them (and giving them "fair warning"):

> "I'll take you on, but you'll probably have to shag with the bloke . . ."
>   A lot of them were undera . . . were young girls, you know.
> I didn't think anything of it. My moral compass was out of sync,
> I think, then.[54] (Charlie Ward)

Ward, who started his alternative YouTube channel *The Charlie Ward Show* in 2020, has been in interviews with many of the leading disinformation artists such as Robert David Steele, Sacha Stone, and the Q-associated General Mike Flynn (national security advisor for the first three weeks in the Trump administration).

To sum it up: people have been waiting for over *two decades* for their NESARA millions *and* for the so-called "white hats" (Dove called them her "white knights") to "arrest the Cabal" and fix everything that is wrong with the world.

Miracle Products

While waiting for your pot of gold in rainbow currency, you could also buy miracle products such as the 5GBioShield, a "full-spectrum radiation balancing technology," for $350.[55] Sold by Charlie Ward and his friend with the lively imagination, Simon Parkes, as well as by Sacha Stone, who claimed it was "invented by KGB and good people in Russia" to "neutralise the harmful radiation from Fukishima."[56] Alas, it turned out to be a regular $6 USB stick with a fancy gold design.[57] Sacha has also offered the "life-prolonging" elixir Immortalis for $825 a bottle. And, through Humanitad, partnered in the development of a "free energy device" called QT-PI, presented at New Earth Festival 2017 and claimed to give 300 percent more energy than put in.[58] This also turned out to be a sham.[59] Today, his new web shop offers other "miracle" products.[60]

Sacha Stone with the magic USB stick on the YouTube channel World Awake, October 10, 2019

Exopolitics and Space Technocracy

Another tribunal that has received much attention is the Natural and Common Law Tribunal for Public Health and Justice. In November 2020, it "sentenced" many national leaders, UN organizations, and heads of leading philanthropies like Bill Gates and David Rockefeller Jr. to long prison sentences for "crimes against humanity" connected to the COVID-19 crisis.[61] Just like the other "people's tribunals," it lacked any power to legally enforce its rulings.

In this tribunal we again find the ever-present Sacha Stone as judge, together with Dolores Cahill and futurist Alfred Lambremont Webre—who also publishes the tribunal's material on his blog *Exopolitics.com*. Webre has long since been closely aligned with the forces he opposes as a judge in the Tribunal for Public Health and Justice.

Webre, a lawyer trained at Yale Law School who labels himself as a space activist, was, in the early 1970s, assistant administrator of the New York City Environmental Protection Administration under New York mayor John Lindsay. He later became a consultant to Ford Foundation, overseeing grantees of Environmental Defense Fund and Natural Resources Defense Council. These organizations were also supported by Rockefeller Brothers Fund, with one of the UFO-movement's most prominent patrons, Laurance Rockefeller, as a board member.[62] Webre would soon assume the position as a key spokesperson for this movement, and later became congressional coordinator of the Rockefeller-funded UFO Disclosure project.[63]

In February 1973, shortly after meeting Phillip H. Liss, a professor in experimental psychology and expert on parapsychology and extraterrestrial civilizations, Webre experienced a multidimensional telepathic interaction with a interdimensional entity identifying as the "Holy Spirit."[64] This took his life in a new (extraterrestrial) direction.

In 1974, Webre wrote the book *The Age of Cataclysm* together with Liss. This book discussed how disasters like earthquakes, floods, tornados, and droughts soon would overwhelm human civilization. These future disasters were based on an integration of earth sciences and the predictions by the famous "sleeping prophet" Edgar Cayce. Webre and Liss also warned about a coming Ice Age and advocated for a "global coordination of disaster preparedness plans" to confront these crises. They argued that "[t]he long range goal of mankind is an establishment of a world federalism in which the energies of the world is directed within a single cohesive and legal social framework."[65]

Their thinking about planning and global governance have a striking similarity to recent proposals from the United Nations to establish emergency platforms with the aim to manage global complex shocks, as well as a major reform of the UN-system.[66]

Between 1977–1978, Webre was a director at the Center for the study of Social Policy at the Stanford Research Institute, where he started to develop the research discipline Exopolitics (the science of relations among intelligent civilizations in the multiverse). The Center is known for the publication *Changing Images of Man* and had a contract with the CIA to study alternative futures, under the directorship of futurist Willis Harman (see chapter 10).

One of Webre's colleagues at Stanford was the futurist Peter Schwartz, who in 1982 moved to London to lead the famous Shell Scenarios Team and who was also coauthor of the highly relevant 2010 Rockefeller Foundation report *Scenarios for the Future of Technology and International Development* (see chapters 10 and 11).

In the late 1970s, Webre lead the (discontinued) Carter White House Extraterrestrial Communication Project. Jimmy Carter claimed to have seen a UFO in 1969 and, during his election campaign, promised to found an institute for UFO observations. These plans were, however, stopped by the Pentagon when Carter became US president.[67]

Webre also claims that that there are secret colonies on Mars and that former US president Barack H. Obama had been enrolled in a Mars training class in 1980.[68] The source is his friend, the lawyer and self proclaimed "Mars visitor," Andrew D. Basiago, who asserts to have been involved with DARPA's secret time travel program Project Pegasus as a child in the 1970s.[69] These statements have no factual backing and are only supported by Basagio's own story, and by his time traveling friend, "crononaut" William B. Stillings. Everything

seems concocted to contaminate the alternative community and associate serious critics with far-fetched theories that are easy to attack
and dismiss.

Basagio was a presidential candidate in 2016 as he had "prior knowledge that not only will I run for president, but that during one of the
elections—which would have to be between 2016 and 2028, because
I'm not running past that—I'm either elected president or vice president."[70] Since he is not a candidate for the 2024 presidency, he only has
one chance left to prove himself right. It's safe to say the odds are not in
his favor.

One of Webre's more recent projects has been the Star Dreams
Initiative, using remote viewing techniques which, according to Webre,
were developed by the Stanford Research Institute, the CIA, and the
American military in order to map the relations between human and
"Off-Planet Cultures on Mars."

> Remote viewing exercises by former US military and intelligence
> remote viewers report the possible existence of a present Martian
> Off-Planet Culture, humanoid in form, living under the surface of
> Mars, as well as on Earth in underground bases in the United States
> of America, and in intentional rural colonies in South America.[71]

One may guess where former CIA-agent Robert David Steele got his
information . . .

In 2010, Webre even sent a petition to the Canadian government
applying for the position as Representative of "New Earth" in the
Regional Galactic Governance Council of advanced human civilizations.
The petition read: "We support Alfred Lambremont Webre as an Earth
Representative to the Regional Galactic Governance Council with of the
Pleiadians, the Alpha Centaurians, the Sirians, and others, and we support
the Living Platform for a New Earth Community."[72]

In his latest book, Webre outlines his theories about how the
"Galactic Governance Council" will save us from the evil "Annunaki/
Archons" that have captured Earth in a "Matrix prison" and are involved

in "Galactic Pedocriminal Trade." The book reads like a mix between the worldviews of David Icke and José Argüelles, as well as Arthur C. Clarke's sci-fi classic *Childhood's End*. Making sense of his logic is not easy. In order to escape the malevolent aliens' transhumanist plans of terraforming the planet, we have to join together in a collective consciousness and choose another timeline: "As a collective consciousness, humanity can find itself on a changed timeline from a more catastrophic lane (global coastal flooding event) to a more positive plane (landing utopia on Earth)."[73]

The narrative of extraterrestrial contact and an impending shift in consciousness has also been spread through films such as *Thrive* (2011) and the Thrive Movement. Sacha Stone appeared in the sequel *Thrive II* (2020) and views the initiators, Kimberly and Foster Gamble, as icons and friends. Sacha has also appeared in several other films together with, among others, Foster Gamble, Michael Tellinger, and Dr. David Martin, where they talk about how new advanced extraterrestrial technology will save humanity.

According to Webre, the solution to humanity's problems and the creation of the "New Earth" include teleportation technology, synthetic meat, digital direct democracy, advanced extraterrestrial health technology, and total debt relief. This sounds like some form of space technocracy, an extraterrestrial great reset. Part of the resistance seems, with the willing assistance of a gang of pseudo-spiritual con artists and UFO-cultists, to have gotten lost in space . . .

"Earth Is Our Common Home"

In many ways, the philosophy of New Earth corresponds with that of Mayan calendar interpreter José Argüelles (1939–2011). Unsurprisingly, Sacha and José were friends. Before the founding of the New Earth Project, both were involved in the 2012 movement with, among others, new age guru and World Future Society members Barbara Marx Hubbard (1929–2019) and Ervin László.

Both Sacha and José were involved in the project Earth Is Our Common Home, an international network of noospheric eco-communities, peace cities, and villages, connected as a single human community for the "total reunification of heaven and earth." Other project members included Russian cult leader Vissarion ("Siberian Jesus"), Rudolf Schneider from the Alice Bailey–inspired Institute for Planetary Synthesis, new age futurist Barbara Marx Hubbard, and Russian Nina Goncharova.[74] In her book about the project, Goncharova quotes Pierre Teilhard de Chardin:

> The outcome of the world, the gates of the future, the entry into the super-human—these are not thrown open to a few of the privileged nor to one chosen people to the exclusion of all others. They will open only to an advance of all together, in a direction in which all together can join and find completion in a spiritual renovation of the earth.[75]

Sacha was described as one of the chosen "world citizens" in this global network which, in cooperation with the UN and UNESCO, was to usher in the shift to a new order and "the birth of a united humanity." The various projects of the 2012 movement were created in anticipation of an expected transition to the noosphere and "the dawn of the Golden Age." As described in the New Earth Project Blueprint:

> For the first time in history, advanced IT solutions, information networking and self-organising communities make it possible for natural actions and reactions to be heard across the planet.
>
> The human family collectively determines the way in which this dynamic network evolves. As an essential aspect of the Noosphere, it becomes a conscious entity in its own right, allowing humanity to guide itself toward the manifestation of NewEarth.[76]

In other words, Sacha's New Earth Project largely overlaps with the ideas of José Argüelles, and was symbolically launched on December 21, 2012.[77] This was the very date popularized by Argüelles as the end of the Mayan calendar and the start of a new enlightened era. Argüelles was also one of the main proponents of Oliver Reiser's vision of a "cosmic temple of wisdom," and Teilhard de Chardin's Omega Point theory, together with Ervin László.

Besides Argüelles writing the postscript of László's book *Worldshift 2012*, they arranged the 2009 Noosphere Forum in Bali as part of the "Earth Is Our Common Home" project, which included transhumanist notions of developing new telepathic abilities through brain-computer interface technology and to "explore the possibilities of a new science based on the expansion of our mental powers synchronized with the solar-terrestrial electromagnetic fields, including preparation for two way communication with ETI (Extra-terrestrial intelligence)."[78]

The extraterrestrial theme has been a part of the new age narrative for many decades. From Argüelles's book *Manifesto for the Noosphere:*

> A common theme of the messages from the extra-terrestrial civilization is that the UFOs will appear en masse in 2012. They will render nuclear weaponry impotent. There will be a quantum shift, a splitting of the worlds. The UFOs will take those who have not completed their learning. The rest will remain here on the New Earth. The Noosphere will be their new consciousness. A new Golden Age will begin. Noosphere is the first stage of the genuinely cosmic civilization on Earth.[79]

Argüelles, planning to gather 144,000 followers to celebrate the Great Shift on December 21, 2012, alas died of peritonitis in March 2011. No visible UFOs appeared on the day of the alleged shift.

Conclusion

It is quite understandable that many who have concerns about the totalitarian direction in which the world seems to be heading may be attracted by new age visions of a better, more just, peaceful, loving, and abundant world. However, just like the green movement and the radical left of the 1960s and 1970s who protested against multinational corporations only to later end up on the same team, there is a risk that *some* of today's freedom fighters and visionaries may be led straight into a rainbow-colored version of the same technocratic world order they are opposing. All roads seem to lead to Rome . . . or Sirius?

Fortunately, however, all through the general confusion both in the mainstream and the alternative sphere during the so-called pandemic, there have also been many serious initiatives and a number of concerned doctors, nurses, psychologists, lawyers, journalists, scientists, economists, politicians, entertainers, entrepreneurs, and private citizens who chose to speak out, in many cases risking their careers, reputations, and livelihoods by doing so.

Most of these were never given a chance to voice their well-founded warnings, personal experiences, or scientific analyses in the mainstream media but have had to use alternative media, independent conferences, and smaller publishing houses to get their messages out, offering level-headed guidance and clarity based on real scientific method, empathy, and common sense.

Some of us who had been researching global power structures for years, or even decades, were less surprised about what happened. Others soon realized that something was seriously wrong and began looking deeper into what could cause a whole world to go crazy overnight.

Here are just a few examples of people who have done excellent reporting, analyses, interviews, writings, or public talks and thereby helped keep their fellow humans sane during one of the most extreme periods in modern times.

Catherine Austin Fitts, economist, USA, *Solari Report*, home.solari
   .com
Derrick Broze, journalist, USA, theconsciousresistance.com/
Dr. John Campbell, former nurse, health educator, UK, youtube
   .com/@Campbellteaching
James Corbett, journalist, Japan, *Corbett Report*, corbettreport.com
Ivor Cummins, biochemical engineer, complex problem solving spe-
   cialist, Ireland, *Fat Emperor podcast*, youtube.com
   /@IvorCumminsScience; thefatemperor.com
Mattias Desmet, psychologist, Belgium, substack.com/@mattiasdesmet

Andrija Klaric, gym owner, lockdown protest organizer, interviewer, Croatia, *Slobodni podcast*, bitchute.com/channel/4LmnJn8cNEif

Philipp Kruse, lawyer, Switzerland, kruse-law.ch/de/ueber-mich.php

Sasha Latypova, ex–pharmaceutical executive, United States, sashalaty-pova.com

Dr. Joseph Mercola, health educator, MD, United States, mercola.com

Dr. Meryl J. Nass, MD, United States, *Door to Freedom*, doortofree-dom.org

Dr. Sven Román, MD, Sweden, *Doctors Appeal*, doctorsappeal.com

Yurie Rosca, politician, Moldova, arcaluinoe.info

Freddie Sayers, journalist, UK, *UnHerd*, youtube.com/c/UnHerd

Johnny Vedmore, journalist, UK, *Unlimited Hangout*, unlimitedhang-out.com/author/johnnyvedmoregmail-com

Whitney Webb, journalist, author, United States, *Unlimited Hangout*, unlimitedhangout.com/author/whitney-webb

Bret Weinstein & Heather Heying, evolutionary biologists, *Darkhorse podcast*, youtube.com/@DarkHorsePod

Richard Werner, economist, UK, professorwerner.org

Ernst Wolff, journalist, author, Germany, ernstwolff.com

Patrick Wood, author, United States, *Technocracy News and Trends*, technocracy.news

Rypke Zeilmaker, journalist, author, Netherlands, *Interessante Tijden*, interessantetijden.nl

There are many more, from all over the world.

Great Transition
The Promise and Lure of the Times Ahead

PAUL RASKIN

TARIQ BANURI

GILBERTO GALLOPÍN

PABLO GUTMAN

AL HAMMOND

ROBERT KATES

ROB SWART

Great Transition cover

10

The Transition

While popular among some environmental and anarchistic sub-cultures, it is difficult to visualize a plausible path from the glo-balizing trends of today to Eco-communalism, that does not pass through some form of Barbarization.[1]

Preparations for achieving the promised utopian paradise have to be meticulously crafted, and all possible outcomes must be considered and planned for. In the end, this means that our existing civilization, with all its arduously accomplished relative equality, justice, democracy, safety, and material well-being, may have to be sacrificed.

"Eco-communalism"

Sacha Stone's New Earth Project has many parallels to the eco-communalism scenario in the Great Transition Initiative.

> Eco-communalism is a vision of bio-regionalism, localism, face-to-face democracy and economic autarky.[2] (Raskin et al. 2002, p. 15)

The project's lead author, Club of Rome member Paul D. Raskin, PhD, from Columbia University in New York, was the founder of Tellus Institute and the American department of Stockholm Environment Institute (SEI), which shared offices in Boston. In 1991, Raskin and Gordon Goodman, former executive director of SEI Stockholm, initiated the Pole Star Project to explore scenarios for the creation of a global civilization.

In 1995, this project led to the formation of a Global Scenario Group initiated by, among others, Steven Rockefeller, professor of religion, with funding from UNEP, the Rockefeller Foundation, and the Nippon Foundation. Their mission was to figure out how a global utopian society could be created, based on the UN *Agenda 21* (Agenda for the 21st Century) and the Earth Charter Project (of which Steven was chairman and Raskin a former member). The scenario group produced the report, *Great Transition: The Promises and Lures of the Times Ahead* (2002), presenting ideas that were later further developed in the network Great Transition Initiative, coordinated by Tellus Institute.

> GTI's message of hope aims to counter resignation and pessimism, and help spark a citizens movement for carrying the transition forward.[3]

Through a historical analysis, Raskin's scenario group concluded that the future might develop along three different paths into six possible scenarios:

- **Conventional Worlds**: development proceeding as before by adopting corporate market solutions. Either through economic growth, deregulation and privatisation (**Market Forces**) or through government-led reforms that create a green economy and eradicate poverty (**Policy Reforms**).
- **Barbarization**: the current system is unable to handle socioeconomic and environmental crises. In one scenario, this means authoritarian responses to the crises, where the elite protect themselves in enclaves, with everyone on the outside living in poverty (**Fortress World**). In the other a complete breakdown of the system, with environmental disasters and collapsed social institutions (**Breakdown**).
- **Great Transitions**: new values and institutions are created based on quality of life, solidarity and sustainability, either in local eco villages (**Eco-Communalism**) or, as in Raskin's ideal scenario

(New Sustainability Paradigm), in sustainable smart cities founded on economic interdependence, cultural cross-fertilization, and global solidarity.

Taxonomy of the Future

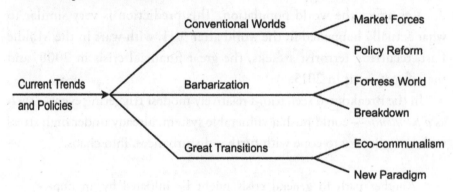

"Barbarization"

The transition to such a sustainable utopia may, however, be painful.

> While popular among some environmental and anarchistic subcultures, it is difficult to visualize a plausible path from the globalizing trends of today to Eco-communalism, that does not pass through some form of Barbarization. (Raskin 2002, p. 15)

When the pandemic was announced, followed by lockdowns and other authoritarian restrictions taking a heavy toll on smaller businesses across the world and dividing both families and nations, we seem to already be in the early stages of the "Fortress World" scenario: a world in a state of emergency, where authoritarian government interventions can suddenly deprive us of our fundamental freedoms.

> The dark belief underlying the Breakdown variant is that the world faces an unprecedented calamity in which unbridled population and economic growth leads to ecological collapse, rampaging conflict and institutional disintegration. (Raskin 2002, p. 18)

According to Raskin, this includes environmental crises, food shortages, and pandemics—leading to a major health crisis!

These crises make the current world order start breaking down. Criminal syndicates and terrorism thrive, violence escalates, polarization between social groups increases, while environmental crises and diseases affect the world population. This prediction is very similar to what actually happened in the world after 9/11, with wars in the Middle East, recurring terrorist attacks, the great financial crisis in 2008, and the refugee crisis in 2015.

In the Breakdown scenario, a relatively modest triggering event—such as *a pandemic*—could push a vulnerable system, already under high stress with low capacity to cope with further disturbances, into chaos.

> Another path to general crisis might be initiated by an unprecedented pandemic; perhaps via an extremely contagious disease vector that emerges from disrupted ecosystems and is carried to the four corners of the Earth by a highly mobile affluent population and by waves of impoverished refugees fleeing the spreading chaos.[4]
> (Raskin et al. 2006)

"Yin-Yang – A Global Citizens Movement"

According to the Great Transition scenarios, in the early 2010s, just before "the 2015 mega-crisis," a global civil rights movement called Yin-Yang would emerge, gathering young people with demands for global change. "Although it was derisively referred to as the Children's Crusade at the time, the unified youth movement was a critical partner in the coalition for a new global deal that led to the Global Reform process."

The parallels to the global climate marches and Greta Thunberg's climate strikes, with their demands on world leaders for reform of the system, are obvious.

> The **YIN** (Youth International Network) was a cultural movement that advanced alternative lifestyles, liberatory values and non-materialistic paths to fulfillment.

> The **YANG** (Youth Action for a New Globalization) was a loose
> political coalition of activist NGOs that eventually were forged into
> a more cohesive network through a long series of global protests and
> actions. (Raskin 2002, p. 85)

YIN is described as having its roots in the 1960s hippie movement while
YANG continues the legacy of political activism for civil rights and the
environment.*

> The Crisis unleashed a widespread social revolt against the domi-
> nance of global corporations, against a quarter century of appalling
> environmental degradation, and against the persistence of poverty
> and social squalor amidst great wealth. (Raskin 2002, p. 80)

Initially, YIN and YANG would be separate movements, but after
2015, they would begin to merge, according to the *Great Transition*
scenarios.

"Alliance for Global Salvation"

In the "Fortress World" scenario, the Yin-Yang movement is not sufficient
to create the necessary changes before the world descends into chaos. At
the peak of the crisis, international military, corporate, and governance
bodies unite in an Alliance for Global Salvation to restore order.

> Using a revamped United Nations as their platform, a state of plan-
> etary emergency is declared. A campaign of overwhelming force,
> rough justice and draconian police measures sweeps through hot
> spots of conflict and discontent. (Raskin 2002, p. 27)

This sounds very much like the global authoritarian governance for creating a sustainable society proposed by the Club of Rome, James Lovelock,

---

* As documented in *Rockefeller: Controlling the Game*, the 1960s youth movements (both hippie
  and activist) have been influenced from above right from the start.

and Swedish utilitarian philosopher Torbjörn Tännsjö, who made the following prediction in 2018:

> The establishment of a global governance may be through a coup, a kind of existential leap, in which the sovereign nation states are forced to cease to exist. A global government in the form of a global despotic rule takes over. Democracy can come later, in the form of a long-term reform project, much like democracy has been established within existing non-democratic nation states.[5]

With an upgraded United Nations as a platform, according to Raskin, a global emergency is declared! Then a campaign is launched in which authoritarian measures and military means are used to end the unrest. This gives rise to a dualistic system—a global apartheid! The rich live in protected and privileged areas (Fortress) while the poor majority forced to live in the police state outside the fort is denied fundamental freedoms. "The authorities use high-tech surveillance and old-fashioned brutality to control social unrest and migration, and to protect valued environmental resources."

"New Earth Order"

In 2016, Raskin wrote a sequel to the *Great Transition* report called *Journey to Earthland: The Great Transition to Planetary Civilization*, envisioning a harsh militant alliance called New Earth Order (NEO).

> The NEO putsch met with pockets of opposition, but organized resistance collapsed in disarray as a planet-wide state of emergency was declared and civil rights suspended. The authorities unified national militaries of the willing into a "peace brigade" to enforce their cynical "3S" program: Stability, Security, and Sustainability. Using the revamped UN as a coordinating platform and legal cover, the NEO forces swept through hot spots, launching sporadic shock and awe attacks.[6] (Raskin 2016, p. 43)

According to an earlier GTI scenario from 1997, such a society benefits only the superrich supranational elite, the 1 percent: "In Barbarization-Fortress World, global income grows very slowly as few become much richer and the many get somewhat poorer."[7]

The scenarios from Great Transition reports clearly overlap with the Rockefeller Foundation report *Scenarios for the Future of Technology and International Development*, especially its "Lock Step" scenario: "A world of tighter top-down government control and more authoritarian leadership, with limited innovation and growing citizen pushback."[8]

According to the most pessimistic of Raskin's scenarios, the brutal regime will last for half a century before the beast begins to falter and pockets of freedom begin to emerge here and there.

In his favorite scenario, on the other hand, the global civil rights movement, in the face of the threat of a possible "Fortress World," succeeds in gathering support for its demands for reform. "Ironically, the authoritarian NEO threat triggered a massive public reaction that further fuelled the GCM and the politics of deep reform."[9]

Thus, the growing pushback ultimately enables the Great Transition. Will real-life movements such as World Freedom Alliance be part of this? How will they avoid becoming used by the very powers they rebel against? According to Raskin, the Global Citizens Movement (GCM) had already initiated sociopolitical experiments with Earthland communities. As described in his essay "Earthland: Scenes from a Civilized Future": "The movement became a living socio-political experiment in creating an Earthlandic community, with each jolt of the Rolling Crisis galvanizing new adherents and enhancing its clout."

This sounds very much like the goals of New Earth Project with "pioneering social experiments serving as nationwide exemplars for the ideal sustainable, conscious community."[10]

"Scenes from a Civilized Future"

If the opposition during the Reform era (2028–2048) in Raskin's final scenario, "Destination: Scenes from a Civilized Future," succeeds in overthrowing the NEO, the UN will establish a New Global Deal, "an enlightened international government," where the old sustainability agenda is resumed, with the goal to create "a resilient economy within the planetary boundaries" (this sounds very much like the Green New Deal proposed in the United States and the EU). In this scenario, the global movement demands reforms to create a "global social democracy" and the creation of an Earthland Parliamentary Assembly.[11]

In 2048 (one hundred years after the first World Constitution was formulated at the University of Chicago), Raskin envisions the creation of a World Constitution, whereafter the Commonwealth of Earthland is instituted. The world constitution is built upon the existing 1948 Universal Declaration of Human Rights, the 1992 Earth Summit's Agenda 21, and the 2000 Earth Charter, and a fictional 2023 Declaration of Interdependence by the GCM.[12] (In real life, David Suzuki wrote a Declaration of Interdependence for the 1992 Earth Summit).[13]

According to Raskin, natural resources should belong to all the world's citizens, while decisions should be based on the wisdom of the people through direct democracy made possible by the internet and mutual cooperation. He stated that: "A third macro-shift in the human condition is underway with implications as far-reaching as those of previous great transformations. History has entered the Planetary Phase of Civilization."

Just as in the old Soviet state propaganda, the sustainable paradise will come later, *after* the rule of harsh authoritarianism. Ideally, the "new sustainability paradigm" will emerge after the reform work is completed. As Raskin describes it:

> The fabric of global society is woven with diverse communities.
> Some are abuzz with cultural experimentation, political inten-
> sity and technical innovation. Others are slow-paced bastions of
> traditional culture, direct democracy and small-is-beautiful tech-
> nology. A few combine reflection, craft skill and high esthetics
> into a kind of "sophisticated simplicity," reminiscent of the Zen
> art of antiquity. Most are admixtures of countless subcultures.
> The plurality of ways is deeply cherished for the choice it offers

individuals and the richness it offers social life. (Raskin et al. 2002, p. 44)

The "old order" of extremes, such as globalism-nationalism and cosmopolitanism-localism, has finally been dissolved and replaced by family-group-region and a global society. Supervising it all is the World Union (formerly the United Nations), the World Court, and the World Regulatory Authority. A global federation for cooperation, security, and sustainability. Governance is handled by a decentralized network of states, corporations, and civil society.[14]

This scenario is eerily similar to the scenario Clever Together from the Rockefeller Foundation's report *Scenarios for the Future of Technology and International Development*:

Nation-states lost some of their power and importance as global architecture strengthened and regional governance structures emerged. International oversight entities like the UN took on new levels of authority, as did regional systems like the Association of Southeast Asian Nations (ASEAN), the New Partnership for Africa's Development (NEPAD), and the Asian Development Bank (ADB). (Rockefeller Foundation 2010, p. 27)

In their version of the future, you are free to manage your affairs—as long as they fall within the framework of what the World Union has defined as right and proper. Back to Raskin: "Social and environmental goals at each scale define the 'boundary conditions' for those nested within it. Subject to these constraints, the freedom to fashion local solutions is considerable—but conditional." (Raskin et al. 2002, p. 44)

If disorder and violence arise, the "peace forces" are called in. The consumer society has been abandoned in favor of a balanced circular economy, where everything is kept within the planetary boundaries of an eco-utopia where human activities are controlled and where the energy system is based on renewable energy such as solar, wind, biomass, and water.

Population stabilization, low-meat diets and compact settlements reduce the human footprint, sparing land for nature. Global warming is abating as greenhouse gas emissions return to pre-industrial levels. Ecosystems are restored and endangered species are returning, although scars remain as reminders of past heedlessness. (Raskin et al. 2002, p. 45)

The coming World State would, according to Raskin, include three systems (with names inspired by Ancient Greece):

- **Agoria**: a Social Democrat–inspired system (like in Sweden) founded in equality and permitting capitalism, but with regulated and socially-ecologically responsible businesses.
- **Ecodemia**: a Socialist-inspired system with large worker-owned corporations, non-profits, highly regulated small businesses and publicly-controlled investment banks for entrepreneurs —if they fulfill social and environmental requirements.
- **Arcadia**: an Anarchist-inspired system with self-sufficient small-scale communities, based on simpler lifestyles with folk crafts and tradition, yet creative, innovative, and connected with cosmopolitan culture and world affairs.[15]

Raskin's time line ends in 2084—exactly two hundred years after the socialist think tank Fabian Society was founded in London and—even more fittingly—one hundred years after the dystopian novel *Nineteen Eighty-Four* by George Orwell.

1980–2001 Takeoff
2001–2023 Rolling Crisis
2023–2028 General Emergency
2028–2048 Reform Era
2028–2084 Commonwealth of Earthland

Like most utopian visions, it all seems hopelessly unrealistic. Clearly inspired by Jesuit transhumanist Pierre Teilhard de Chardin's metaphysical ideas about the "planetary phase," these scenarios reveal a naive idealism and childish belief that humans can be remolded so as to fit snugly into a new "perfect system" of someone else's design.

It is also a sign of pathological megalomania to make a plan for how people in the future will live and organize their lives, and then to try to implement this plan operationally on a global scale. As history has shown us, previous attempts to realize such visions usually do not end well.

The Widening Circle

In 2010, The Great Transition Initiative also initiated the project "The Widening Circle—Campaign for Advancing a Global Citizens Movement," through which the visions of the new global civilization could be spread. "TWC would engage myriad individuals and organizations in articulating a shared planetary consciousness and coordinating actions to elicit public sympathy and influence decision-making.[16]

Through initiatives such as Ervin László's Club of Budapest, *Kosmos Journal*, and Earth Charter (coordinated by Steven Rockefeller in the 1990s), TWC spread to both the New Age movement (loosely associated with the United Nations via Lucis Trust) and the environmental movement.

TWC also included former Soviet leader Mikhail Gorbachev (cochairman of the Earth Charter project), who had previously launched the initiative "Creating a New Civilization" with Japanese Goi Peace Foundation, the Club of Rome, and the Club of Budapest (the latter two of which he was also a member), where he made the following appeal: "We need effective global systems in an interdependent world, where everything is globalized including finance, resources and trade. Without vision and political will to build a new world order, nothing will change, and without a positive push from civil society, politics will not change."[17]

Gorbachev shared similar messages in other fora, including in his position as chairman of the World Political Forum in Turin.

The Hungarian systems philosopher Ervin László, who led the Club of Rome project "Goals for Mankind" in the 1970s (proposing an ideal world population of 500 million) had good connections with some of the more prominent leaders of the New Age movement.[18] He was also involved in the United Nations project "New International Economic Order" and in the creation of a mass movement founded in these visions. According to Laszlo: "The global transformation will require the awakening of a new social actor: a vast movement of global citizens expressing a supranational identity and building new institutions for a planetary age."

In 1993, László founded the Club of Budapest, "dedicated to developing a new way of thinking and a new ethics that will help resolve the social, political, economic, and ecological challenges of the 21st century" and "to be a catalyst for the transformation to a sustainable world through promoting the emergence of planetary consciousness and interconnecting generations and cultures."[19]

László's book *Worldshift 2012* (with a foreword by Gorbachev) outlines his visions of a world system where nation-states will all be included in federations such as the European Union, the African Union, the North American Union, etc., and where the UPO, United Peoples Organization (replacing the United Nations), will govern a World Army and make decisions on global issues concerning peace, security, environmental protection, information/communication, and finance. UPO would politically include representatives from the regional federations, and also thousands of NGOs and business organizations. There is also the vision of a World Environment Organization (WEO) to coordinate environmental programs in the regional federations. However, just like the EU, everything must be based on the "subsidiarity principle," which means that social and political issues should be dealt with at the most immediate or local level. At the lowest level, direct democracy must be applied (digitally if the distances are too long). Regional currencies will replace national and a new global currency called Gaia used for transnational trade (László envisioned this to be realized by 2020).[20]

László's visions bear many similarities with the "cosmic temple of wisdom" described in philosophy professor Oliver Reiser's posthumously published book *Cosmic Humanism and World Unity* (1975), of which László was editor. László has thereafter continued disseminating these ideas through fora such as the Club of Budapest.[21] Reiser in turn was inspired by Alice Bailey's neo-theosophy, allegedly dictated to her telepathically by the Tibetan Djwahl Kuhl. In the foreword to her book *Education in the New Age* Reiser wrote:

> We need not only the political synthesis of a World Federation in which the Eastern and Western hemispheres function like the right and left lobes of man's brain, with the seat of the World Brain serving as the point of decussation of the planetary nerves, but we need also a planetary way of life, a planetary ethics, and a planetary way of feeling to supply the powerful drive we shall require for the great tasks that lie ahead of us.[22]

This is exactly what László preaches. In his latest book *Global Shift NOW* (2020), he views the pandemic as an opportunity: "This is a great experiment, a great experiment in creating the next step in human evolution. So Global Shift NOW is a precious opportunity. It is in a way a blessing in disguise that we have such a crisis."[23]

Using crises as opportunities, a new ethics and a new system will be shaped. This was pointed out by Reiser already in 1942, and again by WEF chairman Klaus Schwab when presenting the Great Reset in June 2020:

> The COVID-19 crisis is affecting every facet of people's lives in every corner of the world. But tragedy need not be its only legacy. On the contrary, the pandemic represents a rare but narrow window of opportunity to reflect, reimagine, and reset our world to create a healthier, more equitable, and more prosperous future.[24]

Schwab's book *Stakeholder Capitalism* (2021) also presents a world system with many similarities to the visions of László and Raskin. Schwab also mentions the subsidiarity principle, ironically referring to the EU.[25] Considering the fact that Schwab's Fourth Industrial Revolution is not something that has been requested by the grassroots, his talk of "subsidiarity" sounds like an empty sales pitch.

How well has this principle worked in the EU, with its leaders coming directly from the WEF and the Trilateral Commission?

For those of us living in the EU, it has proven to be a totally top-down system. The only thing "local" in this system is that the EU member states are required to make EU directives into national law to be enforced by local authorities.

Changing Images of Man

Ervin László also participated as referee in the Stanford Research Institute (SRI) project "Changing Images of Man" in the early 1970s. SRI International at Stanford University had close links to the US federal government, the U.S. Department of Defense, and the CIA and develops surveillance technologies and AI for these entities.[26] Stanford's Center for the Study of Social Policy was established in 1968 by U.S. Department of Education to "investigate alternative future possibilities for the society and their implications for educational policy."[27]

The center studied "World Macro Problems" in order to formulate a plan for how the world needed to develop in order to meet future challenges and to change humankind into one that could better live up to the demands of the postindustrial era. These ambitions, bearing many similarities to the ideas of the Club of Rome, were later included in the 1982 report *Changing Images of Man*. The project was led by futurists Willis Harman, and O.W. Markley. According to their analysis, the future could develop along two different paths:

- **Technological Extrapolation**: A Technocratic central planning system with an expert/elite rule where the free time of citizens have been institutionalized and techniques for behavior modification are used economically, politically, and socially. The social trend is increasing urbanization into mega cities.

- **Evolutionary Transformation**: A balanced, politically and economically decentralized society with less technology and more spare time, fewer behavior modification techniques, except when deemed necessary by the group. Economically egalitarian with dependence on holistic expertise and greater participation from citizens in planning. Technical and scientific development is adapted to the new "moral" paradigm. This includes a greater awareness of the world we live in.

These were the two polar opposites in the dialectical game. Choosing the right course was essential to minimize the negative effects during the Great Transition. An action plan was presented to governments, corporations, and NGOs on using social engineering to lead humankind to the desired utopia. However, a warning was also included:

> Methods of regulation that severely reduce individual freedoms could be welcomed in the face of severe disruptions. We could quickly or, more likely, gradually emerge into the kind of society that Bertram Gross (1970) has termed "friendly fascism." This is a fascism that "will come under the slogans of democracy and 100 percent Americanism . . . in the form of an advanced technological society, supported by its techniques—a techno-urban fascism, American style." (*Changing Images of Man*, p. 169)

The fear was that László's and Willis Harman's vision of an ideal society would be kidnapped by the industrial elite in order to be unilaterally transformed into the Technological Extrapolation (or Fortress World) scenario. Likely, there would be a synthesis of the two possible futures. In any case, some form of authoritarian reaction was considered necessary for the transition to the desired postindustrial society (Evolutionary Transformation).

Regulation and restraint of behavior will be necessary in order to hold the society together while it goes around a difficult corner. The more there can be general understanding of the transitory but inescapable nature of this need, the higher will be the likelihood that a more permanent authoritarian regime can be avoided. (*Changing Images of Man*, p. 198)

For people to endure the transition, the promise of a better world after the ordeal was needed; the vision of a new Paradise.

Funding for *Changing Images of Man* came from the Charles Kettering Foundation, one of the early funders of the Trilateral Commission and a close associate of the Rockefeller sphere. The project can be seen as part of the Trilateral plan to create the Technetronic Society (with the help of SRI's futurists).[28] In this plan, new age thought was to play an important role. As Lynn Picknett and Clive Prince note about the SRI project in their book *Stargate Conspiracy*: "The only resource for those in positions of power and authority was for them to actively hijack the belief systems that underpinned this social unrest, moving it in whatever direction gave them the greatest advantage and retaining their control over the masses."[29]

Sacha Stone's New Earth Project appears to have been inspired by Raskin's and László's Utopian visions of the future.

There would likely be experiments with a diversity of living environments to allow people a greater range of trade-offs in selecting a community. In such a context, there may emerge increasingly sophisticated communal types of living environments which experiment with new institutional forms. (*Changing Images of Man*, p. 177)

Hand circuit board

11

The Digital ID

Digital technologies, such as cloud computing, biometrics, mobile networks and devices, and smartcards, can increase the security, accuracy, and convenience of identifying and authenticating individuals. As public and private service providers increasingly transition into the digital realm, the ability to prove who you are will be essential for participation in the digital environment.[1]

If the coup is successful, full control is achieved. Therefore, it is of essence to make sure that no one escapes the watching eye of the powers that be, and that the new order is respected and its decrees followed to the letter.

ID2020

A digital identity for all citizens of the world has been offered by the World Bank Group and the World Economic Forum as a key component in achieving the 17 Global Goals of Agenda 2030.[2] The right to a legal identity is one of the targets of Goal 16 (Peace, Justice and Strong Institutions), and more precisely, target 9 (Provide universal legal identity for all, including birth registrations).

For this purpose, ID2020 was created — a public-private partnership between UN agencies, the World Economic Forum, private foundations, and Big Tech. Their agenda, however, raises some concerns regarding mass surveillance, population control, and loss of personal integrity. At the helm of this project, we find once again Bill Gates and the Rockefeller Foundation.

ID2020 was founded in New York 2014 by John Edge, an expert on how public-private partnerships can solve the Global Goals using blockchain and artificial intelligence technologies.[3] The organization, supported by law firm Kaye Scholer, technology conglomerate Red Rose Corporation, and merchant bank Broadhaven, held its first meeting in September 2015. This meeting coincided with the adoption of the United Nations Agenda 2030.

The stated mission of ID2020 was to provide a digital identity to everyone through "leveraging start-up models" and in the end create a system that would span the globe, including the 1 billion people that currently have no proper identification.[4]

In May 2016, ID2020 got a more solid foundation at the United Nations annual summit, gathering industry leaders, NGOs, governments, emerging tech pioneers, and cross-industry experts to "build the enabling conditions for the creation of a legal digital identity for all individuals at risk."[5] Speakers came from the World Bank, The European Association for e-Identity & Security, Commonwealth Secretariat, Center for Information Assurance and Cybersecurity, MIT, PSG Solutions, LLC., and Verizon. Several of the speakers were also contributors to the World Economic Forum, which has since been a significant player in the development of a digital ID.

The main topics at the summit were focused on how identities for refugees could be handled and how the Global Goals could be advanced through public-private partnerships. The European refugee crisis in 2015 following the war in Syria had highlighted the problem with "paperless refugees" who could not prove their identity. The solution was soon to be made available—a digital ID, using emerging technologies like blockchain and worldwide broadband connectivity.

The rapid proliferation of smart devices globally, combined with ever-increasing computing power and rapidly expanding broadband coverage, enables new methods of registration and facilitates ongoing interaction between individuals and their identity data. New technologies, including blockchain, when used in conjunction with long-proven technologies, such as biometrics, now make it possible for all people to have access to a safe, verifiable, and persistent form of technology. (ID2020, "Digital identity")

One year later, at the annual summit 2017, held in the UN ECOSOC Chamber, ID2020 adopted the "Platform of Change" and initiated the ID2020 Alliance, with funding from major donor the Rockefeller Foundation and the digital tech consultant firm Accenture. Cofounders were GAVI, Microsoft, and IDEO.org (a design/consultant firm).[6] Alliance partners included Intel, IBM, Verizon, Samsung, NEC, and SAP, exemplifying the tight connection between foundations, Big Tech, and vaccine/health interests. The Alliance had an action plan:

By 2030, the Alliance aims to have facilitated the scaling of a safe, verifiable, persistent digital identity system, consistent with Sustainable Development Goal 16.9. From 2017 to 2020, the Alliance's work will focus on two areas: developing and testing the best technological solutions for digital identity; and, working with governments and existing, established agencies to implement these solutions.[7] (ID2020 Alliance)

Speakers at the summit included representatives from the aforementioned partners as well as UN agencies like UNDP, The UN Refugee Agency, and OCHA (Office for the Coordination of Humanitarian Affairs). A key question was: "What prevented the solution to this challenge?" (The perfect problem for the implementation of their Big Brother solution would soon emerge.)

A white paper from World economic Forum, *Digital Borders*, published 2017, stated that "[i]n the current global geopolitical and security context, the issue of security is foremost. From terrorism to the fear of pandemics, government, business leaders and travellers alike are concerned about security and safety as they cross borders."[8]

Board members of the ID2020 Alliance included Dr. Seth Berkley, CEO of GAVI. He was also a member of CFR and previously involved with the International AIDS Vaccine Initiative (IAVI), the Health Science Division at the Rockefeller Foundation, the Center for Infectious Diseases, and the U.S. Centers for Disease Control (CDC). He was also a longtime contributor and participant at the World Economic Forum. Other board members had been working with the U.S. Department of Defense, JPMorgan Chase, UBS, Microsoft, Accenture, and Morgan Stanley.

Another intriguing coincidence is that one of the advisers of ID2020 is the futurist Peter Schwartz, a specialist "in scenario planning, working with corporations, governments, and institutions to create alternative perspectives of the future and develop robust strategies for a changing and uncertain world" and currently employed as senior vice president of Global Government Relations and Strategic Planning at Salesforce. As mentioned in chapter 10, Schwartz led the Royal Dutch Shell Scenario Team in the 1980s, which famously predicted the fall of the Soviet Union.[9] His climate change report, written for the Pentagon in 2004, forecasting European cities underwater and Britain as a Siberian wasteland by 2020, did, however, somewhat mar his reputation.[10]

As chairman of the company Global Business Network, Peter Schwartz was also involved in the Rockefeller Foundation report *Scenarios for the Future of Technology and International Development* (2010). Schwartz wrote in the foreword of the report:

> The Rockefeller Foundation has already used this project as an opportunity to clarify and advance the relationship between technology and development. Through interviews and the scenario workshops,

they have engaged a diverse set of people—from different geographies, disciplines, and sectors—to identify the key forces driving change, to explore the most critical uncertainties, and to develop challenging yet plausible scenarios and implications.[11]

The Rockefeller Foundation clearly views the crisis as an opportunity to reform the system. This transformation might hurt, but in the end their promised digital utopia will arise out of the ashes of the obsolete system. What now plays out is a part of an old population control agenda, initiated by the Rockefeller foundations and now carried out by close partners like the Bill & Melinda Gates Foundation.

Before the pandemic measures started to wreak havoc on the world economy, GAVI CEO Seth Berkley wrote an article for World Economic Forum, published 16 January 2020, indicating what to expect in the future: "At a time of increasing nationalism and a rejection of globalism, infectious disease is a reminder that we are interconnected and all have a stake in global health security."[12]

The COVID-19 outbreak, with all its tragic consequences, happened to be the perfect trigger event to show the world the need for a global coordination and management of the planet, as well as the need for a technological surveillance regime in order to track and monitor all people and diseases (and the global value chains). The remedy comes with tighter surveillance and control. As Bill Gates was quoted saying in an conversation with TED Talk CEO Chris Anderson: "Eventually we will have some digital certificates to show who has recovered or been tested recently or when we have a vaccine who has received it."[13] Bill knew what he was talking about. On May 24, 2019, the EU Commission presented a road map for strengthened cooperation against vaccine-preventable diseases. The goal was a common vaccination card/passport compatible with electronic immunization systems for EU citizens by 2022.[14]

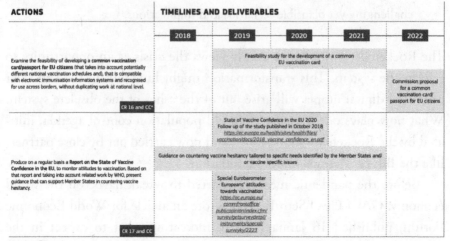

ROADMAP FOR THE IMPLEMENTATION OF ACTIONS BY THE EUROPEAN COMMISSION BASED ON THE COMMISSION COMMUNICATION AND THE COUNCIL RECOMMENDATION ON STRENGTHENING COOPERATION AGAINST VACCINE PREVENTABLE DISEASES

ACTIONS	TIMELINES AND DELIVERABLES				
	2018	2019	2020	2021	2022
Examine the feasibility of developing a **common vaccination card/passport for EU citizens** (that takes into account potentially different national vaccination schedules and), that is compatible with electronic immunisation information systems and recognised for use across borders, without duplicating work at national level. **CR 16 and CC***		Feasibility study for the development of a common EU vaccination card			Commission proposal for a common vaccination card/ passport for EU citizens
Produce on a regular basis a **Report on the State of Vaccine Confidence** in the EU, to monitor attitudes to vaccination. Based on that report and taking into account related work by WHO, present guidance that can support Member States in countering vaccine hesitancy. **CR 17 and CC**		State of Vaccine Confidence in the EU 2020 Follow up of the study published in October 2018 *https://ec.europa.eu/health/sites/health/files/ vaccination/docs/2018_vaccine_confidence_en.pdf*			
		Guidance on countering vaccine hesitancy tailored to specific needs identified by the Member States and/ or vaccine specific issues			
		Special Eurobarometer - Europeans' attitudes towards vaccination *https://ec.europa.eu/ comm/frontoffice/ publicopinion/index.cfm/ survey/getsurveydetail/ instruments/special/ surveyky/2223*			

* Basis for action:
CR for Council Recommendation and the number of the Recommendation in the legal text. CC for Commission Communication

Another issue for the EU Commission was countering vaccine hesitancy, pejoratively called "anti-vaxxers."

The measures for handling the pandemic opened up a path for the ID2020 certification, and in the end for a global digital citizenship—a fundamental pillar in the technocratic Smart Society (4IR) pushed by World Economic Forum to fulfill the 17 goals of Agenda 2030.

Berkley's article coincided with WEF's release of another white paper: *Reimagining Digital Identity: A Strategic Imperative*, written with financial support from the ID2020 partner Accenture. The message was that the world needs a more secure digital identification system due to "fraud, identity theft and misuse or abuse of personal data" in the current fragmented systems.[15]

The white paper partners included ID2020, Accenture, the Bill & Melinda Gates Foundation, Cisco, the World Bank Group, the EU Commission, the UN, and newly founded advocacy groups such as One World Identity, World Identity Network, and Security Identity Alliance. They undertook a big push which, besides refugee identification and disease control, was packaged as a solution to pressing issues like human trafficking and child marriage. But it comes at a price:

> Digital technologies, such as cloud computing, biometrics, mobile networks and devices, and smartcards, can increase the security, accuracy, and convenience of identifying and authenticating individuals. As public and private service providers increasingly transition into the digital realm, the ability to prove who you are will be essential for participation in the digital environment.[16] (World Bank Group, 2020)

In the utopian smart society currently being built, digital identity will be required in order to access all basic human services like healthcare, e-commerce, travel, financial services, and social platforms. This system can then be connected to the "blockchain-enabled citizen loyalty and reward platforms" predicted by the WEF, bringing "peace and order" to the world, just like the social credit system in China.

> The implementation of a global data platform to assess the "risk" level of travellers, if not through actual data, through a type of "credit score," would give governments more accurate information about passengers and better protect their borders and citizens. The ability to effectively prevent the majority of passengers would enable government and border control agencies to more easily single out those that require further investigation.[17]

Some nations, like Sweden and Estonia, are seen as good examples, being ahead of the rest of the world in this regard. Almost everything is done digitally with very small amounts of cash in circulation. In Sweden, it gets increasingly difficult to take part of services and pay for parking tickets or train tickets without a smartphone with a digital bank ID. The communist dictatorship China has been at the forefront with its biometric payment systems, with countries such as Denmark following suit.[18]

In the wake of the COVID-19 crisis, people all over the world, even in countries far behind in terms of digitalization, have during the pandemic been urged to switch from cash to digital payment systems in order to "avoid contagion."

Health Pass

Digital Health Pass

As early as 2016, a health pass had been proposed, to be connected to a WHO database of global vaccination data, enabling countries to refuse any traveler unable to verify an updated vaccination record.[19] The COVID-19 crisis quickly opened up for a rapid implementation of such policies.

In 2019, the Rockefeller Foundation initiated "The Commons Project," focused on using the full potential of digital technology. When the COVID-19 outbreak was announced, the projects CommonHealth, COVIDcheck, and CommonPass were launched, the latter in July 2020 in cooperation with World Economic Forum.

For global travel and trade to return to pre-pandemic levels, travelers will need a secure and verifiable way to document their health status as they travel and cross borders. Countries will need to be able to trust that a traveller's record of a COVID PCR test or vaccination administered in another country is valid.[20] (Common Pass)

In September 2020, the CovidPass was introduced. The app designer, Mustapha Mokass (WEF Global Young Leader 2015), hoped that his app would become "a standardized solution for airlines, airports and border agencies, and eliminate quarantine for healthy travellers. CovidPass could also allow hotels, cinemas, theatres, sporting and concert venues to reopen safely."[21] This means that a digital health pass may be required for virtually all social activity.

Future Chip Implants

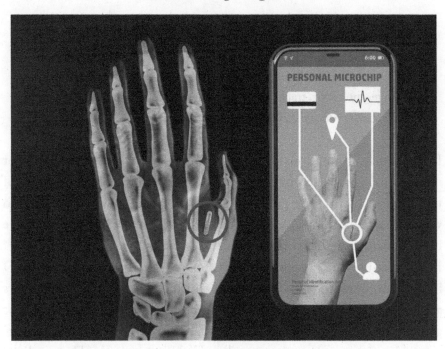

Microchip implant

Pandemics also open up for solutions like new monitoring technology that can be used to count the number of visitors, ensure that distances are kept, and to identify individuals who are unvaccinated or who should be kept from crowds for other reasons, by using data from cell phones, wristbands, and IoT sensors.[22]

For such purposes, a digital ID or pass may also become "necessary." Smartphone devices, smart cards, and biometrics have been used in many current projects for identification, but as a smartphones and cards can be stolen or lost, it is not far-fetched to expect that demands for more secure identification methods, like smart tattoos and implants, will become more frequent as we move closer to 2030. Indeed, this is a development that the World Economic Forum has also predicted in their vision for the Fourth Industrial Revolution. Smart technology devices will, during the coming decade, be integrated with our bodies for behavior monitoring, location data, health functions, and real-time identification.

> Smart tattoos and other unique chips could help with identification and location. Digital tattoos not only look cool but can perform useful tasks, like unlocking a car, entering mobile phone codes with a finger point or tracking body-processes.[23] (Schwab, *The Fourth Industrial Revolution*, 2016)

In the article "Thousands of Swedish people are swapping ID cards for microchips" (published by WEF in 2018), Hannes Sjöblad, founder of the Swedish biohacking group Bionyfiken (Bio-curious), wrote: "Who wants to carry a clumsy smartphone or smartwatch when you can have it in your fingernail? I think that is the direction where it is heading."[24] Early start-ups like Swedish Biohax International have offered RFID implants in humans since 2014, and Danish tech company Bichip offers a chip that can be connected to the internet and has a unique ID for general identification. It can also be used as a payment system "integrateable with cryptocurrency wallets."[25] "BiChip is the First and the Only Distance readable Human Microchip with Internet Connectivity.

Bichip has a unique ID for general identification, and can store your Medical data, Driver license and Passport. It can also be used as an alternative Payment System."[26]

Such invasive technologies are, however, not yet a part of the ID2020 project. For the time being, they are only offered on a voluntary basis for convenience and curiosity by early adopters and tech enthusiasts.

Since 2014, the biohacker movement has arranged conferences, and their initiative Chipster throws parties where people can be "upgraded" with a chip.[27] For now, these "chipsters" constitute only a small fringe group, with its largest following in the progressive Scandinavian countries. This was also noted in 2015 by the Dutch National Office for Identity Data:

> Radio Frequency Identification (RFID) microchip implantation is another mature technology, but its spread is still limited in 2030 due to its invasiveness for users as well as its tagging aspect recalling some inglorious historical precedents. In this respect, biometric technology remains a non-invasive solution for identification and a credible alternative to the use of microchip implants.[28]

In a few years' time, however, that might change. All that is needed, to paraphrase the Club of Rome, is a crisis that fits the purpose.

There is also a new generation with only a vague perception of history and a more positive attitude toward new technologies after growing up with tablets and smart devices. Since the Dutch report was issued, much has changed.

The online ID2020 Summit 2020 is an example of this development, with sessions such as "Digital Immunization Certificates: Designing for a New Era in Global Health" and "Laying the Foundation: Digital ID for the Next Generation." In their vision, no one is to be left behind. It was noted that the pandemic, forcing so many gatherings online, had made the public more aware of digital ID technology and made their joint work "even more urgent."[29]

Internet of Bodies

This development also opens the Internet of Bodies (IoB) where our data can be collected through implanted, swallowed, or worn devices. This is exactly what the World Economic Forum began marketing in connection with the Great Reset.

> With an unprecedented number of sensors attached to, implanted within or ingested into human bodies to monitor, analyse and even modify human bodies and behaviour, immediate actions are needed to address the ethical and legal considerations that come with the IoB. The urgency of such actions is further brought to the forefront by the global COVID-19 pandemic, with extensive IoB technologies and data being enlisted for the surveillance and tracking of coronavirus.[30]

This could have serious consequences for humankind, where our bodies and behaviors may end up in the hands of manipulative forces.

Professor Dirk Helbing from the EU project FuturICT has come to realize how the use of technology is degenerating into serious crimes against humanity. Man becomes reduced to a cell in an almighty world organism or world brain and completely deprived of his autonomy.

> Once a digital ID officially exists, humans could be managed like things. This, however, would fundamentally violate human dignity and contradict the UN Human Rights Charter. Such measures remind of chipped pets or tattoos to mark inmates—and some of the darkest chapters in human history.[31] (Dirk Helbing)

The pursuit of a digital ID ultimately risks fundamentally transforming our place in society, with a humanity that is more or less forced to migrate from the physical to the digital realm. If you as an individual do not accept a digital ID, you risk being denied access to basic services and a decent life.

At the same time, this opens up for solutions such as surveillance technology to count the number of visitors that are unvaccinated, or who are to be kept away from crowds for other reasons. This is already possible by collecting data from mobile phones, bracelets and IoT-sensors.[32] In the near future, there may be demands for a digital ID. This is illustrated by Dutch Royal HaskoningDHV, specialized in the need for surveillance under the slogan "enhancing society together": "Royal HaskoningDHV uses a human-centric design where we harness data to organise space and processes to adapt to the changing needs of inhabitants, visitors and at the same time complying with the strategic policies set by the city's authorities."[33]

Global Health Pass

ID2020 started in 2021, as the Global Health Pass Collaborative with twenty-five leading tech, health, and travel companies and organizations such as Mastercard, IBM, Linux Foundation Public Health, Airports Council International, and Commons Project Foundation.[34]

Former British Prime Minister Tony Blair, chairman of JPMorgan Chase International Council,* gave the project his blessing: "Political leaders should now get behind this. The G20 group of nations should commit to establish a network of globally interoperable health passes, and set up the working groups needed to deliver it."[35]

G20 heeded this call. In August 2021, under the Italian chairmanship, the Digital Economy Working Group was founded, with digital ID as a priority. The G20 Digitalization Ministers wrote in their Declaration:

> We note that during the pandemic, the domestic adoption of digital
> identity to support access to both public and private sector services
> has accelerated. We support technical solutions that are based on
> the users' freely given, specific, and informed consent, and protect

---

* Founded as International Advisory Committee by David Rockefeller in the late 1960s.

citizens' privacy and personal data, within the domestically applicable legal frameworks.[36]

The question was, however, how much informed consent and respect for individual choice their national frameworks would include.

Soon thereafter, US president Joe Biden presented the new controversial vaccine requirements requiring about 100 million Americans, including federal employees, healthcare workers, and some private-sector staff to get vaccinated against the coronavirus in order to keep their jobs.[37]

In the increasingly authoritarian Australia, the Covid Pass was used by authorities to access its citizens' latest health and travel data, and to be able to enforce travel restrictions between states and territories.

The European Digital Identity

On June 3, 2021, the European Commission proposed a European Digital Identity Wallet, a personal digital wallet in the form of an app for storing IDs (such as a driver's license) and official documents (such as medical prescriptions or educational qualifications) in digital form.[38]

The EU Digital COVID Certificate

On June 11, 2022, the Council of the European Union (the second chamber of the European Union) decreed that a vaccine pass (the EU Digital COVID-19 Certificate program) could be used in the EU to facilitate "safe travel" between member states.

By August 2021, the practice had already been adopted by Bulgaria, Denmark, Greece, Croatia, Poland, the Czech Republic, and Germany.[39] Several countries took it even further and implemented what some called a form of "medical apartheid" within their nations.

In France, there were large public protests against (Young Global Leader) Macron's *pass sanitaire*, requiring proof of vaccination or negative test results in order to gain access to hospitals, restaurants, pubs, cafés, shopping malls, museums, cinemas, sports events, amusement parks, libraries, etc.[40] Failure to check guests and enforce this mandate could result in fines up to €45,000 for venue owners.[41] Health workers refusing vaccination risked losing their jobs.

Similar requirements were implemented in Italy. In Cyprus you needed a SafePass for access to supermarkets, taxis, and public transport.

Austria took it a step further. On October 9, 2021, chancellor Sebastian Kurz (Young Global Leader 2009), who was pro-vaccines but opposed *mandatory* vaccinations, had to suddenly resign due to corruption charges. He was swiftly replaced by the federal minister for European and international affairs, the WEF-associated Alexander Schallenberg. On November 19, 2021, the COVID-19 vaccine mandate for residents over eighteen years was announced. It was approved in the Federal Council on February 3, 2022 and included restricted access to public spaces for the unvaccinated and the possibility of issuing fines of up to €3,600 every three months.[42] In early March, only two days before it was to be enforced, it was suspended following the recommendations of a commission of health and legal experts.[43]

In Sweden, the government, media, and social pressure to take the emergency-approved experimental intervention was intense, even though it was "voluntary." After the elderly and then the middle-aged had been treated, the young were next in line (sixteen years or older from autumn 2021 and from twelve years in 2022) even though they were never at risk of getting seriously ill. Vaccine buses would arrive at schools and each student ushered in for their jab. All perfectly voluntary, of course, but who wants to be the odd one out? What teen does not want to help "keep grandma alive"? In order to prevent concerned activists from informing students of potential risks and their right to refuse, police cars would circle the school until the procedure was over.

As for requiring a vaccine pass, Sweden again chose the soft touch. No pass was mandated by the *government* (even though that was called for by the Conservative opposition). Instead, the choice was left to the venue owners themselves. After a dismal year without music concerts, nightclubs, theater, sports matches, etc., many venue owners and event arrangers—and even *churches*—were willing to go along and require a vaccine pass for entry.

International Pandemic Treaty

In September 2020, the Independent Panel for Pandemic Preparedness and Response was established by WHO Director General Tedros Ghebreyesus. The panel was headed by former Prime Minister of New Zealand Helen Clark and former president of Liberia Ellen Johnson Sirleaf.[†] The mission of the panel was to present "an evidence-based path for the future, grounded in lessons of the present and the past to ensure countries and global institutions, including specifically WHO, effectively address health threats."[44] Their report, *Covid-19: Make It the Last Pandemic*, was presented to the World Health Assembly in May 2021.[45]

In March 2022, the WHO initiated a global process to draft and negotiate strengthened International Health Regulations, and a new pandemic prevention, preparedness, and response accord—a legally binding agreement that would afford the WHO nearly unlimited power to keep declaring new pandemics and to regulate in detail the response expected by every region, nation, city, agency, organization, corporation, and individual. The goal was to have the accord adopted at the 77th World Health Assembly in May-June 2024.[46]

However, the negotiations were not finished at the deadline due to disagreements over parts of the treaty. Ghebreyesus blamed "fake news, lies and conspiracy theories" for undermining the process and added that future generations "may not forgive us."[47] Instead, the negotiation period for the Pandemic Treaty was extended and expected to be completed within a year.[48]

The proposal to require a digital vaccine passport was in the end dropped from the International Health Declarations, as well as medical mandates and requirements to pass laws demanded by WHO. As Meryl Nass, MD from Door to Freedom concluded:

> The globalists got essentially nothing that was important to them.
> By brazenly going for broke with the original versions of the treaty

---

†   In 2022, Ellen Johnson Sirleaf also became cochair of the UN High-Level Advisory Board on Effective Multilateralism, see my book *The Digital World Brain*.

and amendments, they not only failed to achieve their goals, but they have lost the advantage of surprise and stealth, which they were counting on to get these treaties passed. Now the world knows what they are up to, and millions of people now understand that "health" and fear of pandemics was being used to effect a global coup.[49]

This doesn't mean that the instigators of the coup have given up. They are instead using other means to achieve their ends. Other global crises loom on the horizon. But they have lost the element of surprise, and time is not on their side.

Vacuum sucking up money

The Robbery

To beat the COVID-19 pandemic, the world needs more than breakthrough science. It needs breakthrough generosity. And that's what we're seeing today as leaders across the public and private sectors are stepping up to support GAVI—especially Prime Minister Johnson. (Bill Gates)

Aside from attaining complete technological control over our lives, and directly or indirectly mandating vaccinations if we wanted to partake in society, we were also being forced to foot the bill. It appears to be part of the greatest theft of public funds in the history of humankind. The COVID-19 crisis, and its predecessor, the climate emergency, created a window of opportunity that was immediately exploited.

The ACT Accelerator

On April 24, 2020, the G20 initiative the Access to COVID-19 Tools (ACT) Accelerator was launched by WHO director-general Dr. Tedros Adhanom Ghebreyesus, French president Emmanuel Macron, the EU Commission president Ursula von der Leyen, and Melinda Gates. The purpose was to speed up the development of COVID-19 vaccines, treatments, and diagnostics on a global scale, with the goal of producing 2 billion vaccine doses by the end of 2021.[1] Organizations such as the World Bank, CEPI, the Wellcome Trust, and GAVI were involved. The initiative was formalized in September by the appointment of a council of governments and partners such as the Bill & Melinda Gates Foundation, the Wellcome Trust, and the World Economic Forum.[2]

The initiative was the result of the G20 leaders' commitment to present a united front against the pandemic: The Coronavirus Global Response. This project required funding. The goal was to raise $35 billion. Global leaders acted in unison by pledging their taxpayers' money in order to ensure the swift vaccination for all.

On May 4, 2020, the G20 members Canada, Germany, Italy, Japan, Saudi Arabia, Great Britain, Norway, Spain, and the European Union held a fundraising event that netted $7.4 billion.[3]

Global Goal: Unite for Our Future

On May 28, the European Commission and Global Citizen launched a new virtual fundraising event called Global Goal: Unite for Our Future, backed by Bloomberg Philanthropies, the Bill & Melinda Gates Foundation, and the Wellcome Trust. Gates praised von der Leyen and emphasized the need for "breakthroughs in generosity and global cooperation."[4] As Bill Gates stated at the International Pledging Event: "The virus doesn't respect borders and it doesn't care about what nationality you are."

All these efforts yielded results during the Global Vaccine Summit in London, June 4, 2020. This conference, organized by Great Britain in association with GAVI and led by Prime Minister Boris Johnson, raised $8.8 billion in pledges from thirty-one governments. Among contributors were G20 states such as India, China, Japan, France, Turkey, Germany, and the EU. The United States joined as the largest single contributor with $1.2 billion. As an echo of Bill Gates and the G20, President Trump, in his address to the Global Vaccine Summit on a link from the White House lawn, declared: "As the coronavirus has shown, there are no borders. It doesn't discriminate. It's mean, it's nasty, but we're going to all take care of it together."

In addition to these, eight foundations, corporations, and organizations (including the Rockefeller Foundation, Unilever, and Mastercard) launched various initiatives to develop vaccines for all citizens of the world.

Global Goal: The Concert

On June 27, 2020, the European Commission and Global Citizen held a conference with world leaders, combined with a fundraising concert with popular performers like Shakira (Young Global Leader 2008), Coldplay, Miley Cyrus, and Charlize Theron (YGL 2014).*

Global Goal: The Concert

Like an echo of Greta Thunberg, Shakira admonished world leaders and implored them to assume responsibility for the situation: "Global Citizens around the world are calling on world leaders to help bring an end to COVID-19 by urging them to commit the billions of dollars needed to deliver testing, treatments, and vaccines to everyone, everywhere."

This was the finale of the campaign "Global Goal: Unite for Our Future." Funds raised would be going to CEPI, GAVI, The Global Fund (a public-private partnership created by Bill Gates in 2002), FIND, UNITAID, Therapeutics Accelerator, and the COVID-19 Solidarity Response Fund for the WHO. All except the Solidarity Response Fund

---

* Event funding came from Analog Devices, Cisco, Citi, CocaCola, GSK, IBM, Johnson & Johnson, P&G, Pepsi, StateFarm, Teneo, Verizon, Vodafone, and Weight Watchers.

(financed by Ted Turner's UN Foundation) were closely associated with the Bill & Melinda Gates Foundation.

On October 28, 2020, Ursula von der Leyen announced that vaccines could be delivered to the EU member states from April 2021. A week earlier, the commission had announced its intention to buy up to 22 million antigen tests to meet EU nations' "immediate needs" and also called for more coordinated requirements for traveling, testing, and quarantines.[5]

COVID-19 Relief Funds

As a consequence of pandemic restrictions, governments soon realized that businesses, artists, and employees needed financial support in order to mitigate some of the income losses due to lockdowns or restrictions on travel, shopping, public venues, and events. Globally, these relief funds were over $9 trillion in May 2020![6]

Even in the more moderately affected Sweden, the government handed out more than 389 billion SEK (over $37.3 billion) in relief funds in 2020 and 2021, which is equivalent to more than 15 percent of our annual state budget.[7]

On top of this, countless billions have been sent in support for Ukraine (SEK 37 billion from Sweden[8] and $95 billion from the United States,[9] just to mention two examples)—much of which has ended up in the pockets of the weapons industry.

In Europe, governments have also had to issue energy relief funds to households and companies after the war outbreak and the timely destruction of the Nord Stream pipelines made energy prices soar. These relief funds were of course not gifts but added to each nation's national debt—*to be repaid by its taxpayers*—just like the previous bank bailouts, and have resulted in increased inflation.

The Funding of Supranational Organizations

Besides funding of vaccine development, national procurements of the finished product, the COVID-19 relief funds etc., member states are already paying billions of dollars to supranational organizations such as the European Union, the African Union, ASEAN, NATO, the WHO, the United Nations, and the Green Climate Fund. Here are just a few examples.

The Green Climate Fund

Even before the WHO's "pandemic," many countries had been persuaded to make substantial commitments to fund "climate mitigation" and the green/digital transition. After the climate summits in Copenhagen 2009 and Cancún 2010, member states pledged to finance the Green Climate Fund with *$10 billion* per year. From 2020, UN member states are expected to pay an additional *$100 billion* annually to the fund!

The European Union Budget

The EU budget for 2023 was 186.6 billion €![10]

This annual influx of European taxpayer funds has helped the EU Commission lay the foundation for the Fourth Industrial Revolution through investments such as Horizon 2020, EU's largest research and innovation program ever with almost 80 billion euro in funding 2014–2020. Within this program, which has existed since 1985, studies have included projects on how emerging technology can be used and implemented, such as HIVE (Brain-Computer Interfaces), The Human Brain Project (with the goal of creating an electronic human brain), and Human-Computer Confluence (how massive data collection can be used to influence citizens). These projects have been conducted mostly under the radar of EU citizens. The program is now largely focused on implementing the European Green Deal, which includes "educating" EU citizens into making the "correct" environmental choices.[11]

The United Nations Budget

The UN budget for 2023 was $3.59 billion.[12] These funds are only partly used for charitable projects. As much as 75 percent of the UN budget is used for salaries and benefits. UN employees enjoy a highly privileged lifestyle. A mid-level official may have subsidized luxury housing for the whole family, first-class travel, health insurance at half price, access to the most expensive private doctors, and free private schools and Ivy League universities for all children.[13] Salaries range from $37,000 to $123,000 annually—*tax free*! Plus generous retirement plans, allowances, vacations, and extra compensations depending on the mission.[14] This creates *very* loyal employees.

Note that this UN budget is only for the UN Secretariat. The other UN agencies, such as the WMO, WHO, UNESCO, UNEP, IMF, World Bank Group, and other UN bodies, each have their own separate budgets and funding.

The WHO Budget

The WHO budget for 2020–2021 was $9.4 billion and for 2022–2023 it was $10.4 billion, of which about a quarter comes from member states.[15]

Footing the bill for the bloated budgets of these supranational organizations and generous commitments are often the ordinary taxpaying citizen. The planet's richest are hardly likely to be affected, having already placed their funds in tax-exempt foundations and invested in the profitable technologies of the Fourth Industrial Revolution, Big Pharma, Big Agro, Big Tech, and public-private partnership projects.[16]

+ 64,8 %
$ 186 bn

+ 18,7 %
$ 116 bn

+ 83,9 %
$ 100 bn

+ 273,8 %
$ 92 bn

+ 45 %
$ 58,8 bn

Jeff Bezos
AMAZON

Bill Gates
MICROSOFT

Mark Zuckerberg
META

Elon Musk
TESLA

Jack Ma
ALIBABA

CLOSED
due to
COVID-19

Restaurants, hotels, travel,
tourism, sports, music, theatre,
shops, and small businesses

Isolation, mental health problems,
increased substance abuse, suicide

+71 million more people in extreme poverty due to pandemic restrictions

Covid winners and losers

Internet

Epilogue

I believe there will be another crisis. It will be more significant and we need to start preparing for that now. When we do see this next crisis it will be faster than we have seen with Covid, the exponential growth rate will be much steeper, the impact will be greater, and as a result the social and economic implications will be even more significant.[1] (Cyber Polygon 2020)

The World in 2025

In July 2020, the Cognizant Center for The Future of Work* released the astounding *After the Virus*—a "report from the future" set in 2025.[2] In this predictive programming scenario, everything that could possibly be done online had been digitalized and remained so after the pandemic. People had kept doing almost everything from home, including office work, business meetings, education, entertainment and social interaction, with the aid of online meeting spaces and virtual reality (VR) goggles. In Cognizant's imaginary future, social distancing and face masks had also remained, business travel had become something shameful, and surveillance increased. There had been overnight nationalization of private companies, and personal integrity was a distant memory.

Just like the establishing of the Transportation Security Agency (TSA) only a few weeks after 9/11 in the real world, Cognizant's scenario included a new "Health Security Agency" for overseeing the health of US

---

* The Center for The Future of Work was launched in New Jersey by former analysts from the IT industry, with board members from PepsiCo, Coca-Cola, Intel, GE Healthcare, Lockheed Martin, McKinsey & Company, Bank of New York, and Aquiline Holdings. Partners are about thirty leading technology and IT businesses, among others Adobe, Amazon Cisco, Dell, IBM, Google Cloud, Microsoft, and Salesforce. Strategic partnerships include the World Economic Forum and TED Talks.

citizens. Airlocks and mandatory temperature checks at the entrances of stores, schools, offices, and public buildings were commonplace, as well as the requirement to prove oneself fever-free four hours ahead of every planned trip.

To lower expenses for the care of the growing elderly population, the scenario emphasized keeping as many as possible at home, aided by AI, sensors, and virtual reality.

In relation to the problem of a growing elderly population, there was also a discussion about *whether we really want to live quite that long or if perhaps some form of freely chosen "deadline" would be more appropriate?* This would in turn force the question for all of us *whether our consumption is counterbalanced by what we contribute?* (compare this with the "demise pill" in appendix B).

During and after "The Great Lockdown," the development of multi-sensory VR could make great progress. We could thereby attend political protests without the risk of arrest or tear gas, and attend concerts online without the hassle of trying to find a parking space or risk missing the last train home. When we are finally let out of house arrest, we will, according to this technocratic vision, have realized how convenient it is to live "inside the machine," and nobody would really miss encountering other people, travel, or actually doing things for real.

The report was published along with a fictitious "Zoom meeting from 2025" in which the participants looked back on the past five years and discussed everything that was now different.[3] These future developments were presented as a done deal, as if no other future was possible.

The Next Crisis—Cyberwar

As shown throughout this book, there has been no shortage of warnings about future crises.

During the WEF exercise Cyber Polygon, held in July 2020, the CEO of WEF's Centre for Global Industries and Strategic Intelligence, Jeremy Jurgens, asserted:

> I believe there will be another crisis. It will be more significant and we
> need to start preparing for that now. When we do see this next crisis

it will be faster than we have seen with Covid, the exponential growth rate will be much steeper, the impact will be greater, and as a result the social and economic implications will be even more significant.[4]

What Jurgens referred to was a massive cyberattack that will paralyze power supplies, transportation, health care, and basically all societal functions that rely on the internet to operate. Among the participants in the exercise were INTERPOL, Ericsson, ABB, IBM, TASS, Russian prime minister Mikhail Mishustin as opening speaker, Sberbank's CEO Herman Gref, and former British prime minister Tony Blair.[5] The participation of several Russian leaders, experts, and organizations during both the 2020 and the 2021 exercises might indicate from where a future cyberattack is to be expected. Keep in mind the intense propaganda campaigns warning of Russian digital threats during the last decade (not least in relation to the US presidential election of 2016). The cooperation between the supposed "enemies" is, however, rather close.

Cyber Polygon

Klaus Schwab, who in relation to the exercise praised WEF's relationship with Vladimir Putin and the Russian Federation, argued that the
COVID-19 crisis would be like a tiny ripple in comparison to the coming
"cyber pandemic."[6] In order to counter the threats looming over "our common digital future," Schwab claimed we need a global response. One can
assume that this has become a priority for the Ministers of Digitalization
within the G20.

During the exercise, Tony Blair, former board member of the World
Economic Forum, called for a digital ID with biometric data in order to
counter COVID-19, as well as online fraud and uncontrolled migration:
"Digital ID is from my perspective a major part of the future."

This in spite of considering COVID-19 was a comparatively mild illness, with the vast majority of infected surviving. The problem, according
to Blair, was that the entire society had to shut down to protect the few
who were at serious risk. A digital ID with which one can prove that the
individual is vaccinated and protected would be the path out of this situation, according to the former prime minister. He considered the development toward a digital ID as inevitable.

This was also predicted by the Rockefeller Foundation in the Lock
Step scenario of the 2010 report *Scenarios for the Future of Technology and
International Development* (see chapter 5). The Cyber Polygon exercise
has immediate parallels to the scenario Hack Attack: "An economically
unstable and shock-prone world in which governments weaken, crimi-
nals thrive, and dangerous innovations emerge." (Rockefeller Foundation
2010, p. 16)

The report describes a world that has already emptied its coffers to
deal with a number of synchronized crises, and thus has no resources
to face this new threat (which is precisely what is ostensibly happening
in relation to COVID-19). National governments can, according to this
scenario, no longer protect its citizens. Instead, the "Decade of Doom"
ensues, with lack of resources, hunger, violence, crime, trade conflicts,
proxy wars, and cybercrime:

Technology hackers were also hard at work. Internet scams and pyramid schemes plagued inboxes. Meanwhile, more sophisticated hackers attempted to take down corporations, government systems, and banks via phishing scams and database information heists, and their many successes generated billions of dollars in losses. (Rockefeller Foundation 2010, p. 36).

This scenario relates to a situation where the internet has major security flaws, and where user identities cannot be verified properly or may be hacked or spoofed, causing major losses to society.

Other forms of hacking such as "DIY biology" (biohacking) and genetic modification are, however, viewed as a positive development. These are transhumanist ideas where the body is modified with various types of implants and neurobiological interventions. Synthetic food is also presented as a promising possibility (something that the Rockefeller Foundation has already begun preparing for).

The report also predicted that bioweapons in the form of pathogens will be used, and that contaminated vaccines due to corruption within states or the WHO will be unleashed in Africa (something Bill Gates has also suggested—see chapter 5). "In 2021, 600 children in Cote d'Ivoire died from a bogus Hepatitis B vaccine, which paled in comparison to the scandal sparked by mass deaths from a tainted anti-malarial drug years later."

The pressure from converging crises leads to widening gaps between the haves and the have-nots, with the wealthy securing themselves in gated communities while slums spread outside. The inability of nation-states to face these issues prepares the ground for a new form of feudalism. Everyone except the ultra-rich will in the end be equally poor, according to this scenario. "By 2030, the distinction between 'developed' and 'developing' nations no longer seemed particularly descriptive or relevant."

There will thus no longer be any wealthy nation to escape to, according to the report.

Our Common Agenda

On January 15, 2022, the government of Canada removed the vaccination requirement exemption for truck drivers crossing the Canadian border. This ignited a large convoy protest in Ottawa with truckers both from the United States and from other parts of Canada. The protest lasted from January 22 to February 23, when Prime Minister Justin Trudeau (WEF Young Global Leader 2005) used Canada's Emergencies Act to end it. In connection with this, fundraising accounts were frozen, just as previously threatened by vice-PM and Minister of Finance Chrystia Freeland (WEF Global Leader of Tomorrow 2000).[7] After the Emergencies Act had already been used, but just *before* it was approved (or risked getting rejected) by the Senate, Trudeau revoked it.

The very next day, on February 24, 2022, Russia attacked its neighbor Ukraine. Literally overnight the world's media and social media attention turned from COVID-19 and the embarrassing debacle in Canada to hyper-focus on the war.

The fear and loathing of the unvaccinated was instantly replaced by an even more intense hatred against Putin and Russia. Now it was the Russians' turn to have their bank accounts and financial services frozen. The West's dependency on Russian gas caused energy and food prices to soar.

And with this new drama to occupy everyone's attention, all the egregious violations to human rights during the pandemic became old news—just as more and more people were sobering up after the mass hysteria, and just as the effects of the lockdowns and the experimental intervention were starting to show in real data.

The next step in the Great Transition had thereby been initiated. During the pandemic, preparations had started to reform the United Nations in order to make the organization more capable of managing global catastrophic risks. On September 10, 2021, Secretary-General António Guterres published the report *Our Common Agenda* and stated with dramatic wording:

> We are at an inflection point in history. In our biggest shared test since the Second World War, humanity faces a stark and urgent choice: a

breakdown or a breakthrough. The coronavirus disease (COVID-19) is upending our world, threatening our health, destroying economies and livelihoods and deepening poverty and inequalities.[8]

His solution was a new global order that included a global digital compact, a universal digital ID, an upgraded digital UN 2.0, an apex body for the world economy, space technology to monitor carbon dioxide emissions, an ombudsman to speak for future generations, expanded use of public-private partnerships, and the establishment of an "Emergency Platform" as a more effective way to deal with global crises such as COVID-19 and climate change. All to be decided by the world leaders at UN Summit of the Future in September 2024. More about this can be found in my book *The Digital World Brain* (published in Swedish in 2022).

Final Words

The United Nations Agenda 2030 for Sustainable Development is in the end a technocratic plan for total control—for a new economic system based on a digital surveillance regime which can have very serious consequences for humankind's freedom and future. In the final analysis, this will be a type of scientific dictatorship that requires the digital interconnectedness of every human and every aspect of society in order to function.

The 2020 COVID-19 crisis has been the perfect trigger event on a historically unprecedented scale, with players like the World Economic Forum, the Rockefeller Foundation, and the Bill & Melinda Gates Foundation, in concert with the UN system (including the WHO) and the G20 nations.

These international organizations and foundations have exploited the situation to the fullest, in order to further their technocratic and transhumanist agendas by using the threat from a virus that turned out to have a mortality comparable to a moderately severe seasonal flu. We have paid, and will continue to pay, a very high price for something that has been exaggerated beyond all proportions in order to implement a new techno-totalitarian order.

Professed philanthropists such as Bill Gates and the Rockefeller family, together with their global circle of fellow billionaires, operate on the principle that "crises bring business opportunities" and have effectively utilized the fear and suffering wrought upon humanity to their own ends.

This tiny number of globally influential individuals act through ostensibly philanthropic programs and initiatives to "stop pollution," "save the climate," and "mitigate pandemics." As a rule, they offer only technological solutions, which on the one hand guarantee themselves enormous short- and long-term profits, and on the other hand entrench the power of the global financial, political, and technological oligarchy to a level that will soon be hard to halt or reverse.

This story has revealed the workings of a shockingly corrupt system, in which the institutions created to protect citizens from harm have been infiltrated or completely surrendered to the oligarchs they were meant to guard us against.

Their actions during the pandemic have shown us that the progenitors of this agenda will use any means necessary in order to bring the world into a state of compliance, even if it means deliberately crashing the global economy, destroying every facet of culture, and leaving hundreds of millions people out of work, homeless, cold, and starving.

All of this misery, just so that a few hundred super-privileged individuals may try to realize their utopian visions of a perfect world, governed according to technocratic principles—which will only create a soulless and dead world, governed and surveilled by AI, robots, and a social credit system. This is utterly unacceptable and one of the most severe crimes ever perpetrated against humanity.

Hoping to avoid the need for suppression by force, they clearly want us to *voluntarily* give up our liberties—despite our individual liberty constituting the very *essence* of being human.

Our Hope

The "pandemic" measures have made more and more people aware of what goes on behind the scenes. The aftermath of the experimental treatment, with a growing number serious side effects,[9] fertility problems, excess mortality,[10] and sudden death among young healthy people, have made many who have tended to believe the official narrative start questioning the reliability of previously trusted and respected authorities, institutions, and media.

Since I wrote this book in 2020, Klaus Schwab and the WEF have become household names, and not in a flattering way. Bill Gates is not exactly popular, and Anthony Fauci has been thoroughly defamed.[11]

This awareness keeps growing for every new crisis, such as the wars in Ukraine and Gaza, and the dramatic increase in militarization.

As the effects of the global goals of Agenda 2030 are starting to manifest in real life, a wave of farmer protests have swept through Europe against proposed environmental regulations (including a carbon tax, nitrogen emissions curbs, and restrictions on water and land usage). Such protests are bound to increase when restrictions reach households and individuals and limit or dictate what we can eat, how we can live, drive, travel, work, shop, learn, etc.

We are getting closer to a breaking point where the number of people waking up to what is happening will reach the masses. The lies and propaganda are no longer working as effectively as before. All that remains for those in power is to use more force. This will only further reveal their true intentions. The resistance is growing. As this happens, many opportunists are likely to falter and switch teams in order to save their own skins.

In the end, the emperor will stand naked and alone. The empire falls. This is like a law of nature. What happens after that is up to us.

HAL

Wardenclyffe
Lyrics: Jacob Nordangård
Music: J. Nordangård & Robert Nadde Karlsson

How did we end like this?
in the garden of misery
With the mark on our hands
didn't learn from our history

When did we lose our ways?
Got trapped in this horrid maze
With tiny steps the trap was set
to give rise to the terror

Take me back to the glory days
Then man was free to choose his ways
Change the course of our history
Awake the souls and break us free

Beneath the veil of philanthropy
lies the deeds of the Devil
He pulls the strings and rules as king
seducing with magic

Dehumanize and robotize
reduce us to subjects
How can we light the spark?
and bring mankind together

Give us the keys to harmony
Share the secrets of alchemy
Bring the knowledge from divinity
Tear down the horrors of technocracy

Available on Bandcamp:
wardenclyffe.bandcamp.com

Appendix A

The Method

The Reece Committee

In 1952, the United States House of Representatives initiated an investigation into tax-exempt foundations to determine if they were using their resources for the purposes for which they were established, if they were using their resources for un-American or subversive activities. What the investigators found was even more shocking than they had anticipated.

The Select Committee to Investigate Tax-Exempt Foundations and Comparable Organizations ("the Cox Committee") was initially led by Rep. Edward E. Cox. It consisted primarily of questionnaires sent to foundations and organizations holding assets exceeding $10 million. According to Cox's report to the Congress in early 1952, based on foundations' obliging replies, these foundations appeared to be using their funds according to each foundation's stated purpose, and the Committee had not found any irregularities.

Rep. B. Carroll Reece, however, was critical of the Cox Committee's methods and conclusions, stating that it had been too short and shallow and that leading foundations had not been included (e.g., the Ford Foundation). Reece wanted to dig deeper. In the spring of 1953, he was granted permission to initiate a new investigation ("the Reece Committee"), led by a former banker, Norman Dodd.

As it was estimated that there were around seven thousand foundations at that time, Dodd and his team decided to focus on those foundations that had been in existence for the longest time, which amounted to twelve. They found that these twelve represented as much as 80 percent of the funds of all foundations combined.

Carnegie Endowment for International Peace

One of these foundations was Carnegie Endowment for International Peace. Instead of replying to the pertinent questions Dodd had sent, the endowment's president, Dr. Joseph Johnson, granted the Committee access to the endowment's library for two weeks. The Committee's legal analyst, Kathryn Casey, was given the task of going through the minutes of the endowment's board meetings from its founding and onward (the endowment was officially registered in 1910 but started holding board meetings in 1908). She was to record the most relevant information on a Dictaphone. The information she brought back was so shocking that she eventually had a nervous breakdown.

In a 1982 interview with G. Edward Griffin, Norman Dodd described what Miss Casey had found in the Carnegie minutes:

> We are now at the year 1908, which was the year that the Carnegie Foundation began operations. And, in that year, the trustees meeting, for the first time, raised a specific question, which they discussed throughout the balance of the year, in a very learned fashion. And the question is this: *"Is there any means known more effective than war, assuming you wish to alter the life of an entire people?"* And they conclude that, *no more effective means to that end is known to humanity, than war.*
>
> So then, in 1909, they raise the second question, and discuss it, namely, *"How do we involve the United States in a war?"*
>
> Well, I doubt, at that time, if there was any subject more removed from the thinking of most of the people of this country, than its involvement in a war. There were intermittent shows in the Balkans, but I doubt very much if many people even knew where the Balkans were. And finally, they answer that question as follows: *"We must control the State Department."*

And then, that very naturally raises the question of *how do we do that?* They answer it by saying, *"We must take over and control the diplomatic machinery of this country."* And, finally, they resolve to aim at that as an objective. Then, time passes, and we are eventually in a war, which would be World War I. At that time, they record on their minutes a shocking report in which they dispatch to President Wilson a telegram cautioning him "to see that the war does not end too quickly."[1]

When the purpose of the war had been accomplished, it was time for the next step.

And finally, of course, the war is over. At that time, their interest shifts over to preventing what they call a reversion of life in the United States to what it was prior to 1914, when World War I broke out. At that point, they come to the conclusion that *"to prevent a reversion, we must control education in the United States."*

And they realize that is a pretty big task. To them it is too big for them alone. So they approach the Rockefeller Foundation with a suggestion: *"That portion of education which could be considered domestic should be handled by the Rockefeller Foundation, and that portion which is international should be handled by the Endowment."*

They then decide that the key to the success of these two operations lay in the alteration of the teaching of American History. So, they approach four of the then most prominent teachers of American History in the country—people like Charles and Mary Byrd. Their suggestion to them is this, *"Will they alter the manner in which they present their subject?"* And, they get turned down, flatly.

So they [Carnegie] then decide that it is necessary for them to do as they say, *i.e.* "build our own stable of historians."

Then, they approach the Guggenheim Foundation, which specializes in fellowships, and say, *"When we find young men in the process of studying for doctorates in the field of American History, and we feel that they are the right caliber, will you grant them fellowships on our say so?*

And the answer is, "*Yes.*"

So, under that condition, eventually they assemble twenty, and they take these twenty potential teachers of American History to London. There, they are briefed in what is expected of them— *when*, *as*, and *if* they secure appointments in keeping with the doctorates they will have earned.

That group of twenty historians ultimately becomes the nucleus of the American Historical Association. And then, toward the end of the 1920's, the Endowment grants to the American Historical Association four hundred thousand dollars ($400,000) for a study of our history in a manner which points to what this country can look forward to in the future. That culminates in a seven-volume study, the last volume of which is, of course, in essence, a summary of the contents of the other six.

The essence of the last volume is this: "*The future of this country belongs to collectivism, administered with characteristic American efficiency.*"

Based on this information, the Reece Committee initiated a full-scale investigation of how these leading foundations had used their enormous resources of tax-exempt funds.

There were several attempts at stopping the investigation.[2] The file with the most compromising material from the Cox Committee vanished, and the Reece Committee's funding dwindled. They initially received $50,000 from Congress, with promises of more later—which never came. Meanwhile, the Ford Foundation, the largest and newest of the tax-free trust funds [led by Robert M. Hutchins, former chancellor of the University of Chicago, involved in the founding the Aspen Institute, and one of the leaders of the World Federalist Movement] appropriated $15 million for critically investigating the investigating powers of the Congress.[3] After the publication of Dodd's preliminary report, there was an intense media campaign trying to discredit the Committee, and the hearings were openly sabotaged by a colleague after he had been visited by someone from the White House.

The Reece Commission's full report, comprising over 1,200 pages (including transcripts from the hearings), as well as Dodd's shorter report to the Commission, his interview with G. Edward Griffin, and the informative summary in the special edition of the *Freemen Digest* from 1978, are all available online. Here are just a few select examples to illustrate the goals and methods of some of the leading foundations and their success in driving social change.

The Education System

Despite the many setbacks, the Reece Committee managed to show how leading foundations, specially the Carnegie and Rockefeller foundations, had been able to influence the US education system with strategic donations of astronomical proportions, as stated in the annual reports from their founding in the early 1900s to 1952.

ORGANISATIONS	CARNEGIE		ROCKFELLER		TOTAL USD
	Corporation	Foundation	Gen. Education Board	Foundation	
US Universities, colleges, schools	56,838,000	62,764,000	257,158,000	335,000,000	711,760,000
Adult education	3,013,000	-	50,000	3,436,000	6,499,000
American Council on Education	1,013,000	92,000	4,841,000	1,236,000	7,182,000
Columbia University	2,687,000	-	7,608,000	33,300,000	43,595,000
Corporative Test Service, Educational Records Bureau, Graduate Record, College Entrance Examination Board	91,000	2,850,000	3,483,000	-	6,424,000
Institute of International Education	2,366,000	-	-	1,406,000	3,872,000
National Citizens Commission for the Public Schools	750,000	-	150,000		900,000
National Education Association	262,000	115,000	979,000	32,000	1,388,000
Progressive Education Association	76,000	92,000	4,09, 000	-	4,259,000
Teachers College, Columbia	3,728,000	-	11,576,000	1,750,000	17,054,000
Lincoln School of Teachers College, Columbia	-	-	6,821,000	60,087,000	66,908,000
University of Chicago	2,420,000	-	118,225,000	-	120,645,000
London School of Economics	-	-	-	4,106,000	4,106,000
TOTAL	73,244,000	65,913,000	414,982,000	440,353,000	994,492,000

Carnegie and Rockefeller appropriations to educational institutions and organisations

These funds were focused primarily on five areas: education, international relations (including international law), politics, public service, propaganda, and economy.[4]

Through generous grants to leading universities and the funding of scholarships, professorships, pensions, lecturers, encyclopedias, textbooks, and research grants, distributed through a handful of central organizations acting as clearing houses (the five in the middle of the chart), they could control virtually *the entire national education system.* These central organizations could in turn include from half-a-dozen to—as in the case of the American Council on Education—*over a thousand* sub-organizations and affiliated institutions. Some of the most influential organizations were the National Education Association (NEA) and the Progressive Education Association (PEA), both funded by the Carnegie and Rockefeller foundations.

INTER-RELATIONSHIPS BETWEEN FOUNDATIONS, EDUCATION AND GOVERNMENT

Interrelationships between foundations, education, and government

So, what did the foundations and organizations want to achieve by centralizing and controlling the education system?

According to the Commission's findings, the goal was a form of socialist paternalism in domestic affairs and an interdependent "one-world" policy in foreign affairs, with the United Nations organization as "our light and our saviour, the hope of humanity." The earlier mentioned Carnegie-funded 1934 *Report of the Commission on Social Studies by the American Historical Society*, the last in a series of seven which were intended as textbooks for classes in History and Social Studies, described an expected development toward increased state control and a possible revocation of property rights.

> Cumulative evidence supports the conclusion that, in the United States as in other countries, the age of individualism and laissez faire in economy and government is closing and that a new age of collectivism is emerging. As to the specific form which this "collectivism," this integration and interdependence, is taking and will take in the future, the evidence at hand is by no means clear or unequivocal. It may involve the limiting or supplanting of private property, extended and distributed among the masses.
>
> Most likely, it will issue from a process of experimentation and will represent a composite of historic doctrines and social conceptions yet to appear. Almost certainly it will involve a larger measure of compulsory as well as voluntary cooperation of citizens in the conduct of the complex national economy, a corresponding enlargement of the functions of government, and an increasing state intervention in fundamental branches of economy previously left to the individual discretion and initiative.[5]

When Norman Dodd in November 1953 was invited to the office of the Ford Foundation, its president, Roman Gaither, told him frankly that they acted under directives from the White House:

The substance of the directives under which we operate is that we shall use our grant-making power to alter life in the United States so that we can be comfortably merged with the Soviet Union.

Upon hearing this, Dodd nearly fell off his chair!

Note: As the investigation was carried out during the early days of the Cold War when the fear of Communism was at its peak in the United States, the Commission's findings were interpreted as Soviet infiltration of the foundations. However, it seems rather that it was the *foundation founders* who harbored such visions and invited board members and staff willing to work for that agenda. Henry Ford, for example, made several attempts at creating small-scale tightly controlled "ideal communities," including his disastrous project Fordlândia in Brazil.

National Central Planning

An important player identified by the Reece Commission was the Rockefeller-funded National Planning Board, founded in 1933–1934, which was succeeded by the National Resources Planning Board in 1939. In its final report in 1943, the NRPB proposed that the US government adopt a series of far-reaching tax-funded utopian reforms, listed in bullet points with detailed subitems such as:

- To underwrite full employment for the employables;
- To guarantee and, when necessary, underwrite:
- Equal access to security
- Equal access to education for all
- Equal access to health and nutrition for all
- Wholesome housing conditions for all

The list reads like an early model for what later evolved (via Earth Charter and the Millennium Goals) into the even more detailed 17 Global Goals of Agenda 2030.

Creating World Citizens

The next step was preparing for central planning on a global level. The Reece Commission cites the report from the President's Commission on Higher Education, led by the president of the American Council of Learned Societies:

> In speed of transportation and communication and in economic interdependence, the nations of the globe are already one world; the task is to secure recognition and acceptance of this oneness in the thinking of the people, as that the concept of one world may be realized psychologically, socially and in good time politically.[6]

One of the many Carnegie-funded internationalists mentioned by the Reece Commission was Stanford economist Eugene Staley. Besides proposing the creation of a World Investment Bank, he recommended using emotionally charged symbols in order to create loyalty to international institutions.[*]

> International civic training: It is all too evident that the measures and devices proposed in this chapter can never succeed, cannot even be tried, unless there is a sufficient sense of world citizen-ship among the different peoples of the earth and among their leaders.
>
> Such a sense of world citizenship may be stimulated by a rational appreciation of the worldwide interdependence of economic, social, and political life, but to be politically effective the emotions must also be touched and loyalties to new supranational symbols must be developed.[7]

Social Science

As a tool for social change, the foundations funded radical educators working to reform education. Part of the plan was to combine courses like history, geography, economics, psychology, sociology, etc. into a new field called "social studies." Success in recruiting teachers in this field to

---

[*] This method had been developed by Harold Lasswell at University of Chicago, see *Rockefeller: Controlling the Game*, p. 25.

work for the "new social order" was expected to yield results beyond all proportions, in relation to the number of teachers involved.[8] Another goal was for sociologists and social engineers to gain the same status as experts in the hard sciences.

> It will take social science and social engineering to solve the problems
> of human relations. Our people must learn to respect the need for spe-
> cial knowledge and technical training in this field as they have come to
> defer to the expert in physics, chemistry, medicine, and other sciences.[9]

From these classes the most promising students were selected to work for the agenda as social engineers within public service. In its annual report from 1940, the Rockefeller Foundation proudly notes how their fund-ing of National Institute of Public Affairs has resulted in 60 percent of their "internes" being accepted into Federal Service, and several into state or local service.[10] The Rockefeller Foundation also describes its funding of Training Scholarships in social engineering for the United Nations Economic Commission for Europe.

> The United Nations Economic Commission for Europe has received
> a grant of $12,000 from the Rockefeller Foundation to provide social-
> science scholarships for selected European students. An operational
> body which deals with virtually all aspects of European recovery and
> development, the Commission has attracted to its staff an interna-
> tional group of competent economists. These men can offer promis-
> ing graduate students an introduction to the international approach
> to economic problems while they are acquiring first-hand knowledge
> of applied economics.
>
> The Research and Planning Division, headed by Mr. Nicholas
> Kalder, formerly of the London School of Economics, carries on
> work which is closely linked with the technical economic problems
> encountered in the operational activities of the Commission. Dr.
> Gunnar Myrdal, of Sweden, Executive Secretary of the Commission,
> has established a special committee to administer the program.[11]

The Fund for Advancement of Education compared the process of identifying, recruiting, and indoctrinating suitable ideologues with military training.

> the preparation of officers to assume responsibility for education in the military services was the key to effectiveness of orientation programs.[12]

To this end, the Ford Foundation founded the Center for Advanced Study in the Behavioral Sciences and stated in a 1953 report:

> training of a moderate number of first-rate people is in the present juncture far more urgent than that of a large number of merely competent people. (p.24)[13] In sum, then, the Foundation's hope and expectation is significantly to advance the behavioral sciences—to get farther faster—through the temporary concentration at one place of the ablest scholars and the most promising younger people studying together in the most effective way that the state of the field now permits. (p.28)

The Reece Committee did find that a disproportional size of the appropriations from the Carnegie, Rockefeller, and Ford foundations had been concentrated to a few top universities, such as Harvard, the University of Chicago, the University of California, and Columbia University. According to the Dodd report, there were originally not many scholars capable of handling these unique subjects and most of them were members of these select institutions.[14]

Harvard and Columbia

The method of selecting and training gifted students to work for a specific agenda is, as we have seen, still used and now on a global scale, through the World Economic Forum and UN youth programs. Harvard University is still used to train Young Global Leaders in the United States as well as other students with global business or political ambitions.

Columbia University (formerly King's College, founded in 1754) is also of special interest. It comprises twenty graduate and professional schools, including Columbia Law School, Columbia Business School, Columbia Climate School, and the Columbia Graduate School of Journalism (founded by Joseph Pulitzer and administering the Pulitzer Prize), and is affiliated with the influential Teachers College.

Columbia University, Morningside Heights, New York

Besides the generous Rockefeller appropriations to Columbia and Teachers College, Rockefeller Center is built on Columbia land and pays rent to the university.[15]

In the 1930s, Columbia hosted both the technocracy movement, which has been an underlying influence on the technological and political development over the last century,[16] as well as the philosophers from the Frankfurt School, invited in 1935 to escape the Nazis.[17] The latter are probably best known as the progenitors of postmodern philosophy, including critical theory and deconstructivism, which have increasingly come to dominate the curriculum of many Western universities. The direction of contemporary architecture has also been greatly influenced in the directive of the willfully destructive deconstruction by leading deconstructionist architect Bernard Tschumi, who was Dean of the Columbia Graduate School of Architecture, Planning and Preservation 1988–2003.[18]

Appendix B

The Plan

New Order of Barbarians

On March 20, 1969, Dr. Lawrence A. Dunegan (1923–2004) and around eighty fellow pediatricians attended an astounding lecture at the Pittsburgh Paediatric Society.

Dr. Dunegan later identified the lecturer as Richard L. Day (1905–1989), Professor of Pediatrics at Mount Sinai School of Medicine in New York, previously lector at the College of Physicians and Surgeons, Columbia University, and Medical Director of Planned Parenthood Federation of America.[1]

Professor Day stated that the purpose of the lecture was to inform his colleges and friends so that as to be better prepared for the "very surprising" changes which were to be brought about in the next thirty years or so, so that "an entirely new world-wide system" would be in operation before the turn of the century. He spoke as an initiate and proponent rather than as a whistleblower. He said that only a few years earlier he would not have been free to speak, but now [in 1969] he could do so [privately, to these trusted colleagues] because "everything is in place and nobody can stop us now."

The professor insisted that no notes be taken and no tape recorder be used. Dr. Dunegan, however, realized the importance of what was conveyed and made an effort to memorize as much as possible. He later revealed the information in interviews recorded in 1988 and 1991 (available online and also published in book format).[2]

What Professor Day revealed to his colleagues was a frightening future planned for humanity. Below follows a summary of the most crucial points (rearranged into categories rather than following the somewhat scattered chronology of Dr. Dunegan's interviews). Added comments in footnotes or brackets.

Personal note: One does not necessarily have to share Dr. Dunegan's conservative worldview to be quite astounded by these social engineers who, according to Professor Day, have had a major influence on the development during the twentieth century—and who now seem very close to realizing their stated ultimate goal.

Introduction

In his introductory remarks, Professor Day stated that "most people don't understand how governments operate and even people in high positions in governments, including our own, don't really understand how and where decisions are made." He said that the people who really influence decisions are names that would be familiar to most of us, but he would not name specific individuals or organizations. Their goals were:

- Population control and eugenics.
- Radical change toward a global totalitarian system.

Professor Day explained that all their plans had a dual purpose: the *ostensible* purpose, formulated to win public approval, and the *real* purpose, designed to further the goals leading up to the establishment of the new system.

He said the new system might sound like Communism but that it was something "much bigger than Communism."* He also indicated that there is a much closer cooperation between the East and the West [the communist Soviet Union and China and capitalist North America and Western Europe] than most people realize.

---

*   Very likely, this referred to the new economic system promoted by Technocracy Inc. since the 1930s and the technocratic New International Economic Order which the Trilateral Commission and the UN have worked for since the 1970s; see Patrick M. Wood, *Technocracy Rising*, 2015.

Population Control

Professor Day was very active in the population control movement. He said that the population was growing too fast and must be curtailed or else we will run out of living space. This British neo-Malthusian view, historically used as an excuse for horrible atrocities against millions,[3] was given as the rationale for the radical measures presented in his lecture as necessary and unavoidable.

The first point on the agenda was that sex must be separated from reproduction. As sex had been found "too pleasurable" and "the urges too strong to expect people to give it up," the plan was to encourage rather than discourage sexual activity, but in such a way that people won't be having babies.[†] Several methods were to be used:

- Clothing styles would be made more revealing, stimulating, and provocative. This was the era of the very short miniskirt.
- "Music will get worse" and lyrics more openly sexual.
- There would be pornographic film in theatres and on TV, later on videos, showing people doing "everything you can think of."
- "People will be given permission to be homosexual." [Not for their own sake but as part of the plan for decreasing child births].

Other strategies included:

- Sex education in schools from an early age, specifically connecting sex with contraceptives.
- Contraceptives easily available in shops and through school.
- Legal and tax-funded abortion. [A highly controversial topic in the United States at this time, four years before *Roe v. Wade*].[‡]

---

† Areas which the Rockefeller's Bureau of Social Hygiene researched in the early 1900s, see Rockefeller Foundation Archives, Bureau of Social Hygiene, rockfound.rockarch.org /bureau-of-social-hygiene.

‡ These last strategies were very similar to the proposals in the Rockefeller Commission's report *Population Growth and the American Future* (1972), population-security.org /rockefeller/001_population_growth_and_the_american_future.htm.

Permission to Have Babies

To the astonishment of Dr. Dunegan, Professor Day went on to state that not everyone would be permitted to have babies just because they wanted to or because they were careless. Most people would be allowed two children [zero growth requires 2.1 children per family]. Some would only be allowed one child.[§] A few exceptional families might have three.

Evolutionary Eugenics

"We think we can push evolution faster and in the direction we want it to go." By pushing children to learn more, it was believed that their brains would evolve and that this trait could be passed down to their children [a form of Lamarckism]. The plan also included accelerating puberty [something which has in fact happened, with about three months per decade].[¶]

Social Change

Professor Day indicated that the group he represented had special insights on how to create social change and affect people's behaviour.

> People can carry in their minds and act upon two contradictory ideas at one time, provided that these two contradictory ideas are kept far enough apart.
>
> You can know pretty well how rational people are going to respond to certain circumstances or to certain information that they encounter. So, to determine the response you want you need only control the kind of data or information that they're presented or the kinds of circumstance that they're in; and being rational people they'll do what you want them to do. They may not fully understand what they're doing or why.

---

§　In China, population control began in 1970, and the one-child policy was adopted in 1980 and lasted until 2021.

¶　Caroline Hopkins, "With puberty starting earlier than ever, doctors urge greater awareness and care," NBC News, December 25, 2023, nbcnews.com/health/kids-health/puberty-starting-earlier-treatment-children-rcna125441.

He also stated in his introductory remarks that people will have to get used to change, so used to change that they'll be passively accepting and even expecting it. Nothing will be permanent anymore.

Family

Marriage would become less important and no longer necessary to have sex. Divorce would be made easier. More women would work outside the home and more men be reassigned to work in other cities, making it harder to keep families together and therefore less willing to have babies. Travel would become easier and less expensive—*for a while*—to make them feel they could easily get back to their families (thereby less reluctant to accept work far away from home).

With a more mobile and rootless population, new ideas would be easier to spread. He said, "We take control first of the port cities—New York, San Francisco, Seattle." The idea was that if you manage to spread your philosophy and new ways of living to the port cities, the heartland would have to follow.

Sports

Using economic and other means, soccer—a world-wide *international* sport—would be promoted, whereas *national* sports such as baseball would be demoted.**

Girls were to be encouraged to get into sports rather than play with dolls (as dolls were associated with having children), and women's sports would be given the same status as men's in the sports pages.

Social Darwinism

Crime

One of the more shocking points presented by Professor Day was to try to re-create pre-civilization conditions to "select out the unfit."

** These attempts have still not managed to kill public interest in baseball in the United States.

This was to be achieved by letting some areas of a city turn to slum, with drug abuse and high crime rates, while other parts would be well maintained and secure due to better policing and new security systems. Those who managed to work themselves out of such an "urban jungle" would thereby have proven their fitness and deserve better conditions. For those who didn't, there was no sympathy.

Drugs & Alcohol

Drug use would increase. At the same time, there would be stricter narcotics laws. Drug use and drug law enforcement would be highlighted in the news and influence people on a subconscious level. With increased crime and the criminalizing of drug use and possession, more prisons would be needed.

Alcohol would also be both encouraged (through advertising, films, etc.) and discouraged. There would be stricter rules against drunk driving. The "unfit" were expected to fall for the temptations. Recognizing that even some of the "fit" may develop undesirable habits, counseling would be made available to those wise enough to seek help. Dr. Dunegan got the impression that Professor Day wanted to justify the plans he presented, as if saying "You think we're bad in promoting these evil things, but look how nice we are—we're also providing a way out!"

Gambling

Gambling laws would be relaxed, leading to increased gambling. State-owned lotteries would become an extra source of revenue.

Food

Eating out instead of at home with the family would become more common. Pre-fixed meals and fast food would be made readily available. The nutritional content would change so that people would have to exercise more and be careful with what they ate in order to keep full health. This would weed out those who were too lazy and stupid to heed the health advice offered by the authorities, whereas the wise would eat right and take up running. Sportswear and sports shoes would be made popular.

Diseases

There would be new diseases, difficult to diagnose and cure. In the 1988 interview, Dr. Dunegan associated this with AIDS, but made it clear that was just his own speculation.

Professor Day also said, "We can cure almost every cancer right now. Information is on file in the Rockefeller Institute." However, there was no intention of releasing that information to the public due to the over-population issue. "You may as well die of cancer as of something else." Treatments would therefore be more focused on pain relief than on cure.[††]

Healthcare

Professor Day announced that there would be major changes in the medical profession. Most doctors would be employed by large institutions and become more of "skilled technicians" than the traditional independent practitioner. The job would in the future include things like executions by lethal injection.

Medicine would become more tightly controlled. Medical care would be closely connected to your employment—no work, no care. Clinics offering free or low-cost healthcare would all but disappear. Medical costs would be forced up so that you need insurance. At the same time, health insurance companies would pay half the price of what a patient without insurance would pay for the same treatment.

Access to hospitals would become tightly controlled so that you'd need an ID to get into the building.

Euthanasia

The professor stated people only had a right to live so long, that the elderly were just a burden and no longer useful, and that an arbitrary age limit might be established. Limiting affordable healthcare was one way of

---

[††] This was a direct reference to a Rockefeller institution. The "we" indicates the professor being part of the Rockefeller family's inner circle. The family has close ties to Columbia University, where the professor had been a lector, and have since the 1920s supported Planned Parenthood, of which the professor was medical director.

getting rid of the elderly. The scenario presented was that when medical costs got too high, their children would hold a farewell party, celebrating the achievements of their parents and then offer them a "demise pill."[‡‡]

Many things, from mandatory forms to fill out to traffic planning, would also be designed so as to make life more difficult and confusing for the elderly, making them feel superfluous and more willing to accept the demise pill.

Social Engineering

Entertainment

Entertainment would be used to influence the young (older people were harder to change). Just like sex, violence on film would become worse and ever more graphic and detailed. The purpose was to desensitize people so that they would more easily accept death and to get used to seeing dead and injured people on the streets.

Education

Students would spend more time in school "but they wouldn't learn anything." The school year would be prolonged and summer vacation become "a thing of the past."

In "better schools" in areas with "better people," students would learn more but competition would increase, again in order to "push evolution." Students would have to choose a path early on in life and become specialists in a narrow field, with little understanding of other fields and even less of the bigger picture. Available literature and information would be restricted to their own field.

[‡‡] Here, it seems that these social engineers project their own psychopathy and misjudge family ties, empathy, and the fundamental respect for life of most normal people. However, as of 2016, Canada permits "medical assistance in dying" (MAID) for seriously or terminally ill or disabled Canadian citizens. The law prohibits it for patients suffering from mental illnesses alone. This limitation was to expire in 2023 but has now been postponed to 2027. canada.ca/en/health-canada/services/health-services-benefits/medical-assistance-dying.html.

There would also be pressure to attend extracurricular activities through the school and become part of a club, rather than spontaneous free play or sports with your siblings and friends at home. The pressures to cram more studies and activities into a day would lead to stress, burnout, and substance abuse among many students. This was again by design in order to weed out the "unfit," whereas the smartest would seek the right help and learn how to cope.

Education would continue through life and adults would attend school.^{§§} There would always be new information to process in order to keep up, otherwise you're too old and should take the euthanasia pill.

Literature

The literary classics and religious literature would be amended in subtle ways.^{¶¶} "Some books would just disappear from the libraries." In the future, not everyone would be allowed to own books.

Religion

Religion would also be changed. Professor Day said that many seem to need religion and would have some form of religion. But the religions that were incompatible with the planned changes would have to go, especially Christianity. "Once the Roman Catholic Church is brought down, the rest of Christianity will follow easily."

The new world religion would contain elements from the old religions to create a sense of familiarity, yet still be something new.

For those in his audience doubting that this could be done, the professor stated with confidence, "The churches will help us."

Science

Professor Day also stated that scientific research data could be, and had been, "falsified" [must have meant "tampered with"] in order to produce

---

§§ "Lifelong learning" is an essential part of SDG 4.

¶¶ This is the same plan that Carnegie Endowment for International Peace initiated after the war, with the help of the Rockefeller Foundation, the Guggenheim Foundation, and the American Historical Association; see appendix A.

specific results. He said that "people don't ask the right questions" and that they were "too trusting." According to Dr. Dunegan, he repeated this several times during the lecture, with a mixture of chagrin and contempt for people's naïveté.

Economic Control

Industry

American industry and self-sufficiency would be curtailed. The heavy industry, including the steel and car industries, would be moved abroad to Japan. The reasons given were:

- to give other countries a chance to catch up and compete;
- to let other countries deal with the heavy pollution;
- to tear down family structures among industry workers, forcing them to move and become more susceptible to new ideas, centralized health care, and other ways of living;
- to decrease patriotic feelings upon discovering that Japanese, German, or imported products, especially cars, were of better quality than American;
- to create global *interdependence* where different parts of the world would be assigned specific roles in production and trade and together form a coordinated global system.***

The United States was still to be kept strong in information, communications, high tech, education, and agriculture and would continue to be a central hub in the global system.

Cars would eventually become more alike and difficult to tell apart.

***

***   Economic *interdependence* has been one of the keystones of David Rockefeller's and other leading globalists' plans, and was achieved through GATT (initiated in 1947) and the Structural Adjustment Programs offered by IMF and the World Bank, requiring each country to produce and export specific products in order to receive loans. This *forced* interdependence went way beyond the natural trade between countries.

New Antitrust Laws

Antitrust laws would be modified and competition would be increased. But not as in a *free* competition but more like competition among members of a club or sports league, like the NBA. No one outside the club would have any chance of even joining the competition.

Housing

Privately owned homes would become a thing of the past. The older generation who had been able to afford to buy or build their own houses would be permitted to keep them, but for younger generations, buying a house would gradually become impossible.

Even in times of recession, many buildings might sit empty but prices would still not go down to an affordable level. A larger portion of the population would be forced to rent small apartments (without space for many children). The renting majority would then have little sympathy for increased regulations or taxation of privately owned property.

Later on, people would simply be assigned living quarters from a central housing authority. It would also become more common to have non-family members as tenants—and not know if they could be trusted.

Electronic Money

There was a recognition that wealth represents power and should therefore be limited to the few. Inflation, interest, and taxes would make it hard for ordinary people to save and become financially independent. Loans and credit would be offered generously, tempting people to spend more than they could afford—again as a means of weeding out those who could not handle credit wisely.

Money would mostly be credit. Earnings would be electronically entered directly into one's bank account and purchases automatically deducted. In order to record everyone's transactions, credit cards would replace cash, especially for larger transactions, leaving only pocket money for smaller purchases. Items of value would also have some form of identification so that they could be identified if stolen.

Once people got used to using credit cards for most purchases, these would be replaced by a single card, controlled by a single banking system. This might have the appearance of plurality [e.g. different banks, credit institutes, and currencies] but it would in effect be one single monetary system. As one's single credit card could be lost, stolen, or lent to someone else, the last step would be a skin implant, sending out radio signals so that the person could also be tracked.[†††]

Total Global Control

World Government

The end goal would be a New International Governing Body, likely through the United Nations, with a World Court, but not necessarily. Public acceptance of the UN was at that time not as wide as anticipated so there would be increased efforts to elevate its importance and get people used to the idea of "giving up some of their national sovereignty."[‡‡‡] Economic interdependence was the means for reaching this goal in a peaceful manner.[§§§]

War

"Good" things about war, according to Professor Day, were that some people were given "a chance to show great courage and heroism" and to delay overpopulation. Because there were now technological means of controlling

---

[†††] RFID chips have been used for livestock since the 1970s and on credit cards and pets since the 1990s. See Mae Kubena, "Tracing the History of RFID Implants," September 14, 2020, medium.com/@mae.kubena/tracing-the-history-of-rfid-implants-49ec1d7f66d5. The next planned step is the Internet of Things with a chip in everything (replacing barcodes)—and eventually in everyone (see chapter 11).

[‡‡‡] In 2015, before the Paris Climate Summit, the Swedish climate advocate Johan Rockström said, "I can see no other way than that 200 countries will have to give up some of their decision-making power to a planetary institutional administration. We have to work with the institutions we have, and there is only one institution that is global, the UN." Anders Bolling, "Johan Rockström är miljörörelsens egen Piketty," article in *Dagens Nyheter*, September 4, 2015.

[§§§] This was the exact recipe described by Richard N. Gardner of the Trilateral Commission in "The Hard Road to World Order," *Foreign Affairs* 52, no. 3 (1974).

the population, and economic interdependence to control countries, war was considered "obsolete." However, if there were too many people "in the right places" who opposed the new global system, "there might be a need to use one or two or possibly more nuclear weapons," making even the most reluctant terrified enough to yield.

Terrorism

Terrorism would be used in Europe and other parts of the world. At the time of the lecture (1969), it was not considered necessary for the United States but it *could* be used if needed. "Americans have had it too good anyway" so a bit of terrorism might help convince them that the world is unsafe—or *can be* unless you hand over control to the proper authorities.

Weapons Control

Not everybody should be permitted the privilege of owning a gun. The few privileged people allowed a hunting permit could rent or borrow a gun from official quarters rather than own their own.

Travel Restrictions

"Traveling is a privilege." People would need a good reason and a special permit to be allowed to travel, and also a special ID.¶¶¶ First in the form of an ID card, to be shown upon request. Later it would be in the form of a skin implant, in order to avoid false IDs and loss—or pretended loss—of the ID card. At that time, there were difficulties finding a material that would not cause infection or be rejected by the body. There were hopes that silicon could be used.

Food Control

Food supplies would become centrally controlled, ensuring that people had enough to be well-nourished, but not enough to support any dissidents from the system. Growing one's own food would become illegal under some pretext, e.g. that it could spread disease.

¶¶¶ See chapter 11 about ID2020.

Weather Control

"We can or soon will be able to control the weather." Not just cloud seeding, but *real* control. Weather was seen as a weapon of war, a weapon for influencing public policy, either by making drought during the growing season or very heavy rains during harvest season.****

Surveillance

Thefts in hospitals and other institutions would result in increased security demands and need of an ID to enter and move around in the building. Later, implantable RFID chips would enable remote tracking.

It would become common with TV monitors that could look back at you and register everything you do.†††† When the general public became alerted to this fact, they would already have become dependent on it for things like shopping from home.

The Global Coup d'État

According to professor Day, the New System would be likely implemented sometime during the winter, over a weekend. It would be initiated on a Friday night and be a fait accompli by Monday morning.

Everyone was expected to pledge allegiance to this New System and not resist. There would be no room for dissidents or martyrs. People resisting will simply disappear, to "special places," where they would be "disposed of humanely."

At that time (1969), the would-be world controllers expected to have the new system in place by the end of the century. "We plan to enter the twenty-first century with a running start." This was clearly too optimistic, but now we appear to be standing on the very brink of it—unless we put a stop to it in time.

**** Klaus Schwab warns about weather weapons in *Shaping the Fourth Industrial Revolution* (2018).

†††† This is already implemented in smart TVs. See Steven J. Vaughan-Nichols, "FBI warns about snoopy smart TVs spying on you," December 3, 2019, zdnet.com, zdnet.com/article /fbi-warns-about-snoopy-smart-tvs-spying-on-you.

Appendix C

The Organizations

The Fabian Society, London, founded in 1884 by George Bernard Shaw and Sidney and Beatrice Webb.

The Roundtable Movement, founded in 1909 by Lord Milner and Lionel Curtis.

The Carnegie Corporation, New York, founded in 1910 by Andrew Carnegie.

The Rockefeller Foundation, New York, founded in 1913 by Frederick Gates, John D. Rockefeller, and John D. Rockefeller Jr.

The Royal Institute of International Affairs (Chatham House), London, founded in 1920 by Lionel Curtis.

The Council on Foreign Relations (CFR), New York, founded in 1921 (unofficially 1918) by Elihu Root.

The Ford Foundation, New York, founded in 1936 by Henry and Edsel Ford.

The Rockefeller Brothers Fund, New York, founded in 1940 by the Rockefeller Brothers.

The Aspen Institute for Humanistic Studies, Aspen, Colorado, founded in 1949 by Walter Paepcke.

The Bilderberg Meeting, initiated in 1954 by Prince Bernhard of the Netherlands, yearly meeting for the European and American elite.

The Club of Rome, Winterthur, Switzerland, founded in 1968 by Aurelio Peccei and Alexander King to highlight challenges facing humanity and propose solutions.

The World Economic Forum (WEF), Geneva, founded in 1971 by Klaus Schwab as the European Management Forum to promote public–private partnership.

The Trilateral Commission, Washington DC, founded in 1973 by David Rockefeller and Harvard professor Zbigniew Brzezinski, to promote a closer cooperation between the United States, Europe, and Japan.

The Open Society Foundation, New York, founded in 1993 by George Soros.

The UN Foundation, founded in 1998 by Ted Turner.

The Bill & Melinda Gates Foundation, Seattle, founded in 2000 by Bill and Melinda Gates.

Bloomberg Philanthropies, founded in 2006 by Michael Bloomberg.

Appendix D

Program Areas

Program Areas of Leading Foundations 2022

Founded by **Andrew Carnegie** 1911
(US$ 3.5 bn 2022)

- Education
- Democracy
- International peace & security
- Higher Education and Research in
  Africa

Founded by **John D. Rockefeller** 1913
(US$ 6.1 bn 2022)

- Food
- Health
- Clean Energy
- Economic Equity
- Emerging Frontiers

Founded by **Henry Ford** 1936
(US$ 16 bn 2022)

- Civic Engagement and Government
- Creativity and Free Expression
- Disability Inclusion
- Future of Work(ers)
- Gender, Racial, and Ethnic Justice
- International Cooperation and
  Global Governance
- Mission Investments
- Natural Resources & Climate Change
- Technology and Society

Founded by brothers **John D. III, Nelson, Laurance, Winthrop, David** 1940
(US$ 1.47 bn 2022)

- Democratic Practice
- Peace Building
- Sustainable Development
- Arts & Culture
- Central America
- China
- Western Balkans

OPEN SOCIETY FOUNDATIONS

Founded by **George Soros** 1993
(US$ 18 bn 2022)

- Democratic Practice
- Human Rights Movements and Institutions
- Economic Equity and Justice
- Information and Digital Rights
- Education
- Journalism
- Equality and Anti-discrimination
- Justice Reform and the Rule of Law
- Health and Rights

UNITED NATIONS FOUNDATION

Founded by **Ted Turner** 1998
(US$ 358 m 2022)

- Sustainable Development Goals
- Climate & Environment
- Girls & Women
- Global Health
- Data & Technology
- UN Reform and Innovation
- Peace, Human Rights and Humanitarian Response
- Emerging Issues

BILL & MELINDA GATES *foundation*

Founded by **Bill & Melinda Gates** 2000
(US$ 50 bn 2022)

- Gender Equality
- Global Development
- Global Growth and Opportunity
- Global Health
- Global Policy and Advocacy
- U.S. Program

Bloomberg Philanthropies

Founded by **Michael Bloomberg** 2006
(US$ 4.24 bn 2022)

- Arts
- Education
- Environment
- Government Innovation
- Public Health
- Founders Projects

Timeline

Year	Date	Title	Subject	Organization
1995		*Outbreak* (film)	Pandemic	
2002		*The Great Transition* (report)	Health crisis	SEI/Tellus Institute
2004		Mapping the Global Future, NIC's 2020 Project	Pandemic, Climate, Cyberwar	National Intelligence Council
2006		*The Global Technology Revolution 2020*	Emerging technologies	RAND Corporation
2006		*Global Risks* (report)	Pandemics, climate, terrorism	World Economic Forum
2009		Foresight for Smart Globalization (workshop report)	Emerging technologies, Global challenges	Rockefeller Foundation, Institute for Alternative Futures
2010	May	*Scenarios for the Future of Technology and International Development* (report)	Health crisis (Lock Step scenario)	Rockefeller Foundation
2010		*Contagion* (film)	Pandemic	
2012		New Earth Project	Alternative lifestyles	Humanitad
2015		*Managing the Risks and Impact of Future Pandemics: Options for Public-Private Cooperation*	Pandemic	World Economic Forum
2015		TED Talk	Pandemics	Bill Gates
2016		Shaping the Future of Health and Healthcare (system initiative)	Health	World Economic Forum
2016		Global Health Challenges	Health	Trilateral Commission

Year	Date	Title	Subject	Organization
2017		*Digital Borders: Enabling a Secure, Seamless and Personalized Journey*	Digital ID	World Economic Forum
2017	20–17 Jan	Coalition for Epidemic Preparedness Innovations (CEPI)	Pandemic	WEF; Wellcome Trust; Bill & Melinda Gates Foundation
2017	Feb	Security Conference in Munich	Pandemic	Bill Gates
2017	Oct	The SPARS Pandemic 2025–2028 (simulation)	Pandemic	Johns Hopkins Center for Health Security
2018	March	Meeting between Bill Gates and Donald Trump	Pandemic	United States/White House
2018	May	*Om krisen eller kriget kommer* (Swedish crisis pamphlet)	Crisis, war	MSB (Swedish Civil Contingencies Agency)
2018	15 May	Clade X Tabletop Exercise (simulation)	Pandemic	Johns Hopkins Center for Health Security
2019	18 Jan	*Outbreak Readiness and Business Impact* (white paper)	Pandemic	World Economic Forum
2019	19–12 March	Co-creating the Future of Vaccines	Vaccines	WHO
2019	23 May	Road Map on vaccination	Vaccines	EU
2019	12 Sep	Global Vaccines Summit	Vaccines	EU/WHO
2019	18 Oct	EVENT 201 (live simulation)	Pandemic	WEF, Gates Foundation; Johns Hopkins University
2020	16 Jan	*Reimagining Digital Identity: A Strategic Imperative* (report)	Digital ID	World Economic Forum
2020	11 Mar	Pandemic Declared	Pandemic	WHO
2020	1 Apr	Immunisation Agenda 2030	Vaccines	WHO
2020	24 Apr	The Access to COVID-19 Tools (ACT) Accelerator	Vaccines	G20
2020	18 Apr	One World: Together at Home	Pandemic	Global Citizen
2020	28 May	International Pledging Event	Vaccines	European Commission & Global Citizen
2020	4 June	Global Vaccine Summit	Vaccines	UK and GAVI

Year	Date	Title	Subject	Organization
2020	27 Jun	Global Goal—The Concert	Vaccines	Global Citizen
2020	1 July	Vaccination Program	Vaccines	EU
2020	July	Cyber Polygon (exercise)	Cyberattack Management	Russia, World Economic Forum
2020	Aug	Operation Warp Speed	Vaccines	USA
2020	Sep	The Independent Panel for Pandemic Preparedness and Response	Pandemic	WHO
2020	Oct	Great Barrington Declaration	Resistance	
2020	Oct	Founding of World Doctors Alliance	Resistance	World Doctors Alliance
2020	Nov	Founding of World Freedom Alliance	Resistance	World Freedom Alliance
2020		*Principles on Identification for Sustainable Development toward the Digital Age* (report)	Digital ID	World Bank
2021	7 Jan	Implementing IA 2030	Vaccines	WHO
2021	Jan	G20 High Level Independent Panel on Financing the Global Commons for Pandemic Preparedness and Response	Pandemic	G20
2021	9 Feb	Good Health Pass	Covid Pass	ID2020
2021	May	*COVID-19: Make It the Last Pandemic* (report)	Pandemic	WHO
2021	July	*A Global Deal for Our Pandemic Age* (report)	Pandemic	G20
2021	1 July	EU Digital COVID Certificate Regulation	Health Pass	EU
2021	Sep	*Our Common Agenda* (report)	Global Governance	UN
2022	Mar	HLAB on Effective Multilateralism	Global Governance	UN
2023	Apr	*A Breakthrough for People and Planet* (report)	Global Governance	UN

Year	Date	Title	Subject	Organization
2024	May	Pandemic Prevention, Preparedness and Response Accord	Pandemic	WHO
2024	Sep	Summit of the Future/ Pact for the Future	Global Governance	UN

Bibliography

Books

Argüelles, José. *Manifesto for the Noosphere*. Berkeley, CA: Evolver Editions, 2011.

Bailey, Alice. *Education in the New Age*. New York: Lucis Trust, 1954. bailey.it/files
/Education-in-the-New-Age.pdf.

Bezold, Clement et al. *Foresight for Smart Globalization: Accelerating & Enhancing Pro-Poor Development Opportunities*. Alexandria, VA: Institute for Alternative Futures, 2009.

Christian, Robert. *Common Sense Renewed*. Lake Hills, IA: Graphic Publishing Company, 1986.

Erdman, Martin. *Ecumenical Quest for World Federation*. Greenville, SC: Vera Vox Media, 2016

Gates, William H. *Showing Up for Life: Thoughts on the Gifts of a Lifetime*. New York: Crown Currency, 2010

Goncharova, Nina. *Rainbow Earth: Vision from the Future*, Earth Is Our Common Home Project. New Delhi: Sanbun Publishers, 2010.

Harman, Willis, and O. W. Markley. *Changing Images of Man*. Oxford: Pergamon Press, 1982.

Kennedy, Robert F. Jr. *The Real Anthony Fauci: Bill Gates, Big Pharma, and the Global War on Democracy and Public Health*. New York: Skyhorse Publishing, 2021.

Lambremont Webre, Alfred. *The Omniverse: Transdimensional Intelligence, Time Travel, the Afterlife, and the Secret Colony on Mars*. Rochester, VT: Bear & Company, 2015.

Lambremont Webre, Alfred. *Emergence of the Omniverse: Universe–Multiverse–Omniverse*. Universe Books.com, 2020.

Lambremont Webre, Alfred and Phillip H. Liss. *The Age of Cataclysm*. New York: Berkley Pub. Corp, 1974.

László, Ervin. *Worldshift 2012*. Rochester, VT: Inner Traditions, 2009.

László, Ervin et al. *Goals for Mankind: A Report to the Club of Rome on the New Horizons of Global Community*. New York: Dutton, 1977.

Martinus. *Livets bok*, Band 1. Hässelby, Stockholm: Världsbild förlag, 1964.

Nordangård, Jacob. *Rockefeller: Controlling the Game.* Norrköping: Stiftelsen Pharos, 2019.

Penn, Lee. *False Dawn: The United Religions Initiative, Globalism, and the Quest for a One-World Religion.* Hillsdale, NY: Sophia Perennis, 2004.

Picknett, Lynn and Clive Prince. *Stargate Conspiracy.* Boston: Little, Brown & Co., 1999.

Public Record. *The New Order of Barbarians: The New World System,* 2013.

Quigley, Carroll. *Tragedy & Hope.* San Pedro, CA: GSG, 1966.

Reiser, Oliver L. *Cosmic Humanism and World Unity.* World Institute Creative Findings. New York: Gordon and Breach, 1975.

Reiser, Oliver L. *The World Sensorium: The Social Embryology of World Federation.* Whitefish, MT: Kessinger Publishing, 1946.

Rockefeller Brothers Fund, *Prospect for America: The Rockefeller Panel Reports.* Garden City, NY: Doubleday & Co., 1961.

Schwab, Klaus. *Shaping the Fourth Industrial Revolution.* Geneva: World Economic Forum Publishing, 2018.

Schwab, Klaus. *Stakeholder Capitalism.* Hoboken, NJ: Wiley, 2021.

Schwab, Klaus. *The Fourth Industrial Revolution.* Geneva: World Economic Forum Publishing, 2016.

Schwab, Klaus and Thierry Malleret. *COVID-19: The Great Reset.* Geneva: World Economic Forum Publishing, 2020.

Smuts, J. C. *Holism & Evolution.* London: Macmillan and Company Ltd., 1927.

Spielvogel, Jackson J. *Hitler and Nazi Germany: A History.* Abingdon: Routledge, 2020.

Suitters, Beryl. *Be Brave and Angry: Chronicles of the International Planned Parenthood Federation.* London: International Planned Parenthood Federation, 1973.

Teilhard de Chardin, Pierre. *The Phenomenon of Man.* New York: Harper & Brothers, 1955.

Wells, H. G. *The New World Order—Whether It Is Attainable, How It Can Be Attained, and What Sort of World a World at Peace Will Have to Be.* London: Secker & Warburg, 1940.

Wells, H. G. *The Open Conspiracy: Blue Prints for a World Revolution.* Garden City, NY: Doubleday & Co, 1928.

Wells, H. G. *World Brain.* London: Methuen & Co., Ltd., 1938.

Wood, Patrick M. *Technocracy Rising: The Trojan Horse of Global Transformation.* Mesa, AZ: Coherent Publishing, 2015.

Political Sources

A UNA Environment and Development Conference to provide broad public and support for United Nations Earth Summit '92. (1991): Initiative for ECO-92

Earth Charter (The Cobden Clubs, Secretariat for World Order), Midwest Public Hearing on Environment and Development. House Chambers, States Capitol, Des Moines, Iowa, September 22, 1991. archive.org/details/1991-una-environment /page/n1/mode/2up.

EU LISA. *Smart Borders Pilot Project Report on the Technical Conclusions of the Pilot, 2015.* European Agency for the operational management of large-scale IT systems in the area of freedom, security and justice. eulisa.europa.eu/Publications/Reports /Smart%20Borders%20-%20Technical%20Report.pdf.

European Commission. "A European Green Deal," 2020. ec.europa.eu/info/strategy /priorities-2019-2024/european-green-deal_en.

European Commission. "Coronavirus Global Response: €7.4 billion raised for universal access to vaccines" (press release). Brussels, May 4, 2020.

European Commission. "Coronavirus Global Response International Pledging Event—Bill Gates, Co-Chair and Trustee of the Bill & Melinda Gates Foundation." May 28, 2020. global-response.europa.eu/coronavirus-global-response-international-pledging-event-bill-gates-co-chair-and-trustee-bill -2020_mt.

European Commission. "Enabling citizens to act on climate change, for sustainable development and environmental protection through education, citizen science, observation initiatives, and civic engagement." September 18, 2020. cordis.europa. eu/programme/id/H2020_LC-GD-10-3-2020.

European Commission. "European Digital Identity—Questions and Answers." June 3, 2021. ec.europa.eu/commission/presscorner/detail/en/QANDA_21_2664.

European Commission. "European industrial strategy," 2020. commission.europa.eu /strategy-and-policy/priorities-2019-2024/europe-fit-digital-age/european -industrial-strategy_en.

European Commission, "European Travel Information and Authorisation System (ETIAS)." October 15, 2022. travel-europe.europa.eu/etias_en. ec.europa.eu /commission/presscorner/detail/en/SPEECH_92_81.

European Commission. "Making Europe's businesses future-ready: A new Industrial Strategy for a globally competitive, green and digital Europe" (press release). March 10, 2020. competitionpolicyinternational.com/making-europes-businesses -future-ready-a-new-industrial-strategy-for-a-globally-competitive-green-and -digital-europe/.

European Commission. "Opening Statement in the European Parliament Plenary Session by Ursula von der Leyen, Candidate for President of the European Commission" (transcript). July 16, 2019. ec.europa.eu/commission/presscorner /detail/en/SPEECH_19_4230.

European Commission. "Proposal for a Regulation of the European Parliament and of the Council establishing the framework for achieving climate neutrality and amending Regulation (EU) 2018/1999" (European Climate Law). 2020.

European Commission. "Roadmap for the implementation of actions." 2019. ec.europa .eu/health/sites/health/files/vaccination/docs 2019-2022_roadmap_en.pdf.

European Commission. "'THE EUROPEAN COMMUNITY AND THE NEW WORLD ORDER', address by President Jacques Delors to the Royal Institute of International Affairs – LONDON, 7 SEPTEMBER 1992" (transcript).

European Commission. "What is Horizon 2020?" 2020. ec.europa.eu/programmes /horizon2020/what-horizon-2020.

European Council. "Infographic—2023 EU budget: Main areas," November 14, 2022. consilium.europa.eu/en/infographics/2023-eu-budget-main-areas/.

European Parliament. "P9_TA(2019)0078, European Parliament resolution of 28 November 2019 on the climate and environment emergency, 2019/2930(RSP)." europarl.europa.eu/doceo/document/TA-9-2019-0078_EN.html.

European Parliament. "The European Parliament declares climate emergency" (press release). November, 29, 2019. europarl.europa.eu/news/en/press-room /20191121IPR67110/the-european-parliament-declares-climate-emergency.

European Union. "EU institutions and bodies in brief." europa.eu/european-union /about-eu/institutions-bodies.

G20 Information Centre. "Declaration of G20 Digital Ministers: Leveraging Digitalisation for a Resilient, Strong, Sustainable and Inclusive Recovery," Trieste, August 5, 2021. g20.utoronto.ca/2021/210805-digital.html.

G20 Information Centre. "Extraordinary G20 Digital Economy Ministerial Meeting: COVID-19 Response Statement" (virtual meeting). April 30, 2020. g20.utoronto. ca/2020/2020-g20-digital-0430.html.

G20 Information Centre. "Extraordinary Leaders Summit: Statement on COVID-19." March 26, 2020, g20.utoronto.ca/2020/2020-g20-statement-0326.html.

G20 Information Centre. "G20 New Industrial Revolution Action Plan, 2016 Hangzhou Summit Hangzhou." September 5, 2016. g20.utoronto. ca/2016/160905-industrial.html.

G20 Information Centre. "G20 Leaders' Declaration Shaping an interconnected world: Hamburg, 7–8 July 2017." g20.utoronto.ca/2017/2017-G20-leaders -declaration.pdf.

G20 Information Centre. "G20 Leaders Unite To Enhance Pandemic Preparedness: Riyadh, Kingdom of Saudi Arabia, November 22, 2020." g20.utoronto. ca/2020/2020-g20-leaders-declaration-1121.html.

G20 Information Centre . "G20 Ministerial Statement on Trade and Digital Economy." 2019. g20.utoronto.ca/2019/2019-g20-trade.html.

Government of Canada, "Medical assistance in dying: Overview," updated March, 5, 2024.

Government Offices of Sweden. "Sweden's support to Ukraine." government.se /government-policy/swedens-support-to-ukraine/.

Guterres, António. "Remarks to High-Level Political Forum on Sustainable Development" (transcript). United Nations Secretary-General. September 24, 2019. un.org/sg/en/content/sg/speeches/2019-09-24/remarks-high-level -political-sustainable-development-forum.

Huxley, Julian. *UNESCO: Its purpose and its philosophy*. Preparatory Commission of UNESCO, London, 1946, unesdoc.unesco.org/ark:/48223/pf0000068197.

New Zealand Parliamentary Office. "COVID-19 Public Health Response Act 2020." May 13, 2020. legislation.govt.nz/act/public/2020/0012/latest/LMS344193.html.

Schengen Visa Info. "France Requires Tourists to Hold Vaccination Passport to Access Certain Activities & Services." August 10, 2021. schengenvisainfo.com/news /france-requires-tourists-to-hold-vaccination-passport-to-access-certain-activities -services/.

Trump White House Archives. "Executive Order 13887—Modernizing Influenza Vaccines in the United States To Promote National Security and Public Health." September 19, 2019.

Trump White House Archives. "Executive Order Protecting the Nation from Foreign Terrorist Entry into the United States." March 6, 2017. trumpwhitehouse. archives.gov/presidential-actions/executive-order-protecting-nation-foreign -terrorist-entry-united-states-2/.

Trump White House Archives. *Peace and Prosperity: A Vision to Improve the Lives of the Palestinian and Israeli People*. January 2020. trumpwhitehouse.archives.gov /wp-content/uploads/2020/01/Peace-to-Prosperity-0120.pdf.

Trump White House Archives. "Remarks by President Trump During an Update on Operation Warp Speed." 13 November 2020. trumpwhitehouse.archives.gov /briefings-statements/remarks-president-trump-update-operation-warp-speed.

Trump White House Archives. "Remarks by President Trump on Vaccine Development." May 15, 2020. trumpwhitehouse.archives.gov/briefings-statement s/remarks-president-trump-vaccine-development/.

Trump White House Archives. "Remarks by President Trump to the 74th Session of the United Nations General Assembly." September 25, 2019. trumpwhitehouse. archives.gov/briefings-statements/remarks-president-trump-74th-session -united-nations-general-assembly/.

Trump White House Archives. "Remarks by President Trump, Vice President Pence, and Members of the Coronavirus Task Force in Press Briefing." April 7, 2020.

trumpwhitehouse.archives.gov/briefings-statements/remarks-president-trump-vice
-president-pence-members-coronavirus-task-force-press-briefing-april-7-2020/.

UNCTAD, *Trade and Development Report 2019: Financing a Global Green New Deal*.
UN Trade & Development, September 25, 2019. unctad.org/en/pages
/PublicationWebflyer.aspx?publicationid=2526.

UNCTAD. *A New Multilateralism for Shared Prosperity: Geneva Principles for a Global
Green New Deal*. UNCTAD & The Global Development Policy Center at Boston
University. 2019. unctad.org/publication/new-multilateralism-shared-prosperity
-geneva-principles-global-green-new-deal.

United Nations. "Careers." careers.un.org/lbw/home.aspx?viewtype=sal.

United Nations. "Decade of Action." 2020. un.org/sustainabledevelopment
/decade-of-action.

United Nations. "ID2020 Summit 2016." May 20, 2016. un.org/partnerships/ar/news
/id2020-summit-2016.

United Nations. "Launching the decade of action at a time of crisis: Keeping the
focus on the SDGs while combatting COVID-19" (Secretariat Background Note).
sustainabledevelopment.un.org/content/documents/26298HLPF_2020_impact
_COVID19.pdf.

United Nations. "Member States Approve USD 3.59 Billion UN Budget for 2024"
(press release). January 10, 2024. news.un.org/en/story/2023/12/1145072.

United Nations. *Our Common Agenda: Report of the Secretary-General*, Department of
Global Communications. United Nations. New York, NY. September 10, 2021.
un.org/en/content/common-agenda-report.

United Nations. "Secretary-General Appoints High-Level Panel on Global Response
to Health" Crises (press release). un.org/press/en/2015/sga1558.doc.htm.

United Nations, *Strengthening the global health architecture: implementation of
the recommendations of the High-Level Panel on the Global Response to Health
Crises: report of the Secretary-General*. April 8, 2016. digitallibrary.un.org/
record/826896?ln=en&v=pdf.

United Nations. *The age of digital interdependence: report of the UN Secretary-General's
High-level Panel on Digital Cooperation*. UN High-Level Panel on Digital
Cooperation, 2019. un.org/en/pdfs/DigitalCooperation-report-for%20web.pdf.

United Nations. "The Global Goals for Sustainable Development: Partners."
globalgoals.org/partners. United Nations. *The Sustainable Development Goals
Report 2020*. unstats.un.org/sdgs/report/2020/The-Sustainable-Development
-Goals-Report-2020.pdf.

United Nations. "The UN Charter." un.org/en/about-us/un-charter/full-text.

United Nations. "The UN Secretary-General's Roadmap on Digital Cooperation."
May 11, 2021. un.org/en/digital-cooperation-panel.

United Nations. "Transforming our world: the 2030 Agenda for Sustainable Development." Resolution adopted by the General Assembly on September 25, 2015.

United Nations Department of Global Communications. "The UN System." un.org /en/pdfs/18-00159e_un_system_chart_17x11_4c_en_web.pdf.

United Nations Department of Economic and Social Affairs. "The 17 Goals." sdgs. un.org.

United Nations High-level Panel on Digital Cooperation. "UN Secretary-General launches a Roadmap for Digital Cooperation." June 11, 2020. digitalcooperation. org/un-secretary-general-launches-a-roadmap-for-digital-cooperation.

UNRIC (UN Regional Information Office for Western Europe). unric.org.

US Congress. "H. RES. 109: Recognizing the duty of the Federal Government to create a Green New Deal." 2019. congress.gov/116/bills/hres109/BILLS -116hres109ih.pdf.

US Congress. "H.R.6666, COVID–19 Testing, Reaching, and Contacting Everyone (TRACE) Act." May 1, 2020. congress.gov/116/bills/hr6666/BILLS-116hr6666ih. pdf.

US Department of Defense. "Michael J.K. Kratsios: Acting Under Secretary of Defense for Research and Engineering." 2020. defense.gov/About/Biographies /Biography/Article/2279091/michael-jk-kratsios/.

US Department of Health and Human Services. "Fact Sheet: Explaining Operation Warp Speed." August 13, 2020. web.archive.org/web/20201025022616/ https ://www.hhs.gov/coronavirus/explaining-operation-warp-speed/index.html.

US House of Representative. *Report of the Special Committee to Investigate Tax-Exempt Foundations and Comparable Organizations*, Staff report no. 1-4, United States, US Govt. Print. Off. Washington, DC.

W20 Japan. "Women20." Tokyo, 2019. web.archive.org/web/20221205234708/ https://w20japan.org/en.

WHO. "ACT-Accelerator Facilitation Council, Terms of Reference." September 21, 2020. web.archive.org/web/20201119234526/https://www.who.int/docs/default-source/coronaviruse/act-accelerator/act-a-facilitation-council-terms-of-reference-21 -september-2020.pdf.

WHO. "COVID-19—virtual press conference—30 March 2020, 00:49:04" (transcript). who.int/docs/default-source/coronaviruse/transcripts/who-audio -emergencies-coronavirus-press-conference-full-30mar2020.pdf.

WHO. "Decade of Vaccines – Global Vaccine Action Plan 2011–2020." who.int /immunization/global_vaccine_action_plan/DoV_GVAP_2012_2020/en.

WHO. "Financing of General Programme of Work 2020–2025." open.who. int/2024-25/budget-and-financing/gpw-overview.

WHO. "Pandemic prevention, preparedness and response accord" (press release). who.
    int/news-room/questions-and-answers/item/pandemic-prevention—preparedness
    -and-response-accord.

WHO. "Seventy-seventh World Health Assembly – Daily update: 1 June 2024." June
    1 2024 .who.int/news/item/01-06-2024-seventy-seventh-world-health-assembly
    —daily-update—1-june-2024.

WHO. "The top 10 causes of death." World Health Organization. December 9, 2020.
    who.int/news-room/fact-sheets/detail/the-top-10-causes-of-death.

WHO. "WHO Director-General's opening remarks at the media briefing on COVID
    -19—11 March 2020." who.int/dg/speeches/detail/who-director-general-s
    -opening-remarks-at-the-media-briefing-on-covid-19—11-march-2020.

Reports

American Academy of Art & Sciences. *Our Common Purpose*. 2020. amacad.org
    /ourcommonpurpose/report.

Aspen Institute Congressional Program. *Africa's Economic, Security, and Development
    Challenges and the US Role, August 12–19, 2019*. Kigali, Musanze, and Muhanga,
    Rwanda. 2019. assets.aspeninstitute.org/content/uploads/2020/02/Africa-2019
    -Report.pdf.

Bill & Melinda Gates Foundation. *Annual Report 2006*. gatesfoundation.org/about
    /financials/annual-reports.

Bill & Melinda Gates Foundation. *Annual Report 1998*.

Club of Rome. *Planetary Emergency Plan: Securing a New Deal for People, Nature
    and Climate*, Club of Rome & Potsdam Institute for Climate Impact, 2019.
    clubofrome.org/publication/the-planetary-emergency-plan.

Club of Rome. *Planetary Emergency 2.0: Securing a New Deal for People, Nature and
    Climate*, The Club of Rome & Potsdam Institute for Climate Impact Research,
    September 2020. clubofrome.org/wp-content/uploads/2020/09/COR-PEP
    _Sep2020_A4_16pp-v2.pdf.

Cognizant. *After the Virus: A Special Report Looking Back on the Next Five Years*.
    Cognizant Center for The Future of Work, July 2020. cognizantcfow.turtl.co
    /story/after-the-virus/page/1.

Council on Foreign Relations. *War & Peace Studies of the Council on Foreign Relations*.
    New York: The Harold Pratt House, 1946.

DiEM25. *Blueprint for Europe's Just Transition*, Green New Deal for Europe. 2019.
    report.gndforeurope.com/#3.4.5.

Dixson-Declève, S., Ian Dunlop, and Anders Wijkman. *The Club of Rome Climate
    Emergency Plan: A Collaborative Call for Climate Action*. 2018. clubofrome.org/
    publication/the-climate-emergency-plan.

Dodd, Norman. *The Dodd Report to the Reece Committee on Foundations*. New York: The Long House, Inc., 1954. illinoisfamily.org/wp-content/uploads/2020/04/ Dodd-Report-to-the-Reece-Committee-on-Foundations-1954.pdf.

Dutch National Office for Identity Data, *Identity Management in 2030*. November 6, 2015. secureidentityalliance.org/publications-docman /public/6-November-15-paper-identity-management-2030/file.

Ferguson, Neil et al. *Report 9: Impact of non-pharmaceutical interventions (NPIs) to reduce COVID-19 mortality and healthcare demand*. London: Imperial College COVID-19 Response Team. March 16, 2020.

Great Transition Initiative. *Imagine all the People: Advancing a global citizens movement*. Tellus Institute. 2010. greattransition.org/archives/perspectives /Perspective_Imagine_All_the_People.pdf.

GSMA. *GSMA Cities Guide: Crowd Management*. 2018. gsma.com/iot/wp-content /uploads/2016/10/GSMA-Crowd-management-case-study-web.pdf.

The Independent Panel. *Covid-19: Make It the Last Pandemic*. 2022. theindependentpanel.org/wp-content/uploads/2021/05/COVID-19-Make-it-the -Last-Pandemic_final.pdf.

M4BL. *A Vision for Black Lives: Policy Demands for Black Power, Freedom and Justice*. 2016. archive.org/details/20160726M4blVisionBookletV3/mode/2up.

MRC Centre for Outbreak Analysis and Modelling, *Annual Report 2015-16*. 2016. imperial.ac.uk/media/imperial-college/medicine/sph/ide/2015-16.pdf.

MSB. *Konspirationsteorier och covid-19: mekanismerna bakom en snabbväxande samhällsutmaning*, Enheten för skydd mot informationspåverkan. 2021.

National Influenza Vaccine Modernization Task Force. *National Influenza Vaccine Modernization Strategy 2020–2030*. 2020. aspr.hhs.gov/MCM/Documents /nivms-2020-2030.pdf.

PNAC. *Rebuilding America's Defenses: Strategy, Forces and Resources For a New Century*. A Report of The Project for the New American Century, September 2000. archive. org/web/20130501130739/http://newamericancentury.org /RebuildingAmericasDefenses.pdf.

Radermacher, Franz Josef. *Global Marshall Plan—A Planetary Contract: For A Worldwide Eco-Social Market Economy*. 2004. files.globalmarshallplan.org/gmp _text/global_marshall_plan_e_I_eng.pdf.

Raskin, Paul. *The Great Transition Today: A Report from the Future* Tellus Institute. 2006, p. 81. greattransition.org/archives/papers/The_Great_Transition_Today.pdf.

Raskin, Paul, et al. *Branch Points: Global Scenarios and Human Choice*, A Resource Paper of the Global Scenario Group. 1997. greattransition.org/archives/other /Branch%20Points.pdf.

Raskin, Paul. *Journey to Earthland: The Great Transition to Planetary Civilization.* Tellus Institute. 2016. greattransition.org/images/GTI_publications/Journey-to -Earthland.pdf.

Raskin, Paul, et al. *Great Transition: The Promises and Lures of the Times Ahead.* Stockholm Environment Institute. 2002. greattransition.org/documents/Great _Transition.pdf.

Raskin, Paul, et al. *World Lines: Pathways, Pivots, and the Global Future* Tellus Institute. 2006. greattransition.org/archives/papers/World_Lines.pdf.

Rockefeller Foundation. *Digital Health.* 2020. rockefellerfoundation.org/wp-content /uploads/2020/09/v7_RF-Final-Report_AHI_2020903_reduced.pdf.

Rockefeller Foundation. *Scenarios for the Future of Technology and Inter-national Development.* Rockefeller Foundation and Global Business Network. May 2010. nommeraadio.ee/meedia/pdf/RRS/Rockefeller%20Foundation.pdf.

Rockefeller, John D. III. *Population and the American Future: The Rockefeller Commission Report.* Center for Research on Population and Security. July 27, 1972. population-security.org/rockefeller/001_population_growth_and_the_american _future.htm.

Schoch-Spana, Monica et al. *The SPARS pandemic 2025–2028: A Futuristic Scenario for Public Health Risk Communicators.* Johns Hopkins Center for Health Security, October 2017. centerforhealthsecurity.org/sites/default/files/2022-12/spars-pandemic-scenario.pdf.

Trilateral Commission. *Global Health Challenges* (Triangle Papers/Task Force Reports). July 30, 2016. web.archive.org/web/20160610100531/trilateral.org /file/197/Global-Health-Challenges.

World Bank Group. *Decarbonizing Development: Three Steps to a Zero-Carbon Future.* September 2015. worldbank.org/content/dam/Worldbank/document/Climate/dd /decarbonizing-development-report.pdf.

World Bank Group. *Principles on Identification for Sustainable Development: Toward the Digital Age.* World Bank Group and Center for Global Development February 2017. documents1.worldbank.org/curated/en/213581486378184357/pdf/Principles -on-identification-for-sustainable-development-toward-the-digital-age.pdf.

World Economic Forum. *Global Risks 2006: A World Economic Forum Report in collaboration with MMC (Marsh & McLennan Companies, Inc.), Merrill Lynch and Swiss Re.* 2006. www3.weforum.org/docsWEF_Global_Risks_Report_2006.pdf.

World Economic Forum. *Managing the Risk and Impact of Future Epidemics: Options for Public-Private Cooperation.* World Economic Forum & Boston Consulting Group (BCG). June 2015. www3.weforum.org/docs/WEF_Managing_Risk _Epidemics_report_2015.pdf.

World Economic Forum. *Digital Borders: Enabling a secure, seamless and personalized journey* (White Paper). 2017. www3.weforum.org/docs/IP/2017/MO/WEF_ATT _DigitalBorders_WhitePaper.pdf .

World Economic Forum. *Health and Healthcare in the Fourth Industrial Revolution: Global Future Council on the Future of Health and Healthcare 2016–2018.* May 2019. www3.weforum.org/docs/WEF__Shaping_the_Future_of_Health _Council_Report.pdf.

World Economic Forum. *Globalization 4.0: Shaping a Global Architecture in the Age of the Fourth Industrial Revolution*, Annual Meeting 2019, January 2019. www3. weforum.org/docs/WEF_AM19_Report.pdf.

World Economic Forum. *Outbreak Readiness and Business Impact: Protecting Lives and Livelihoods across the Global Economy.* 2019. www3.weforum.org/docs/WEF%20 HGHI_Outbreak_Readiness_Business_Impact.pdf.

World Economic Forum. *Reimagining Digital Identity: A Strategic Imperative.* January 16, 2020. www3.weforum.org/docs/WEF_Digital_Identity_Strategic_Imperative. pdf.

World Economic Forum. *Accelerating Digital Inclusion in the New Normal*, Playbook, July 2020. www3.weforum.org/docs WEF_Accelerating_Digital_Inclusion_in _the_New_Normal_Report_2020.pdf.

World Economic Forum. *Unlocking Technology for the Global Goals*, Antonia Gawel & Celine Herweijer, World Economic Forum, in collaboration with PwC. January 2020. www3.weforum.org/docs/Unlocking_Technology_for_the_Global_Goals.pdf.

Journal Articles

Brzezinski, Zbigniew. "America in the Technetronic Age." *Childhood Education* 45, no. 1 (1968): 6–10. doi.org/10.1080/00094056.1968.10729371.

Czech, Herwig, and Christiane Druml. "A pandemic is no private matter: the COVID-19 vaccine mandate in Austria." *The Lancet 10,* no. 4 (2022): 322–24. https://doi.org/10.1016/S2213-2600(22)00063-7.

Doshi, Peter. "The elusive definition of pandemic influenza." *Bulletin of the World Health Organization* 89 (2011): 532–38. doi.org/10.2471/BLT.11.086173.

Du Bois, W. E. B. "Neuropa: Hitler's New World Order." *The Journal of Negro Education* 10, no. 3 (1941): 380–86. doi.org/10.2307/2292742.

Faksova, K. et al. "COVID-19 vaccines and adverse events of special interest: A multinational Global Vaccine Data Network (GVDN) cohort study of 99 million vaccinated individuals." *Vaccine* 42, no. 9 (2024): 2200–2211. ISSN 0264-410X. doi.org/10.1016/j.vaccine.2024.01.100.

Gardner, Richard N. "The Hard Road to World Order." *Foreign Affairs* 52, no. 3 (1974): 556–76. doi.org/10.2307/20038069.

Gosine, Andil. "Dying Planet, Deadly People: 'Race'–Sex Anxieties and Alternative Globalizations." *Social Justice* 32, no. 4 (102): 69. https://www.jstor.org/stable/29768337.

Mostert, Saskia et al. "Excess mortality across countries in the Western World since the COVID-19 pandemic: 'Our World in Data' estimates of January 2020 to December 2022." *BMJ Public Health* 2, no. 1 (2024): e000282. doi.org/10.1136/bmjph-2023-000282.

Rabinowitch, Eugene. "Scientists and World Government." *Bulletin of the Atomic Scientists* 3, no. 12 (1947): 345–46. doi.org/10.1080/00963402.1947.11459139.

Steffen, W. et al. "Trajectories of the Earth System in the Anthropocene." *Proceedings of the National Academy of Sciences (USA)* 115, no. 33 (2018): 8252–59. doi.org/10.1073/pnas.1810141115.

Wheatland, Thomas. "The Frankfurt School's Invitation from Columbia University." *German Politics & Society* 22, no. 3 (Fall 2004): 1-32, Berghahn Books.

Wilson, Kumanan, Katherine Atkinson, and Cameron Bell. "Travel Vaccines Enter the Digital Age: Creating a Virtual Immunization Record." *American Journal of Tropical Medicine and Hygiene* 94, no. 3 (2015): 485–88. doi.org/10.4269/ajtmh.15-0510.

Articles

Alexander, Dan. "New Details About Wilbur Ross' Business Point to Pattern of Grifting." *Forbes*, August 7, 2018.

Alter, C., S. Haynes, and J. Worland. "Person of the Year: Greta Thunberg." *Time Magazine,* December 23, 2019.

Atkinson, Claire. "David Rockefeller hosts some of the world's wealthiest at MOMA." *New York Post*, April 10, 2016.

Atterstam, Inger. "Epidemiolog: Alla tycks ha tappat omdömet." *Svenska Dagbladet*, May 9, 2016.

Auken, Ida. "Welcome to 2030: I Own Nothing, Have No Privacy and Life Has Never Been Better." *Forbes*, November 10, 2016.

Barbero, Michele. "Macron's Big Vaccination Gamble." *Foreign Policy,* July 27, 2021.

Barron's. "Rockefeller Capital Management Opens, Chasing $100 Billion." *Barron's*, March 1, 2018.

BBC. "Covid: Austria suspends compulsory vaccination mandate," March 9, 2022. bbc.com/news/world-europe-60681288.

Biddle, Sam, and Ryan Devereaux. "Peter Thiel's Palantir Was Used to Bust Relatives of Migrant Children, New Documents Show." *The Intercept*, May 2, 2019.

Bolling, Anders. "Johan Rockström är miljörörelsens egen Piketty." *Dagens Nyheter*, September 4, 2015.

Brewis, Harriet. "Piers Corbyn, 73, arrested and handed £10k fine over Trafalgar Square 'anti-lockdown protests.'" *Evening Standard*, August 30, 2020.

Bruhns, Anette, et al. "Fridays for Future Is About to Turn One." *Der Spiegel*, August 1, 2019.

Cao, Sissi. "Rockefeller Family Deepens Ties in Silicon Valley through Elite Merger." *Observer*, September 19, 2019.

Chini, Maïthé. "'Best-case scenario': EU could have Covid-19 vaccine by April." *The Brussels Times*, October 28, 2020.

Crilly, Rob. "Robert Mercer: From computer programmer to Trump backer." *The National*, March 20, 2018.

Flitter, Emily, and Matthew Goldstein. "Long Before Divorce, Bill Gates Had Reputation for Questionable Behavior." *New York Times*, May 16, 2021.

Friedman, Thomas L. "The power of green." *New York Times*, April 15, 2007.

Fund, John. "'Professor Lockdown' Modeler Resigns in Disgrace." *National Review*, May 6, 2020.

Gates, Bill. "How to Fight the Next Pandemic." *New York Times*, March 18, 2015.

Gripenberg, Pia. "Hitler spökar i bakgrunden när Europaparlamentet ska besluta om klimatnödläge." *Dagens Nyheter*, November 28, 2019.

Goldstein, Matthew. "The Fed Asks for BlackRock's Help in an Echo of 2008." *New York Times*, March 25 2020

The Guardian. "Bill Gates becomes honorary knight." *The Guardian*, March 2, 2005.

The Guardian. "Melbourne stage 4 restrictions and Covid lockdown rules explained." *The Guardian*, October 16, 2020.

The Guardian. "'Our house is on fire': Greta Thunberg, 16, urges leaders to act on climate." *The Guardian*, January 25, 2019.

Harris, Paul. "They're called the Good Club—and they want to save the world." *The Guardian*, May 31, 2009.

Hauptfuhrer, Fred. "Vanishing Breeds Worry Prince Philip, but Not as Much as Overpopulation." *People*, December 21, 1981.

Huang, Joyce. "Chinese Diplomat Accuses US of Spreading Coronavirus." Voice of America, March 13, 2020. voanews.com/science-health/coronavirus-outbreak /chinese-diplomat-accuses-us-spreading-coronavirus.

Kaiser, Charles. "The Truth Is, Columbia Owns Rockefeller Center Buildings, Too." *New York Times*, March 21, 1976. nytimes.com/1976/03/21/archives/the-truth-is -columbia-owns-rockefeller-center-buildings-too.html.

Kampeas, Ron. "Treasury pick Steven Mnuchin was mentored by two of Trump's 'global' villains." *Times of Israel*, December 1, 2016.

Khiss, Peter. "Gifts of John D. Rockefeller 3d Totaled $94 Million Over His Lifetime." *New York Times*, July 10, 1979.

Kilgore, Ed. "Jimmy Carter Saw a UFO on This Day in 1973." *Intelligencer*, September 18, 2019

Kissinger, Henry. "The chance for a new world order." *New York Times*, January 12, 2009.

Koetsier, John. "$350 '5G Bioshield' Radiation Protection Device Is a . . . $6 USB Stick." *Forbes*, May 28, 2020.

Larsson, Simon. "Kravet: Bryt lockdown—ge oss flockimmunitet." *Expressen*, October 16, 2020.

MacMillan, Douglas, "Michael Kratsios Plays Peacemaker Between Trump and Tech." *Wall Street Journal*, November, 13, 2017.

Maremba, Maciej. "Varför fick de äldre dö utan läkarvård?" *Dagens Nyheter*, October 18, 2020.

Mathers, Matt. "Covid vaccine: Bill Gates says several more shots 'likely' to show strong efficacy." *The Independent*, November 18, 2020.

New York Times. "Biden's New Vaccine Requirements Draw Praise, Condemnation and Caution." *New York Times*, September 9, 2021.

New York Times. "How George Floyd Died, and What Happened Next." *New York Times*, July 29, 2020.

Nordberg, Jenny. "FN är Sveriges jultomte." *Svenska Dagbladet*, September 20, 2013.

Peterson-Withorn, Chase. "Getting Donald out of Debt: The 25-Year-Old Ties That Bind Trump and Wilbur Ross." *Forbes*, December 8, 2016.

Peterson-Withorn, Chase. "The $132 Billion Dinner: Meet the Tycoons Who Ate with Trump Last Night." *Forbes*, April 25, 2018.

Pirttisalo Sallinen, Jani. "Så byggde Balimannen sin propagandamaskin." *Svenska Dagbladet*, May 9, 2021.

Popovich, Nadj, and Henry Fountain. "What Is the Green Climate Fund and How Much Does the US Actually Pay?" *New York Times*, June 2, 2017.

Rockström, Johan. "Corona—och klimatkrisen har samma grundorsak." *Svenska Dagbladet*, March 28, 2020.

Robert Scheaffer. "Carl Sagan, Laurance Rockefeller, and UFOs." *Skeptical Enquirer*, September/October, 2014.

Schultz, Abby. "The Rockefeller Legacy." *Barron's*, June 20, 2018.

Schwab, Klaus. "The Fourth Industrial Revolution: What It Means and How to Respond." *Foreign Affairs*, December 12, 2015.

Simos, Andriana. "Michael Kratsios named as Pentagon's top technology official." *The Greek Herald*, July 14, 2020.

Stewart, James B. and Emily Flitter. "Gates Met with Epstein Many Times, Despite His Criminal Past." *New York Times*, October 13, 2019.

Stewart, James, et al. "Epstein Envisioned Seeding Human Race with His DNA." *New York Times*, August 1, 2019.

Stiernstedt, Jenny. "Gretas hälsa blev starten för Ernmans klimatkamp."*Svenska Dagbladet*, April 21, 2018.

Sutton, Matthew. "Jerusalem: Trump's gift to evangelicals." *The Seattle Times*, December 16, 2016.

Tännsjö, Torbjörn. "Så kan klimatkrisen leda fram till en global despoti." *Dagens Nyheter*, November 28, 2018.

Thomas, Ken, and Sabrina Siddiqui. "Biden Says Rioters Who Stormed Capitol Were Domestic Terrorists." *The Wall Street Journal*, January 7, 2021.

Thunberg, Greta. "Greta Thunberg: 'Vi vet—och vi kan göra något nu.'" *Svenska Dagbladet*, May 30, 2018.

Townsend, Mark, and Paul Harris. "Now the Pentagon tells Bush: climate change will destroy us." *The Observer*, February 22, 2004.

Vanhainen, Ida. "Trumps nya ambassadör—Elon Musks ex-kollega." *Svenska Dagbladet*, October 18, 2018.

Wigen, Malin. "Greta, 15, skolkar—för klimatets skull." *Aftonbladet*, August 20, 2018.

Winkler, Rolfe. "Investor Peter Thiel is Helping Mold Tech's Ties to Donald Trump." *Wall Street Journal*, December 13, 2016.

Online Articles

Agarwal, Kabir. "Not Just the Aurangabad Accident, 383 People Have Died Due to the Punitive Lockdown." *The Wire*, May 10, 2020. thewire.in/rights /migrant-workers-non-coronavirus-lockdown-deaths.

"Donald Trump acknowledges Biden election win: Full transcript." Al Jazeera, January 8, 2021. aljazeera.com/news/2021/1/8/donald-trumps-video -statement-on-capital-riot-full-transcript.

AP and ToI staff. "Israel group mints Trump coin to honor Jerusalem recognition." *Times of Israel.* February 28, 2018. timesofisrael.com/israeli-group-mints-trump -coin-to-honor-jerusalem-recognition.

Battersby, B., E. Ture, and R. Lam."Tracking the $9 Trillion Global Fiscal Support to Fight COVID-19" (blog post). *IMF BLOG.* May 20, 2020. imf.org/en/Blogs /Articles/2020/05/20/tracking-the-9-trillion-global-fiscal-support-to-fight-covid-19.

Berke, Rick. "Watch: In prescient move, Bill Gates urged Trump to invest in pandemic preparedness two years ago." STAT, March 10, 2020. statnews. com/2020/03/10/bill-gates-president-trump-pandemic-preparedness-investment.

Berkley, Seth. "We all have a stake in global health security." World
    Economic Forum, January 16, 2020. weforum.org/agenda/2020/01/
    we-all-have-a-stake-when-it-comes-to-global-health-security.

Bill & Melinda Gates Foundation. Statement from CEO Mark Suzman about
    Melinda French Gates. May 13, 2024, gatesfoundation.org/ideas/media-center
    /press-releases/2024/05/melinda-french-gates.

Branswell, Helen. "Bill Gates got President Trump fired up about a universal flu
    vaccine—and also (maybe) got a job offer." STAT, April 30, 2018. statnews.
    com/2018/04/30/bill-gates-vaccine-trump-meeting.

Branswell, Helen. "With cash and a call for new ideas, Bill Gates tries to boost
    the campaign for a universal flu vaccine." STAT, April 27, 2018. statnews.
    com/2018/04/27/bill-gates-universal-flu.

Brett, Lindsey. "Ciro Orsini blog." August 23, 2006. corsini222.blogspot.com.

Broom, Douglas. "Could this COVID-19 'health passport' be the future of travel and
    events?" World Economic Forum, July 30, 2020. weforum.org/agenda/2020/07
    /covid-19-passport-app-health-travel-covidpass-quarantine-event.

Broom, Douglas. "Most adults agree with vaccine passports for travel, survey show."
    World Economic Forum, April 28, 2021. weforum.org/agenda/2021/04
    /vaccine-passport-travel-covid-19/.

Burt, Chris. "Spoof attacks top this week's biometrics and digital ID news.
    BiometricUpdate, November 8, 2019. biometricupdate.com/201911
    /spoof-attacks-top-this-weeks-biometrics-and-digital-id-news.

Cann, Oliver. "Who Pays for Davos?," World Economic Forum, 2017. weforum.org
    /agenda/2017/01/who-pays-for-davos.

Chatzky, Andrew, and Anshu Siripurapu. "Envisioning a Green New Deal: A Global
    Comparison." Council on Foreign Relations. May 1, 2019. cfr.org/backgrounder
    /envisioning-green-new-deal-global-comparison.

Cilluffo, A., and N. G. Ruiz. "World's population is projected to nearly stop
    growing by the end of the century." Pew Research Center, June 17, 2019.
    pewresearch.org/fact-tank/2019/06/17/worlds-population-is-projected-to
    -nearly-stop-growing-by-the-end-of-the-century.

Claims of the Living. "The ITNJ Rears Its Ugly Head: A Warning" (blog post). June
    25, 2017. claimsoftheliving.blogspot.com/2017/06/the-itnj-international-tribunal
    -for.html.

Club of Rome. "Club of Rome Releases Its Climate Emergency Plan at the European
    Parliament." Club of Rome, December 3, 2018. clubofrome.org/impact-hubs
    /climate-emergency/the-club-of-rome-launches-its-climate-emergency-plan-at-the
    -european-parliament.

Dixson-Declève, Sandrine, H. J. Shellnhuber, and Kate Raworth. "Could COVID-19 give rise to a greener global future?" World Economic Forum, March 2020. weforum.org/agenda/2020/03/a-green-reboot-after-the-pandemic.

Eggerton, John. "Rockefeller Welcomes Markey." Next TV, July 17, 2013. nexttv.com /news/rockefeller-welcomes-markey-380814.

Ekholm, Börje, and Johan Rockström. "Digital technology can cut global emissions by 15%. Here's how." World Economic Forum, January 2019. weforum.org /agenda/2019/01/why-digitalization-is-the-key-to-exponential-climate-action.

Elias, Jennifer. "Sanofi partners with GSK for developing coronavirus vaccine." CNBC, April 14, 2020.

Exopolitics. "Mars visitors Basiago and Stillings confirm Barack Obama traveled to Mars." November 2011, exopolitics.blogs.com/exopolitics/2011/11/mars-visitors -basiago-and-stillings-confirm-barack-obama-traveled-to-mars-1.html.

Farrow, Anna. "Who Killed Granny? Pandemic Death Protocols in Canada's Long -term Care Facilities." C2C Journal, March 7, 2022. c2cjournal.ca/2022/03/ who-killed-granny-pandemic-death-protocols-in-canadas-long-term-care-facilities/.

Folkers, Richard. "Xanadu 2.0, Bill Gates's stately pleasure dome and futuristic home." US News, November 23, 1997. money.usnews.com/money /business-economy/articles/1997/11/23/xanadu-20.

Ford, Wayne. "Elbert County won't rebuild bombed Georgia Guidestones, will donate monument's remains." Athens Banner-Herald, October 8, 2020. eu.onlineathens. com/story/news/2022/08/10/georgia-guidestones-bombing-elbert-county-decides -not-rebuild-donating-remains/10279337002/.

Gasparino, Charles. "Trump Touts Henry Kravis as Treasury Secretary Again . . . and Again He Declines." Fox Business, May 1, 2016. foxbusiness.com/politics /trump-touts-henry-kravis-as-treasury-secretary-again-and-again-he-declines.

Gates, Bill. "Bill Gates: A new kind of terrorism could wipe out 30 million people in less than a year—and we are not prepared." *Business Insider*, February 18, 2017.

Gates, Bill. "3 lessons from COVID-19 to help us tackle climate change." World Economic Forum, August 2020. weforum.org/agenda/2020/08/ covid19-global-health-climate-change.

Gates, Bill. "Remembering Bill Gates Senior" (blog post). *Gates Notes*, September 15, 2020. gatesnotes.com/About-Bill-Gates/Remembering-Bill-Gates-Sr.

Glaser, April. "Palantir's pandemic contracts stir concern ahead of IPO." NBC News, July 22, 2020. nbcnews.com/tech/tech-news/palantir-s-pandemic-contracts -stir-concern-ahead-ipo-n1234537.

Green, Matthew."Military-style Marshall Plan needed to combat climate change, says Prince Charles." Reuters, September 21, 2020. reuters.com/article /us-climate-change-new-york-idUSKCN26C2DP.

Hamilton, Isobel. "Trump's closest Silicon Valley ally, Peter Thiel, is reportedly abandoning the president's reelection campaign." Business Insider, July 3, 2020. businessinsider.com/peter-thiel-reportedly-cutting-trump-loose-2020-7.

Haselton, Todd. "President Trump announces new 5G initiatives: It's a race 'America must win.'" CNBC, April 12, 2019, cnbc.com/2019/04/12/trump-on-5g -initiatives-a-race-america-must-win.html.

Helbing, Dirk, and Peter Seele. "Digital ID, Global Resilience, and Human Dignity" (blog post). futurict.blogspot.com/2020/09/digital-id-global-resilience-and -human.html.

Herszenhorn, David M. "Vaccinate America first, Trump tells G20," Politico, November 21, 2020. politico.eu/article/coronavirus-vaccinate-america -first-trump-tells-g20.

Hill, Josh P. "'Divest For Paris' Challenges Leaders To Show Climate Leadership." September 3, 2015, cleantechnica.com/2015/09/03/divest-paris-challenges -leaders-show-climate-leadership.

History Channel. "Rudy Guiliani," February 10, 2014. history.com/topics/21st -century/rudy-giuliani

Holden, Constance, "Rockefeller Finances Crop Circle Survey." 21 May 1999, Science, www.science.org/content/article/rockefeller-finances-crop-circle-survey.

Hopkins, Caroline. "With puberty starting earlier than ever, doctors urge greater awareness and care." NBC News, December 25, 2023, nbcnews.com/health /kids-health/puberty-starting-earlier-treatment-children-rcna125441.

Ivanova, Irina. "U.N. blasts Blackstone Group for worsening the US housing crisis." CNN News, March 26, 2019. cbsnews.com/news/blackstone-group-is -making-u-s-housing-crisis-worse-the-un-says.

Jackson, Abby. "The 13 most powerful members of 'Skull and Bones.'" Business Insider, March 19, 2017. businessinsider.com/most-powerful-members-yale-skull -and-bones-2017-3?r=US&IR=T#steven-mnuchin-class-of-1985-12.

Jacobo, Julia. "This is what Trump told supporters before many stormed Capitol Hill." January 7, 2021, ABC News, abcnews.go.com/Politics /trump-told-supporters-stormed-capitol-hill/story?id=75110558.

Johnstone, Caitlin. "The Boot Is Coming Down Hard and Fast." January 9, 2021. caitlinjohnstone.com/2021/01/09/the-boot-is-coming-down-hard-and-fast/.

Kelland, Kate. "Africa's rapid population growth puts poverty progress at risk, says Gates." Reuters, September 18, 2018.

Kleiner, Art. "The man who saw the future." Strategy+Business, February 12, 2003.

Kozul-Wright, Richard, and Kevin P. Gallagher. "Toward a Global Green New Deal." Project Syndicate, April 9, 2019. project-syndicate.org/commentary /global-green-new-deal-by-richard-kozul-wright-and-kevin-p-gallagher-2019-04.

Kubena, Mae. "Tracing the History of RFID Implants." September 14, 2020, medium.com/@mae.kubena/tracing-the-history-of-rfid-implants-49ec1d7f66d5.

Lambremont Webre, Alfred. "Canadian UFO researcher creates official Petition to have Canadian government designate him 'an Earth representative to Galactic Council.'" March 20, 2021. newsinsideout.com/2021/03/canadian-ufo-researcher -creates-official-petition-to-have-canadian-government-designate-him-an-earth -representative-to-galactic-council/.

The Local. "EXPLAINED: What is Denmark's proposed 'epidemic law' and why is it being criticised?" The Local, November 13, 2020.

Loh, Matthew. "Canada says it will freeze the bank accounts of 'Freedom Convoy' truckers who continue their anti-vaccine mandate blockades." Business Insider, February 15, 2022.

Ma, Alexandra. "Thousands of Swedish people are swapping ID cards for microchips." World Economic Forum, May 16, 2018. weforum.org/agenda/2018/05/thousands -of-people-in-sweden-are-embedding-microchips-under-their-skin-to-replace-id -cards.

Mangan, Dan. "Trump blames China for coronavirus pandemic: 'The world is paying a very big price for what they did.'" CNBC, March 19, 2020.

McGee, Patrick, "Becoming One With Your Robot." *Wired Magazine*, October 30, 2000.

Modarressy-Tehrani, Caroline, and Grace Murray. "'It just feels surreal': Military posted at checkpoints as Australian state extends COVID-19 lockdown." NBC News, August 19, 2020.

Moskovitz, Dan. "Impact Investing vs. Venture Philanthropy." Investopedia, February 2020. investopedia.com/articles/personal-finance/060915/impact-investing-vs -venture-philanthropy.asp.

Moulson, Geir. "Thousands of Germans took to Berlin's streets to protest the government's coronavirus restrictions." Associated Press, August 1, 2020.

Myers, Joe. "This member of the British Royal Family has a vital message if we are to save the planet." January 22, 2020, World Economic Forum, weforum.org/agenda/2020/01/prince-charles-the-crucial-lesson -we-have-to-learn-from-the-climate-crisis.

Nasiripour, Shahien. "Schwarzman's Wallet Props Up Wall Street Elite's Giving to Trump." Bloomberg, August 6, 2020. bloomberg.com/news/articles/2020-08-06 /schwarzman-s-wallet-props-up-wall-street-elite-s-giving-to-trump.

Natarajan. Sridhar. "BlackRock's Larry Fink delivers a grim outlook for corporate America." Financial Review, May 7, 2020. afr.com/world/north-america /blackrock-s-larry-fink-delivers-a-grim-outlook-for-corporate-america-20200507 -p54qlc.

Nation and State. "PIH, Bobby Rush, and The Truth Behind Contact Tracing Surveillance." May 15, 2020. web.archive.org/web/20200516234445 /https://nationandstate.com/2020/05/15/pih-bobby-rush-and-the-truth -behind-contact-tracing-surveillance.

Nass, Meryl. "Door to Freedom—where to now? Can we aspire to even bigger things?" June 9, 2024, Meryl's COVID Newsletter. merylnass.substack.com/p /door-to-freedom-where-to-now-can.

Pascu, Luana. "Facial recognition payment systems rolled out in Denmark, growing rapidly in China." BiometricUpdate.com, December 10, 2019. biometricupdate. com/201912/facial-recognition-payment-systems-rolled-out-in-denmark-growing -rapidly-in-china.

Pomeroy, Robin. "At Davos, Trump urges the world to ignore the 'prophets of doom'." World Economic Forum. January 21, 2020. weforum.org/agenda/2020/01 /trump-davos-apocalypse-greta-climate.

Rockefeller Foundation. "Rebuilding toward the Great Reset" (blog post). June 19, 2020. rockefellerfoundation.org/blog/rebuilding-toward-the-great-reset-crisis -covid-19-and-the-sustainable-development-goals.

Rogers, Taylor Nicole. "Davos 2021 is postponed—here's what you need to know about the invitation-only conference that brings billionaires together with business and political leaders at a Swiss ski resort." Business Insider, August 26, 2020. www.businessinsider.com/what-is-davos-world-economic-forum-conference -2020-1.

Rognerud, Nils. "Free Energy Device by Sacha Stone?" November 2017. electrogravityphysics.com/free-energy-energy-qt-pi-device/.

Sardana, Saloni. "US billionaires' wealth grew by $845 billion during the first six months of the pandemic." Business Insider, September 17, 2020.

Sault, Samantha. "What we know about the Wuhan coronavirus and urgent plans to develop a vaccine." World Economic Forum, January 24, 2020. weforum.org /agenda/2020/01/wuhan-coronavirus-china-cepi-vaccine-davos.

Singularity Hub. "Silicon Valley's Transhumanist Movement Uncovered." Singularity-Hub, January 19, 2009. singularityhub.com/2009/01/19/silicon-valleys-transhumanist -movement-uncovered.

Stakston, Brit. "Så skadar pandemin demokratin i världen." April 10, 2020. Blankspot, blankspot.se/sa-skadar-pandemin-demokratin-i-varlden-hela-listan.

Stone, Ken. "Time-Traveling Truth Candidate for President Wins 1 Vote Locally." *Times of San Diego.* July 7, 2016. timesofsandiego.com/politics /2016/07/07/time-traveling-truth-candidate-for-president-wins-1-vote-locally/.

The Guardian. "Global pandemic agreement at risk of falling apart, WHO warns." January 22, 2024, theguardian.com/world/2024/jan/22/global-pandemic -agreement-at-risk-of-falling-apart-who-warns.

True Pundit. "Exclusive: Bill Gates Negotiated $100 Billion Contact Tracing Deal with Democratic Congressman Sponsor of Bill Six Months BEFORE Coronavirus Pandemic." June 11, 2020. truepundit.com/exclusive-bill-gates-negotiated-100 -billion-contact-tracing-deal-with-democratic-congressman-sponsor-of-bill-six -months-before-coronavirus-pandemic.

Varley, Alana. "Margaret Sanger: More Eugenic than Fellow Eugenicists" (blog article). January 16, 2018. care-net.org/abundant-life-blog/margaret-sanger -more-eugenic-than-fellow-eugenicists.

Vaughan-Nichols, Steven J. "FBI warns about snoopy smart TVs spying on you." December 3, 2019. zdnet.com/article/fbi-warns-about-snoopy-smart-tvs -spying-on-you/.

Wall, Mic. "New Conspiracy Theory: Children Kidnapped for Mars Slave Colony." July 1, 2017. web.archive.org/web/20170702051044/https://www.space .com/37366-mars-slave-colony-alex-jones.html.

Weidmo Uvell, Rebecca. "Bo Thorén—Spindeln i nätet." February 12, 2019. uvell. se/2019/02/12/bo-thoren-spindeln-i-natet.

Wilcock, David. "Disclosure Imminent? Two Underground NWO Bases Destroyed." (blog post), September 16, 2011. web.archive.org/web/20120422144337/http ://www.divinecosmos.com/start-here/davids-blog/975-undergroundbases.

Wilner, Michael. "'We're good to go.' The diplomatic push to release Kushner's Mideast peace plan." Impact2020, January 30, 2020, mcclatchydc.com/news /politics-government/white-house/article239781943.html.

Winter, Jessic. "Greed Is Bad. Bad!" *Slate*, September 25, 2007. slate.com /culture/2007/09/how-wall-street-s-gordon-gekko-inspired-a-generation-o -imitators.html.

World Economic Forum. "Now is the time for a Great Reset." WEF, June 3, 2020. weforum.org/agenda/2020/06/now-is-the-time-for-a-great-reset.

Thomson, Alex. "Coronavirus lockdown: German lawyer detained for opposition." April, 14 2020. www.ukcolumn.org/article/coronavirus-lockdown-german -lawyer-detained-opposition.

Zubrin, Robert. "The Population Control Holocaust." The New Atlantis, Spring 2022. thenewatlantis.com/publications/the-population-control-holocaust.

Internet Sources

2030Vision. "Advancing Fourth Industrial Revolution Technology for the Global
    Goals." 2030vision.com.

5G Bioshield. web.archive.org/web/20210816042515/https://5gbioshield.com.

AGRA. "Leadership: Rajiv J. Shah." agra.org/who-we-are-our-leadership-old
    /dr-rajiv-j-shah/.

American Frontline Nurses. "Rememberance Project." americanfrontlinenurse.org
    /remembranceproject.

American Frontline Nurses. "Archive." Substack. afln.substack.com/archive.

American Humanist Association. "The Humanist Manifesto I." americanhumanist.
    org/what-is-humanism/manifesto1.

Avanti. avantiplc.com.

Bill & Melinda Gates Foundation. "About Event." gatesfoundation.org/goalkeepers
    /about-event/awards.

Bill & Melinda Gates Foundation. "About Goalkeepers." gatesfoundation.org
    /goalkeepers/about-goalkeepers.

Biohax International. facebook.com/BiohaxInternational.

Black Lives Matters. "Herstory." blacklivesmatter.com/herstory.

Boudreau, John. "Elihu Root—1912 Nobel Peace Prize." hamilton.edu/about/history
    /elihu-root.

Carnegie Medal of Philanthropy. "The Gates Family." 2001. medalofphilanthropy.org
    /the-gates-family.

Carnegie Medal of Philanthropy. "Kravis, Marie-Josée and Henry R."
    medalofphilanthropy.org/marie-josee-and-henry-r-kravis.

Chipster. chipster.nu.

Climate Strike. "Partners." climatestrike.net/partners.

Club of Budapest. "Our Mission." clubofbudapest.com/our-mission.

Co-Impact. "Funding Partners." co-impact.org/partners.

The Commons Project (2020). "CommonPass." thecommonsproject.org/commonpass.

Corona Schadensersatzklage. corona-schadensersatzklage.de.

The COVID-19 Humanity Betrayal Memory Project. "Cases." chbmp.org/cases.

David Suzuki Foundation. "Declaration of Interdependence." davidsuzuki.org/about
    /declaration-of-interdependence.

DiEM25. "About us." diem25.org/about-us.

DiEM25. *Blueprint for Europe's Just Transition*. Democracy in Europe Movement
    2025, 2019. gnde.diem25.org.

Earth Is Our Common Home. "Vision." present5.com/rio-20-earth-is-our
    -common-home-vision.

Earth Sanctuary. web.archive.org/web/20140626125741/http://www.humanitad.org
/programs/earth_sanctuary.

Earth Sanctuary. "Address problem." web.archive.org/web/20140618215333/http
://earth-sanctuary.org/address-problems.html.

Ekonomifakta. "Statsbudget & statsskuld: Stödåtgärder Coronakrisen." 22 mars
2022. ekonomifakta.se.

El Hassan Bin Talal. "Biography." elhassanbintalal.jo/en-us/HRH-Prince
-EL-Hassan-Bin-Talal/Biography.

Exemplar Zero. "Administration." web.archive.org/web/20110128184112/http://www
.exemplarzero.org/index.php?p=team&ref=admin.

Exemplar Zero. "Initiative Overview." web.archive.org/web/20110211204009/http
://www.exemplarzero.org.

Exopolitics. "Star Dreams Initiative." exopolitics.blogs.com/star_dreams_initiative.

Forum of Young Global Leaders. "Community." younggloballeaders.org/community.

Forum of Young Global Leaders "Community." 2012. web.archive.org/web
/20120806113309if_/http://www.weforum.org/community/forum-young-
global-leaders.

Forum of Young Global Leaders. "Concept." 2005. web.archive.org
/web/20050114005555/http://www.younggloballeaders.org/scripts/page48.html.

Forum of Young Global Leaders. "Nomination Committee." 2005. web.archive.org
/web/20050113113223/http://www.younggloballeaders.org/scripts/page36.html.

Forum of Young Global Leaders. "Our Alumni Community." www.younggloballeaders.org/
our-alumni-community/.

Forum of Young Global Leaders. "Young Global Leaders and Alumni Annual Summit
2018 Co-Creating a Sustainable Future." San Francisco, USA. 15–18 October.
web.archive.org/web/20181128222743/https://www.weforum.org/events
/young-global-leaders-and-alumni-annual-summit/.

GAVI. "COVAX explained." 2020. gavi.org/vaccineswork/covax-explained.

GAVI. "Proceeds to Gavi from Donor Contributions & Pledges (2021–2025) as of 30
June, 2023," gavi.org/investing-gavi/funding/donor-profiles/united-states-america.

The Giving Pledge. "About." givingpledge.org/About.aspx.

Global Citizen. "One World: Together at Home." Global Citizen, April 18, 2020.
globalcitizen.org/en/connect/togetherathome.

Global Goals Week. globalgoalsweek.org.

Global Shapers Community. "The power of youth in action." globalshapers.org.

GND Group. "History of the Green New Deal." greennewdealgroup.org
/history-of-the-green-new-deal.

Goi Peace Foundation. "Our Approach." goipeace.or.jp/en/about/approach.

Good Health Pass. "Good Health Pass Collaborative." Feb 8, 2021. web.archive.org
/web/20210208222630/https://goodhealthpass.org.

Graham, Javier. "ID2020 Alliance at a glance" (presentation). readkong.com/page
/alliance-committed-to-improving-lives-through-digital-1380992.

Great Barrington Declaration. "The Great Barrington Declaration." 2020.
gbdeclaration.org.

Great Transition Initiative. greattransition.org.

Hague Academic Coalition. "Members: The Carnegie Foundation." haguecoalition.
org/Members/the-carnegie-foundation.

Heintz, Stephen. "Earned Knowledge: The Intersection of Learned Knowledge and
Lived Experience." Rockefeller Brothers Fund. February 4, 2020. rbf.org/news
/earned-knowledge-intersection-learned-knowledge-and-lived-experience.

Humanitad. "Initiatives." humanitad.org/initiatives.

Humanitad. "Mission." humanitad.org/mission.

Humanitad. "People." humanitad.org/people.

Humanitad. "QT-PI." humanitad.org/wp-content/uploads/2017/03/qtpi.pdf.

ID2020. "ID2020." 2015. web.archive.org/web/20151108233202/https://id2020.org.

ID2020. "Digital Identity." 2017. web.archive.org/web/20170912122929/http
://id2020.org/digital-identity-1.

ID2020. "ID2020 Summit 2017." web.archive.org/web/20171013132643/http
://id2020summit.org.

ID2020. "ID2020 Summit 2020: Sessions" (webinars). id2020.org
/summit/2020-id2020-summit-sessions-webinar-series.

ID2020 "ID2020." 2020. id2020.org.

ID2020 (2021). "Good Health Pass: A New Cross-Sector Initiative to Restore Global
Travel and Restart the Global Economy." February 9, 2021. medium.com/id2020
/good-health-pass-a-new-cross-sector-initiative-to-restore-global-travel-and-restart
-the-global-8b59eb1050a0.

The Independent Panel for Pandemic Preparedness and Response. "About."
theindependentpanel.org/about-the-independent-panel.

ITNJ. "International Tribunal of Natural Justice." itnj.org.

ITNJ. "Judicial Commission." commission.itnj.org.

Johns Hopkins Center for Health Security. "Event 201: A Global Pandemic Exercise."
October 18, 2019. centerforhealthsecurity.org/event201.

Johns Hopkins Center for Health Security. "The SPARS Pandemic 2025–2028:
A Futuristic Scenario to Facilitate Medical Countermeasure Communication."
October 2017, centerforhealthsecurity.org/our-work/Center-projects/completed
-projects/spars-pandemic-scenario.html.

Läkaruppropet. "The Doctors' Appeal." March 12, 2021, lakaruppropet.se.

Masters, Jonathan, and Will Merrow. "How Much Aid Has the U.S. Sent Ukraine? Here Are Six Charts." Council on Foreign Relations. February 23, 2024. cfr.org /article/how-much-aid-has-us-sent-ukraine-here-are-six-charts.

Medic Debate. "Peoples Court." medicdebate.org/node/1102.

MERA25. "What is MERA25?" diem25.org/mera25.

Modern Money Network. "Bernhard Lietaer." modernmoneynetwork.org/content /bernard-lietaer.

New Earth Festival. newearthfestival.com.

New Earth Horizon. "Locations." newearthhorizon.com/locations.

New Earth Horizon Shop. newearthhorizon.com/shop.

New Earth Nations. web.archive.org/web/20210323211204/http://newearthnations .org/.

New Earth Nations. "Statement of Clarification." newearthnations.org /statement-of-clarification.

New Earth Project. "About Us." web.archive.org/web/20130820194747/http ://www.new-earth-project.org/about-us.

New Earth University. "Fellows." newearth.university/fellows.

Newman, Caroline. "Rajiv Shah. Thomas Jefferson medal in Citizen leadership." University of Virginia, April 2, 2020. hnews.virginia.edu/content /dr-rajiv-j-shah-thomas-jefferson-foundation-medalist-citizen-leadership.

Noosphere Forum. web.archive.org/web/20130210100117/http://www .noosphereforum.org/main.html.

Participant Media. "About Participant." participant.com/about-participant#block -views-team-block-1.

Plant for the Planet. "About us." plant-for-the-planet.org/en/about-us/aims-and-vision.

Project Everyone. project-everyone.org.

Q-map. web.archive.org/web/20180807020442/https://qmap.pub.

Right Livelihood Awards. "Greta Thunberg." rightlivelihoodaward.org/laureates /greta-thunberg.

Rockefeller Brothers Fund. "Grantees: Tides Foundation $250,000 for 24 months, awarded Sep 19, 2019, For the Electoral Justice Project of its project, the Movement for Black Lives." rbf.org/grantees/tides-foundation.

Rockefeller Brothers Fund. "Rockefeller Brothers Fund Increases Spending to Seize 'Hinge Moment in History'" (announcement). June 29, 2020. www.rbf.org/news /rockefeller-brothers-fund-increases-spending-seize-hinge-moment-history.

Rockefeller Family Fund. "Environment." rffund.org/programs/environment.

Rockefeller Foundation Archives. "Bureau of Social Hygiene." rockfound.rockarch .org/bureau-of-social-hygiene.

Rockefeller Foundation Archives. "A Digital History: Childhood Immunization."
    rockfound.rockarch.org/childhood-immunization.

Royal HaskoningDHV. "Crowd Management: Shaping the Normal in Public Space."
    June 21, 2020. web.archive.org/web/20200621174729/https
    ://www.royalhaskoningdhv.com/en-gb/specials/people-flows/social-distancing.

Sønstebø. David (2017). "Welcome John Edge to IOTA." blog.iota.org
    /welcome-john-edge-to-iota-d378fb8f0b2.

SRI International. National Security. sri.com/national-security.

StandUpX. standupx.info.

Sunrise Movement (2019). "Green New Deal Resources." sunrisemovement.org
    /gnd-resources.

Supermajority. "About Us." supermajority.com/about-us/#about-us-6.

Synergos. "David Rockefeller Bridging Leadership Award." www.synergos.org
    /david-rockefeller-bridging-leadership-award.

Team Blackbird (2020). "Our Work." teamblackbird.org/our-work.

Team Malizia. "Greta Thunberg arrives in New York after 14 days crossing the
    Atlantic aboard Malizia II." team-malizia.com/en/greta-thunberg-arrives-in-new
    -york-after-14-days-crossing-the-atlantic-aboard-malizia-ii.

United Nations Foundation. "Our Mission." unfoundation.org/who-we-are
    /our-mission.

University of Chicago Library. "Guide to the Committee to Frame a World
    Constitution Records 1945–1951." www.lib.uchicago.edu/e/scrc/findingaids
    /view.php?eadid=ICU.SPCL.CFWC.

Venus Project. thevenusproject.com.

WhaleWisdom. "Rockefeller Capital Management." whalewisdom.com/filer
    /rockefeller-capital-management-lp#tabholdings_tab_link.

World Economic Forum. Centre for the Fourth Industrial Revolution. 2020.
    weforum.org/centre-for-the-fourth-industrial-revolution.

World Economic Forum. CEO Action Group for the European Green Deal. 2020.
    weforum.org/communities/ceo-action-group-for-a-european-green-deal.

World Economic Forum. Shaping the Future of Digital Economy
    and New Value Creation. 2020. weforum.org/platforms/
    shaping-the-future-of-digital-economy-and-new-value-creation.

World Economic Forum. "Ai-jen Poo, Director, National Domestic Workers Alliance."
    weforum.org/people/ai-jen-poo.

World Economic Forum. "Antonia Gawel." www.weforum.org/agenda/authors
    /antonia-gawel.

World Economic Forum. "Dr Celine Herweijer." www.weforum.org/agenda/authors
    /celineherweijer.

World Economic Forum. "Frontier 2030." weforum.org/projects/frontier-2030. weforum.org/agenda/authors/celineherweijer.

World Economic Forum. "Global Future Councils." weforum.org/communities /global-future-councils.

World Freedom Alliance. "Youth For Freedom." youth.worldfreedomalliance.org.

Yachtfan, Peter. "Bill Gates Private Jets." July 19, 2020, superyachtfan.com/bill-gates -private-jet.html.

Yale Law School. "The Covenant of the League of Nations." avalon.law.yale.edu/20th _century/leagcov.asp.

Film & Video

After Burner. "Charlie Ward. underage girls & Jimmy Savile" (video). Bitchute, March 5, 2021. www.bitchute.com/video/NvNKNO6fBDUp/.

Aghoutane, Ismail. "World Doctors Alliance Hearing #3 in Berlin. Germany 10 10 2020" (video). YouTube, December 6, 2020. youtu.be/HBcidqig5kk.

The American Presidency Project. "Remarks During a Meeting With Former Secretary of State Henry A. Kissinger and an Exchange with Reporters." October 10, 2017. UC Santa Barbara. presidency.ucsb.edu/documents/remarks-during-meeting-with-former-secretary-state-henry-kissinger-and-exchange-with-.

Bay, Michael (2020). *Songbird*—Official Trailer (film trailer). October 29, 2020. youtu.be/hzTYZTXGQeU.

Bridgespan. "For the Sake of Sustainability: Ted Turner makes an urgent appeal to reverse population growth" (video). November 27, 2019. bridgespan.org/insights /ted-turner/for-the-sake-of-sustainability-ted-turner-makes-a.

Cahill, Dolores. "World Freedom Alliance: Stockholm - Part 2" (video). November 20, 2020. facebook.com/663251520811711/videos/132652364972091.

CNN Business. "See how drones are helping fight coronavirus" (video). April 20, 2020. edition.cnn.com/videos/business/2020/04/30/drones-coronavirus -pandemic-lon-orig-tp.cnn.

Club of Budapest. "Ervin László: Global Shift NOW! A new book announcement" (video). July 20, 2020. youtu.be/gOL2d65I0tA.

Cognizant (2020). "After the Virus: A Discussion Looking Back on the Next 5 Years" (fictitious zoom meeting). Cognizant. July 28, 2020. youtu.be/oNxFJt5aYI4.

Columbia Journalism Review, "Covering Climate Change" (livestream). April 30, 2019. youtu.be/FO9DKk07SCY; coveringclimatenow.org.

C-SPAN. "President Trump Remarks on Election Results." November 5, 2020 (video & transcript). c-span.org/video/?477858-1/president-trump-remarks -election-results.

Cyber Polygon 2020, "Live Stream Agenda" (videos), July 8, 2020. 2020.
    cyberpolygon.com/agenda.

Cyber Polygon 2021, "Live Stream Agenda" (videos), July 9, 2021. 2021.cyberpolygon.
    com/agenda.

Cyber Polygon 2020, "Trust or fear: what will be the main incentive for cooperation
    after the crisis?" with Jeremy Jurgens (video), July 2020. 2020.cyberpolygon.com
    /gallery/video/?roistat_visit=941241#LAvq7X6UBcw.

Cyber Polygon 2020. "Welcoming Remarks by Klaus Schwab" (video). July 2020.
    2020.cyberpolygon.com/gallery/video/#EOvz1Flfrfw.

Demokrati utan gränser. "Idén om världsparlamentet" by Andreas Önnerfors (video
    presentation). YouTube, April 25, 2020. youtu.be/_AOBPvgW-gQ.

Gates, Bill. "How we must respond to the coronavirus pandemic" (TED Talk).
    March 24, 2020. ted.com/talks/bill_gates_how_we_must_respond_to_the
    _coronavirus_pandemic#t-475854.

Global Economic. "Robert David Steele Confirm! Donald Trump Start Arrest—
    Hillary Clinton—On Deep State in March 2019." March 4, 2019 (video). youtu.
    be/Sq3mdRyVwoE.

Grossman, Nathan. *I Am Greta: A Force of Nature* (documentary). B-Reel Films.
    November 13, 2020.

The Intercept. "A Message From the Future with Alexandria Ocasio-Cortez." (official
    video, illustrated by Molly Crabapple). *The Intercept* & Naomi Klein, April 17,
    2019. youtu.be/d9uTH0iprVQ.

marekdjw (2020). "Sacha Stone Interview with John and Irina Mappin from Camelot
    TV Network" (video). YouTube, April 25, 2020. youtu.be/DuIIGOw4myM.

Narayani, Marzia. "Sacha Stone: 'We will see the end of all governments' (interview).
    2020. bewusst.tv. youtube.com/watch?v=AZ2zVC8FN0A.

Ossebaard, Janet. *Fall of the Cabal* ("documentary" series). 2019. web.archive.org
    /web/20200822151347/https://en.valcabal.nl.

Pinto, Christian J., and Mike Bennett. (2015). *Dark Clouds over Elberton: The True Story
    of the Georgia Guidestones* (documentary). Adullam Films, September 18, 2015.

Soderbergh, Steven. *Contagion* (film). Participant Media. Imagenation Abu Dhabi.
    Double Feature Films, 2011.

Steele, Robert David. "Sacha Stone Update On Virus. 5G and Fall of Cabal" (video).
    April 1, 2020. altcensored.com/watch?v=m4Qx_7FDunE.

Steele, Robert David. "Declaration of NESARA/GESARA Coming? Sacha Stone
    Thinks So!" (video). Bitchute, April 13, 2020. bitchute.com/video/6IjdpaLAQQQ.

Stone, Sacha. "Message to the Stockholm Rally. Sweden," (video). November 18,
    2020. facebook.com/sacha.stone.7/videos/10159315741808487.

Teunissen, Fred. "Sacha Stone interview" (video). Vimeo, October 13, 2013. vimeo.
com/77732706.

Vaken.se. "Maneka JC Helleberg om lösningar på världens problem" (video).
Facebook, juli 16, 2020. facebook.com/vakenpunktse/videos/288677812337376.

Ward, Charlie. "Health Technology. EMF Medbed Devices With John Baxter"
(video). Before It's News, May 2023. beforeitsnews.com/alternative/2023/05/
charlie-ward-health-technology-emf-medbed-devices-with-john-baxter-
video-3792692.html.

World Awake. "5G Apocalypse Protection with Sacha Stone on Trump.
Sovereignty. Income Tax & More!" (video). YouTube, October 10, 2019. youtu.
be/_DVn9xXpTLk.

World Doctors Alliance. "World Freedom Alliance." 2020 (video). web.archive.org
/web/20201126132800/https://worlddoctorsalliance.com/blog
/theworldfreedomalliance2020announcementvideo/.

World Doctors Alliance. "Hearing #3 in Berlin, Germany" (video). October 10, 2020.
onevsp.com/watch/uYTDU74AzhxeGFe.

World Economic Forum. "COVID-19: The Great Reset." June 3, 2020. weforum.org/
great-reset and youtu.be/VHRkkeecg7c.

World Economic Forum. "Greta Thunberg: 'Our house is still on fire and you're
fuelling the flames'" (video and transcript). January 21, 2020. weforum.org
/agenda/2020/01/greta-speech-our-house-is-still-on-fire-davos-2020.

World Economic Forum. "Prince Charles says we need a global Marshall Plan to
save the environment" (video). World Economic Forum, September 25, 2020.
weforum.org/videos/prince-charles-says-we-need-a-global-marshall-plan
-to-save-the-environment.

X22 Report Spotlight. "Deep State Panic. Arrests & Military Tribunals Around The
Corner: Robert David Steele" (video). Dailymotion, 2018. dailymotion.com/video
/x6ux5ff.

Other

American Presidency Project. "Remarks During a Meeting With Former Secretary of
State Henry A. Kissinger and an Exchange With Reporters. October 10, 2017"
(transcript). UC Santa Barbara. presidency.ucsb.edu/documents/remarks-during
-meeting-with-former-secretary-state-henry-kissinger-and-exchange-with-0.

Bichip. "Bichip coin BCHI." January 21, 2019. bichip.store/uploads/LSESOJXONL.
pdf.

Bilderberg Meetings. "67th Bilderberg Meeting to take place 30 May–2 June 2019 in
Montreux, Switzerland" (press release). bilderbergmeetings.org/press/press-release
/press-release.

Bill & Melinda Gates Foundation. "Bill & Melinda Gates Foundation Dedicates Additional Funding to the Novel Coronavirus Response" (press release). February 2020. www.gatesfoundation.org/Media-Center/Press-Releases/2020/02/Bill-and -Melinda-Gates-Foundation-Dedicates-Additional-Funding-to-the-Novel -Coronavirus-Response.

Bill & Melinda Gates Foundation. "Life Sciences Companies Commit Expertise and Assets to the Fight Against COVID-19 Pandemic Alongside Bill & Melinda Gates Foundation" (press release). March 25, 2020.

Borealis Foundation. "Borealis Philanthropy Launches New Fund to Strengthen Racial Equity in Nonprofits" (press release), Business Wire. June 5, 2019. borealisphilanthropy.org/borealis-philanthropy-launches-fund-to-advance-racial -equity-in-philanthropy.

Carnegie Corporation of New York. "First Andrew Carnegie Medals Awarded to Seven Visionaries of Modern Philanthropy." 2001 (press release). www.carnegie. org/news/articles/first-andrew-carnegie-medals-awarded-to-seven-visionaries-of -modern-philanthropy.

Carnegie Corporation of New York. "Strengthening the Work of the United Nations: A Sustained Strategy for Peace." Carnegie Results (quarterly newsletter), 2006. carnegie.org/publications/strengthening-the-work-of-the-united-nations-a -sustained-strategy-for-peace.

CBS News (2016). "Face the Nation Transcript December 18, 2016: Conway. Kissinger. Donilon" (transcript). www.cbsnews.com/news/face-the-nation -transcript-conway-kissinger-donilon.

Eco-Social Forum & PIK. "A Global Contract Based on Climate Justice. Conference on November 11, 2008. European Parliament/Hemicycle, Brussels, Belgium." Conference program. biopolitics.gr/biowp/wp-content/uploads/2013/04/ seminars.-participation-Global-Contract-on-Climate-Justice.New-Approach. -programme.pdf.

Gates, Bill. "About David Rockefeller" (tweet). March 21, 2017. twitter.com/billgates /status/844311407399223296.

GAVI (2011). Donors commit vaccine funding to achieve historic milestone (press release). gavi.org/donors-commit-vaccine-funding-to-achieve-historic -milestone-in-global-health.

Dixson-Declève. Sandrine. "Letter to Ursula von der Leyen from the Chairman of the Club of Rome." December 11, 2019. listas.unizar.es/pipermail/cdr-aragon /attachments/20200224/6a67996d/attachment-0001.pdf.

Financial Times. "Transcript: Bill Gates speaks to the FT about the global fight against coronavirus" (interview). *Financial Times*. April 9, 2020.

The Freemen Institute. "Tax-Exempt Foundations." *The Freemen Digest*. June 1978. Interviews and summary of the Reece Commission report. web.archive.org /web/20170302090737/http://www.freedomforallseasons.org/TaxFreedomEmail /TaxExemptFoundationsTakingsFinal.pdf.

French. Jedediah. "Q&A: Andreas Önnerfors" (interview). *The Gavel* 20, no. 3 (March 2020).

French. Jedediah (2020). Final Word. *The Gavel* 20, no. 3 (March 2020).

Gates, Bill, and Melinda Gates. "Why we swing for the fences. 2020 Annual Letter. Gates Notes" (newsletter). gatesnotes.com/2020-Annual-Letter.

Griffin, G. Edward. "Norman Dodd Interview" (transcript). 1982. supremelaw.org /authors/dodd/interview.htm.

Harvard Kennedy School. "Schwab's Wiener Lecture points to challenges and opportunities of new industrial revolution" (interview). October 2, 2017.

ITNJ. Bombshell Nuclear Coverup on the Scale of Fukushima (press release). September 25, 2019. itnj.org/blog/2019/09/25/carolyn_tyler_testmony_on _nuclear_cover_up/.

Johns Hopkins School of Public Health. "Experts Issue Urgent Call to Adopt New Principles to Aid and Protect World's Most Vulnerable Populations from Influenza Pandemic" (press release). September 29, 2006. jhsph.edu/news/news -releases/2006/faden-bellagio.html.

Klimatriksdagen. "Program 2018" (program leaflet). klimatriksdagen.se/wp-content/.

lightgreenleaf. "August, 29th 2020 Trafalgar Square. Unite for Freedom Rally." Twitter. 15 September 2020. peakd.com/hive-196427/@lightgreenleaf/lshpfrgd.

New Earth Nations. (Facebook post). May, 25 2020. www.facebook.com/ newearthnations/posts/2874059096040637.

New York Times. "Obituaries: Dr. Richard Day. 84. Ex-Pediatrics Professor." *New York Times*. June 16, 1989.

New York Times. "Transcript of Donald Trump's Immigration Speech." *New York Times*. February 9, 2016.

The Nobel Prize. "Elihu Root: Nobel Lecture" (transcript). www.nobelprize.org /prizes/peace/1912/root/lecture.

NPR. "Greta Thunberg's Speech At The U.N. Climate Action Summit" (transcript). September 23, 2019. npr.org/2019/09/23/763452863/ transcript-greta-thunbergs-speech-at-the-u-n-climate-action-summit

PBS. "Transcript: Bill Moyers Interviews Bill Gates" (interview). 2003. www.pbs.org /now/transcript/transcript_gates.html.

Peaceinspace.org (2020). "Judgment of the Tribunal in the matter of Genocidal Technologies Pandemic." November 29, 2020. exopolitics.blogs.com/files/final -judgment—natural-and-common-law-tribunal–November-29-2020.pdf.

Plant for the Planet & UNEP (2015). "Endorse our Manifesto of the World's Youth" (letter to Chancellor Merkel). May 25, 2015. tunza.eco-generation.org/file /IMG_20150609_014115.png.

Plant for the Planet. "Youth Manifesto." May 25, 2015. web.archive.org /web/20150910044323/http:/www.pftp2014-prod.plant-for-the-planet.org/media /files/news/40154307-youth-manifesto.pdf.

Plant for the Planet. "Youth Summit 2015" (conference brochure). global-youth-climate-plan.org/media/files/program/youth_summit_program_flyer_20150513_ web.pdf.

Potsdam Institute for Climate Impact Research, "A Global Contract Based on Climate Justice: Policy paper prepared for the conference on 11 November 2008." researchgate.net/publication/252106419_A_Global_Contract_on _Climate_Change.

Rockefeller Capital Management. "Rockefeller Capital Management to Acquire Silicon Valley Multi-Family Office Financial Clarity" (press release). September 18, 2019. businesswire.com/news/home/20190918005288/en/Rockefeller-Capital-Management-to-Acquire-Silicon-Valley-Multi-Family-Office-Financial-Clarity.

Rockefeller Capital Management. "Rockefeller Capital Management Adds Three Highly Acclaimed Advisory Teams to Growing Private Wealth Platform" (press release). September 8, 2020. businesswire.com/news/home/20200908005119/en /Rockefeller-Capital-Management-Adds-Highly-Acclaimed-Advisory.

Rockefeller Foundation. "Using Data to Save Lives: The Rockefeller Foundation and Partners Launch $100 Million Precision Public Health Initiative" (press release). September 25, 2019. rockefellerfoundation.org/news/using-data-save -lives-rockefeller-foundation-partners-launch-100-million-precision-public-health -initiative.

Rockefeller Foundation. "The Rockefeller Foundation Launches Covid-19 Action Plan to Reopen Workplaces. Protect Lives" (press release). April 21, 2020. rockefellerfoundation.org/news/the-rockefeller-foundation-launches-covid-19 -action-plan-to-reopen-workplaces-protect-lives.

Rockefeller University. "Epstein, Kandel and Kissinger Join Rockefeller University Board of Trustees" (press release). November 22, 1995. newswire.rockefeller. edu/1995/11/22/epstein-kandel-and-kissinger-join-rockefeller-university -board-of-trustees/.

Shah, Rajiv J. "COVID-19: Meeting This Moment." (President's Annual Letter.) Rockefeller Foundation. April 4, 2020. rockefellerfoundation. org/2020-annual-letter.

StandUpX. Rally message on Twitter. September 5, 2020. twitter.com/StandUpX2 /status/1302168398965678080/photo/1.

Stiftelsen Pharos & Malone Institute. World Economic Forum's Young Global Leaders (complete list), May, 2022. blog.jacobnordangard.se/wef-ygl-list/.

Trilateral Commission. "The Trilateral Commission at 25: Between Past . . . and Future." Anniversary Evening sponsored by US Group. December 1, 1998. web.archive.org/web/20160519221402/trilateral.org/download/files/anniversary_evening.pdf.

Trilateral Commission. "Frequently Asked Questions." archive.is/6Iktb.

Trilateral Commission. "Member List." 2015. web.archive.org/web/20151129042629/https://www.trilateral.org/download/files/TC_list_11_15.pdf.

vsblty.net. "VSBLTY and PHOTON-X Developing Advanced Thermal Camera Technology" (press release). April 21. 2020. https://vsblty.net/news/vsblty-and-photon-x-developing-advanced-thermal-camera-technology/.

World Economic Forum. Shape a Better Future (recruitment brochure). 2016. www3.weforum.org/docs/WEF_Shape_a_Better_Future_business.pdf.

World Economic Forum (2019). World Economic Forum and UN Sign Strategic Partnership Framework (press release). weforum.org/press/2019/06/world-economic-forum-and-un-sign-strategic-partnership-framework.

World Economic Forum. The Great Reset: A Unique Twin Summit to Begin 2021 (press release). June 3, 2020. weforum.org/press/2020/06/the-great-reset-a-unique-twin-summit-to-begin-2021.

Image Credits

Chapter 1. The Vision

World Control, Shutterstock

Georgia Guidestones, photo by Dina Eric/Flickr (CC 0)

Chapter 2. The Threats

Atomic bomb, wallpaperflare.com (CC 0)

Edward Teller 1958, Lawrence Livermore National Laboratory (CC 3.0)

Chapter 3. The Partnership

Handshake, Shutterstock

UN–WEF partnership 2019, World Economic Forum. weforum.org/press

Chapter 4. The Emergency

Extinction Rebellion, Shutterstock

School strike, Fridays For Future, 2020, photo by Frankie Fouganthin (CC 4.0)

Franz-Josef Radermacher 2016, photo by Manfred Werner/Tsui (CC4.0)

Reichstagsbrand 1933, Records of the Office of War Information (CC 0)

Ursula von der Leyen presents her vision to MEPs, 19 July 2019, EU (CC 4.0)

Chapter 5. The Trigger

Coronavirus, Shutterstock

Chapter 6. The Coup

Earth in the hands, Getty Images
Klaus Schwab, The Great Reset (video screenshot), WEF (Fair Use)

Chapter 7. The Club

Bill Gates with vaccine deal, Shutterstock
Bill Gates about David Rockefeller, Twitter, March 21, 2017 (Fair Use)
   twitter.com/billgates/status/844311407399223296

Chapter 8. The Trump Card

Donald Trump and Henry Kissinger, 10 October 2017, photo by Sheala
   Graighead/The White House (CC0)

Chapter 9. The Resistance

Stockholm rally, 6 June 2021, photo by Almanova (Fair Use)
London rally poster, 19 September 2020, standupx.info (Fair Use)
Sacha Stone (video screenshot), World Awake, Youtube, 10 Oct 2019
   (Fair Use)

Chapter 10. The Transition

Great Transition (report cover), Stockholm Environment Institute, 2002
   (Fair Use)

Chapter 11. The Digital ID

Digital ID, Shutterstock

EU Vaccine Roadmap, European Commission, 2019 (Fair Use) health. ec.europa.eu/publications/roadmap-implementation-actions_en

GAVI fundrasing summit, June 2011, Ben Fisher/GAVI Alliance (CC2.0)

Digital Health Pass, Shutterstock

Microchip implant, Shutterstock

Chapter 12. The Robbery

Vacuuming money, Getty Images

Global Goal Concert poster 2020, Global Citizen (Fair Use)

Jack Ma, New York, 23 September 2018, photo by Ben Hider/WEF (CC2.0)

Elon Musk, JD Lasica, Pleasanton, CA (CC 2.0)

Mark Zuckerberg 2008, photo by Jason McELweenie/Flickr (CC 2.0)

Bill Gates in Tokyo 2015, Wikimedia (CC 4.0)

Jeff Bezos 2013, photo by Steve Jurvetson (CC 2.0)

Closed due to COVID-19, Shutterstock

Lockdown, Shutterstock

Begging woman in Italy, pxhere.com (CC 0)

Epilogue

Internet, Gerd Altman, pixabay.com (CC0)

Cyber Polygon exercise, World Economic Forum (Fair Use)

Appendix A

Columbia University, Beyond My Ken, Wikimedia (CC4.0)

Appendix D

Andrew Carnegie 1913 (CC 0)
John D. Rockefeller 1914 (CC 0)
Henry Ford 1919 (CC 0)
Rockefeller Brothers, Smithsonian National Portrait Gallery, Philippe Halsman Archive (Fair Use)
George Soros, photo by Paul Hogroian/US Government (CC 0)
Ted Turner 2019, photo by John Mathew Smith/celebrity-photos.com (CC 2.0)
Bill & Melinda Gates 2009, photo by Kjetil Ree (CC 3.0)
Michael Bloomberg 2015 (CC 0)

About the Author

Jacob Nordangård is a Swedish researcher, author, and musician. He has a PhD in technology and social change from Linköping University, a master's of social science in geography, and a master's of social science in culture and media production. He is the founding chairman of Stiftelsen Pharos (Pharos Foundation), CEO of Pharos Media Productions, and former senior lecturer at the universities of Norrköping, Jönköping, and Stockholm.

Nordangård is the author of six books about the historical roots and development of the global management system that has emerged in recent years, including *An Inconvenient Journey* (2015), *Rockefeller: Controlling the Game* (2019), *The Global Coup d'État* (2020, in Swedish), and *The Digital World Brain* (2022, in Swedish).

He is also the bandleader, singer, and songwriter of the Swedish doom metal band Wardenclyffe, with lyrics inspired by his research and originally offered as soundtracks to his books. The latest project was the concept album *Temple of Solomon*, released one song per month (from July 2021) with a public lecture about the subject of each song. This story will also be published as a book.

jacobnordangard.se
drjacobnordangard.substack.com

Endnotes

Prologue

1   "WHO Director-General's opening remarks at the media briefing on COVID-19," World Health Organization, March 11, 2020, who.int/dg/speeches/detail/who-director-general-s-opening-remarks-at-the-media-briefing-on-covid-19—11-march-2020.

Chapter 1

1   G. Edward Griffin, "Transcript of Norman Dodd Interview," 1982, supremelaw.org/authors/dodd/interview.htm.

2   Martin Erdmann, *Ecumenical Quest for a World Federation* (Greenville, SC: Verax Vox Media, 2016).

3   Carroll Quigley, *Tragedy & Hope* (San Pedro, CA: GSG, 1966).

4   Hague Academic Coalition, "Members: The Carnegie Foundation," haguecoalition.org/Members/the-carnegie-foundation.

5   Karen Theroux, "Strengthening the Work of the United Nations: A Sustained Strategy for Peace," Carnegie Results (quarterly newsletter), 2006, carnegie.org/publications/strengthening-the-work-of-the-united-nations-a-sustained-strategy-for-peace.

6   US House of Representatives, *Report of the Special Committee to Investigate Tax-Exempt Foundations and Comparable Organizations,* Staff report no. 1-4, United States, US Govt. Print. Off, Washington, DC, 1954.

7   John Boudreau, "Elihu Root—1912 Nobel Peace Prize," hamilton.edu/about/history/elihu-root.

8   John P. Finnegan, *Against the Specter of a Dragon: The Campaign for American Military Preparedness 1914–1917,* 1974 (Westport, CT: University of Michigan/Greenwood Pres.)

9   Nobel Prize: "Elihu Root Nobel Lecture" (transcript), nobelprize.org/prizes/peace/1912/root/lecture.

10   Yale Law School, "The Covenant of the League of Nations," avalon.law.yale.edu/20th_century/leagcov.asp.

11   Jacob Nordangård, *Rockefeller: Controlling the Game* (Norrköping: Stiftelsen Pharos, 2019).

12   Council on Foreign Relations, *War & Peace Studies of the Council on Foreign Relations* (New York: The Harold Pratt House, 1946).

13   J. C. Smuts, *Holism & Evolution* (London: Macmillan and Company Ltd., 1927).

14   United Nations Department of Global Communications, "The UN System," 2019, un.org/en/pdfs/18-00159e_un_system_chart_17x11_4c_en_web.pdf.

15   United Nations, "United Nations Charter," un.org/en/about-us/un-charter/full-text.

16   UNRIC (UN Regional Information Centre for Western Europe), unric.org.

17   European Commission (1992), "THE EUROPEAN COMMUNITY AND THE
     NEW WORLD ORDER, address by President Jacques Delors to the Royal Institute of
     International Affairs—LONDON, 7 SEPTEMBER 1992" (transcript), ec.europa.eu
     /commission/presscorner/detail/en/SPEECH_92_81.

18   The Freemen Institute, "Tax-Exempt Foundations," *The Freemen Digest*, June 1978,
     interviews and summary of the Reece Commission report, web.archive.org
     /web/20170302090737/http://www.freedomforallseasons.org/TaxFreedomEmail
     /TaxExemptFoundationsTakingsFinal.pdf.

19   Trilateral Commission,"Frequently Asked Questions," archive.is/6Iktb.

20   Richard N. Gardner, "The Hard Road to World Order," *Foreign Affairs* 52, no. 3 (1974):
     556-76, doi.org/10.2307/20038069.

21   H. G. Wells, *World Brain* (London: Methuen & Co., Ltd., 1938).
     H. G. Wells, *The Open Conspiracy: Blue Prints for a World Revolution* (Garden City, NY:
     Doubleday, Doran & Company, Inc., 1928).

22   H. G. Wells, *The New World Order: Whether It Is Attainable, How It Can Be Attained, and
     What Sort of World a World at Peace Will Have to Be* (London: Secker & Warburg, 1940).

23   Pierre Teilhard de Chardin, *The Phenomenon of Man* (New York: Harper & Brothers, 1959).

24   Oliver L. Reiser, *The World Sensorium: The Social Embryology of World Federation* (Whitefish,
     MT: Kessinger Publishing, 1946).

25   American Humanist Association, "Humanist Manifesto I," americanhumanist.org
     /what-is-humanism/manifesto1.

26   Oliver L. Reiser, *Cosmic Humanism and World Unity,* World Institute Creative Findings
     (New York: Gordon and Breach, 1975).

27   Julian Huxley, *UNESCO: Its Purpose and Its Philosophy*, Preparatory Commission of
     UNESCO, London, 1946, unesdoc.unesco.org/ark:/48223/pf0000068197.

28   Patrick M. Wood, *Technocracy Rising: The Trojan Horse of Global Transformation* (Mesa, AZ:
     Coherent Publishing, 2015).

29   Reiser, *Cosmic Humanism and World Unity.*

30   Ervin László et al., *Goals for Mankind: A Report to the Club of Rome on the New Horizons of
     Global Community* (New York: Dutton, 1977).

31   Robert Christian, *Common Sense Renewed* (Lake Hills, IA: Graphic Publishing Company,
     1986).

32   Christian J. Pinto and Mike Bennett, *Dark Clouds over Elberton: The True Story of the
     Georgia Guidestones*, Adullam Films, September 18, 2015.

33   Wayne Ford, "Elbert County won't rebuild bombed Georgia Guidestones, will donate
     monument's remains," *Athens Banner-Herald*, August 10, 2022, eu.onlineathens.com/
     story/news/2022/08/10/georgia-guidestones-bombing-elbert-county-decides-not-rebuild-
     donating-remains/10279337002/.

34   A UNA Environment and Development Conference to provide broad public and support
     for United Nations Earth Summit '92. (1991): Initiative for ECO-92 Earth Charter (The
     Cobden Clubs, Secretariat for World Order), Midwest Public Hearing on Environment and
     Development. House Chambers, States Capitol, Des Moines, Iowa, September 22, 1991,
     archive.org/details/1991-una-environment/page/n1/mode/2up.

Chapter 2

1 Eugene Rabinowitch, "Scientists and World Government," *Bulletin of the Atomic Scientists* 3, no. 12 (1947): 345–46, tandfonline.com/doi/abs/10.1080/00963402.1947.11459139.

2 Rockefeller Brothers Fund, *Prospects for America: The Rockefeller Panel Reports* (New York: Doubleday & Co., 1961).

3 Rabinowitch, "Scientists and World Government."

4 "Guide to the Committee to Frame a World Constitution Records 1945–1951," University of Chicago Library, 2014, lib.uchicago.edu/e/scrc/findingaids/view.php?eadid=ICU.SPCL. CFWC.

5 Andil Gosine, "Dying Planet, Deadly People: 'Race'–Sex Anxieties and Alternative Globalizations," *Social Justice* 32, no. 4 (2005): 69.

6 John D. Rockefeller III, *Population and the American Future: The Rockefeller Commission Report*, Center for Research on Population and Security, July 27, 1972, population-security. org/rockefeller/001_population_growth_and_the_american_future.htm.

7 Nordangård, *Rockefeller.*

8 A. Cilluffo and N. G. Ruiz, "World's population is projected to nearly stop growing by the end of the century," Pew Research Center, June 17, 2019, pewresearch.org/fact-tank/2019/06/17/worlds-population-is-projected-to-nearly-stop-growing-by-the-end -of-the-century.

9 Nordangård, *Rockefeller.*

10 Ibid.

11 PNAC (2000), *Rebuilding America's Defenses: Strategy, Forces and Resources For a New Century*, A Report of The Project for the New American Century, September 2000, p. 51.

12 EU LISA, *Smart Borders Pilot Project Report on the Technical Conclusions of the Pilot, 2015*, European Agency for the operational management of large-scale IT systems in the area of freedom, security and justice, eulisa.europa.eu/Publications/Reports/Smart%20Borders%20 -%20Technical%20Report.pdf.

13 European Commission, "European Travel Information and Authorisation System (ETIAS)," ec.europa.eu/home-affairs/what-we-do/policies/borders-and-visas/smart -borders/etias_en.

14 Henry Kissinger (2009), "The chance for a new world order," article in *New York Times*, January 12, 2009.

Chapter 3

1 United Nations, "Transforming our world: the 2030 Agenda for Sustainable Development," Resolution adopted by the General Assembly on September 25, 2015.

2 Oliver Cann, "Who Pays for Davos?" World Economic Forum, January 2017 weforum.org /agenda/2017/01/who-pays-for-davos.

3 Taylor Nicole Rogers, "Davos 2021 is postponed—here's what you need to know about the invitation-only conference that brings billionaires together with business and political leaders at a Swiss ski resort," Business Insider, August 26, 2020, businessinsider.com /what-is-davos-world-economic-forum-conference-2020-1.

4   World Economic Forum, "Shaping the Future of Health and Healthcare" (platform), weforum.org/platforms/shaping-the-future-of-health-and-healthcare.

5   World Economic Forum, "Shaping the Future of Digital Economy and New Value Creation" (platform), 2020, weforum.org/platforms/shaping-the-future-of-digital-economy -and-new-value-creation.

6   World Economic Forum, *Shape a Better Future*, 2016, www3.weforum.org/docs/WEF _Shape_a_Better_Future_business.pdf.

7   Forum of Young Global Leaders, "Nomination Committee," 2005, web.archive.org /web/20050113113223/http://www.younggloballeaders.org/scripts/page36.html.

8   Forum of Young Global Leaders, 2012, web.archive.org/web/20120806113309if_/http ://www.weforum.org/community/forum-young-global-leaders.

9   Harvard Kennedy School, "Schwab's Wiener Lecture points to challenges and opportunities of new industrial revolution," October 2, 2017, https://www.hks.harvard.edu/more/alumni/ alumni-stories/collaboration-fractured-world-klaus-schwab-mcmpa-speaks-harvard-kennedy.

10   Forum of Young Global Leaders, "Concept," 2005, web.archive.org/web/20050114005555 /http://www.younggloballeaders.org/scripts/page48.html.

11   Forum of Young Global Leaders, "Community," younggloballeaders.org/community.

12   Forum of Young Global Leaders, "Our Alumni Community," younggloballeaders.org /our-alumni-community/.

13   Forum of Young Global Leaders, "Young Global Leaders and Alumni Annual Summit 2018: Co-Creating a Sustainable Future, San Francisco, USA 15–18 October, 2018," web.archive. org/web/20181128222743/https://www.weforum.org/events/young-global-leaders-and -alumni-annual-summit/.

14   Global Shapers Community, "The power of youth in action," globalshapers.org.

15   Klaus Schwab, "The Fourth Industrial Revolution: What It Means and How to Respond," article in *Foreign Affairs*, December 12, 2015.

16   Klaus Schwab, *Fourth Industrial Revolution* (Geneva: World Economic Forum Publishing, 2016).

17   World Economic Forum, "Global Future Councils," weforum.org/communities /global-future-councils.

18   Klaus Schwab, *Shaping the Fourth Industrial Revolution* (Geneva: World Economic Forum Publishing, 2018).

19   Patrick McGee, "Becoming One With Your Robot," article in Wired Magazine, October 30, 2000.

20   World Economic Forum, "Centre for the Fourth Industrial Revolution," 2020, weforum. org/centre-for-the-fourth-industrial-revolution.

21   World Economic Forum, "World Economic Forum and UN Sign Strategic Partnership Framework," June 13, 2019, weforum.org/press/2019/06/world-economic-forum -and-un-sign-strategic-partnership-framework.

22   United Nations, "The Global Goals for Sustainable Development: Partners," globalgoals. org/partners.

23   2030Vision, "Advancing Fourth Industrial Revolution Technology for the Global Goals," 2030vision.com.

24   Project Everyone, project-everyone.org.

25   Global Goals Week, globalgoalsweek.org.

26   United Nations Foundation, "Our Mission and History," unfoundation.org/who-we-are /our-mission/.

27   Bridgespan, "For the Sake of Sustainability" (video), November 27, 2019, bridgespan.org
      /insights/library/remarkable-givers/profiles/ted-turner/for-the-sake-of-sustainability
      -ted-turner-makes-a.

28   Bill & Melinda Gates Foundation, "About Goalkeepers," gatesfoundation.org/goalkeepers
      /about-goalkeepers.

29   Bill & Melinda Gates Foundation, "About Event," gatesfoundation.org/goalkeepers
      /about-event/awards.

30   United Nations, "Decade of Action," un.org/sustainabledevelopment/decade-of-action.

31   António Guterres, "Remarks to High-Level Political Forum on Sustainable Development,"
      September 24, 2019, United Nations Secretary-General (transcript). un.org/sg/en/content
      /sg/speeches/2019-09-24/remarks-high-level-political-sustainable-development-forum.

32   United Nations, "Digital Cooperation Panel," un.org/en/digital-cooperation-panel.

33   United Nations, *The Age of Digital Interdependence: Report of the UN Secretary-General's
      High-level Panel on Digital Cooperation*, UN High-Level Panel on Digital Cooperation,
      2019, un.org/en/pdfs/DigitalCooperation-report-for%20web.pdf.

34   World Economic Forum, "Frontier 2030," web.archive.org/web/20210419154836/
      weforum.org/projects/frontier-2030.

35   W20 Japan, "Women20," Tokyo, 2019, web.archive.org/web/20221205234708/https
      ://w20japan.org/en.

36   G20 Information Centre, "G20 New Industrial Revolution Action Plan," Hangzhou
      Summit, September 5, 2016, g20.utoronto.ca/2016/160905-industrial.html.

37   G20 Information Centre, "G20 Leaders' Declaration Shaping an interconnected world,"
      Hamburg, 7–8 July 2017, g20.utoronto.ca/2017/2017-G20-leaders-declaration.pdf.

38   G20 Information Centre, "G20 Ministerial Statement on Trade and Digital Economy,"
      2019, web.archive.org/web/20240220002553/https://www.g20.utoronto.ca/2019/2019-
      g20-trade.html.

Chapter 4

1   NPR, "Greta Thunberg's Speech At The U.N. Climate Action Summit, 23 September
     2019" (transcript), npr.org/2019/09/23/763452863/transcript-greta-thunbergs-speech-at
     -the-un-climate-action-summit.

2   Plant for the Planet, "Youth Summit 2015" (conference brochure), global-youth-climate
     -plan.org/media/files/program/youth_summit_program_flyer_20150513_web.pdf.

3   Plant for the Planet, "Youth Manifesto," May 25, 2015, web.archive.org/
     web/20150910044323/http:/www.pftp2014-prod.plant-for-the-planet.org/media/files
     /news/40154307-youth-manifesto.pdf.

4   Plant for the Planet & UNEP, "Endorse our Manifesto of the World's Youth" (letter to Chan-
     cellor Merkel), May 25, 2015, tunza.eco-generation.org/file/IMG_20150609_014115.png.

5   Plant for the Planet, "About us," plant-for-the-planet.org/en/about-us/aims-and-vision.

6   Eco-Social Forum & PIK, "A Global Contract Based on Climate Justice," Conference on
     November 11, 2008, European Parliament/Hemicycle, Brussels (program), biopolitics.gr/
     biowp/wp-content/uploads/2013/04/seminars.-participation-Global-Contract-on-Climate
     -Justice.New-Approach.-programme.pdf; Potsdam Institute for Climate Impact Research,
     "A Global Contract Based on Climate Justice," November 2008, Policy paper prepared for

the conference, researchgate.net/publication/252106419_A_Global_Contract_on
_Climate_Change.

7   Climate Strike, "Partners," climatestrike.net/partners.

8   Rebecca Weidmo Uvell, "Bo Thorén—Spindeln i nätet," February 12, 2019, uvell.
se/2019/02/12/bo-thoren-spindeln-i-natet.

9   Jenny Stiernstedt, "Gretas hälsa blev starten för Ernmans klimatkamp" (Greta's health was
the start of Ernman's climate activsm), article in *Svenska Dagbladet*, April 21, 2018.

10   Klimatriksdagen, "Program 2018," klimatriksdagen.se/wp-content/uploads/pdf/program
/Program.pdf?sprak=eng.

11   Greta Thunberg, "Vi vet—och vi kan göra något nu" ("We know—and we can do
something now"), opinion piece in *Svenska Dagbladet*, May 30, 2018.

12   Malin Wigen, "Greta, 15, skolkar—för klimatets skull" ("Greta, 15, plays truant—for the
climate"), article in *Aftonbladet*, August 20, 2019.

13   Nathan Grossman, *I Am Greta: A Force of Nature*. B-Reel Films, November 13, 2020.

14   The Guardian, "'Our house is on fire': Greta Thunberg, 16, urges leaders to act on climate,"
article in *The Guardian,* January 25, 2019.

15   Anette Bruhns et al., "Fridays for Future Is About to Turn One," article in *Der Spiegel,*
August 1, 2019.

16   Team Malizia, "Greta Thunberg arrives in New York after 14 days crossing the Atlantic
aboard Malizia II," August 28, 2019, team-malizia.com.

17   W. Steffen et al., *Trajectories of the Earth System in the Anthropocene: Proceedings of the
National Academy of Sciences (USA),* 2018, doi.org/10.1073/pnas1810141115.

18   World Economic Forum, *Globalization 4.0: Shaping a Global Architecture in the Age of
the Fourth Industrial Revolution,* Annual Meeting 2019, World Economic Forum, www3.
weforum.org/docs/WEF_AM19_Report.pdf.

19   Börje Ekholm, & Johan Rockström, "Digital technology can cut global emissions by 15%.
Here's how," World Economic Forum, 2019, weforum.org/agenda/2019/01
/why-digitalization-is-the-key-to-exponential-climate-action.

20   Right Livelihood Awards: "Greta Thunberg 2019," rightlivelihoodaward.org/laureates
/greta-thunberg. .

21   C. Alter, S. Haynes, and J. Worland, "Person of the Year: Greta Thunberg," article in *Time
Magazine,* December 23, 2019.

22   UNCTAD, *Trade and Development Report 2019: Financing a Global Green New Deal.* UN
Trade & Development, September 25, 2019. unctad.org/en/pages/PublicationWebflyer.
aspx?publicationid=2526.

23   Thomas L.Friedman, "The power of green," opinion piece in *New York Times*, April 15,
2007; Andrew Chatzky and Anshu Siripurapu, "Envisioning a Green New Deal: A Global
Comparison," Council on Foreign Relations, May 1, 2019, cfr.org/backgrounder
/envisioning-green-new-deal-global-comparison.

24   United States Congress, H.RES.109: Recognizing the duty of the Federal Government to
create a Green New Deal, 2019.

25   John Eggerton, "Rockefeller Welcomes Markey," Next TV, July 17, 2013, nexttv.com/news
/rockefeller-welcomes-markey-380814.

26   Rockefeller Family Fund, "Environment," rffund.org/programs/environment.

27   Sunrise Movement, "Green New Deal Resources," 2019, sunrisemovement.org
/gnd-resources.

28 Richard Kozul-Wright and Kevin P. Gallagher, "Toward a Global Green New Deal," Project Syndicate, April 9, 2019, project-syndicate.org/commentary/global-green-new-deal-by-richard-kozul-wright-and-kevin-p-gallagher-2019-04.

29 UNCTAD, *A New Multilateralism for Shared Prosperity: Geneva Principles for a Global Green New Deal*, UNCTAD & The Global Development Policy Center at Boston University, 2019, unctad.org/publication/new-multilateralism-shared-prosperity-geneva-principles-global-green-new-deal.

30 The Intercept, "A Message From the Future with Alexandria Ocasio-Cortez" (official video, illustrated by Molly Crabapple), *The Intercept* and Naomi Klein April 17, 2019, youtu.be/d9uTH0iprVQ.

31 Columbia Journalism Review, "Covering Climate Change" (livestream), April 30, 2019, youtu.be/FO9DKk07SCY; coveringclimatenow.org.

32 DiEM25, "About us," diem25.org/about-us/.

33 MERA25, "What is MERA25?" diem25.org/mera25.

34 DiEM25, *Blueprint for Europe's Just Transition*, Green New Deal for Europe, December 2019, report.gndforeurope.com/#3.4.5.

35 DiEM25, *The Green New Deal for Europe: A Blueprint for Europe's Just Transition* Democracy in Europe Movement 2025, gnde.diem25.org.

36 Radermacher, Franz Josef, *Global Marshall Plan—A Planetary Contract: For A Worldwide Eco-Social Market Economy*, 2004, files.globalmarshallplan.org/gmp_text/global_marshall_plan_e_I_eng.pdf.

37 Nordangård, *Rockefeller*, 194–97.

38 El Hassan Bin Talal, "Biography," elhassanbintalal.jo/en-us/HRH-Prince-EL-Hassan-Bin-Talal/Biography.

39 S. Dixson-Declève, I. Dunlop, and A. Wijkman, *The Club of Rome Climate Emergency Plan: A Collaborative Call for Climate Action*, Club of Rome, 2018, clubofrome.org/publication/the-climate-emergency-plan.

40 Club of Rome, "Club of Rome releases its Climate Emergency Plan at the European Parliament," December 3, 2018, clubofrome.org/impact-hubs/climate-emergency/the-club-of-rome-launches-its-climate-emergency-plan-at-the-european-parliament.

41 Club of Rome and PIK, *Planetary Emergency Plan: Securing a New Deal for People, Nature and Climate*, Club of Rome and Potsdam Institute for Climate Impact Research, 2019, clubofrome.org/publication/the-planetary-emergency-plan.

42 Ibid.

43 European Parliament, "The European Parliament declares climate emergency," November, 29, 2019, europarl.europa.eu/news/en/press-room/20191121IPR67110/the-european-parliament-declares-climate-emergency.

44 European Parliament, "European Parliament resolution of November 28, 2019 on the climate and environment emergency" (2019/2930(RSP)).

45 Josh P. Hill, "'Divest For Paris' Challenges Leaders To Show Climate Leadership," September 3, 2015, cleantechnica.com/2015/09/03/divest-paris-challenges-leaders-show-climate-leadership.

46 Pia Gripenberg, "Hitler spökar i bakgrunden när Europaparlamentet ska besluta om klimatnödläge" (Hitler's ghost hovers in the background when the EU Parliament is to vote on declaring a climate emergency)," article in *Dagens Nyheter*, November 28, 2019.

47   W. E. B. Du Bois (1941), "Neuropa: Hitler's New World Order," *The Journal of Negro Education* 10, no. 3 (1941): 380–86. doi.org/10.2307/2292742.

48   Jackson J. Spielvogel, *Hitler and Nazi Germany: A History* (Abingdon: Routledge, 2020).

49   European Union, "EU institutions and bodies in brief," europa.eu/european-union /about-eu/institutions-bodies.

50   European Commission, "Opening Statement in the European Parliament Plenary Session by Ursula von der Leyen, Candidate for President of the European Commission" (transcript), July 16, 2019, ec.europa.eu/commission/presscorner/detail/en/SPEECH_19_4230.

51   Sandrine Dixson-Declève, "Letter to Ursula von der Leyen," December 11, 2019, listas. unizar.es/pipermail/cdr-aragon/attachments/20200224/6a67996d/attachment-0001.pdf.

52   European Parliament, "The European Parliament declares climate emergency" (press release), November 29, 2019, europarl.europa.eu/news/en/press-room/20191121IPR67110 /the-european-parliament-declares-climate-emergency.

53   Robin Pomeroy, "At Davos, Trump urges the world to ignore the 'prophets of doom,'" World Economic Forum, 2020.

54   World Economic Forum, "Greta Thunberg: 'Our house is still on fire and you're fuelling the flames,'" January 21, 2020, weforum.org/agenda/2020/01/greta-speech-our-house -is-still-on-fire-davos-2020.

55   World Bank Group, *Decarbonizing Development: Three Steps to a Zero-Carbon Future*, 2015, worldbank.org/content/dam/Worldbank/document/Climate/dd/decarbonizing -development-report.pdf.

56   Joe Myers, "This member of the British Royal Family has a vital message if we are to save the planet," World Economic Forum, January 2020, weforum.org/agenda/2020/01 /prince-charles-the-crucial-lesson-we-have-to-learn-from-the-climate-crisis.

57   World Economic Forum, "CEO Action Group for the European Green Deal," 2020, weforum.org/communities/ceo-action-group-for-a-european-green-deal.

58   Antonia Gawel and Celine Herweijer, *Unlocking Technology for the Global Goals*, World Economic Forum & PwC, January 2020, www3.weforum.org/docs/Unlocking _Technology_for_the_Global_Goals.pdf.

59   World Economic Forum, "Antonia Gawel," weforum.org/agenda/authors/antonia-gawel.

Chapter 5

1   Samantha Sault, "What we know about the Wuhan coronavirus and urgent plans to develop a vaccine," World Economic Forum, January 24, 2020, weforum.org/agenda/2020/01 /wuhan-coronavirus-china-cepi-vaccine-davos.

2   MRC Centre for Outbreak Analysis and Modelling, *Annual Report 2015–16*, imperial. ac.uk/media/imperial-college/medicine/sph/ide/2015-16.pdf.

3   Neil Ferguson et al., *Report 9: Impact of non-pharmaceutical interventions (NPIs) to reduce COVID-19 mortality and healthcare demand.* Imperial College COVID-19 Response Team, March 16, 2020.

4   John Fund, "'Professor Lockdown' Modeler Resigns in Disgrace," article in *National Review*, May 6, 2020.

5   Brit Stakston, "Så skadar pandemin demokratin i världen" ("How the pandemic harms democracy all over the world"), April 10, 2020, https://blankspot.se/sa-skadar-pandemin -demokratin-i-varlden-hela-listan.

6   CNN Business, "See how drones are helping fight coronavirus" (video), April 20, 2020, edition.cnn.com/videos/business/2020/04/30/drones-coronavirus-pandemic-lon-orig-tp .cnn.

7   Kabir Agarwal, "Not Just the Aurangabad Accident, 383 People Have Died Due to the Punitive Lockdown," The Wire, May 10, 2020, https://thewire.in/rights/ migrant-workers-non-coronavirus-lockdown-deaths.

8   Alex Thomson,"Coronavirus lockdown: German lawyer detained for opposition," April 14, 2020, UK Column, ukcolumn.org/article/coronavirus-lockdown-german -lawyer-detained-opposition.

9   Caroline Modarressy-Tehrani and Grace Murray, "'It just feels surreal': Military posted at checkpoints as Australian state extends COVID-19 lockdown," NBC News, August 19, 2020, https://www.nbcnews.com/news/world/it-just-feels-surreal-military-posted -checkpoints-australian-state-extends-n1237068.

10 The Guardian, "Melbourne stage 4 restrictions and Covid lockdown rules explained," article in *The Guardian*, October 16, 2020.

11 The Local, "EXPLAINED: What is Denmark's proposed 'epidemic law' and why is it being criticised?" *The Local*, November 13, 2020, https://www.thelocal.dk/20201113/ explained-what-is-denmarks-proposed-epidemic-law-and-why-is-it-being-criticised.

12 New Zealand Parliamentary Office, "COVID-19 Public Health Response Act 2020," May 13, 2020, legislation.govt.nz/act/public/2020/0012/latest/LMS344193.html.

13 Stakston, "Så skadar pandemin demokratin i världen."

14 WHO, "COVID-19—virtual press conference, March 30, 2020" (transcript).

15 Joyce Huang, "Chinese Diplomat Accuses US of Spreading Coronavirus," VOA News, March 13, 2020, voanews.com/science-health/coronavirus-outbreak/chinese-diplomat- accuses-us-spreading-coronavirus; Dan Mangan "Trump blames China for coronavirus pandemic: 'The world is paying a very big price for what they did,'" CNBC, March 19, 2020.

16 Maciej Maremba, "Varför fick de äldre dö utan läkarvård?" ("Why were our elderly left to die without medical care"), opinion piece in *Dagens Nyheter*, October 18, 2020.

17 Anna Farrow, "Who Killed Granny? Pandemic Death Protocols in Canada's Long-term Care Facilities," article in C2C Journal, March 7, 2022.

18 American Frontline Nurses, "Rememberance Project," americanfrontlinenurse.org /remembranceproject; American Frontline Nurses, Substack Archive, afln.substack.com /archive.

19 The COVID-19 Humanity Betrayal Memory Project, "Cases," chbmp.org/cases.

20 Rockefeller Brothers Fund, *Prospect for America: the Rockefeller Panel reports*, Garden City, NY: Doubleday & Co, 1961.

21 Nordangård, *Rockefeller.*

22 World Economic Forum, *Global Risks 2006: A World Economic Forum Report*, in collaboration with MMC, Merrill Lynch and Swiss Re, www3.weforum.org/docs/WEF _Global_Risks_Report_2006.pdf.

23 Johns Hopkins School of Public Health, "Experts Issue Urgent Call to Adopt New Principles to Aid and Protect World's Most Vulnerable Populations from Influenza Pandemic" (press release), September 29, 2006, jhsph.edu/news/news-releases/2006/faden -bellagio.html.

24   Peter Doshi, "The elusive definition of pandemic influenza," *Bulletin of the World Health Organisation* 2011:89, 532–38. doi.org/10.2471/BLT.11.086173.

25   Inger Atterstam, "Skattemiljoner gick upp i rök—miljonrullning fortsätter" ("Tax millions up in smoke—spending continues," article in *Svenska Dagbladet*, May 10, 2016.

26   Rockefeller Foundation, *Scenarios for the Future of Technology and International Development*. Rockefeller Foundation and Global Business Network, May 2010, nommeraadio.ee/meedia /pdf/RRS/Rockefeller%20Foundation.pdf.

27   Clement Bezold et al., *Foresight for Smart Globalization: Accelerating & Enhancing Pro-Poor Development Opportunities* (Alexandria, VA: Institute for Alternative Futures, 2009).

28   Steven Soderbergh, *Contagion*, Participant Media, Imagenation Abu Dhabi, Double Feature Films, 2011.

29   Participant Media, "About Participant," participant.com/about-participant#block -views-team-block-1.

30   Co-Impact, "Funding Partners," co-impact.org/partners.

31   World Economic Forum, *Managing the Risk and Impact of Future Epidemics: Options for Public-Private Cooperation*, World Economic Forum & Boston Consulting Group, June 2015, www3.weforum.org/docs/WEF_Managing_Risk_Epidemics_report_2015.pdf.

32   Bill Gates, "How to fight the next Pandemic," article in *New York Times*, March 18, 2015.

33   United Nations, "Secretary-General Appoints High-Level Panel on Global Response to Health Crises" (press release), April 2, 2015, un.org/press/en/2015/sga1558.doc.htm.

34   United Nations, *Strengthening the global health architecture: implementation of the recommendations of the High-Level Panel on the Global Response to Health Crises: report of the Secretary-General*, April 8, 2016, digitallibrary.un.org/record/826896?ln=en&v=pdf.

35   Trilateral Commission, *Global Health Challenges*, July 30, 2016, web.archive.org /web/20160610100531/trilateral.org/file/197/Global-Health-Challenges.

36   Bill Gates, "A new kind of terrorism could wipe out 30 million people in less than a year— and we are not prepared," opinion piece in *Business Insider*, February 18, 2017, https://www .businessinsider.com/bill-gates-op-ed-bio-terrorism-epidemic-world-threat-2017-2.

37   Kate Kelland, "Africa's rapid population growth puts poverty progress at risk, says Gates," Reuters, September 18, 2018, https://www.reuters.com/article/us-health -global-gates/africas-rapid-population-growth-puts-poverty-progress-at-risk-says-gates -idUSKCN1LY0GU.

38   Johns Hopkins Center for Health Security, "The SPARS Pandemic 2025–2028: A Futuristic Scenario to Facilitate Medical Countermeasure Communication," October 2017, centerforhealthsecurity.org/our-work/Center-projects/completed-projects/spars-pandemic -scenario.html.

39   Monica Schoch-Spana et al., *The SPARS pandemic 2025–2028: A Futuristic Scenario for Public Health Risk Communicators*, Johns Hopkins Center for Health Security, October 2017, centerforhealthsecurity.org/sites/default/files/2022-12/spars-pandemic-scenario.pdf.

40   World Economic Forum, *Outbreak Readiness and Business Impact: Protecting Lives and Livelihoods across the Global Economy*, January 2019, www3.weforum.org/docs/WEF%20 HGHI_Outbreak_Readiness_Business_Impact.pdf.

41   World Economic Forum, *Health and Healthcare in the Fourth Industrial Revolution: Global Future Council on the Future of Health and Healthcare 2016–2018*, April 2019, www3 .weforum.org/docs/WEF__Shaping_the_Future_of_Health_Council_Report.pdf.

42 Rockefeller Foundation, "Using Data to Save Lives: The Rockefeller Foundation and Partners Launch $100 Million Precision Public Health Initiative," (press release), September 25, 2019, rockefellerfoundation.org/news/using-data-save-lives-rockefeller-foundation -partners-launch-100-million-precision-public-health-initiative.

43 Johns Hopkins Center for Health Security, "Event 201: A Global Pandemic Exercise," October 18, 2019, centerforhealthsecurity.org/event201.

44 European Commission, "Proposal for a Regulation of the European Parliament and of the Council establishing the framework for achieving climate neutrality and amending Regulation (EU) 2018/1999 (European Climate Law)," April 3, 2020, https://eur-lex. europa.eu/legal-content/EN/TXT/?uri=CELEX%3A52020PC0080.

45 European Commission, "European industrial strategy," 2020, https://commission.europa. eu/strategy-and-policy/priorities-2019-2024/europe-fit-digital-age/european-industrial -strategy_en#documents..

46 European Commission, "The European Green Deal," 2020, https://commission.europa.eu/ strategy-and-policy/priorities-2019-2024/european-green-deal_en.

47 European Commission, "Making Europe's businesses future-ready: A new Industrial Strategy for a globally competitive, green and digital Europe" (press release), March 10, 2020, competitionpolicyinternational.com/making-europes-businesses-future-ready-a-new -industrial-strategy-for-a-globally-competitive-green-and-digital-europe/.

48 Johan Rockström, "Corona- och klimatkrisen har samma grundorsak" ("The Corona and climate crisis have the same root cause"), chronicle in *Svenska Dagbladet*, March 29, 2020, https://www.svd.se/a/70A7ow/coronakrisen-och-klimatkrisen -har-samma-grundorsak.

49 S. Dixson-Declève, H. J. Shellnhuber, and K. Raworth, "Could COVID-19 give rise to a greener global future?" World Economic Forum, March 25, 2020.

50 Club of Rome, *Planetary Emergency 2.0: Securing a New Deal for People, Nature and Climate*, The Club of Rome & Potsdam Institute for Climate Impact Research, September 2020, cluboffrome.org/wp-content/uploads/2020/09/COR-PEP_Sep2020_A4_16pp-v2.pdf.

51 G20 Information Centre, "Extraordinary Leaders Summit: Statement on COVID-19," March 26, 2020, g20.utoronto.ca/2020/2020-g20-statement-0326.html.

52 G20, "Extraordinary G20 Digital Economy Ministerial Meeting: COVID-19 Response Statement," virtual meeting, April 30, 2020, g20.utoronto.ca/2020/2020-g20-digital-0430. html.

53 Financial Times, "Transcript: Bill Gates speaks to the FT about the global fight against coronavirus" (interview), *Financial Times*, April 9, 2020, https://www.ft.com/ content/13ddacc4-0ae4-4be1-95c5-1a32ab15956a.

54 Rockefeller Foundation, "The Rockefeller Foundation Launches Covid-19 Action Plan to Reopen Workplaces, Protect Lives" (press release), April 21, 2020, rockefellerfoundation. org/news/the-rockefeller-foundation-launches-covid-19-action-plan-to-reopen-workplaces- protect-lives.

55 COVID–19 Testing, Reaching, and Contacting Everyone (TRACE) Act, H. R. 6666, 116th Cong. (2020), congress.gov/116/bills/hr6666/BILLS-116hr6666ih.pdf.

56 Nation and State, "PIH, Bobby Rush, and the Truth Behind Contact Tracing Surveillance," May 15, 2020, web.archive.org/web/20200516234445/https://nationandstate. com/2020/05/15/pih-bobby-rush-and-the-truth-behind-contact-tracing-surveillance/.

57 True Pundit, "Exclusive: Bill Gates Negotiated $100 Billion Contact Tracing Deal With Democratic Congressman Sponsor of Bill Six Months BEFORE Coronavirus Pandemic," June 11, 2020, https://truepundit.com/exclusive-bill-gates-negotiated-100-billion-contact-tracing-deal-with-democratic-congressman-sponsor-of-bill-six-months-before-coronavirus-pandemic.

58 Aspen Institute Congressional Program, *Africa's Economic, Security, and Development Challenges and the US Role, August 12–19, 2019*, Kigali, Musanze, and Muhanga, Rwanda.

59 GlobeNewsWire, "VSBLTY and PHOTON-X Developing Advanced Thermal Camera Technology," April 21, 2020, https://www.globenewswire.com/news-release/2020/04/21 /2019206/0/en/VSBLTY-AND-PHOTON-X-DEVELOPING-ADVANCED-THERMAL -CAMERA-TECHNOLOGY.html.

60 New York Times, "How George Floyd Died, and What Happened Next," *New York Times*, July 29, 2020, https://www.nytimes.com/article/george-floyd.html.

61 Black Lives Matters, "Herstory," blacklivesmatter.com/herstory.

62 Heintz, Stephen, "Earned Knowledge: The Intersection of Learned Knowledge and Lived Experience," Rockefeller Brothers Fund, rbf.org/news /earned-knowledge-intersection-learned-knowledge-and-lived-experience.

63 Team Blackbird, "Our Work," web.archive.org/web/20240622221848mp_/ https://www.teamblackbird.or.

64 Supermajority: "About Us," web.archive.org/web/20200731214514/https://supermajority.com/ about-us/.

65 World Economic Forum, "Ai-jen Poo, Director, National Domestic Workers Alliance," weforum.org/agenda/2013/04/taking-care-of-the-carers/.

66 Rockefeller Brothers Fund, "Grantees: Tides Foundation $250,000 for 24 months, awarded Sep 19, 2019, For the Electoral Justice Project of its project, the Movement for Black Lives," rbf.org/grantees/tides-foundation.

67 Borealis Foundation, "Borealis Philanthropy Launches New Fund to Strengthen Racial Equity in Nonprofits," (press release), June 5, 2019, borealisphilanthropy.org/2019/06/05/ borealis-philanthropy-launches-new-fund-to-strengthen-racial-equity-in-nonprofits.

68 M4BL, *A Vision for Black Lives: Policy Demands for Black Power, Freedom and Justice*, 2016, archive.org/details/20160726M4blVisionBookletV3/mode/2up.

Chapter 6

1 World Economic Forum, "The Great Reset" (video), June 3, 2020, weforum.org/great-reset and youtu.be/VHRkkeecg7c.

2 World Economic Forum, "The Great Reset: A Unique Twin Summit to Begin 2021" (press release), June 3, 2020, weforum.org/press/2020/06/ the-great-reset-a-unique-twin -summit-to-begin-2021.

3 United Nations High-Level Panel on Digital Cooperation, "UN Secretary-General launches a Roadmap for Digital Cooperation," June 11, 2020, digitalcooperation.org /un-secretary-general-launches-a-roadmap-for-digital-cooperation.

4 World Economic Forum, *Accelerating Digital Inclusion in the New Normal*, Playbook, July 2020, www3.weforum.org/docs WEF_Accelerating_Digital_Inclusion_in_the_New _Normal_Report_2020.pdf.

5   United Nations, *The Sustainable Development Goals Report 2020*, unstats.un.org/sdgs
    /report/2020/The-Sustainable-Development-Goals-Report-2020.pdf.
6   United Nations, "Launching the decade of action at a time of crisis: Keeping the focus
    on the SDGs while combatting COVID-19," Secretariat Background Note, 2020,
    sustainabledevelopment.un.org/content/documents/26298HLPF_2020_impact
    _COVID19.pdf.
7   Klaus Schwab, & Thierry Malleret, *COVID-19: The Great Reset* (Geneva: World Economic
    Forum Publishing, 2020).
8   WHO, "The top 10 causes of death," World Health Organization, December 9, 2020, who.
    int/news-room/fact-sheets/detail/the-top-10-causes-of-death.
9   Matthew Green "Military-style Marshall Plan needed to combat climate change, says Prince
    Charles," Reuters, September 21, 2020.
10 World Economic Forum, "Prince Charles says we need a global Marshall Plan to save the
    environment" (video), September 25, 2020, weforum.org/videos
    /prince-charles-says-we-need-a-global-marshall-plan-to-save-the-environment.
11 G20 Information Centre, "Declaration of G20 Digital Ministers: Leveraging Digitalisation
    for a Resilient, Strong, Sustainable and Inclusive Recovery," Trieste, 5 August 2021, g20.
    utoronto.ca/2021/210805-digital.html.

Chapter 7

1   Rockefeller Foundation, "Rebuilding toward the Great Reset," June 19, 2020,
    rockefellerfoundation.org/blog/rebuilding-toward-the-great-reset-crisis-covid
    -19-and-the-sustainable-development-goals.
2   Abby Schultz, "The Rockefeller Legacy," *Barron's*, June 20, 2018, https://www.barrons.com
    /articles/the-rockefeller-legacy-1529467230.
3   William H. Gates, *Showing Up for Life: Thoughts on the Gifts of a Lifetime* (New York:
    Crown Currency, 2010).
4   Dan Moskovitz, "Impact Investing vs. Venture Philanthropy," 2020. investopedia.com
    /articles/personal-finance/060915/impact-investing-vs-venture-philanthropy.asp.
5   Bill & Melinda Gates Foundation, *Annual Report*, 1998.
6   Rajiv J. Shah, "COVID-19: Meeting This Moment," President's Annual Letter, Rockefeller
    Foundation, April 4, 2020, rockefellerfoundation.org/2020-annual-letter.
7   PBS (2003), "Transcript: Bill Moyers Interviews Bill Gates" (interview), web.archive.org
    /web/20030601125846/www.pbs.org/now/transcript/transcript_gates.html.
8   Bill Gates, "Remembering Bill Gates Senior," *Gates Notes*, September 15, 2020, gatesnotes.
    com/About-Bill-Gates/Remembering-Bill-Gates-Sr.
9   Peter Khiss, "Gifts of John D. Rockefeller 3d Totaled $94 Million Over His Lifetime,"
    article in *New York Times*, July 10, 1979.
10 Alana Varley, "Margaret Sanger: More Eugenic than Fellow Eugenicists," January 16, 2018,
    care-net.org/abundant-life-blog/margaret-sanger-more-eugenic-than-fellow-eugenicists.
11 Beryl Suitters, *Be Brave and Angry: Chronicles of the International Planned Parenthood
    Federation*, International Planned Parenthood Federation, London, 1973, p. 18.
12 Rockefeller Foundation, A Digital History—Childhood Immunization, rockfound.
    rockarch.org/childhood-immunization.

13 GAVI, "Donors commit vaccine funding to achieve historic milestone" (press release), 2011, gavi.org/donors-commit-vaccine-funding-to-achieve-historic-milestone-in-global-health.

14 Carnegie Medal of Philanthropy, "The Gates Family," 2001, medalofphilanthropy.org /the-gates-family.

15 Carnegie Corporation of New York, "First Andrew Carnegie Medals Awarded to Seven Visionaries of Modern Philanthropy" (press release), 2001, www.carnegie.org/news/articles /first-andrew-carnegie-medals-awarded-to-seven-visionaries-of-modern-philanthropy.

16 The Guardian (2005), "Bill Gates becomes honorary knight," article in *The Guardian,* March 2, 2005.

17 Fred Hauptfuhrer, "Vanishing Breeds Worry Prince Philip, but Not as Much as Overpopulation," article in *People,* December 21, 1981.

18 Bill & Melinda Gates Foundation (2006), *Annual Report* 2006, gatesfoundation.org /about/financials/annual-reports.

19 Rockefeller Foundation, Alliance for a Green Revolution in Africa, rockefellerfoundation. org/initiative/alliance-for-a-green-revolution-in-africa.

20 AGRA, "Leadership: Rajiv J. Shah," agra.org/who-we-are-our-leadership-old/dr-rajiv-j-shah; University of Virginia, "Caroline Newman, Rajiv Shah, Thomas Jefferson medal in Citizen leadership," UVA Today, April 2, 2020.

21 Trilateral Commission, "Member List," 2015 trilateral.org/download/files/TC_list_11 _15.pdf.

22 Synergos, "David Rockefeller Bridging Leadership Award," synergos.org /david-rockefeller-bridging-leadership-award.

23 Paul Harris, "They're called the Good Club—and they want to save the world," article in *The Guardian,* May 31, 2009.

24 The Giving Pledge, "About the Giving Pledge," givingpledge.org/About.aspx.

25 WHO (2012), "Decade of Vaccines—Global Vaccine Action Plan 2011–2020," who.int /immunization/global_vaccine_action_plan/DoV_GVAP_2012_2020/en.

26 Trilateral Commission, "The Trilateral Commission at 25, Between Past . . . and Future, Anniversary Evening sponsored by US Group," December 1, 1998, web.archive.org /web/20160519221402/trilateral.org/download/files/anniversary_evening.pdf.

27 Rockefeller University, "Epstein, Kandel and Kissinger Join Rockefeller University Board of Trustees" (press release), November 22, 1995, newswire.rockefeller.edu/1995/11/22 /epstein-kandel-and-kissinger-join-rockefeller-university-board-of-trustees/.

28 James B. Stewart and Emily Flitter, "Gates Met with Epstein Many Times, Despite His Criminal Past," article in *New York Times,* October 13, 2019.

29 Emily Flitter and Matthew Goldstein, "Long Before Divorce, Bill Gates Had Reputation for Questionable Behavior," article in *New York Times,* May 16, 2021.

30 James Stewart et al., "Epstein Envisioned Seeding Human Race with His DNA," article in *New York Times,* August 1, 2019.

31 Bill & Melinda Gates Foundation, "Bill & Melinda Gates Foundation Dedicates Additional Funding to the Novel Coronavirus Response" (press release), February 2020, gatesfoundation.org/Media-Center/Press-Releases/2020/02/Bill-and-Melinda-Gate s-Foundation-Dedicates-Additional-Funding-to-the-Novel-Coronavirus-Response.

32 Bill Gates and Melinda Gates, "Why we swing for the fences," 2020 Gates Notes Annual Letter, February 10, 2020, gatesnotes.com/2020-Annual-Letter.

33 Bill Gates, "Bill Gates: 3 lessons from COVID-19 to help us tackle climate change," World Economic Forum, weforum.org/agenda/2020/08/covid19-global-health-climate -change.

34 Peter Yachtfan, "Bill Gates Private Jets," July 19, 2020, superyachtfan.com/bill-gates-private -jet.html.

35 Rickard Folkers, "Xanadu 2.0, Bill Gates's stately pleasure dome and futuristic home," US News, November 23,1997, money.usnews.com/money/business-economy/articles/1997 /11/23/xanadu-20.

36 Bill & Melinda Gates Foundation, Statement from CEO Mark Suzman about Melinda French Gates, May 13, 2024, gatesfoundation.org/ideas/media-center/press-releases/2024/05 /melinda-french-gates.

37 Rockefeller Brothers Fund, "Rockefeller Brothers Fund Increases Spending to Seize 'Hinge Moment in History,'" 2020. rbf.org/news/rockefeller-brothers-fund-increases-spending -seize-hinge-moment-history.

38 American Academy of Art & Sciences, *Our Common Purpose,* 2020. amacad.org /ourcommonpurpose/report.

39 Rockefeller Foundation, "Rebuilding toward the Great Reset," 2020, rockefellerfoundation .org/insights/perspective/rebuilding-towards-the-great-reset-crisis-covid-19-and-the- sustainable-development-goals.

40 Rockefeller Foundation, *Digital Health,* September 2020.

41 Business Wire, "Rockefeller Capital Management to Acquire Silicon Valley Multi-Family Office Financial Clarity" (press release), September 18, 2019, businesswire.com/news/ home/20190918005288/en/Rockefeller-Capital-Management-to-Acquire-Silicon-Valley -Multi-Family-Office-Financial-Clarity.

42 Sissi Cao, "Rockefeller Family Deepens Ties in Silicon Valley Through Elite Merger," article in *Observer,* September 19, 2019.

43 Business Wire, "Rockefeller Capital Management Adds Three Highly Acclaimed Advisory Teams to Growing Private Wealth Platform" (press release), September 8, 2020, businesswire.com/news/home/20200908005119/en/Rockefeller-Capital-Management -Adds-Highly-Acclaimed-Advisory.

44 Barron's, "Rockefeller Capital Management Opens, Chasing $100 Billion," article in *Barron's,* March 1, 2018.

45 Jennifer Elias, "Sanofi partners with GSK for developing coronavirus vaccine," CNBC, April 14, 2020.

46 Bill & Melinda Gates Foundation, "Life Sciences Companies Commit Expertise and Assets to the Fight Against COVID-19 Pandemic Alongside Bill & Melinda Gates Foundation" (press release), March 25, 2020.

47 WhaleWisdom, "Rockefeller Capital Management 2022," whalewisdom.com/filer/ rockefeller-capital-management-lp#tabholdings_tab_link.

48 White House, "Remarks by President Trump on Vaccine Development," May 15, 2020, trumpwhitehouse.archives.gov/briefings-statements/remarks-president-trump -vaccine-development/.

49 US Department of Health and Human Services, "Fact Sheet: Explaining Operation Warp Speed," https://public3.pagefreezer.com/content/HHS.gov/31-12-2020T08:51/https:// www.hhs.gov/coronavirus/explaining-operation-warp-speed/index.html.

Chapter 8

1   White House, "Remarks by President Trump to the 74th Session of the United Nations General Assembly," September 24, 2019, trumpwhitehouse.archives.gov/briefings-statements/remarks-president-trump-74th-session-united-nations-general-assembly.

2   Rob Crilly, "Robert Mercer: From computer programmer to Trump backer," article in *The National*, March 20, 2018.

3   Ida Vanhainen, "Trumps nya ambassadör—Elon Musks ex-kollega" ("Trump's new ambassador—Elon Musk's former colleague"), article in *Svenska Dagbladet*, October 18, 2018.

4   Rolfe Winkler, "Investor Peter Thiel Is Helping Mold Tech's Ties to Donald Trump," article in *Wall Street Journal*, December 13, 2016.

5   World Economic Forum, "Centre for the Fourth Industrial Revolution," weforum.org/centre-for-the-fourth-industrial-revolution.

6   Singularity Hub, "Silicon Valley's Transhumanist Movement Uncovered," SingularityHub, January 19, 2009, singularityhub.com/2009/01/19/silicon-valleys-transhumanist-movement-uncovered.

7   Sam Biddle and Ryan Devereaux, "Peter Thiel's Palantir Was Used to Bust Relatives of Migrant Children, New Documents Show," article in *The Intercept*, May 1, 2019.

8   April Glaser, "Palantir's pandemic contracts stir concern ahead of IPO," NBC News, July 22, 2020.

9   Isobel Hamilton, "Trump's closest Silicon Valley ally, Peter Thiel, is reportedly abandoning the president's reelection campaign," article in Business Insider, July 3, 2020.

10 Charles Gasparino, "Trump Touts Henry Kravis as Treasury Secretary Again . . . and Again He Declines," *Fox Business*, May 1, 2016. foxbusiness.com/politics/trump-touts-henry-kravis-as-treasury-secretary-again-and-again-he-declines.

11 Jessica Winter, "Greed Is Bad. Bad!," article in *Slate*, September 25, 2007, slate.com/culture/2007/09/how-wall-street-s-gordon-gekko-inspired-a-generation-of-imitators.html.

12 Chase Peterson-Withorn, "The $132 Billion Dinner: Meet the Tycoons Who Ate with Trump Last Night," article in *Forbes*, April 25, 2018.

13 Abby Jackson, "The 13 most powerful members of 'Skull and Bones,'" article in Business Insider, March 19, 2017.

14 Ron Kampeas, "Treasury pick Steven Mnuchin was mentored by two of Trump's 'global' villains," article in *Times of Israel*, December 1, 2016.

15 Shahien Nasiripour, "Schwarzman's Wallet Props Up Wall Street Elite's Giving to Trump," Bloomberg, August 6, 2020.

16 Irina Ivanova, "U.N. blasts Blackstone Group for worsening the US housing crisis," CNN News, March 26, 2019.

17 Sridhar Natarajan, "BlackRock's Larry Fink delivers a grim outlook for corporate America," article in *Financial Review*, May 7, 2020.

18 Matthew Goldstein, "The Fed Asks for BlackRock's Help in an Echo of 2008," article in *New York Times*, March 25, 2020.

19 Claire Atkinson, "David Rockefeller hosts some of the world's wealthiest at MOMA," article in *New York Post*, April 10, 2016.

20 Chase Peterson-Withorn, "Getting Donald out of Debt: The 25-Year-Old Ties That Bind Trump and Wilbur Ross," article in *Forbes*, December 8, 2016.

21   Dan Alexander, "New Details About Wilbur Ross' Business Point To Pattern Of Grifting,"
     article in *Forbes*, August 8, 2018.

22   Bilderberg Meetings, "67th Bilderberg Meeting to take place 30 May–2 June 2019 in
     Montreux, Switzerland" (press release), bilderbergmeetings.org/press/press-release
     /press-release.

23   The American Presidency Project, "Remarks During a Meeting with Former Secretary of
     State Henry A. Kissinger and an Exchange with Reporters," October, 10 2017, presidency.
     ucsb.edu/documents/remarks-during-meeting-with-former-secretary-state-henry
     -kissinger-and-exchange-with-0.

24   CBS News, "Face the Nation Transcript December 18, 2016: Conway, Kissinger,
     Donilon" (transcript), CBS News, December 18, 2016, cbsnews.com/news/
     face-the-nation-transcript-conway-kissinger-donilon/.

25   Todd Haselton,"President Trump announces new 5G initiatives: It's a race 'America must
     win,'" CNBC, April 12, 2019, cnbc.com/2019/04/12/trump-on-5g-initiatives-a-race
     -america-must-win.html.

26   New York Times, "Transcript of Donald Trump's Immigration Speech," *New York Times*,
     February 9, 2016.

27   White House, "Executive Order Protecting the Nation from Foreign Terrorist Entry into
     the United States," March 6, 2017.

28   Andriana Simos, "Michael Kratsios named as Pentagon's top technology official," article in
     The Greek Herald, July 14, 2020.

29   Chris Burt, "Spoof attacks top this week's biometrics and digital ID news," Biometric
     Update, November 8, 2019, biometricupdate.com.

30   Douglas MacMillan, "Michael Kratsios Plays Peacemaker Between Trump and Tech," article
     in *Wall Street Journal*, November 13, 2017.

31   Rick Berke, "Watch: In prescient move, Bill Gates urged Trump to invest in pandemic
     preparedness two years ago," statnews.com, March 10, 2020.

32   Helen Branswell, "Bill Gates got President Trump fired up about a universal flu vaccine—
     and also (maybe) got a job offer," statnews.com, April 30, 2018.

33   Helen Branswell, "With cash and a call for new ideas, Bill Gates tries to boost the campaign
     for a universal flu vaccine," statnews.com, April 27, 2018.

34   White House, "Executive Order 13887: Modernizing Influenza Vaccines in the United
     States to Promote National Security and Public Health," September 19, 2019.

35   Ibid.

36   Ibid.

37   National Influenza Vaccine Modernization Task Force, *National Influenza Vaccine
     Modernization Strategy 2020–2030*. 2020. aspr.hhs.gov/MCM/Documents/nivms
     -2020-2030.pdf.

38   Michael Wilner, "'We're good to go.' The diplomatic push to release Kushner's Mideast
     peace plan," *Impact2020*, January 30, 2020, mcclatchydc.com/news/politics-government
     /white-house/article239781943.html.

39   White House, *Peace and Prosperity: A Vision to Improve the Lives of the Palestinian and Israeli
     People* (report), January 2020.

40   Matthew Sutton, "Jerusalem: Trump's gift to evangelicals," article in *The Seattle Times*,
     December 16, 2016.

41   AP & ToI staff, "Israel group mints Trump coin to honor Jerusalem recognition," *Times of Israel*, February 28, 2018, timesofisrael.com/israeli-group-mints-trump-coin-to-honor -jerusalem-recognition.

42   White House, "Remarks by President Trump, Vice President Pence, and Members of the Coronavirus Task Force in Press Briefing," April 7, 2020, trumpwhitehouse.archives.gov /briefings-statements/remarks-president-trump-vice-president-pence-members-coronavirus -task-force-press-briefing-april-7-2020/.

43   C-Span, "President Trump News Conference," November 5, 2020 (video), c-span.org /video/?477858-1/president-trump-challenges-latest-election-results-claims-voter-fraud.

44   History Channel (2014), "Rudy Guiliani," February 10, 2014, history.com/ topics/21st-century/rudy-giuliani.

45   White House, "Remarks by President Trump During an Update on Operation Warp Speed," November 13, 2020, trumpwhitehouse.archives.gov/briefings-statements /remarks-president-trump-update-operation-warp-speed.

46   Matt Mathers, "Covid vaccine: Bill Gates says several more shots 'likely' to show strong efficacy," article in *The Independent*, November 18, 2020.

47   G20, "G20 Leaders Unite To Enhance Pandemic Preparedness," Riyadh, Kingdom of Saudi Arabia, November 22, 2020.

48   David M. Herszenhorn, "Vaccinate America first, Trump tells G20," *Politico*, November 21, 2020.

49   Julia Jacobo, "This is what Trump told supporters before many stormed Capitol Hill," ABC News, January 7, 2021.

50   Al Jazeera, "Donald Trump acknowledges Biden election win," January 8, 2021.

51   Ken Thomas and Sabrina Siddiqui, "Biden Says Rioters Who Stormed Capitol Were Domestic Terrorists," article in *The Wall Street Journal*, January 7, 2021.

52   Caitlin Johnstone, "The Boot Is Coming Down Hard and Fast," January 9, 2021, caitlinjohnstone.com/2021/01/09/the-boot-is-coming-down-hard-and-fast/.

Chapter 9

1   Geir Moulson, "Thousands of Germans took to Berlin's streets to protest the government's coronavirus restrictions," Associated Press, August 1, 2020.

2   Great Barrington Declaration, "The Great Barrington Declaration," 2020, gbdeclaration. org.

3   Läkaruppropet, "The Doctors' Appeal," March 12, 2021, lakaruppropet.se.

4   Corona Schadensersatzklage, corona-schadensersatzklage.de.

5   lightgreenleaf, "29th August 2020 Trafalgar Square, Unite for Freedom Rally" (video), September 15, 2020 peakd.com/hive-196427/@lightgreenleaf/lshpfrgd.

6   Harriet Brewis, "Piers Corbyn, 73, arrested and handed £10k fine over Trafalgar Square 'anti-lockdown protests,'" article in *Evening Standard*, August 30, 2020.

7   StandUpX, standupx.info.

8   StandUpX, Rally message on Twitter, September 5, 2020, twitter.com/StandUpX2 /status/1302168398965678080/photo/1.

9   World Doctors Alliance, "Hearing #3 in Berlin, Germany," October 10, 2020, brandnewtube.com/watch/uYTDU74AzhxeGFe.

10 World Doctors Alliance, "World Freedom Alliance 2020" (video), web.archive.org /web/20201126132800/https://worlddoctorsalliance.com/blog /theworldfreedomalliance2020announcementvideo/.

11 Dolores Cahill, "World Freedom Alliance: Stockholm—Part 2" (video), November 20, 2020, facebook.com/663251520811711/videos/132652364972091.

12 World Freedom Alliance, "Youth For Freedom," youth.worldfreedomalliance.org.

13 MSB, *Konspirationsteorier och covid-19: mekanismerna bakom en snabbväxande samhällsutmaning* ("Conspiracy theories and COVID-19: mechanisms behind a rapidly growing challenge to society"), Enheten för skydd mot informationspåverkan, 2021, p. 39.

14 Demokrati utan gränser, "Idén om världsparlamentet" (video), presentation by Andreas Önnerfors, April 25, 2020, youtu.be/_AOBPvgW-gQ.

15 Jedediah French, "Q&A: Andreas Önnerfors" (interview), *The Gavel* 20, March 3, 2020, p. 11, nyadagbladet.se/wp-content/uploads/2021/06/O%CC%88nnerforsintervju-2020-3 -Gavel-March-2020.pdf.

16 Jani Pirttisalo Sallinen, "Så byggde Balimannen sin propagandamaskin" ("How the Bali man built his propaganda machine"), article in *Svenska Dagbladet*, May 9, 2021.

17 New Earth Festival, "New Earth project," newearthfestival.com/pages/newearth-project.

18 New Earth Nations, web.archive.org/web/20210323211204/http://newearthnations.org.

19 Natural World Organization, web.archive.org/web/20120119094904/http://nwo-igo.org.

20 New Earth Horizon, newearthhorizon.com.

21 Humanitad.org, "Mission," humanitad.org/mission.

22 Lindsey Brett, "Bali 7th Aug–12th Aug," Ciros Orsini (blog), August 23, 2006, web.archive. org/web/20231124193053/https://corsini222.blogspot.com/2006/08/.

23 Modern Money Network, "Bernhard Lietaer," modernmoneynetwork.org/content /bernard-lietaer.

24 Lee Penn, *False Dawn* (Hillsdale, NY:Sophia Perennis, 2004), 306–15.

25 Humanitad: "People," humanitad.org/people.

26 Exemplar Zero, "Administration," web.archive.org/web/20110128184112/http ://www.exemplarzero.org/index.php?p=team&ref=admin.

27 Fred Teunissen, "Sacha Stone interview," October 13, 2013, vimeo.com/77732706.

28 New Earth Horizon, "Locations," newearthhorizon.com/locations.

29 The Venus Project, thevenusproject.com.

30 New Earth Festival, newearthfestival.com.

31 Humanitad, "Initiatives," humanitad.org/initiatives.

32 Earth Sanctuary, web.archive.org/web/20140626125741/http://www.humanitad.org /programs/earth_sanctuary.

33 Earth Sanctuary, "Address problem," web.archive.org/web/20140618215333/http ://www.earth-sanctuary.org/address-problems.html.

34 Exemplar Zero, "Initiative Overview," web.archive.org/web/20110211204009/http://www .exemplarzero.org.

35 Sacha Stone, "Message to the Stockholm Rally" (video), November 18, 2020, facebook. com/sacha.stone.7/videos/10159315741808487.

36 ITNJ, "International Tribunal of Natural Justice," itnj.org

37 ITNJ, "Judicial Commission," commission.itnj.org.

38 Vaken.se, "Maneka JC Helleberg om lösningar på världens problem" (video), Facebook, 16 juli 2020, facebook.com/vakenpunktse/videos/288677812337376.

39 ITNJ, Bombshell Nuclear Coverup on the Scale of Fukushima (press release), September 25, 2019, itnj.org/blog/2019/09/25/carolyn_tyler_testmony_on_nuclear_cover_up/.

40 ITNJ. "Closed Cases." itnj.org/itnj-cases/closed-cases.

41 Claims of the Living, "The ITNJ Rears Its Ugly Head: A Warning" (blog post), 25 juni 2017, claimsoftheliving.blogspot.com/2017/06/the-itnj-international-tribunal-for.html.

42 marekdjw, "Sacha Stone Interview with John and Irina Mappin from Camelot TV Network" (video), April 25, 2020, youtu.be/DuIIGOw4myM.

43 Marzia Narayani, "Sacha Stone: 'We will see the end of all governments'" (interview), bewusst.tv, 2020, youtube.com/watch?v=AZ2zVC8FN0A.

44 Q-map, web.archive.org/web/20180807020442/https://qmap.pub.

45 US Department of State, "Report on U.S. Government Efforts to Combat Trafficking in Persons," December 1, 2017, state.gov/report-on-u-s-government-efforts-to-combat -trafficking-in-persons/#1.

46 Derrick Bronze, "Vaccine Bait & Switch: As Millions Pulled From WHO, Trump Gives Billions To Gates-Founded GAVI," July 7, 2020, The Last American Vagabond, thelastamericanvagabond.com/vaccine-bait-switch-millions-pulled-from-who-trump -gives-billions-gates-founded-gavi; GAVI, "Proceeds to Gavi from Donor Contributions & Pledges (2021–2025) as of 30 June, 2023," gavi.org/investing-gavi/funding/donor-profiles/ united-states-america.

47 Janet Ossebaard, "Fall of the Cabal" ("documentary" series), 2019, web.archive.org /web/20200822151347/https://en.valcabal.nl.

48 David Wilcock, "Disclosure Imminent? Two Underground NWO Bases Destroyed" (blog post including interview with Ben Fulford), September 16, 2011. web.archive.org/ web/20120422144337/http://www.divinecosmos.com/start-here/davids-blog/975 -undergroundbases.

49 Global Economic, "Robert David Steele Confirm! Donald Trump Start Arrest—Hillary Clinton—On Deep State in March 2019," March 4, 2019 (video), youtu.be /Sq3mdRyVwoE.

50 Mick Wall, "New Conspiracy Theory: Children Kidnapped for Mars Slave Colony," Space. com, July 1, 2017, web.archive.org/web/20170702051044/https://www.space.com/37366 -mars-slave-colony-alex-jones.html.

51 Steele, Robert David, "Declaration of NESARA/GESARA Coming? Sacha Stone Thinks So!" (video), April 13, 2020, bitchute.com/video/6IjdpaLAQQQ/.

52 Robinson, Sean, "Snared by a cybercult queen," *The News Tribune*, July 18, 2004.

53 Writeside Blonde, Rachel, "The Quantum Financial System According to Charlie Ward," article in *George*, December 19, 2021, georgeonline.com/2022/12/19 /the-quantum-financial-system-according-to-charlie-ward.

54 After Burner, Charlie Ward, underage girls & Jimmy Savile, Bitchute, 5 March 2021, www .bitchute.com/video/NvNKNO6fBDUp.

55 5G Bioshield, web.archive.org/web/20200721194355/https://5gbioshield.com/.

56 World Awake, "5G Apocalypse Protection with Sacha Stone on Trump, Sovereignty, Income Tax & More!," October 10, 2019, youtu.be/_DVn9xXpTLk.

57 John Koetsier, "$350 '5G Bioshield' Radiation Protection Device Is a . . . $6 USB Stick," article in *Forbes*, May 28, 2020.

58 Humanitad, "QT-PI," humanitad.org/wp-content/uploads/2017/03/qtpi.pdf.

59 Nils Rognerud, "Free Energy Device by Sacha Stone?," November 2017, electrogravityphysics.com/free-energy-energy-qt-pi-device/.

60 New Earth Horizon Shop, newearthhorizon.com/shop.

61 Peaceinspace.org, "Judgment of the Tribunal in the matter of Genocidal Technologies Pandemic," November 29, 2020, exopolitics.blogs.com/files/final-judgment—natural-and -common-law-tribunal–november-29-2020.pdf.

62 Holden, Constance, "Rockefeller Finances Crop Circle Survey," 21 May 1999, *Science*, www.science.org/content/article/rockefeller-finances-crop-circle-survey.

63 Robert Scheaffer, "Carl Sagan, Laurance Rockefeller, and UFOs," September/October 2014, *Skeptical Enquirer,* https://skepticalinquirer.org/wp-content/uploads/sites/29/2014/09/p19. pdf.

64 Alfred Lambremont Webre, *The Omniverse: Transdimensional Intelligence, Time Travel, the Afterlife, and the Secret Colony on Mars* (Rochester, VT: Bear & Company, 2015).

65 Alfred Lambremont Webre and Phillip H. Liss, *The Age of Cataclysm* (New York: Berkley Pub. Corp, 1974).

66 United Nations, *Our Common Agenda: Report of the Secretary-General,* Department of Global Communications, United Nations, New York, 2021, un.org/en/content /common-agenda-report/.

67 Kilgore, Ed, "Jimmy Carter Saw a UFO on This Day in 1973," article in *Intelligencer,* September 18, 2019.

68 Webre, *The Omniverse.*

69 Exopolitics, "Mars visitors Basiago and Stillings confirm Barack Obama traveled to Mars," exopolitics.blogs.com/exopolitics/2011/11/mars-visitors-basiago-and-stillings-confirm-barack-obama-traveled-to-mars-1.html

70 Ken Stone "Time-Traveling Truth Candidate for President Wins 1 Vote Locally," article in *Times of San Diego,* July 7, 2016, timesofsandiego.com/politics/2016/07/07 /time-traveling-truth-candidate-for-president-wins-1-vote-locally/

71 Exopolitics, Star Dreams Initiative, web.archive.org/web/20120301031954/ http ://exopolitics.blogs.com/star_dreams_initiative/.

72 Alfred Lambremont Webre, "Canadian UFO researcher creates official Petition to have Canadian government designate him 'an Earth representative to Galactic Council'" (self-authored 'news article' from his own newsinsideout.com and exopolitics.com), March 20, 2021.

73 Alfred Lambremont Webre, *Emergence of the Omniverse: Universe–Multiverse–Omniverse* (Universe Books, 2020).

74 Earth Is Our Common Home, "Vision," present5.com/rio-20-earth-is-our-common -home-vision.

75 Nina Goncharova, *Rainbow Earth: Vision from the Future,* Earth Is Our Common Home Project (New Delhi: Sanbun Publishers, 2010), p. 215.

76 New Earth Project, "Blueprint," p. 18, newearthproject.org/wp-content/assets/docs/ne _blueprint.pdf.

77 New Earth Nations, "Statement of Clarification," newearthnations.org /statement-of-clarification.

78 Noosphere Forum, web.archive.org/web/20130210100117/http://www.noosphereforum .org/main.html.

79 José Argüelles, *Manifesto for the Noosphere* (Evolver Editions, 2011).

Chapter 10

1   Paul Raskin et al., *Great Transition: The Promises and Lures of the Times Ahead*, Stockholm Environment Institute, 2002, greattransition.org/documents/Great_Transition.pdf.

2   Paul Raskin et al. *Great Transition*, p. 15

3   Paul Raskin, *The Great Transition Today: A Report from the Future*, Tellus Institute, 2006, greattransition.org/archives/papers/The_Great_Transition_Today.pdf.

4   Paul Raskin et al., *World Lines: Pathways, Pivots, and the Global Future*, 2006, p. 10, greattransition.org/archives/papers/World_Lines.pdf.

5   Tännsjö, Torbjörn, "Så kan klimatkrisen leda fram till en global despoti" ("How the climate crisis may lead to global despotism"), article in *Dagens Nyheter*, 28 November 28, 2018.

6   Paul Raskin, *Journey to Earthland: The Great Transition to Planetary Civilization*, Tellus Institute, 2016, p.43, greattransition.org/images/GTI_publications/Journey-to-Earthland .pdf.

7   Paul Raskin et.al., *Branch Points—Global Scenarios and Human Choice,* A Resource Paper of the Global Scenario Group, 1997, p. 13, greattransition.org/archives/other/Branch%20 Points.pdf.

8   Rockefeller Foundation, *Scenarios for the Future of Technology and International Development*, 2010, p. 18.

9   Paul Raskin et al., *Branch Points*, p. 74.

10 New Earth Project, "About Us," web.archive.org/web/20130820194747/http://www.new -earth-project.org/about-us.

11 Paul Raskin, *Journey to Earthland: The Great Transition to Planetary Civilization*, Tellus Institute, 2016, p. 73, greattransition.org/images/GTI_publications/Journey-to-Earthland .pdf.

12 Paul Raskin, *Journey to Earthland*, pp. 78–79.

13 David Suzuki Foundation, Declaration of Interdependence, davidsuzuki.org/about /declaration-of-interdependence.

14 Paul Raskin et al., *Great Transition*, p. 81.

15 Paul Raskin, *Great Transition Today*, p. 4.

16 Great Transition Initiative, *Imagine all the People: Advancing a global citizens movement*, 2010, Tellus Institute, greattransition.org/archives/perspectives/Perspective_Imagine_All _the_People.pdf.

17 Goi Peace Foundation, Our Approach, goipeace.or.jp/en/about/approach/.

18 Ervin László, *Goals for Mankind* (London: Hutchinson & Co, 1977).

19 The Club of Budapest, "Our Mission," clubofbudapest.com/our-mission.

20 Ervin László, *Worldshift 2012* (Rochester, VT: Inner Traditions, 2009), pp. 80–83.

21 Oliver Reiser, *Cosmic Humanism and World Unity*, World Institute Creative Findings (New York: Gordon and Breach, 1975).

22 Alice Bailey, *Education in the New Age* (New York: Lucis Trust, 1954), bailey.it/files/ Education-in-the-New-Age.pdf.

23 The Club of Budapest, "Ervin László: Global Shift NOW! A new book announcement" (video), July 20, 2020, youtu.be/gOL2d65I0tA.

24 World Economic Forum, "Now Is the time for a Great Reset," June, 3, 2020, weforum.org /agenda/2020/06/now-is-the-time-for-a-great-reset.

25 Klaus Schwab, *Stakeholder Capitalism* (Hoboken, NJ: Wiley, 2021), pp. 178–81.

26   SRI International, "National Security," sri.com/national-security.

27   Willis Harman and O. W. Markley, *Changing Images of Man* (Oxford: Pergamon Press, 1982), p. xvii.

28   Zbigniew Brzezinski, "America in the Technetronic Age," *Childhood Education* 45, no. 1 (1968): 6–10, doi.org/10.1080/00094056.1968.10729371.

29   Lynn Picknett and Clive Prince, *Stargate Conspiracy* (Boston: Little, Brown & Co. 1999), p. 219.

Chapter 11

1   World Bank Group, *Principles on Identification for Sustainable Development: Toward the Digital Age*, World Bank Group and Center for Global Development, February 2017, documents1.worldbank.org/curated/en/213581486378184357/pdf/Principles-on -identification-for-sustainable-development-toward-the-digital-age.pdf.

2   ID2020, id2020.org.

3   David Sønstebø, "Welcome John Edge to IOTA," 2017, blog.iota.org/ welcome-john-edge-to-iota-d378fb8f0b2.

4   ID2020, web.archive.org/web/20151108233202/https://id2020.org.

5   United Nations, "ID2020 Summit 2016," May 20, 2016, un.org/partnerships/ar/news /id2020-summit-2016.

6   ID2020 Summit, "ID2020 Summit 2017," web.archive.org/web/20171013132643/http ://id2020summit.org.

7   Javier Graham, "ID2020 Alliance at a glance" (presentation), 2017, readkong.com/page /alliance-committed-to-improving-lives-through-digital-1380992.

8   World Economic Forum, *Digital Borders: Enabling a secure, seamless and personalized journey* (White Paper).

9   Art Kleiner, "The man who saw the future," Strategy+Business, February 12, 2003.

10   Mark Townsend and Paul Harris, "Now the Pentagon tells Bush: climate change will destroy us," article in *The Observer*, February 22, 2004.

11   Rockefeller Foundation, *Scenarios for the Future of Technology and International Development*, 2010.

12   Seth Berkley, "We all have a stake in global health security," World Economic Forum, January 16, 2020, weforum.org/agenda/2020/01/we-all-have-a-stake-when-it -comes-to-global-health-security.

13   Bill Gates: "How we must respond to the coronavirus pandemic" (TED Talk), March 24, 2020.

14   European Commission, "Roadmap for the implementation of actions," 2019, ec.europa.eu /health/sites/health/files/vaccination/docs/2019-2022_roadmap_en.pdf.

15   World Economic Forum, *Reimagining Digital Identity: A Strategic Imperative*, 2020.

16   World Bank Group, *Principles on identification for sustainable development toward the digital age*, 2020.

17   World Economic Forum, *Digital Borders: Enabling a secure, seamless and personalized journey* (white paper), 2017.

18   Luana Pascu, "Facial recognition payment systems rolled out in Denmark, growing rapidly in China," December 10, 2019, biometricupdate.com/201912/ facial-recognition-payment-systems-rolled-out-in-denmark-growing-rapidly-in-china.

19　K. Wilson, K. Atkinson, and C. Bell, "Travel Vaccines Enter the Digital Age: Creating a Virtual Immunization Record," *American Journal of Tropical Medicine and Hygiene* 94, no. 3 (2015): 485–88, doi.org/10.4269/ajtmh.15-0510.

20　The Commons Project, "CommonPass," 2020, thecommonsproject.org/commonpass.

21　Douglas Broom, "Could this COVID-19 'health passport' be the future of travel and events?," World Economic Forum, July 30, 2020.

22　GSMA, *Smart Cities Guide: Crowd Management,* 2018, gsma.com/iot/wp-content /uploads/2016/10/GSMA-Crowd-management-case-study-web.pdf.

23　Klaus Schwab, *The Fourth Industrial Revolution* (Geneva: World Economic Forum Publishing, 2016).

24　Alexandra Ma, "Thousands of Swedish people are swapping ID cards for microchips," World Economic Forum, May 16, 2018.

25　Biohax International, facebook.com/BiohaxInternational.

26　BiChip, "Bichip coin BCHI," bichip.store/uploads/LSESOJXONL.pdf.

27　Chipster, chipster.nu.

28　Dutch National Office for Identity Data, *Identity Management in 2030,* 2015, p. 13.

29　ID2020, "ID2020 Summit Sessions 2020" (webinar series), id2020.org/ summit/2020-id2020-summit-sessions-webinar-series.

30　World Economic Forum, *Shaping the Future of the Internet of Bodies: New challenges of technology governance,* 2020, www3.weforum.org/docs/WEF_IoB_briefing_paper_2020.pdf.

31　Dirk Helbing & Peter Seele, "Digital ID, Global Resilience, and Human Dignity," September 2020, futurict.blogspot.com/2020/09/digital-id-global-resilience-and-human .html.

32　GSMA, *Smart Cities Guide.*

33　Royal HaskoningDHV, "Crowd Management: Shaping the Normal in Public Space," June 21, 2020, web.archive.org/web/20200621174729/https://www.royalhaskoningdhv.com /en-gb/specials/people-flows/social-distancing.

34　ID2020, "Good Health Pass: A New Cross-Sector Initiative to Restore Global Travel and Restart the Global Economy," February 9, 2021, medium.com/id2020/good-health-pass-a -new-cross-sector-initiative-to-restore-global-travel-and-restart-the-global-8b59eb1050a0.

35　Good Health Pass, "Good Health Pass Collaborative," Feb 8, 2021, web.archive.org /web/20210208222630/https://goodhealthpass.org.

36　G20 Italia, "Declaration of G20 Digital Ministers: Leveraging Digitalisation for a Resilient, Strong, Sustainable and Inclusive Recovery," August 5, 2021, g20.utoronto. ca/2021/210805-digital.html.

37　New York Times, "Biden's New Vaccine Requirements Draw Praise, Condemnation and Caution," article in *New York Times,* September 9, 2021.

38　European Commission, "European Digital Identity—Questions and Answers," June 3, 2021, ec.europa.eu/commission/presscorner/detail/en/QANDA_21_2664.

39　Ny Teknik, "Vaccinpass för corona—här är allt du behöver veta," article in *Ny Teknik,* August 18, 2021.

40　Schengen Visa Info, "France Requires Tourists to Hold Vaccination Passport to Access Certain Activities & Services," August 10, 2021, schengenvisainfo.com/news /france-requires-tourists-to-hold-vaccination-passport-to-access-certain-activities-services/.

41　Michele Barbero, "Macron's Big Vaccination Gamble," *Foreign Policy,* July 27, 2021.

42 Herwig Czech and Christiane Druml, "A pandemic is no private matter: the COVID-19 vaccine mandate in Austria," *The Lancet*, February 17, 2022.

43 BBC, "Covid: Austria suspends compulsory vaccination mandate," March 9, 2022, bbc .com/news/world-europe-60681288.

44 The Independent Panel for Pandemic Preparedness and Response, "About," theindependentpanel.org/about-the-independent-panel/.

45 The Independent Panel, *Covid-19: Make It the Last Pandemic,* theindependentpanel.org /wp-content/uploads/2021/05/COVID-19-Make-it-the-Last-Pandemic_final.pdf.

46 WHO, "Pandemic prevention, preparedness and response accord, Q&A," February 24, 2023. who.int/news-room/questions-and-answers/item/pandemic-prevention –preparedness-and-response-accord.

47 The Guardian, "Global pandemic agreement at risk of falling apart, WHO warns," January 22 2024, theguardian.com/world/2024/jan/22/global-pandemic-agreement-at-risk-of -falling-apart-who-warns.

48 WHO, "Seventy-seventh World Health Assembly – Daily update: 1 June 2024," June 1 2024, who.int/news/item/01-06-2024-seventy-seventh-world-health-assembly—daily -update–1-june-2024.

49 Meryl Nass, "Door to Freedom–where to now? Can we aspire to even bigger things?," June 9, 2024, Meryl's COVID Newsletter, merylnass.substack.com/p/door-to-freedom -where-to-now-can.

Chapter 12

1 GAVI, "COVAX explained," 2020 gavi.org/vaccineswork/covax-explained.

2 ACT-Accelerator Facilitation Council, "Terms of Reference," September 10, 2020, WHO, who.int/docs/default-source/act/act-a-facilitation-council-terms-of-reference-21 -September-2020.pdf.

3 European Commission, "Coronavirus Global Response: €7.4 billion raised for universal access to vaccines" (press release), Brussels, May 4, 2020.

4 European Commission, "Coronavirus Global Response International Pledging Event—Bill Gates, Co-Chair and Trustee of the Bill & Melinda Gates Foundation," May 28, 2020, global-response.europa.eu/coronavirus-global-response-international-pledging-event-bill -gates-co-chair-and-trustee-bill-2020_mt.

5 Maïthé Chini, "'Best-case scenario': EU could have Covid-19 vaccine by April," *The Brussels Times*, October 28, 2020.

6 B. Battersby, E. Ture, and R. Lam, "Tracking the $9 Trillion Global Fiscal Support to Fight COVID-19," *IMF BLOG*, 2020, imf.org/en/Blogs/Articles/2020/05/20/ tracking-the-9-trillion-global-fiscal-support-to-fight-covid-19.

7 Ekonomifakta (2022), "Statsbudget & statsskuld: Stödåtgärder Coronakrisen," March 22, 2022, ekonomifakta.se/Fakta/Offentlig-ekonomi/Statsbudget/stodatgarder-coronakrisen.

8 Government Offices of Sweden, "Sweden's support to Ukraine," government.se /government-policy/swedens-support-to-ukraine/.

9 Jonathan Masters and Will Merrow, "How Much Aid Has the U.S. Sent Ukraine? Here Are Six Charts," Council on Foreign Relations, February 23, 2024, cfr.org/article /how-much-aid-has-us-sent-ukraine-here-are-six-charts.

10 European Council, "Infographic—2023 EU budget: Main areas," November 14, 2022, consilium.europa.eu/en/infographics/2023-eu-budget-main-areas/.

11 European Commission, "Enabling citizens to act on climate change, for sustainable development and environmental protection through education, citizen science, observation initiatives, and civic engagement," September 18, 2020, cordis.europa.eu/programme/id /H2020_LC-GD-10-3-2020.

12 United Nations, "Member States Approve USD 3.59 Billion UN Budget for 2024" (press release), January 10, 2024. news.un.org/en/story/2023/12/1145072.

13 Jenny Nordberg, "Sverige är FN:s jultomte" ("Sweden is the UN's Santa Claus"), *Svenska Dagbladet,* September 20, 2013.

14 United Nations, "Careers," careers.un.org/lbw/home.aspx?viewtype=sal.

15 WHO, "Financing of General Programme of Work 2020–2025," open.who.int/2024-25 /budget-and-financing/gpw-overview.

16 Saloni Sardana, "US billionaires' wealth grew by $845 billion during the first six months of the pandemic," article in *Business Insider,* September 17, 2020.

Epilogue

1 Cyber Polygon 2020, "Trust or fear: what will be the main incentive for cooperation after the crisis?," with Jeremy Jurgens (video), July 2020, 2020.cyberpolygon.com/gallery /video/?roistat_visit=941241#LAvq7X6UBcw.

2 Cognizant, "After the Virus: A Special Report Looking Back on the Next Five Years", Cognizant Center for The Future of Work, July 2020, ognizantcfow.turtl.co/story/ after-the-virus/page/1.

3 Cognizant, "After the Virus: A Discussion Looking Back on the Next 5 Years" (video), Cognizant, July 28, 2020. youtu.be/oNxFJt5aYI4.

4 Cyber Polygon 2020, "Trust or fear."

5 Cyber Polygon 2020, "Live Stream Agenda" (videos), July 8, 2020, 2020.cyberpolygon. com/agenda.
Cyber Polygon 2021, "Live Stream Agenda" (videos), July 9, 2021, 2021.cyberpolygon.com /agenda/.

6 Cyber Polygon 2020, "Welcoming Remarks by Klaus Schwab" (video), July 2020, 2020. cyberpolygon.com/gallery/video/#EOvz1Flfrfw.

7 Matthew Loh, "Canada says it will freeze the bank accounts of 'Freedom Convoy' truckers who continue their anti-vaccine mandate blockades," article in Business Insider, February 15, 2022.

8 United Nations, *Our Common Agenda: Report of the Secretary-General,* Department of Global Communications, United Nations, New York, 2021, un.org/en/content /common-agenda-report/.

9 K. Faksova et al. "COVID-19 vaccines and adverse events of special interest: A multinational Global Vaccine Data Network (GVDN) cohort study of 99 million vaccinated individuals," *Vaccine* 42, no. 9 (2024): 2200–2211, ISSN 0264-410X, doi. org/10.1016/j.vaccine.2024.01.100.

10 Saskia Mostert, Marcel Hoogland, Minke Huibers, Gertjan Kaspers, "Excess mortality across countries in the Western World since the COVID-19 pandemic: 'Our World in Data' estimates of January 2020 to December 2022," *BMJ Public Health* 2, no. 1 (2024):2:e000282, doi.org/10.1136/bmjph-2023-000282.

11 Robert F. Kennedy Jr., *The Real Anthony Fauci: Bill Gates, Big Pharma, and the Global War on Democracy and Public Health* (New York: Skyhorse Publishing, 2021).

Appendix A

1 Supreme Law.org, "Transcript of Norman Dodd Interview 1982 with G. Edward Griffin" (transcript), supremelaw.org/authors/dodd/interview.htm.

2 The Freemen Institute, Tax-Exempt Foundations, *The Freemen Digest*, June 1978, p. 2-3. web.archive.org/web/20170302090737/http://www.freedomforallseasons.org/TaxFreedomEmail/TaxExemptFoundationsTakingsFinal.pdf.

3 US House of Representatives, *Report of the Special Committee to Investigate Tax-Exempt Foundations and Comparable Organizations;* Staff report No. 1-4, United States, Washington: US Govt. Print. Off, 1954, p. 31.

4 US House of Representatives, Tax-Exempt Foundations, p. 669.

5 *Report of the Commission on the Social Studies: Conclusions and Recommendations of the Commission*, May 1934, Scribners; cited in Tax-Exempt Foundations (1954), p. 476.

6 *Report of the President's Commission on Higher Education*, 1947; cited in Tax-Exempt Foundations (1954), p. 483.

7 Eugene Staley, *War and the Private Investor*, Doubleday, 1935, pt. 3: Toward a Policy, pp. 517–18; cited in Tax-Exempt Foundations (1954), p. 923.

8 Tax-Exempt Foundations (1954), p. 480.

9 George F. Zook, "The President's Commission on Higher Education," *Bulletin of the American Association of University Professors* 1915–1955 33, no. 1 (1947); cited in Tax-Exempt Foundations, p. 483.

10 Rockefeller Foundation, *Annual Report* 1940, p. 273–277; cited in Tax-Exempt Foundations (1954), p. 931.

11 Rockefeller Foundation (1948), *Annual Report* 1948, p. 247–248; in Tax-Exempt Foundations (1954), p. 939.

12 Fund for Advancement of Education, *Annual Report* 1951–52, p. 6; in Tax-Exempt Foundations (1954), p. 480.

13 Ford Foundation, *Report on the Behavioral Sciences Division of the Ford Foundation*, June 1953; cited in Tax-Exempt Foundations (1954), p. 481.

14 Norman Dodd, *The Dodd Report to the Reece Committee on Foundations, 1954.*

15 Charles Kaiser, "The Truth Is, Columbia Owns Rockefeller Center Buildings, Too," article in *New York Times*, March 21, 1976, nytimes.com/1976/03/21/archives/the-truth-is-columbia-owns-rockefeller-center-buildings-too.html.

16 Patrick M. Wood, *Technocracy Rising*, p. 3.

17 Thomas Wheatland, "The Frankfurt School's invitation from Columbia University," *German Politics & Society* 22, no. 3 (72) (Fall 2004): 1–32, Berghahn Books.

18 Nikos A. Salingaros, *Anti-Architecture and Deconstruction: The Triumph of Nihilism*, Katmandu: Vajra Books, 2010.

Appendix B

1   New York Times, "Obituaries: Dr. Richard Day, 84, Ex-Pediatrics Professor," *New York Times*, June 16, 1989.
2   Public Record, *The New Order of Barbarians: The New World System, 2013.*
3   Robert Zubin, "The Population Control Holocaust," article in *The New Atlantis*, 2012, thenewatlantis.com/publications/the-population-control-holocaust.

Index